# ski atlas of the world

the complete reference
to the best resorts

# ski atlas of the world

### the complete reference to the best resorts

contributing editor arnie wilson

**abbeville press publishers**
new york london

*For the original edition*

Editorial Direction: Clare Hubbard
Design: Peter Crump
Resort maps: Andrew Reeves
Other maps: Stephen Dew
Production: Marion Storz

*For the North American edition*

Production manager: Louise Kurtz
Production editor: Austin Allen
Jacket designer: Misha Beletsky

First published in the United States of America in 2008 by Abbeville Press, 137 Varick Street, New York, NY 10013

First published in Great Britain in 2007 by New Holland Publishers (UK) Ltd, Garfield House, 86–88 Edgware Road, London, W2 2EA United Kingdom

First edition
10 9 8 7 6 5 4 3 2 1

Library of Congress Cataloging-in-Publication Data

Ski atlas of the world : the complete reference to the best resorts / contributing editor Arnie Wilson.
      p. cm. — (Ski atlas of the world)
  Includes index.
  ISBN 978-0-7892-0986-3 (hardcover : alk. paper)
  1. Ski resorts—Directories. 2. Ski resorts—Guidebooks. I. Wilson, Arnie, 1944–

  GV854.35.S55 2007
  796.93025—dc22
                    2008014290

For bulk and premium sales and for text adoption procedures, write to Customer Service Manager, Abbeville Press, 137 Varick Street, New York, NY 10013, or call 1-800-Artbook.

Visit Abbeville Press online at www.abbeville.com.

Jacket front: Photograph © The Canyons Resort, Park City, Utah.

Jacket back: Photograph © Tourismusverband St Anton am Arlberg.

Jacket spine: Photograph © Val Thorens/Oddoux.

page 2: Klosters, linked with the historic ski town of Davos. These two traditional ski areas provide one of the most popular and well-established wintersports regions in Switzerland – for many years a favourite haunt of the Prince of Wales.

pages 4–5: Fresh tracks at Bad Gastein: few resorts in the Alps have such extensive and easy powderfields as this classic Austrian resort in the Gasteinertal. Here, skiers and boarders pause to look back at their handiwork.

# Contents

ARCTI

**ASIA**

Verkhoyansk Range

Sikhote Alin Range

EUROPE: p.20

Ural Mountains

**EUROPE**

Altai

Alps

Carpathians

Tien Shan

Pyrenees

Appenines

Caucasus

Hindu Kush

Kunlun Shan

Atlas Mts.

Taurus

Zagros Mts.

Himalaya

Tropic of Cancer

**AFRICA**

Western Ghats

Arakan

Mitumba Mts.

Equator

INDIAN

OCEAN

SOUTH

ATLANTIC

Great Dividing Range

OCEAN

Drakensberg Mts.

**AUSTRAL**

Australian
Alps

**REST OF THE WORLD: p.270**

0    1000    2000    3000    4000 miles

0    2500    5000 kilometres

S O U T H E R N

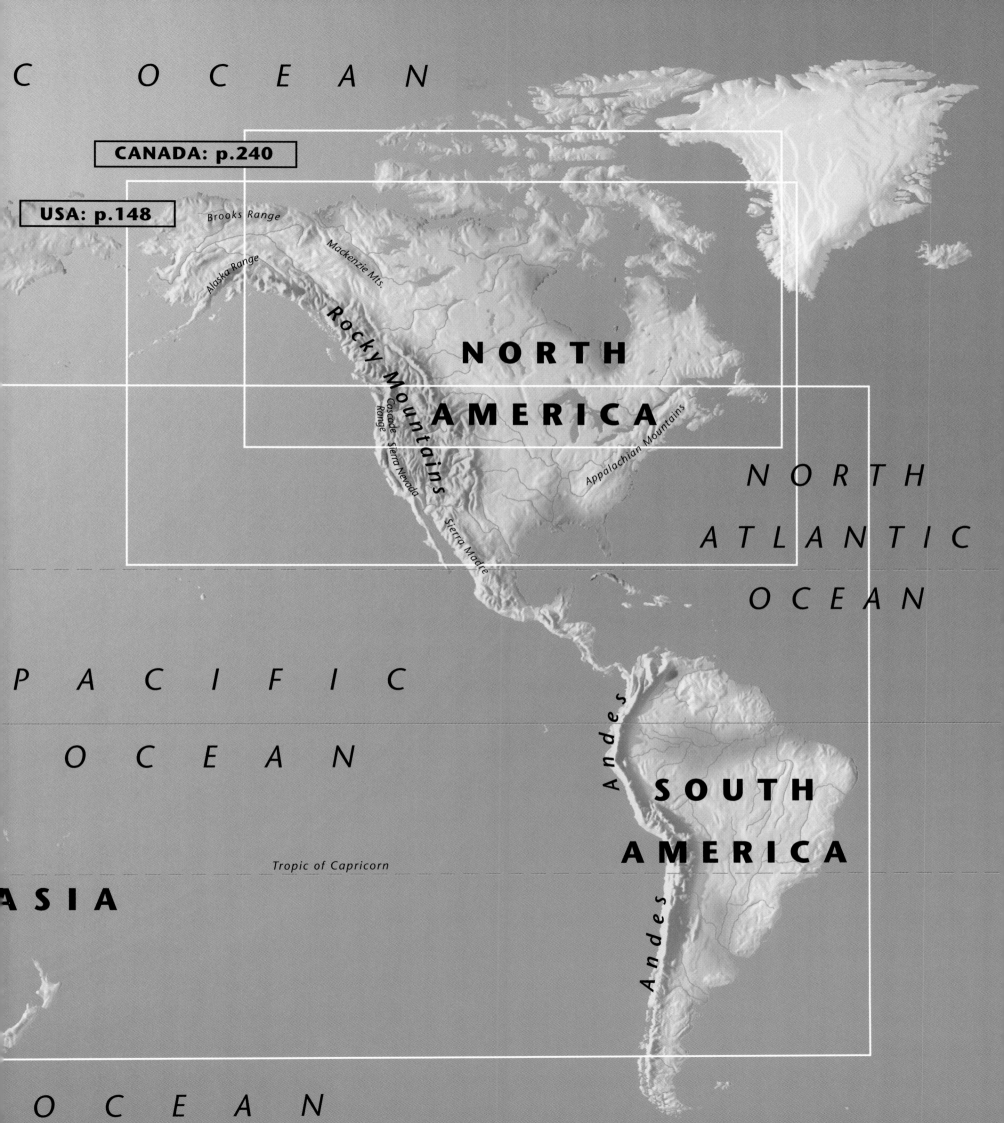

C  O C E A N

CANADA: p.240

USA: p.148

*Brooks Range*

*Alaska Range*

*Mackenzie Mts.*

# NORTH
# AMERICA

*Rocky Mountains*

*Cascade Range*

*Sierra Nevada*

*Appalachian Mountains*

*N O R T H*

*A T L A N T I C*

*O C E A N*

*Sierra Madre*

*P A C I F I C*

*O C E A N*

*Andes*

# SOUTH
# AMERICA

Tropic of Capricorn

A S I A

*Andes*

C  O C E A N

# INTRODUCTION

BY ARNIE WILSON

Skiing is a strange but truly exhilarating phenomenon. It would be difficult to explain it to a visitor from another world. What pleasure could the human race possibly get from deliberately venturing outside – for pretty much the entire day, during the coldest and often most inhospitable time of the year – and sliding down frozen water at considerable financial cost, vulnerable to avalanche, frostbite, collision, rocks and cliffs?

And yet – visit any ski area in the world – large or small, glitzy or run-of-the-mill, world-class or ma-and-pa ski hill, with phenomenal powder or relying on man-made snow, with stunning scenery or a road running along the top of the slopes – and you will see men, women and children doing pretty much the same thing: skiing or snowboarding, to the best of their very mixed abilities, down a slope covered in snow.

The quality of that snow can be as varied as their own level of skill. It's not just the Inuit people who have many words for snow. We do too. Or at least skiers and snowboarders do. It can be powder, granulated, icy, wind-packed, sun crust, breakable crust, bullet-proof, mashed-potatoes, corn snow, surface hoar, crud, loose or chopped up. And there are many other descriptions – some desirable, some not. But as long as you can slide a ski or snowboard down it, it is all part of the magical winter sport that millions have found so addictive. The French, eager for a word to incorporate all forms of snow-sliding, have a word for it – or rather two: *la glisse*.

## In the beginning

But where did it all start? There are many places – or 'cradles'– where skiing is said to have originated. And 'fathers' of skiing too. But which one? Was it Sondre Auversen Norheim, the Norwegian ski-maker who in 1866 gave the first known demonstration of the Telemark and Christiania turn? The Austrian army offcer, Matthias Zdarsky, who pioneered so called 'stem-Christiania' turns? His pupil, Hannes Schneider, who developed the classic Austrian style? Or even Britain's Sir Arnold Lunn, who gave us the 'modern slalom'?

In terms of skiing 'cradles', it seems to be a toss-up between Scandinavia and Mongolia as to where man first strapped on primitive skis. Skiing has an incomparably longer history than snowboarding (a very recent phenomenon, the snowboard evolved from something called the snurfer – two skis bound together with a rope at the nose to enable the rider to keep it more stable).

The snow that skiers and snowboarders rely on comes in many forms, but for most the sought after variety is fresh powder.

In its very early form, skiing was not a sport but a method of transport. The ski was invented to get from A to B – when the terrain between them was otherwise almost impassable because of deep snow. Primitive skis helped Mongolian peasants to fish, hunt, farm and even go into battle.

There has been a long history of foot-soldiers using skis to facilitate the fight against the enemy during the winter months. As recently as the 20th century, troops on skis fought in both world wars. The Americans still venerate their 10th Mountain Division, which, indirectly, helped spawn their post-war ski industry. (The division was still in action as recently as 2006 in both the Iraq and Afghanistan theatres of conflict.)

The Pahsimi, who lived in the hills south-east of the Kirghiz steppes, strapped on footwear called *mu-ma* (wooden horses) when they were out hunting. In the *Kuang Chi*, an encyclopaedia of the Sung dynasty, it was said that "when the hunter has bound these boards under his feet…and goes over the snow on the flat, he prods the earth with a stick, and glides like a ship…and overtakes the fleeing deer".

In a contemporary description of the use of skis by a 13th-century Siberian tribe known as the Urianguts (whose most famous leader was Genghis Khan) Rashid ad-Din, a Persian physician wrote: "Their country being very cold, they hunt much over the snow. They bind to their feet long lengths of wood that they call *chana*, using a staff in their hands to push them along the snow, like the pole of a boat. They shoot down the mountainsides so swiftly that they catch up with animals. This is something you must see, in order to believe it."

Centuries later, in 18th-century Finland, Laplanders were said to "travel over the very highest mountains by the swiftest speed, and faster than thought. By a certain wooden machine, of an oblong figure, fastened to their feet, commonly called wooden sandals, they are carried

with such rapidity over the highest mountains, through the steepest hills…and the winds whizz about their ears, and their hair stands on end".

Californian miners, heavily influenced by Scandinavian immigrants, raced each other down the slopes on primitive skis at alarming speeds. Men with names like 'Cornish Bob' Oliver, Napoleon 'Little Corporal' Norman, 'French Pete' Riendeau, 'Quicksilver' Handel and 'Gray Flash' Pollard, introduced reckless but exhilarating races to the High Sierras as long ago as the 1860s. Hurtling down the slopes at speeds of up to 128kph (80mph), they battled for cash prizes and the champion's title.

At the turn of the 19th century, British aristocrats, gentlemen, and not long afterwards, a good number of army and naval officers, started what was arguably the most influential ski club in the world: the Ski Club of Great Britain. Odd, in a way, for a nation with precious few mountains (the only ones that qualify for skiing are in Scotland, which does have a handful of ski areas).

Even when the Norwegians started using 'ski' for jumping and cross-country, they were rarely used for downhill racing. It was the British, and Sir Arnold Lunn in particular, who helped make such a concept popular. British climbers specialized in conquering the Alps, and many took skis with them to combine the two activities – skiing down after climbing up. This was not at all the Norwegian *modus operandi*. Before Lunn helped revolutionize the whole concept of skiing, the Norwegians held that *langlauf* (cross-country) and jumping were sacrosanct. For them, said Lunn, "downhill racers were pariahs, despised as weaklings who lacked the strength to compete in the *langlauf* or the courage to jump".

## Looking ahead

Today the skiing (and snowboarding) industry is on what might be described as a fairly even keel, but looking over its shoulder. Changes in climate and ethnic population have to be dealt with, if not embraced. On the meteorological front, there are many scare-stories which – if accurate – may play havoc with skiing as we know it. In the worst-case scenario, hundreds, perhaps thousands of ski areas may be compromised by climate change. Although artificial snow technology has become very sophisticated, producing snow of very high quality, you still need temperatures that are close to freezing point to produce it: some resorts may still have to close, while others may have to broaden their scope to provide an ever-wider array of alternative activities like paragliding (parapenting), 'wellness' (spa) treatments and a greater emphasis on other sports such as skating, swimming, riding and even walking.

There is also concern about the changing profile of skiers in the USA. The discussion is not about ethics but hard business sense. In the next 15 years, says America's *Ski Area Management* magazine (*SAM*), the US Census Bureau projects that the US population will grow by about 38 million. Nearly 90 per cent will come from Hispanic, African-American and Asian-American populations. The Caucasian population under 18 will actually shrink by 16 per cent. "As a result" says the magazine, "by 2020, Caucasian youth will represent just 54 per cent of the youth population."

"In 1980, nearly three-quarters of the youth population was Caucasian. Ours was a largely white world. It's a different landscape now…many of us still wonder 'Can these ethnic communities afford to ski and ride? Don't they dislike the cold?' These questions reflect stereotypes that don't fit the modern world."

"African-Americans and Hispanics are willing to spend freely on products that matter to them. They spend as much – and often more than – Caucasian customers on shoes, cell-phones and service. Cycling, hiking, backpacking and camping are drawing interest and participation from ethnic communities. Skiing and snowboarding can too."

"So why", the magazine asks, "have we been slow to follow suit? Probably because most of us are white guys. To serve a multi-ethnic audience, many feel it helps to have a multi-ethnic staff. These populations are growing, and they can afford to become our customers – they *need* to become our future customers or our sports will wither. Diversity is the future. The sooner we embrace this concept, the better."

It is no surprise to find the Americans are concerned about their ski industry. Skiing produces few millionaires. Resorts themselves are not money spinners, as the closure, over the years, of scores of American ski areas illustrates. (In America, unlike Europe, many resorts are owned by individuals whose personal fortunes can fluctuate, or who have been unable to modernize lifts, introduce sufficient snowmaking or survive a sudden hike in oil prices.) In general, the only way to make serious money out of ski resorts is through associated real estate developments, which explains the proliferation of new ski villages, particularly in North America.

FACING PAGE: **The Nordic way: for the early Norwegian skiers, cross-country was sacrosanct and downhill anathema.**

ABOVE: **Young, skillful and white. But the demographic of people who ski is slowly changing.**

## Where to go

Choosing the right resort for a ski or snowboarding holiday is no easy matter, especially for a newcomer to the sport. Among the most important criteria for beginners perhaps, are: what else is there to do apart from ski if it turns out that you don't like it? (This is where Swiss resort villages like Zermatt and Grindelwald, the French resort of Chamonix, Austria's Kitzbühel and Italy's Cortina – where you can have an enjoyable holiday without going near the slopes – can be a blessing.) How big is the area? If it's vast, like France's Les Trois Vallées, there is absolutely no point in buying an expensive lift ticket giving you access to myriad runs when you only need the nursery slopes.

Each resort, of course, has its own particular flavour and charm – or possibly, particularly in the uglier French resorts, lack of charm. This is the paradox of resorts like Flaine, Avoriaz, La Plagne, Les Arcs, Val Thorens and Les Menuires. They provide some of the finest skiing in the Alps – along with some of the ugliest architecture. At the other end of the scale, many of the resorts in Italy's stunning Dolomites are not as demanding as the major French resorts but have buckets of charm, and outstanding food and scenery.

The resorts you will find in this book certainly include a good cross-section of both categories, and few major resorts have been left out. The most important resorts pretty much pick themselves. But the 'lesser' resorts are to a certain extent the personal selection of the writers. There are, inevitably, some paradoxes. Who would have guessed, for example, that you could ski in the deep south of America. The states of Viginia, North Carolina, Tennessee, Indiana, Maryland and even Alabama all have ski hills, and have to make most if not all of their own snow. But in the land which speaks of ski areas as 'breeders, feeders and leaders' any ski hill, however small, is worth having. And who would have guessed that New York State has almost twice as many ski areas as Colorado – (it has 45 compared with Colorado's 25). But New York's ski areas are considerably smaller than Colorado's and we list only two compared with a dozen in Colorado (including four separate ski areas in Aspen).

As for the now time-honoured quandary – the choice between Europe and North America – this is perhaps partly a question of aspirational skiing. My theory is that most European skiers, particularly those from the UK, will eventually want to try skiing in the USA or Canada at least once. This is partly based, I believe, on wanting to relive some of the great Western movies that have almost certainly been part of their childhood. How exciting to be able to ski in, say, Jackson Hole, where a number of celebrated Westerns, including *Shane*, were filmed. Or to visit Lake Tahoe, where the famous TV

**BELOW LEFT: The town of Steamboat Springs, Colorado: so-called because the original settlers thought the sound of the river resembled the chug of a paddle-steamer**

**BELOW: Heavenly powder: in a good snow year, hundreds of acres of lightly forested slopes across the California-Nevada border become skiable at Heavenly.**

Courchevel 1850: gateway to the vast French ski *domaine* of Les Trois Vallées. The resort is linked with Méribel, Saint Martin de Belleville, Les Menuires and Val Thorens, which together form the biggest resort complex in the world.

series *Bonanza* was set at the Ponderosa Ranch (although this is now closed to the public). Hundreds of films, of course, have been shot in the Rockies, and it takes little imagination to imagine the likes of Charlton Heston urging his horse through the powder as he rides to cut some villain off at the pass. If you visit Sun Valley, Idaho, you might even encounter the 'real thing'– Clint Eastwood or Arnold Schwarzenegger making turns on a slope near you. Visit Sundance, Utah, and it is not improbable that you might find yourself skiing the same slope – or even sharing the same chairlift – as the owner, a certain Robert Redford.

Meanwhile, as Europeans 'cross the salty pond' to enjoy their wild-west fantasies – and of course the well-organized and friendly North American resorts – a sub-

stantial number of Americans and Canadians will be winging their way in the opposite direction. They have their sights set on a different adventure: history and tradition. They are fascinated by the mountains where skiing really started, and such magnificent nearby towns and cities as Salzburg, Innsbruck, Zurich, Venice, Interlaken and Montreux.

They may, however, be confused by the European colour coding for identifying the relative difficulty of slopes. In North America, a green run is the easiest, blue indicates an intermediate run, and anything more or 'most' difficult is flagged up by black diamonds. A single black diamond indicates a fairly difficult run. A double-black is really for experts only, and the occasional triple-black is usually a gimmick and no more challenging than

**Though not quite in the same league as its glamorous neighbour, Aspen, or other iconic Colorado resorts such as Vail, Breckenridge or Copper Mountain, the picturesque old mining town of Crested Butte provides excellent skiing.**

a double-black. The major difference between the two continents is that in North America there are no red runs – used to signify intermediate runs in the Alps. An American blue run would be a red in Europe, where a blue would be an easy run. (Green is used for a very easy slope in North America and often in Europe too.)

There are other differences. By and large, the Rockies, especially those in the USA, are not as dramatic as the Alps. They may be just as high, but because many ranges – particularly in Colorado – start from a plateau which is already a mile in elevation, this prevents them appearing to be so high. In Canada, conversely, they start lower and therefore look higher, even though they are, in general, not actually as lofty as their counterparts across the border.

The runs in the Rockies are generally shorter than those in the Alps, and the demarcation zones – ski area perimeter, in-bounds and out-of-bounds – more clearly defined. In general, too, mountain food and the huts where it is served is vastly superior in the Alps, where lunch is a major event rather than a pit stop for refuelling. On the other hand the North Americans are almost invariably more friendly, and the queues, or lift lines, much more civilized. No pushing and jostling here as there is in Europe. There are big differences too between skiing America's east coast and west coast. The skiing in New England cannot really be compared with the Rockies. It rarely gets the same quantities of powder. The resorts are lower, and, with one or two exceptions like Killington, Vermont, smaller. And yet

LEFT: **Lake Louise – where skiers and snowboarders can enjoy Alberta's biggest ski area and some of the most dramatic scenery in the whole of Canada.**

ABOVE: **Far above the highest ski resort in the Alps at Val Thorens, the giant cable car whisks skiers and boarders to some of the best slopes in the French Alps.**

# Heliskiing

BY ALF ALDERSON

Two things prevent most skiers from heliskiing: lack of cash and lack of confidence in their skiing ability. But given the choice between waiting around in lift queues to take on uncertain snow conditions and carving fresh tracks through pristine, untouched powder, this has got to be an option any serious skier should consider at least once in their life.

First let's dispose of the myth that you need to have been on skis since the age of two to deal with deep, untracked snow. If you're a good intermediate – say you can tackle black runs without too much trepidation and have dabbled off-piste once or twice – a pair of fat skis will take you into a new world, and these will be provided by your heliski company (in many cases, the use of fat skis is actually compulsory).

Clipping into what feel and look like ski-jumping 'planks' will feel strange at first, but as soon as you set off through the powder you'll discover that they really do work – given a little adjustment to your technique. A good heliskiing guide will ensure that no-one in the group ends up out of their depth (literally) at the same time as moving onto progressively harder runs as the day develops. As your feel for your new skis improves and your confidence grows you may find yourself tackling the kind of terrain you'd normally associate with ski magazines and videos.

The pure excitement of heliskiing is not just confined to the skiing and the inspirational landscapes, though. Travelling into the mountains in a helicopter is a truly intense experience – exiting in a flurry of rotor-whipped snow atop a remote mountain peak is like something out of an action movie, and seeing your craft shrink in the distance as it 'whump-whumps' its way down to the distant valley where you'll eventually meet it again is certain to bring a buzz of excitement to any skier.

Heliskiing is invariably associated with the more remote and exotic mountain ranges of destinations such as Alaska, Russia and neighbouring former Soviet bloc states, British Columbia, New Zealand and the Himalaya, but Europe's more crowded peaks have companies offering to fly you into the alpine backcountry in Switzerland and Italy. You can heliski in Sweden too.

Although heliskiing is undeniably expensive by the standards of a regular package ski holiday, most heliski companies offer one, two or three-day options as well as a full week, and some will also do single drop-offs which allow pretty much anyone to experience this most exciting form of skiing. If you shop around, you'll find there are prices to suit almost any budget.

If you decide to take the plunge try and go the whole hog and spend at least one night at a heliski lodge, for this is almost as much a part of the experience as the skiing. You'll invariably be housed in luxurious surroundings, with features such as hot tubs, roaring fires, sports masseurs, fine dining and good wines, and it's a great chance to get to know your fellow guests at the end of what may well be the best skiing of your life. You'll find that heliskiers come from all walks of life, and are not necessarily rich doctors, lawyers and captains of industry, just mad keen skiers. You'll also get to spend more time with your guide and pilot, who invariably have all sorts of tales to impart about their exotic mountain life.

And there'll be one thing that everyone present has in common – after heliskiing once they just can't get enough of it, since for a skier there simply isn't a more thrilling and memorable way to spend a day in the mountains.

The helicopter is Swiss, the guide is French, and the location is Turkey. Now that heliskiing is discouraged or even banned in much of the Alps, the Kaçkar mountains of north-east Turkey provide an exciting alternative.

skiing in colder, sometimes icier climes in birch, beech or larch woods can be addictive. And the New England welcome is every bit as warm as that of the Rockies.

There is, unfortunately, no room to more than touch on the southern hemisphere resorts of Australasia or South America. Nor on Japan, although perhaps surprisingly to some, this Pacific island actually has some 600 ski areas, and has hosted two winter Olympics – in 1972 at Sapporo, and in 1998 at Nagano. Instead we concentrate on the main European ski nations of Austria, France, Switzerland and Italy, with a good selection too from Scandinavia and Germany. Andorra, for so long the 'cheap-and-cheerful' destination for skiers on a budget is featured. This small principality has gone up-market in recent years, and skiers and snowboarders in search of less expensive holidays are casting their eyes towards Eastern European ski nations like Bulgaria, Romania, Slovakia, Poland, Serbia and, perhaps in the not too distant future, even Russia. For the time being, however, the Russians continue their obsession with the Alps.

Bulgaria's skiing is surprisingly good, and the cost of eating out and the cost of living in general is an eye-opener. Borovets and Pomporovo are old favourites – Bansko is the big new attraction (old town but new lifts). Romania has only one serious resort – Poiana Brasov. It is a little limited, but provides a good few days for beginners and intermediates. And Brasov is an attractive and interesting medieval town. The skiing in Serbia, Slovakia and its neighbour the Czech Republic is also limited, and Poland's skiing reputation is based on one major resort just across the Slovakian border: Zakopane. Sarajevo, Bosnia, which enjoyed the Winter Olympics of 1984, is still recovering from the shattering events of the Yugoslav wars of the 1990s.

In Europe, the majority of skiers and snowboarders traditionally head for France and Austria. In the USA, Colorado is the big favourite, although following the 2002 Salt Lake City Winter Olympics, more visitors are trying Utah, with its legendary though not always justified 'Greatest Snow On Earth' tag. In Canada, Whistler in British Columbia and Lake Louise (Alberta) are still the big favourites – in both senses of the word.

But wherever you ski, from Andermatt to Alabama, and Wyoming to Wengen, there's nothing quite like it. Somehow, if that alien from another world ever turns up, you'll just have to persuade this bemused visitor in the best possible way, by taking him…her…or even it…to the nearest snow-capped peak.

ABOVE: **Portillo (Chile) is so close to the Argentine border that in some places you can see Aconcagua, the highest mountain in both western and southern hemispheres.**

SWEDEN/NORWAY: p.124

ITALY/SLOVENIA/SWITZERLAND/
AUSTRIA/GERMANY: p.60

SPAIN/ANDORRA/FRANCE: p.24

BULGARIA/SLOVAKIA/ROMANIA: p.140

# EUROPE

BY ARNIE WILSON

Europe (10 million sq km/4 million sq miles) is the second smallest continent (after Australia), and only the fourth most heavily populated – but has one of the highest population densities. Its 46 countries form the 'Western extension' of Eurasia. Although Europe is dominated by the Alps, there are other important mountain ranges. Apart from the Caucasus – generally regarded as the dividing line between Europe and Asia, these include the Pyrenees, Apennines and Carpathians. You can ski in at least 35 of the 46 countries – from Albania and Armenia to the Ukraine…and even the United Kingdom (mainly Scotland).

Those who have skied in the Caucasus, be it in Russia or Turkey (which have territory in both continents – as has even Azerbaijan), have sometimes wondered whether they are skiing in Europe or Asia: it is not always clear. Officially the border runs from the Urals to the Caspian and Black Seas. The highest mountain is Elbrus at 5,643m (18,510ft) – easily the highest peak in Europe. Despite Mont Blanc's fame, at 4,811m (15,780ft) the French/Italian peak is significantly lower.

Europe, of course, is home to the Alps – glorious and awe-inspiring natural barriers which both separate and contain countries, regions, languages and cultures – and create lush and picturesque valleys through which snowmelt sends torrents, streams and rivers.

The Alps are natural frontiers: it is no accident that some of Europe's most famous mountains, such as Mont Blanc and the Matterhorn, are shared by more than one country, and that peaks like the Gemsstock (Andermatt) stand sentinel-like above four Swiss cantons, prompting the proud locals to boast that in a single day you can 'eat *ossobuco Ticinese*, *raclette* with Valaisian bread and barley soup from the Grisons'.

There are hundreds of ski resorts in Europe: although the principal ski nations are France, Austria, Switzerland and Italy, there is also excellent skiing in Scandinavia, Spain and the Pyrenees (including Andorra). And an increasing interest in lesser-known resorts in Bulgaria, Romania, Slovakia, Slovenia, Poland and Serbia. The principal skiing gateways are Geneva, Zurich, Munich, Lyon, Salzburg, Milan, Turin, Venice and Toulouse.

Historically, it was Norway that provided the principal impetus for the emergence of skiing as a sport, concentrating almost entirely on the Nordic disciplines of cross-country and ski-jumping. Alpine skiing was still anathema to the Norwegians – they had no time for the concept, regarding any downhill sections of cross-country as opportunities merely to give their tired muscles a break and have a rest. No longer, of course, as any visitor to the Norwegian resorts of Hemsedal, Trysil or Oppdal will quickly discover. Sweden too has many good ski areas, including Åre, and Riksgränsen above the Arctic Circle,

No time to waste! A skier enjoys the challenge of getting round the extensive Saalbach-Hinterglemm circuit in Austria's Salzburgerland.

Space-age city: the major French resort of Les Menuires, a vital link in the vast Trois Vallées region, all lit up for some open-air après-ski.

where the sun never sets during the mid-summer months and you can even heliski in the middle of the night. Even Finland, a pretty flat country, has a number of ski resorts, although with the exception of Levi and Ylläs, the vertical drop is not at all substantial.

It was in Switzerland, the home of such glorious resorts as Zermatt, St Moritz, Wengen, Grindelwald and Verbier, and Austria (where skiing is the national sport) in such resorts as St Anton, Lech and Kitzbühel, that downhill skiing took root. In these countries, mountain villages inevitably acquired some of the early ski lifts, and some gradually evolved into famous ski resorts. Others remained obscure and undeveloped, with a handful of lifts or less. The Austrian Alps in particular, although celebrated for world-famous resorts, are also dotted with tiny, little-known ski villages.

In spite of two world wars (the first of which had a huge impact on the Dolomites, one of the key front lines between Austria and Italy, both in loss of life and national borders) skiing continued to develop. Italy produced one of the earliest purpose-built ski communities at Breuil-Cervinia, on the 'other side' of the Matterhorn, and Sestriere, which hosted many of the 2006 Winter Olympic events. France was very much a late starter. With relatively few traditional ski villages, the

way was open, in the 1960s, to start a 'brave new world' of 'third generation' purpose-built resorts. They came thick, fast and mostly ugly: La Plagne, Tignes, Les Menuires, Avoriaz, Les Arcs and Flaine.

The good thing about being able to start a ski resort from scratch was that, unlike the gradual evolution of Austrian and Swiss villages – not necessarily close to the best slopes – you could 'cherry pick' the highest, most snow-sure slopes. The bad thing was the belief that rather brutal architecture was the way forward. Today it is regarded by most as unsightly.

In recent decades, the French have tried to achieve substantial damage-limitation. La Plagne introduced pretty new satellite villages to try to detract from the horrors of its earlier construction, particularly Aime La Plagne, which looked as though some vast ocean-going liner had gone aground. Intrawest, the huge Canadian ski village developer, built an attractive North American-style village at Arc 1950, and went on to design a new village to soften the harshness of Flaine's grim architecture too – although many skiers and snowboarders were and still are prepared to

Not all high-alpine French architecture is unsightly! These attractive mountain homes are in the chic resort of Courchevel, aka 'Paris on ice'.

overlook such architectural blunders in order to enjoy some of the finest skiing in the world.

These days the tiny principality of Andorra has some big-hearted skiing, and is striving to throw off its cheap-and-cheerful image. It has deliberately taken itself up-market in an attempt to attract wealthier skiers. One result of this has been something of an exodus by its traditional clients in search of cheaper skiing elsewhere. It seems that Andorra's 'loss' is Eastern Europe's gain. Countries like Bulgaria, Serbia, Slovakia and Romania are the new playgrounds of skiers looking for cut-price lift tickets, accommodation and meals. Slovenia, although less inexpensive, is also becoming a popular destination with holiday skiers.

With climate change potentially threatening all resorts, it is difficult to forecast the long-term future of skiing in Europe. But judging by recent years, although rising temperatures during the summer months are melting glaciers, this does not automatically mean seriously diminishing snowfalls. Indeed the winter of 2005–6 produced so much snow that the number of fatal avalanches reached almost record proportions. This is a tragic statistic, but it does seem to indicate that skiing in Europe is by no means doomed. At least hopefully not for the foreseeable future.

ATLANTIC OCEAN

Bay of

Biscay

Golfe de Gascogne

**KEY**

-  Ski resort
- Peak
- – National border
- ✈ Airport
- — Main road
- —·—·— Main railway
- —— Local railway

**SPAIN/ANDORRA**

Baqueira Beret: p.26
Soldeu-El Tarter: p.28
Pas de la Casa-Grau Roig : p.32
Arcalis: p.34

Vannes

Loir

Angers ✈

Blois

Tours ✈

Loire

Vierzon

Montluçon

**FRANCE**

Poiters ✈

La Rochelle

Gironde

Aquitane Basin

Limoges ✈

Brive-la-Gaillarde

Cère

**MASSIF**

Bordeaux ✈

Bergerac ✈

Dordogne

Lot

Marmande

Garonne

Cahors

Aveyron

**CENTRAL**

Landes

Adour

Montauban

Tarn

Santander

Biarritz

Bayonne ✈

Toulouse ✈

Garonne

Ariège

Carcassonne

Aude

Bilbao ✈

San Sebastián

Pau ✈

Tarbes

St. Gaudens

Narbonne

**Cantabrian Mountains**

Vitoria ✈

Ebro

Lourdes

**P**

**Y**

**R**

Pic de Vignemale

**E**

**N**

Foix

Limoux

Miranda de Ebro

Pamplona ✈

Cerro de Mulhacén

Arcalis

Perpignan ✈

Jaca

**Baqueira Beret**

**Soldeu-El Tarter**

**E**

Burgos

Logroño

Tafalla

Pico de Aneto

**Andorra la Vella**

**Pas de la Casa-Grau Roig**

**ANDORRA**

Figueras

**S**  **P**  **A**  **I**  **N**

Gerona ✈

Manresa

Saragossa ✈

| 0 | 25 | 50 | 75 | 100 miles |

| 0 | 50 | 100 kilometres |

Auxerre

Avallon

PLATEAU DE LANGRES

Dijon

Nevers

Chalon-sur-Saône

Besançon

*Saône*

*Doubs*

Basel

**LEICHTENSTEIN**

Bern

**SWITZERLAND**

Lausanne

Montreux

Mâcon

Bourg-en-bresse

Geneva

Lapalisse

Villefranches

*Saône*

*Loire*

**Chamonix**

*Monte Rosa*

A
L
P
S

**Lyon**

Clermont-Ferrand

*Rhône*

*Matterhorn*

*Mont Blanc*

Aosta

Milan

Vienne

Chambéry

*Chartreuse*

*Isère*

**Paradiski**

St.-Étienne

Voiron

**Val d'Isère and Tignes**

**Les Trois
Vallées**

A
L
P
S

**ITALY**

*Isère*

Tournon

Grenoble

**La Grave and
Les Deux Alpes**

Turin

Alessandria

Valence

*Drac*

*Cottan
Alps*

*Po*

*Lot*

Gap

*Durance*

Cuneo

Genoa

Mondovi

Montélimar

La Spezia

*Rhône*

CÉVENNES

Orange

*Durance*

**Maritime Alps**

*Golfo
di Genova*

Avignon

*Verdon*

Lodève

Nîmes

Monte Carlo

L
A
N
G
U
E
D
O
C

Montpellier

Aix-en-Provence

Nice

**MONACO**

**LIGURIAN
SEA**

Brignoles

Cannes

Pisa

St.Tropez

**Marseille**

Toulon

*Côte d'Azur*

**Golfe du Lion**

*Corsica*

| FRANCE |
| --- |
| **Val d'Isère & Tignes : p.36** |
| **Les Trois Vallées: p.40** |
| **Chamonix: p.46** |
| **Paradiski: p.50** |
| **La Grave & Les Deux Alpes: p.56** |

M E D I T E R R A N E A N   S E A

# SPAIN

# Baqueira Beret

BY ARNIE WILSON

Since its conception in the 1960s, Baqueira Beret, on the winding road leading to the high Port de la Bonaigua Pass in the Pyrenees, has arguably become Spain's most celebrated ski area. This purpose-built resort is set in the beautiful Val d'Aran, in northwestern Catalonia, near Romanesque churches, mountain lakes and the Aiguestortes National Park. There are three connected ski areas – Baqueira, Beret and Bonaigua. The skiing is wide open, mainly above the tree line, and extensive – but in general not fiercely challenging. So for the vast majority of visitors – from lower- to high-end intermediates – the skiing is a joy. So, too, is the eating. The delicious Spanish tapas tradition is alive and well here – and prices for most commodities are relatively low.

The Spanish royal family are regular visitors to the resort. King Juan Carlos himself does not ski so much these days, but the heir to the throne, Felipe, his wife Leticia, his sisters Elena and Cristina and their families, are regular visitors, staying in their own royal mountainside enclave, La Pleta de Ley (The King's Hamlet). Even though France has plenty of world-class skiing of its own, Baqueira is popular with skiers from the neighbouring Bordeaux region.

One of the attractive satellite communities that has sprung up recently on the mountain at Baqueira Beret.

The resort has some of the best and most extensive bowl skiing in the Pyrenees. Its 1,9ha (4,750 acres) of skiable terrain are divided into the separate, but linked, sections of Baqueira, Beret and the recently developed Bonaigua section. Baqueira is the main hub, but both Beret and Bonaigua have their own bases.

## The starting point

The initial key to the slopes is the Bosque chair from the main Baqueira base area. This brings you up to a bustling plateau and meeting point where you can pause for meals and other refreshments, discover the main nursery slopes, or continue up the mountain on a network of higher lifts, including the Mirador and Pla de Baqueira chairs that take skiers and boarders to the Cap de Baqueira – at 2,500m (8,202ft) the resort's main peak and highest lift-served point.

From here runs fan out in most directions – mostly exhilarating reds, with links on one side to Bonaigua, and Beret on the other. Some of the best off-piste skiing can be found in the small valley between Baqueira and Bonaigua, where four chairs take strong skiers and boarders to some of the best pow-

der. These include the Manaud lift that also reaches the Cap de Baqueira. Another way to reach this area is to take the chair from the Port de la Bonaigua base.

Altogether there's 104km (64 miles) of skiing on 77 mainly intermediate runs, with unexpectedly extensive off-piste (including the exhilaratingly steep Escornacrabes – 'Where Goats Tumble' – couloir, also from the Cap de Baqueira) and an impressive vertical drop of 1,010m (3,313ft) – all served by 31 lifts. Baqueira's snow record is good, but just to be on the safe side there are 522 snow cannon. The resort has 200 instructors and there are three kindergartens.

A classic mile-and-a-half long double-black diamond run on the Baqueira slopes is named after the resort's founder, Luis Arias. There is a superb off-piste run down the north face of Dossau (Beret) to the deserted village of Mongarri, but you will need transport for the return. A helicopter is an option! The cost of heliskiing, like prices in general in Baqueira Beret, is significantly less than in most of the Alps.

In the winter of 2005–06, the resort continued with its expansion plans by opening the upper stage of a new gondola eventually connecting the resort base at Val de Ruda residential complex with the mid-mountain. From there, it continues to 1,800m (5,906ft) where it connects with the Bosque chairlift. The new gondola has 78 cabins that each take up to nine people. Baqueira's nursery slopes, at 1,800m (5,906ft), were updated for the winter of 2005–06 with lifts and conveyor belts (magic carpets) removed or relocated.

Apart from skiing and snowboarding, winter activities include helicopter skiing, mountain guide excursions, paragliding, bowling, squash, ice skating and swimming. Those with any energy remaining will be tempted by the Spanish party scene: Baqueira has a variety of vibrant nightspots which often stay open until the small hours.

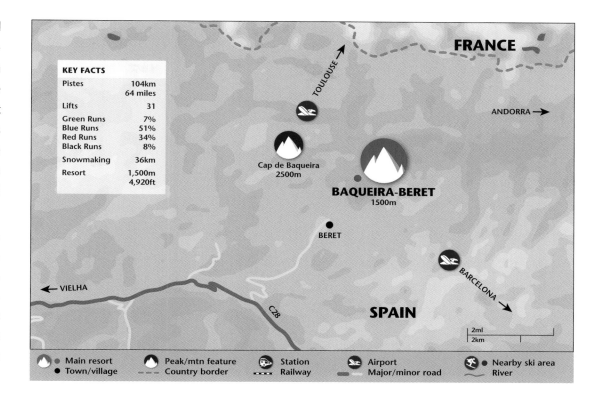

| KEY FACTS | |
|---|---|
| Pistes | 104km |
| | 64 miles |
| Lifts | 31 |
| Green Runs | 7% |
| Blue Runs | 51% |
| Red Runs | 34% |
| Black Runs | 8% |
| Snowmaking | 36km |
| Resort | 1,500m |
| | 4,920ft |

## REFUELLING

*Off the slopes, this being Spain, there are numerous tapas bars, offering a wide selection of delicious lunchtime and après-ski snacks. Thursdays are* marisco *or seafood day in Baqueira. Giant prawns, crabs, cockles and* perecebes *(goose barnacles) arrive here, at 1,500 m (4,920ft), in deep-frozen containers from the Galician coast, to be distributed to the many restaurants and tapas bars in the area.*

*Most people get up late and eat late in Spain – 9pm or even 10pm is the norm for dinner. Lunch is late too, so visiting Americans, for example, who prefer to eat early, can enjoy uncrowded slopes when the lifts open, uncrowded restaurants at noon and uncrowded slopes again after lunch. Because of the region's proximity to France, the local cuisine has much in common with that of Gascony. In spite of the excellent fish available, meat is still the staple of the valley. Lamb, veal and duck are popular.* Olha Aranesa *– a pot of soup-cum-stew with all kinds of pork sausage and potatoes – can take up to four hours to cook properly. Rioja is the traditional wine to wash it down.*

**Easy pickings: Baqueira Beret enjoys some unusually extensive powderfields sufficiently easy for off-piste novices to practise turns in deep snow.**

# ANDORRA

# Soldeu-El Tarter

BY FRANCIS JOHNSTON

Soldeu-El Tarter is Andorra's most internationally renowned, most progressive ski station and home to one of the best ski schools in the world. As a major player in the expansive Grandvalira linked ski domain, Soldeu-El Tarter also ranks in Europe's top 20 resorts for sheer extent of pistes and facilities, with 110 well-maintained linked runs stretching to almost 200km (124 miles), shared with Pas de la Casa-Grau Roig.

The resort made its name catering for young first-timers on a budget, with Soldeu village as the area's principal resort, dominated by British and Irish package-tour clients. Now maturing more gracefully, Soldeu is developing steadily into Andorra's most up-market resort, although it is still rather plain and lacks true Pyrenean charm. Its appeal as a young-and-lively destination remains noticeably strong, with more than a dozen late-night music bars and unpretentious eateries lining the busy main street, but this former entry-level resort now also boasts five four-star hotels and a sumptuous spa to cater for an increasingly cosmopolitan clientele.

As the double-barrelled name implies, Soldeu-El Tarter consists of two main linked ski areas, accessible from the principal resort or from the more tranquil, and slightly more attractive, base station at El Tarter, just 3km (2 miles) west of Soldeu. Both villages straddle the road that links the bustling Andorran capital, Andorra la Vella, with the French border at Pas de la Casa. Strictly speaking, the station now has an even more long-winded triple-barrelled name: Soldeu-El Tarter-Valls de Canillo. The local government of this parish, based at the nearby parochial capital, Canillo, has been a major shareholder in the Soldeu-El Tarter ski station for many years. In 2000, a gondola lift was inaugurated to link the town with a compact beginners' zone at El Forn, on the southwestern margin of the ski area. This small satellite zone has a sheltered, family-oriented feel and is ideal for nervous novices and weekend dabblers. It has its own branch of the highly respected Soldeu-El Tarter ski school, a crèche, a café, a self-service canteen and a good quality à la carte restaurant, all focused around a brace of short green-graded pistes. There are no home-run pistes down to Canillo, but there is a chairlift link into the upper El Tarter ski area snowbowl and a testing blue, plus a fast black piste linking in the opposite direction.

The open and frequently sunny snowbowl at El Tarter forms the core of the ski area, offering wide cruising pistes and almost limitless inter-piste powder pockets. A unique

El Tarter's buzzing Riba Escorxada plateau; the central mid-altitude services hub for the Soldeu-El Tarter ski area.

feature of this sector is the weekend-only 'Ratrac' service, whereby a piste-grooming machine (snowcat) tows off-piste powder seekers to the non-lift-served summit of Pic d'Encampadana, high above the main snow-bowl. There are four tried and tested ungroomed routes marked on the local piste map – two red- and two black-graded – although riders are free to choose any line they like over the exciting and varied terrain. The tow service is included in the price of the ski pass but is subject to favourable weather conditions and avalanche risk approval from the station's snow patrol.

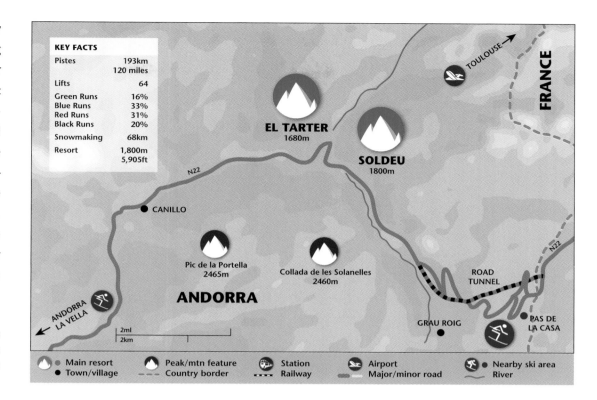

| KEY FACTS | |
|---|---|
| Pistes | 193km |
| | 120 miles |
| Lifts | 64 |
| Green Runs | 16% |
| Blue Runs | 33% |
| Red Runs | 31% |
| Black Runs | 20% |
| Snowmaking | 68km |
| Resort | 1,800m |
| | 5,905ft |

**A pure Pyrenean powder morning: first tracks off the *arête* between Soldeu-El Tarter and Grau Roig in the Grandvalira domain.**

El Tarter's prime attraction is its well-maintained and full-featured snowpark, overlooking the busy restaurants and services zone close to the gondola upper station at Riba Escorxada. The park is served by a six-pack chairlift and a button draglift, both just a short slide from the gondola station and services area. Simple low rails, boxes and kickers have been positioned just inside the entrance to the park to ease novices into their first freestyle experience. The main park boasts a full-sized halfpipe, a huge spine, gap jumps, various kickers and a good selection of rails and boxes. The station sponsors its own freestyle team and, by having undoubtedly the best snowpark in the Pyrenees, often hosts major international competitions.

Away from the freeride and freestyle features, the most noteworthy pistes in this sector are the summit-to-base Esquirol blue and Aliga black home runs. The Esquirol is an epic tour manageable by confident beginners after the first few days of tuition, while the Aliga is a fairly full-on blast that delivers a testing workout for those of competent intermediate standard and above. Younger visitors will love the 'Mickey Snow Club' piste immediately above Riba Escorxada: a fantastic

themed adventure trail through the woods, designated for the under-12s only – grown-ups are forbidden! The course has colourful obstacles and cartoon decorations. Features include a little slalom and some gently banked bends, a series of rolling bumps under low-hanging banners, hoops forming a tunnel and a finish schuss with flashing lights and sirens.

Further to the northeast, and well linked with the expansive El Tarter sector, lies Soldeu's equally large and varied home sector. As at El Tarter, the main uplift is provided by a gondola lift departing from a sizeable base station, just off the resort's main street, arriving at a sunny yet snow-sure plateau at the buzzing Espiolets area. These wide and gentle Espiolet snowfields are the station's main beginners' zone and house the headquarters of the world-class Soldeu ski school. The school employs a large number of English-speaking instructors, most of British or Commonwealth nationality. Mother-tongue English helps create a more flowing rapport with the instructors and the effectiveness of instruction and rate of learner progress are therefore consistently very high. One of the most effective systems developed by the school is their group lessons' management on

the first day. Unlike in many other ski resorts, where beginners are simply grouped into ski school classes on a first-come-first-served basis, here they take groups of 44 guests with four instructors jointly hosting an initial light-hearted 'team teach' to observe each person's natural ability. Only then are these large groups split into smaller classes, matched to each individual's aptitude, age and character and led by a dedicated instructor.

The busy Espiolet plateau is also the main on-mountain services hub for this sector, and is served by two cafés, a fast food and self-service restaurant, plus a more refined à la carte restaurant. All slope users, from beginners to all-mountain riders, must pass through this area at least once before ranging out to the rest of the ski area. A single, gentle blue piste leads from Espiolets towards El Tarter, providing confident beginners with an ideal first tour away from the nursery slopes; in the opposite direction, a broad blue cruises down to Soldeu's principal chairlift, connecting with

**Flowing out of Soldeu's wide and often sunny Espiolets beginners' snowfields for the gentle excursion to El Tarter.**

this sector's upper Solana del Forn slopes. These open slopes flow over fairly tame terrain above the tree line, accessing two further chairlifts – one to the summit of Tossal de la Llosada, the highest point in the Soldeu-El Tarter ski area at 2,560m (8,399ft); the other towards the Collada de les Solanelles ridge, marking the crossover point with the linked Grau Roig sector towards Pas de la Casa.

The face of the mountain directly above Soldeu is north-facing and sheltered by mature pine forest. A good selection of home runs trace down these wooded slopes, allowing visitors of all abilities to return on-piste to the resort, schussing the final few metres across a pisted bridge over a ravine to reach the foot of the gondola base station at Soldeu village. Advanced-ability visitors should try the steep Avet black down the line

**Andorra's trademark Mediterranean blue skies and enviable snow record will put a spring in your step.**

of the gondola lift pylons, regarded by many as Soldeu's signature run.

With its huge well-integrated ski domain, ever-improving high-quality accommodation, lively après-ski and reasonable prices, Soldeu-El Tarter still reigns as Andorra's best all-round snowsports destination.

# Pas de la Casa-Grau Roig

BY FRANCIS JOHNSTON

Pas de la Casa is Andorra's largest and liveliest resort, well established as one of the most popular snowsport resorts in the Pyrenees. It is the only Andorran resort with home-run slopes to the heart of the town, and its wide super-pistes flow down to the base of all main chairlifts. The resort itself is a busy frontier town, packed with bustling duty-free shops and buzzing bars, with a reputation for providing Andorra's most raucous après-ski.

The town sits at the northeastern edge of this tiny principality, almost straddling the Franco-Andorran border, meaning that it is the closest Andorran ski station to the airports at Toulouse, Pau, Carcassonne and Perpignan; Toulouse is the most convenient entry point, lying around two hours away by road (160km/99 miles).

In many ways, Pas de la Casa is reminiscent of similar-sized resorts in the Alps. It is a popular jaunt for French shoppers and snow-sports enthusiasts who throng its streets and slopes every weekend, giving the resort a more Gallic ambience than any of Andorra's other ski stations. The French feel is further reflected in the purpose-built nature of the resort and in the extensive ski area, set against an impressive backdrop of classically-shaped Alpine peaks. The town itself, however, is not attractive, and its austere blocks of plain apartments and basic hotels are located above rows of brash duty-free shops in a sprawl of ill-conceived 1970s architecture. Thankfully, however, there are also plenty of well-run refurbished and new hotels and a good number of quality boutiques, top-of-the-range sports shops, welcoming cafés and restaurants, which contribute to a more positive impression once you get in amongst the vibrant streets.

Pas de la Casa is a thriving border trading post and, with such an established and regular flow of year-round visitors, it was natural that it was the first Andorran village to develop as a ski station. Founded in 1957, Pas de la Casa was also the first ski area in Andorra to install mechanical ski lifts and automatic snowmaking equipment. The pistes were gradually extended over the high Envalira pass into the neighbouring valleys surrounding Grau Roig, eventually intertwining with the pistes belonging to the resort's longstanding rival, Soldeu-El Tarter. In 2004, Pas de la Casa-Grau Roig and Soldeu-El Tarter finally came to a commercial agreement and combined their ski areas, together forming the impressive Grandvalira ski domain. Spread over 110 pistes (extending

Shredding through the crux of the Jordi Anglés black run, towards Pas de la Casa and the Franco-Andorran border.

to almost 200km/124 miles), the entire domain is now fully accessible on one ski pass, putting Grandvalira among Europe's top 20 ski areas for extent of pistes and facilities.

Pas de la Casa's home sector, immediately above the resort, is characterized by long straight blues and reds offering easy cruising down to the town. This sector is also expanding internationally: in a recent initiative, the ski area has crept over the French border as part of a scheme to link with the nearest French ski station, Porte Puymorens. The Grau Roig sector is more varied and extensive than Pas de la Casa's home sector, although it is also mainly characterized by wide ribbons of well-groomed cruising pistes.

Grau Roig is not actually a resort, merely a linked access station with just one hotel and a couple of day lodges serving busy day-tripper car parks. Both stations lie within Andorra's Encamp parish, although Encamp itself is located at the geographical centre of Andorra, close to the cosmopolitan capital, Andorra la Vella. To save skiers from having to drive all the way from Encamp to reach the slopes, the 'Funicamp' cable car stretches over 6km (4 miles) from Encamp Grau Roig.

Beginners are well catered for in both sectors, the standard of tuition provided is

| KEY FACTS | |
|---|---|
| Pistes | 193km |
| | 120 miles |
| Lifts | 64 |
| Green Runs | 16% |
| Blue Runs | 33% |
| Red Runs | 31% |
| Black Runs | 20% |
| Snowmaking | 68km |
| Resort | 2,050m |
| | 6,725ft |

ANDORRA

SOLDEU

TOULOUSE

N22

ROAD TUNNEL

Port d'Envalird 2405m

GRAU ROIG

Coll Blanc 2530m

PAS DE LA CASA 2050m

FRANCE

2000ft
500m

● Main resort / ● Town/village      Peak/mtn feature / Country border      Station / Railway      Airport / Major/minor road      ● Nearby ski area / River

high and the Andorran ski schools have developed some of the best snowsports teaching systems in the world. The whole ski area is fairly accessible to novices, whilst intermediates should appreciate the long sweeping reds and the high mileage achievable thanks to the easy links with Soldeu-El Tarter.

Pas de la Casa has consolidated its position as one of the best-value destinations in the

world of snowsports: it may not be sophisticated, but it offers something for everyone in a lively and fun environment. Leave space in your luggage for the duty-free shopping and remember to pack something to help dull the hangover.

*Grandvalira's stable twin-cable 'Funicamp' super gondola, connecting the village of En Camp with the pistes at Grau Roig.*

# Arcalis

BY FRANCIS JOHNSTON

Arcalis is a Pyrenean paradox: it is Andorra's smallest and least-known ski station, yet it offers this mountain micro-state's purest Alpine experience. This region is endowed with a very favourable microclimate, blessing Arcalis with reliable snowfall, but without extremes of temperature. As a result, Arcalis can usually be relied on consistently to be more than 90 per cent open throughout the winter season and almost never suffers from icy pistes.

## Off the beaten track

Andorrans have long regarded Arcalis as their own secret snowsports playground, thanks to the station's remote location tucked away in the less touristy parish of Ordino, draped over the rugged snow-sure peaks that mark Andorra's northwestern border with France. Now, however, the secret is out. Arcalis has recently been linked commercially with the more internationally renowned Pal-Arinsal ski area, and is now marketed together with that more established destination as the Vallnord ski domain. The Vallnord ski pass covers both ski areas, although Arcalis still remains physically separate from Pal-Arinsal.

Arcalis is reminiscent of some small North American ski stations, having no accommodation or actual 'resort' village to speak of, with just a couple of base-station day-lodges housing all main services immediately next to the car parks and roadside ski-lift access points. Public transport to the station is infrequent so hiring a car is definitely the best way to reach this less-visited corner of Andorra; a car also allows you to make the most of the Ski Andorra pass, which permits access to all of Andorra's ski stations. This option lets you take a 'ski safari' approach to your visit, whereby you ski in a different resort each day; Ski Andorra ski passes can be purchased from all main ski pass sales kiosks throughout the principality.

The nearest accommodation can be found at the handful of quiet family-run hotels strung out in a series of sleepy hamlets along the picturesque Valira del Nord valley, leading up to the ski station, or 14km (9 miles) away in the pretty French-influenced village of Ordino. Most visitors, however, choose to stay in the livelier resort of Arinsal or its neighbouring parish town of La Massana, a 16-km (10-mile) drive from Arcalis.

## On- and off-piste

Arcalis' well-groomed ski area is quite compact, with 14 lifts serving just 25 mainly blue- and red-graded pistes, but it offers something for all ability levels. An imposing cirque directly above the base station provides the most demanding marked trails and inter-piste terrain, including the station's snowpark, a couple of high-end blues and a web of fast reds, plus the seriously steep La Portella del Mig and La Canal Gran black runs – two of Andorra's best. A further linked sector lies in the higher, and frequently

FRANCE

TOULOUSE →

**ARCALIS**
1940m

Pic d'Arcalis
2776m

**ANDORRA**

● EL SERRAT

● LES SALINES

ARINSAL

LA MASSANA/
ANDORRA LA VELLA

| KEY FACTS | |
|---|---|
| Pistes | 26km |
| | 16 miles |
| Lifts | 14 |
| Green Runs | 24% |
| Blue Runs | 24% |
| Red Runs | 44% |
| Black Runs | 8% |
| Snowmaking | 74 guns |
| Resort | 1,940m |
| | 6,360ft |

1ml
1km

| | | | |
|---|---|---|---|
| ● Main resort | ● Peak/mtn feature | ● Station | ● Airport | ● Nearby ski area |
| ● Town/village | --- Country border | ▬ Railway | ▬ Major/minor road | ～ River |

sunnier, open La Coma snowbowl close to the French border, offering easy cruising on gently undulating motorway-wide blues. The long La Basera green run flows gently out of this upper sector down into the base area cirque, passing a huge metal ring perched precariously on the edge of the cliffs above the base station – an incongruous and whimsical sculpture which is one of Arcalis's signature landmarks.

The station's main draw is its almost legendary lift-served off-piste. A specially designated free-ride initiation zone (marked as the *Zona Fora Pista* on the piste map) is served by a single draglift and provides a couple of tried-and-tested red-equivalent routes on ungroomed slopes between the two sectors; while the impressive arc of peaks, accessible using the westernmost Creussans chair-lift, positively drip with extreme couloirs and untamed descents.

Although Arcalis has a couple of sheltered childrens' and beginners' zones, the station primarily appeals to, and is best suited to, competent intermediates and experts. The well-respected ski school is noted for providing the highest-level tuition in Andorra, with a focus on off-piste and backcountry touring, and offers regular training sessions in the use of avalanche search and rescue equipment.

Arcalis really adds interest to a snow-sports trip to this historic Pyrenean principality. This is where Andorra's ski instructors and extreme sports enthusiasts come to ride on their day off – we recommend you pack a camera and follow their example.

**Preparing for the off at the top of La Coma snowbowl, on the lift-linked watershed between the Arcalis and La Coma Cirques.**

**The sweeping snowbowl in Arcalis' La Coma sector, a powder paradise for all abilities.**

# Val d'Isère and Tignes (Espace Killy)

BY FRANCIS JOHNSTON

The Tarentaise valley, east of Chambéry in France's historically important Savoie *département*, houses some of the world's greatest ski resorts and is the principal gateway to France's premier national park, the spectacular Vanoise. At the uppermost end of the valley lies the Espace Killy ski domain, named after one of skiing's most respected champions, Jean-Claude Killy, triple gold medallist at the 1968 Winter Olympics, held in Grenoble. The Espace Killy consists of the combined ski areas of Val d'Isère and Tignes, forming one of the world's most extensive linked ski domains, spread over 300km (186 miles) of Europe's most thrilling and technically demanding terrain.

## Val d'Isère

Val d'Isère occupies a pivotal position in the history of modern snowsports and has shared in some of snowsports' defining moments. The French national ski school was conceived here in 1932 and a local baker's son, Henri Oreiller, became France's first Olympic gold medal skier in 1948. The station hosted the blue-riband skiing events for the 1992 Winter Olympics, held in Albertville, and will host the 2009 Alpine World Championships. It is also home to the annual *Critérium de la Première Neige* race, which has marked the start of every Alpine World Cup season since 1955.

The town is an extensive mountain resort, attracting a fairly even mix of French and English-speaking visitors, yet, since it is based around a traditional Savoyard village, it retains the feel of a working mountain community. Much effort has gone into preserving the traditional regional architecture of the original village and towards gentrifying the pedestrian-friendly heart of the resort. Quality restaurants, delicatessens and

designer boutiques sit alongside snack bars, souvenir shops and sports outlets, enhancing the feel of cosmopolitan exclusivity for which the resort is renowned. There are many luxury chalets and high-quality hotels to cater for those attracted by the up-market cachet, however, there is a good balance of more affordable accommodation too. The resort has a reputation for some of the liveliest après-ski in the French Alps, attracting plenty of younger visitors intent on partying the night away in the bars and late-night venues.

The extensive ski area is easily accessible directly from the bustling town slopes, close to the resort centre. This is the finish area for the Olympic and World Championship courses, providing challenging home runs back to the resort. Gentler snowfields here at the edge of town house the main beginners' zone: this is quite limited in extent and suffers

See and be seen at Val d'Isère's buzzing *front de neige* base slopes, just a stroll from the resort centre.

FACING PAGE: As the sun slowly sinks behind the Rocher du Charvet and the Bellevarde Massif, the après-ski heat quickly rises in Val d'Isère below.

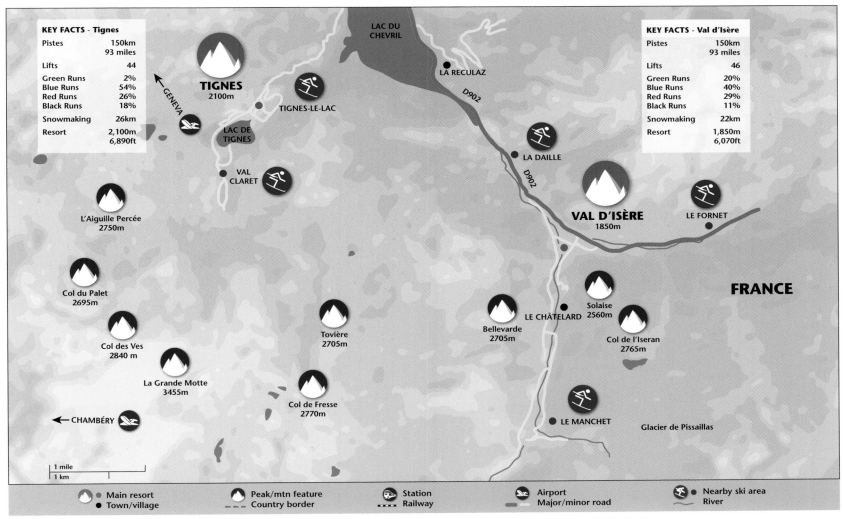

**KEY FACTS - Tignes**

| Pistes | 150km |
| | 93 miles |
| Lifts | 44 |
| Green Runs | 2% |
| Blue Runs | 54% |
| Red Runs | 26% |
| Black Runs | 18% |
| Snowmaking | 26km |
| Resort | 2,100m |
| | 6,890ft |

**KEY FACTS - Val d'Isère**

| Pistes | 150km |
| | 93 miles |
| Lifts | 46 |
| Green Runs | 20% |
| Blue Runs | 40% |
| Red Runs | 29% |
| Black Runs | 11% |
| Snowmaking | 22km |
| Resort | 1,850m |
| | 6,070ft |

LAC DU CHEVRIL

LA RECULAZ

D902

**TIGNES** 2100m

TIGNES-LE-LAC

GENEVA

LAC DE TIGNES

VAL CLARET

LA DAILLE

D902

L'Aiguille Percée 2750m

**VAL D'ISÈRE** 1850m

LE FORNET

Col du Palet 2695m

**FRANCE**

Bellevarde 2705m

LE CHÂTELARD

Solaise 2560m

Col des Ves 2840 m

Tovière 2705m

Col de l'Iseran 2765m

La Grande Motte 3455m

Col de Fresse 2770m

CHAMBÉRY

LE MANCHET

Glacier de Pissaillas

1 mile
1 km

Main resort • Town/village   Peak/mtn feature — — Country border   Station · · · Railway   Airport Major/minor road   Nearby ski area River

from busy piste traffic, but the beginners' lifts are free and all resort facilities are just a stroll away. This attractive base area is lined with restaurant terraces and sun-lounger patios, buzzing with slope users and locals enjoying the views and the lively ambience.

To the east, directly above the town, lies the Solaise ski sector; characterized by wide, gentle cruising pistes in an open and often sunny snowbowl, with testing reds and mogul-heavy black runs down the fir-lined skirts of the mountain back to base. Beyond Solaise, the high-altitude Pissaillas Glacier tops off the quieter lift-linked Le Fornet sector, ensuring snow-sure conditions and giving access to some demanding off-piste itineraries on the margins of the wild and beautiful Vanoise National Park, close to the border with Italy.

Immediately to the west of Val d'Isère is the expansive Bellevarde ski sector, draped over the imposing Bellevarde Massif that towers above the town. Principal access to this sector is via a swift gondola-style cable-car directly from the town slopes, or via a fast

funicular tube train from the nearby satellite resort base station at La Daille. Val d'Isère's most famous pistes are on Bellevarde: the testing Face black run (the Olympic course), sweeping straight down to the town slopes, and the fast OK red run (the *Critérium de la Première Neige* course) down to La Daille.

La Daille is only a five-minute ski bus ride (free) from Val d'Isère and is marketed to those on a budget. Its monstrously huge accommodation blocks are not to everyone's taste, but it offers a very convenient and affordable alternative to the main resort, right at the heart of this world-class ski domain. Two fast chair-lifts, one of them an eight-seater, depart from the wide snowbowl above La Daille to link towards Tignes.

## Tignes

Tignes is a complete contrast to Val d'Isère: a high-altitude sports station dominated by huge modernist accommodation blocks and displaying little in the way of traditional Alpine charm. It might have less perceived class, but it still occupies a key position amongst the world's top ski resorts: it was one of the first purpose-designed ski-in/ski-out resorts and was one of the first to exploit a glacier, allowing the resort to operate from

late September to early May. Not so long ago, Tignes boasted of being open for skiing 365 days a year, but has been forced to reduce the number of days the glacier is open because of climate change. The resort is situated at a snow-sure altitude of 2,100m (6,890ft) and is split into two main clusters, Val Claret and Tignes-le-lac, located on either side of a central lake. Val Claret consists of mostly high-rise accommodation blocks and lacks central focus, but is within strolling distance of Tignes' innovative freeride/freestyle zone and has a fast funicular tube train direct to the glacier. Tignes-le-lac is more pedestrian-friendly and has a discernible community spirit in its open lakeside setting. Both resort centres have home-run pistes and direct links into Val d'Isère's ski area above La Daille.

Rising above Val Claret is Tignes' signature ski sector, La Grande Motte. This glacial realm of permanent snow is accessible by all visitors using the funicular, giving even absolute beginners and non-skiers the opportunity to experience the breathtaking splendour of the high Alps. Also overlooking Val Claret is Tignes' innovative 'Le SPOT' freeride/freestyle zone: this consists of a search and rescue training area, a lift-served ungroomed powder valley, a BorderCross/SkierCross course and a full-featured snowpark. This zone, a laudable effort by the station to embrace freeride and freestyle snowsports, provides the safest possible introduction to backcountry touring for those wishing to progress beyond the pisted ski area into the Espace Killy's almost limitless off-piste terrain.

Tignes has another side to its personality, far removed from the high-rise severity of the main resort. Deep in the Isère valley lie two sleepy villages that offer a more traditional Savoyard experience: Tignes-les-Boisses and Tignes-les-Brévières. Both are lift- and piste-linked with Tignes-le-lac and both have home-run pistes. The epic Sache black run is particularly noteworthy, marking the western-most boundary of the Espace Killy and providing a long cruise through a peaceful

**Tignes' Grande Motte cable-car to the roof of the Espace Killy. Open for snowsports in high summer on La Grande Motte Glacier.**

side valley before dropping steeply on heavily mogulled wooded slopes down to Les Brévières on the valley floor. Les Brévières is the larger of the two valley villages and offers a viable, lower-cost base from which to explore this extensive and varied domain.

Tignes may not have the same reputation for nightlife as its glitzy neighbour, but with over 60 restaurants and lively late-night music bars and nightclubs, there's certainly plenty of action, particularly in Val Claret.

Both Tignes and Val d'Isère offer a plethora of alternative activities: dog-sledding, snow-mobiling, helicopter and paragliding flights, frozen waterfall climbing and even scuba-diving under the ice at Tignes' lake. Those seeking more relaxing distractions can indulge themselves at one of the growing number of spas and wellness suites, or simply soak up the atmosphere of the spectacular surroundings in this privileged Alpine paradise. Although best suited to experienced snowsports enthusiasts seeking a big mileage ski area and some of Europe's best lift-accessible off-piste, the Espace Killy also

offers family-friendly facilities and vibrant après-ski too. Beginners are more suitably catered for at other more novice-focused resorts. All things considered, this is still one of Europe's best all-round wintersports destinations.

ABOVE: A powder paradise under a perfect sky: above Le Fornet and Le Laisinant in one of Val d'Isère's quieter sectors.

BELOW: Mogul bashing at Tignes, the Espace Killy's centre of snowsports innovation and the capital of summer skiing.

# Les Trois Vallées

BY FELIX MILNS

In terms of scale, no ski area on earth can compete with the sheer magnitude of Les Trois Vallées (the Three Valleys). Boasting 600km (372 miles) of prepared terrain spread over 334 pistes and serviced by over 200 ski lifts, together comprising skiing's most comprehensive lift infrastructure, the mountains are also superbly laid out for almost endless skiing odysseys around the slopes. Strong intermediates who consistently want to explore mile after mile of different pistes have come to the right place. Both beginners and experts are well catered for.

The ski area can be roughly subdivided into three parts; Courchevel, Méribel and the Vallée de Belleville, comprising Val Thorens and Les Menuires. However, with the development of the 'fourth valley' of Maurienne (off the back of Val Thorens) and the maturing of the many smaller satellite villages, this catch-all area requires more explanation.

Courchevel sits to the left on the piste map and is made up of five key residential centres: 1850 is the resort's heartbeat; 1550 a cheaper base feeding directly into 1850; and 1650, a calmer alternative on the fringes of the three-valley network. Lower down are the almost entirely separate villages of Le Praz (aka 1300), famous for gourmet restaurants and ski jumps, and La Tania (1,350m/4,429ft), a pretty, purpose-built development with fabulous tree-lined skiing. Courchevel is the most chi-chi of the three valleys and the favourite winter destination of Parisian high society, with 1850 the focal point. Not surprisingly it is also by far the most expensive port of call.

Méribel is the central valley, meaning skiers staying here can easily drop into either adjoining valley as well as exploring Méribel itself.

**Distinctive timber chalets sit half-hidden in a forest of pine under the jagged Saulire peaks.**

There are two major areas; the picture-post-card chalet style of Méribel (1,450m/4,757ft) and the more high-rise, high-altitude Méribel Mottaret (1,750m/5,741ft). However, the price you pay for high altitude and an undeniably better location is a lack of resort charm and ambience. Below Méribel are several smaller, historic villages. Méribel village (1,400m/4,593ft) now has pistes to the village and a speedy chair linking into the beginner area but is still rather isolated. Lower down are the villages of Les Allues and Le Raffort, both of which have intermediary stops on the bubble coming up from the valley town of Brides-Les-Bains (600m/1,968ft). All of these are becoming increasingly popular as more budget family-friendly bases for this formidable ski area.

Val Thorens is king of the Belleville valley, a not very attractive purpose-built but wood-clad resort, which, at 2,300m (7,546ft), is the highest resort in the Alps with a virtual guarantee of good snow. However, being so high above the tree line also means the risk of lift closure and white-outs is correspondingly higher. The unflattering name of Les Menuires reflects the historically rather ugly character of the mid–resort (1,800m/5,905ft), though much has changed since the architectural atrocities of the 1970s, with sympathetic new developments replacing the old eyesores. Still comparatively cheaper, this high-altitude gateway is beginning to look more attractive. In sharp architectural contrast is Saint-Martin-de-Belleville (1,400m/4,593ft), an old village positively resplendent with alpine charm, excellent value accommodation and the focus of much investment in recent years.

Across the ski area, there are over 1,500 snow cannons and 75 snowcats that work tirelessly to ensure that most runs are freshly groomed every day. While this is a point of contention with advanced skiers, who would prefer to see more pistes left to develop moguls, the great majority of visitors really appreciate the corduroy slopes. Advanced skiers can't complain too much: there are many off-piste areas of a sharp pitch

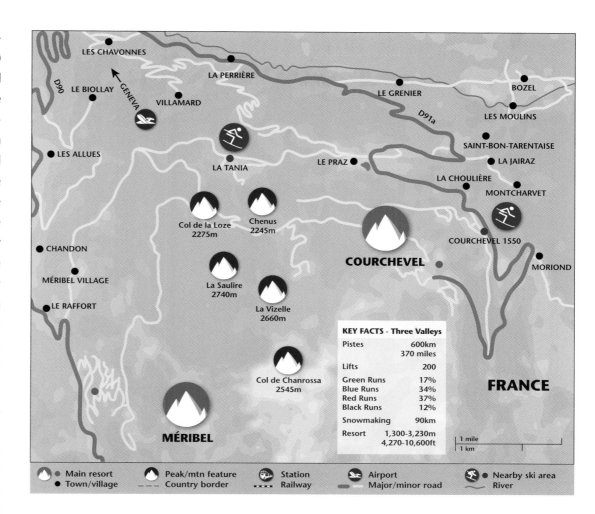

and bumpy façade, as well as myriad itineraries, six glaciers and no less than 25 skiable summits.

## Courchevel

Courchevel is the most glamorous section of Les Trois Vallés, with a private airstrip (altiport) that spits out a constant stream of celebrities and Parisian high society throughout the season, most of whom head to private chalets or deluxe hotels like Byblos in 1850. However, though you could spend your mortgage deposit in a week of glamorous excess here, there are many cheaper accommodation and culinary alternatives, even in 1850, though prices drop considerably in the other resorts. The atmosphere is certainly not stuffy yet remains resolutely more French than the thoroughly anglicised Méribel over the hill.

Most seasoned three-valley veterans would agree that Courchevel has the best breadth and variety of skiing. Starting with the magnificent couloirs from the top of Saulire

(2,738m/8,983ft) down to some tremendously characterful woodland runs down to Le Praz and La Tania, it also encompasses secluded powder bowls, intermediate favourites and high-quality nursery slopes.

The heart of the resort is the area directly above 1850, leading up to the twin peaks of Vizelle and Saulire, from where there are some excellent steep reds and a whole phalanx of steep-sided couloirs. Heading skier's right takes you down the ever-popular Creux, from where you can continue up Chanrossa before dropping down into 1600's wonderfully secluded reds around Bel Air. Here are also found several excellent mountain restaurants; Bel Air has a multi-tiered south-facing sun terrace, exquisite but by no means exorbitant food and a wonderful house rosé. Casserole, the restaurant at the bottom of the Signal lift, is also excellent.

The best restaurant for star-spotting is the mega-expensive Chalet de Pierres, halfway down Verdons above 1850. Skier's right of here is the main beginners' area of Pralong, which has recently been specially customized to focus almost wholly on beginners, with rope tows and other short lifts designed to help novices maximize their time with their instructors. There are also good beginner facilities at 1650, and there is an excellent choice of English-speaking ski schools throughout the valley.

Though the slopes are primarily north-facing (meaning good snow conditions), there is great variety. Skier's left of 1850, gentle runs feed back to the centre, while looping around the underside of Loze opens up an entire flank of excellent runs pirouetting out from 1550 all the way around to La Tania. The blacks of Jockeys and Jean Blanc are sensational runs in good conditions, as are all the reds and blues dropping down to La Tania. Above here is the Col de la Loze, which is one of the two points where you can drop into Méribel, the other being off the back of Saulire.

There are some excellent ski touring opportunities up in the Vallée des Avals, and one of the best non-skiing alpine experiences must surely be a tandem skydive above the winter beauty of Courchevel.

## Méribel

Méribel's greatest virtue is its central location; piste-hungry intermediates will be in all kinds of heaven here. From either of the two main resort bases, one two-stage lift will get you to the top of the adjoining valleys, in some cases more quickly than those staying in the other valleys can get there themselves. The skiing may not be as diverse as at Courchevel or as high-altitude as Val Thorens, but experienced skiers will more than likely drop into at least one of the other valleys every day. That said, there is also plenty of skiing for all levels in the Méribel valley.

This is perhaps best exemplified in the case of a mixed-ability group. There are countless itineraries different skiing levels can follow while still arranging to meet for lunch. It is only real beginners who are tied to a particular area, with the gentle slopes of Altiport an ideal learning ground. It is definitely recommended that beginners should stay in Méribel, with Méribel Village a suitable cheaper option. The slopes around Mottaret are not geared towards beginners, but from a purely skiing perspective this is the best base from which to explore Les Trois Vallées.

The skiing in the Méribel Valley takes place along both flanks and, as the valley runs from north to south, you can ski in the sun all day long, though the largely intermediate west-facing Saulire slopes do tend to get busy in the afternoon sun. Across the valley, Tougnète (2,435m/7,694ft) has a good variety of slopes, from the rolling Choucas (excellent for progressing beginners) to the steep pistes next to the Roc de Tougne drag, together sandwiching a clutch of characterful runs. It is also a top spot for dropping down towards Saint Martin de Belleville, either through some pleasantly graded off-piste or down one of two excellent reds, Jerusalem being a particular favourite. In good snow,

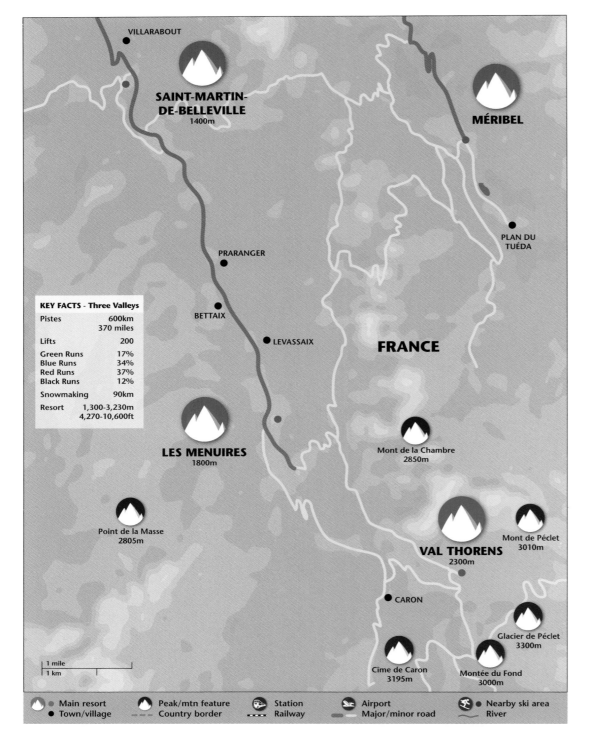

VILLARABOUT

**SAINT-MARTIN-DE-BELLEVILLE**
1400m

**MÉRIBEL**

PLAN DU TUÉDA

PRARANGER

| KEY FACTS - Three Valleys | |
|---|---|
| Pistes | 600km |
| | 370 miles |
| Lifts | 200 |
| Green Runs | 17% |
| Blue Runs | 34% |
| Red Runs | 37% |
| Black Runs | 12% |
| Snowmaking | 90km |
| Resort | 1,300-3,230m |
| | 4,270-10,600ft |

BETTAIX

LEVASSAIX

**FRANCE**

**LES MENUIRES**
1800m

Mont de la Chambre
2850m

Point de la Masse
2805m

Mont de Péclet
3010m

**VAL THORENS**
2300m

CARON

Glacier de Péclet
3300m

Cime de Caron
3195m

Montée du Fond
3000m

1 mile
1 km

| | | | | | | | | |
|---|---|---|---|---|---|---|---|---|
| ▲● | Main resort | ▲ | Peak/mtn feature | 🚉● | Station | ✈ | Airport | 🎿● Nearby ski area |
| ● | Town/village | | Country border | | Railway | | Major/minor road | River |

the women's downhill and itineraries down to the low-altitude villages can all be excellent.

The east-facing slopes above Mottaret are largely intermediate, with the best of them feeding down to the Val Thorens links and also Mont du Vallon (2,952m/9,685ft), imperious head and highest point of the Méribel valley. Only two reds officially come down from the top (with Combe generally regarded as the superior), but there are also lots of off-piste routes under, to the left and right of the lift, plus a scenic itinerary winding round the back.

Méribel itself has a curiously English heritage. The first lift was built in 1945 under the command of Colonel Peter Lindsay, who had fallen in love with the valley before the war and returned immediately afterwards. He then worked with the locals to ensure a strict architectural style, using local stone and wood, producing one of the most picturesque chalet-driven resort developments in the Alps. Lindsay was certainly ahead of his time, although one slightly negative aspect is that today the resort can seem more British than French.

The majority of the chalets are of a very high standard, and there are also self-catering apartments and a reasonable selection of hotels. Méribel has the best ambience, with English bars like the Taverne and Le Pub providing a warm-up to the expensive Dick's Tea-Bar. Rond Point is a good spot for a late-season après-ski drink on the sun terrace above the town. Check out Rastros if you're in Mottaret. Olympic investment also yielded benefits here, with a large ice rink, indoor climbing, bowling and swimming facilities.

ABOVE RIGHT: **The two-stage Saulire bubble runs from Meribel's La Chaudanne up to the distinctive 'Cadbury's Flake' peak separating Meribel and Courcheval.**

RIGHT: **Early morning shadows spill across the piste while a light dusting of snow sprays up from the skis on the approach to Belvedere.**

## Val Thorens, Les Menuires and Saint Martin

As the highest resort in the Alps, Val Thorens can generally guarantee its guests good snow conditions, the only drawback being the complete absence of trees. This means that whiteouts can completely wipe out skiing days, and high winds can force the top lifts to close. However, the proportion of skiers who actually want to ski in these conditions, and would benefit from the help of a little guidance from trees, is comparatively small.

Fortunately for the resort, French developers had seen the error of their ways and chose to clad many of the buildings in wood in an effort not to create another soulless ski resort. Les Menuires, built six years earlier (in 1967), was not so fortunate, but is undergoing something of a facelift. The charming village of Saint Martin predates the idea of recreational skiing itself. Saint Martin offers family-friendly alpine charm, Les Menuires high altitude for low prices and Val Thorens boasts higher altitude, atmosphere and prices.

FACING PAGE: **Val Thorens, the highest resort in the French Alps, sits high above the tree line in the middle of a snow-sure bowl.**

In skiing terms, this valley is bigger than both of the other two (Courchevel and Méribel) put together, with over 330km (205 miles) of pistes, 71 ski-lifts and eight peaks above 3,000m (9,842ft). Starting in Val Thorens, most of the skiing takes place across north- and east-facing slopes, spreading out across the valley from the resort base built below the Méribel ridge. The linking lifts and slopes here are generally less interesting. Val Thorens is the market leader in big gondolas, and the 25-seater up to the Peclet Glacier (3,101m/10,174ft) is no exception. From here, there are some excellent reds off-piste and the bumpy black of Cascades. The greater proportion of the skiing takes place along the flank from the glacier under the Point de Thorens down to the Cime de Caron which, until the fourth valley expansion, was the highest skiable point in the three valleys. That accolade now falls to the Sommet des Pistes, 3,230m (10,597ft), at the top of the Bouchet chair in the fourth valley.

Across the flank, the high-altitude pistes are largely intermediate, with excellent off-piste runs off the ridge and between the marked trails. There are also some exhilarating runs and itineraries off the back into the fourth valley, notably from the top of Cime de Caron.

How low can you go? Carve those turns and cut fresh tracks in the morning corduroy above Val Thorens.

Often overlooked are the fast and furious reds leading down to Les Menuires. Les Menuires itself comprises two main ski areas, a predominantly west-facing flank stretching all the way from the Tougnète peak above Saint Martin to Mont de la Chambre (2,850m/9,350ft) with the greater proportion of runs situated directly over the resort and wide flanks of off-piste between the resort and Saint Martin. Stay high on this flank for the best snow and don't be afraid to drop over the other side into Méribel.

The long back-country haul from Val Thorens to Méribel across the Gebroulaz glacier is not difficult, but there are crevasses, so you need a guide.

The real feather in the Les Menuires cap is the mountain on the other side of the valley, one that surprisingly few people visit. Pointe de la Masse (2,804m/9,199ft) is a wonderfully sculpted mountain with the runs twisting around steep couloir-rich rock formations. The runs are challenging but rewarding and there is excellent off-piste, both from the main lift, under the Lac Noir chair and a sublime itinerary looping round the back of the mountain.

# Chamonix

### BY FELIX MILNS

Chamonix has an almost revered place in the skiing lexicon. Sitting at the base of a steep-sided valley at the foot of Mont Blanc, at 4,810m (15,780ft) the highest peak in the Alps, it has long attracted adventure seekers of all persuasions. As much a summer base for climbers as a winter base for skiers, Chamonix is a town rather than a resort and is arguably busier during the summer, making it almost unique among ski resorts.

The very fabric of the town seems imbued with a sense of adventure; craning your neck upwards you see the fabled Chamonix Aiguilles – inspiring and intimidating in equal measure – almost daring you to test yourself against the awesome power of the mountain. It is this lure that pulls people to Chamonix; it is quite common for people to arrive for a week only to become permanent residents. In this cosmopolitan town, people are united by respect and love for the mountains above.

Only an hour's drive from Geneva airport, the town itself, at an elevation of 1,035m (3,396ft), is relatively low as it is situated on the valley floor rather than up a winding mountain road. This has its obvious advantages but there are also drawbacks. This is not your typical alpine ski resort: there is no ski-in/ski-out accommodation, the ski areas are far apart and are not lift-linked (a car is definitely recommended as otherwise you will have to rely on taking a bus every day), and the imposing slopes, very few of which have intimate knowledge of a piste-basher, are not for everyone. It is not ideal for beginners, and mixed-ability groups will find it difficult to ski together. This is not where you find mile after mile of easy piste cruising, but if you want to be taken out of your comfort zone you have come to the right place.

That said, these minor inconveniences pale into insignificance against the sheer quality of the skiing. There is a vertical drop of 2,807m (9,209ft) and most of the skiing is high, long and steep. Add in the dramatic scenery and incredible off-piste opportunities and it is easy to see why Chamonix is held in such high regard.

The awe-inspiring Chamonix valley cuts a swathe through the Mont Blanc massif and the Massif des Aiguilles Rouges and measures 23km (14 miles) from the ski area of Les Houches up to Le Tour. Often overlooked, Les Houches is no longer covered by the Chamonix skipass but has the best tree-lined pistes in the valley and is the only place to offer night-skiing. The valley is rounded off by the Domaine de Balme, at 2,270m (7,447ft) the top of the more gentle Le Tour ski area. The disparate parts spread along both sides of the valley and include the lift-linked areas of Le Brévent and La Flégère and, on the Mont Blanc side, Argentière's Les Grands Montets and the iconic Aiguille du Midi, start of the Vallée Blanche – the world's most famous off-piste run.

The statue of Dr Gabriel Michel Paccard, one of the first men to summit Mont Blanc, looks over the river in Chamonix town centre.

No other ski area has such a high proportion of glaciers – and their accompanying crevasses. In fact, the Mer de Glace, fed by avalanches and other glaciers, is the second largest glacier in Europe, and one of the more compelling reasons why many people say a mountain guide is more important than a piste map here. Anyone planning to tackle the off-piste described below should seriously consider hiring a guide.

Officially there are 47 lifts servicing 80 marked runs, totalling 152km (94 miles), but in reality this means very little as much of the skiing takes place off-piste. Les Grands

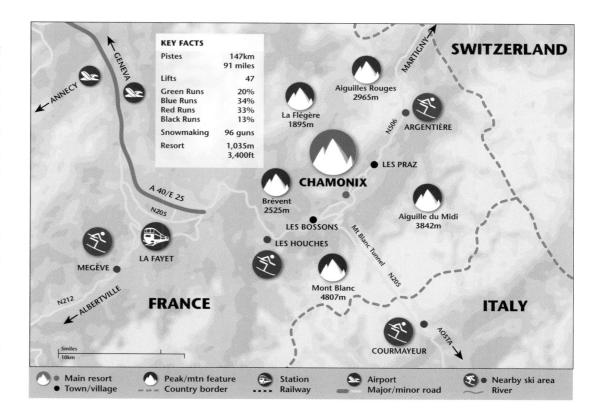

**KEY FACTS**

| | |
|---|---|
| Pistes | 147km |
| | 91 miles |
| Lifts | 47 |
| Green Runs | 20% |
| Blue Runs | 34% |
| Red Runs | 33% |
| Black Runs | 13% |
| Snowmaking | 96 guns |
| Resort | 1,035m |
| | 3,400ft |

**Main resort** • **Town/village** — **Peak/mtn feature** — **Country border** — **Station** — **Railway** — **Airport** — **Major/minor road** — **Nearby ski area** • **River**

**Famous for all things extreme, you need a good head for heights and an insane lack of fear to conquer the fabled Chamonix cliffs.**

Montets is where the toughest slopes are found, and, more than anywhere, it is here that Chamonix's reputation for fearsome steeps and sublime powder fields was formed. Most of the slopes are north-or northwest-facing so often have the best snow. The line between on- and off-piste soon blurs; after a snowfall, bumps develop across the mountain (most of the entire mountainside is skiable), not least because it is here that most Chamonix visitors come to ski. Fortunately there is plenty to go around.

Over 2,000m (6,562ft) of vertical gets you to the summit at 3,275m (10,745ft), though you have to pay extra for the privilege of taking the final lift and gaining an extra 500m (1,640ft) of altitude. From here, you can drop down onto either the Argentière or the Mer de Glace glacier or simply follow the Point du Vue itinerary alongside the glacier. Check out the 'Italian bowl' from the top of the Herse chair or veer left and right from L4 under the Bochard gondola. Both lifts offer many different lines, and it is by no means essential always to take the fee-paying lift.

At the foot of the mountain is the alternative resort base of Argentière (1,252m/ 4,107ft), the closest that Chamonix gets to a traditional resort. Developed largely along one main road, Argentière has local restaurants, a couple of bars and a welcoming atmosphere. If you are planning a short break focusing on this ski area, it is worth considering staying here, particularly as Chamonix itself is only 10–15 minutes' drive away.

In contrast, Le Tour's west-facing slopes are good for intermediates and progressing beginners. This is also a good area for those looking to attempt off-piste for the first time. The new gondola from Vallorcine has also opened up the north-facing slopes and some more adventurous tree-lined off-piste (the best in the valley, but beware of the avalanche risk) down that face.

**The view of the Vallée Blanche from the Cosmiques refuge, with the Grands Jorasses and the Dent du Géant peaks in the background.**

The lift-linked areas of Le Brévent and La Flégère offer another perspective on Chamonix; spectacular scenic views across the valley towards Mont Blanc, the Aiguille du Midi and the Chamonix Aiguilles. They are also the best areas for intermediates although there are plenty of steep chutes and couloirs to navigate here, too. Most of the slopes are south-facing and the skiing takes place above the tree line between 1,877m and 2,500m (6,158–8,202ft). The majority of the flank gets sun all day, making for pleasant skiing but slushy snow at the end of the season. Some of the runs, however, lose the after-noon sun, including the mighty black of Charles Bozon (Le Brévent), one of the steepest runs in the valley. Ski this run in the sun before rewarding yourself with a long tartiflette lunch at the Bergerie.

Le Brévent is also the only pisted ski area with a lift directly from town, in the shape of a cable-car built in 1932. There are some truly testing routes down under this lift, including the famous ENSA couloir. A proportion of Le Brévent's upper slopes have been re-sculpted to make them more intermediate-friendly, a good example being the run down from Col Cornu (2,414m/7,920ft).

The areas are linked by a short cable-car that is liable to be closed in high winds but very handy when open. La Flégère is short on lifts but long on terrain, with the familiar Chamonix trademark of minimal pistes and maximum powder. The terrain is less sharp and the slopes wider than its neighbour, however. Nonetheless, here you will find reds that anywhere else would probably be the toughest blacks in the resort – but in Chamonix everything is relative. The best of the runs are accessed from the top of the Index lift, with the 3,500-m (11,483-ft) long Combe Lachenal a particular highlight. Be warned that the Index face is quite exposed and can be cold in the depths of winter. There is plenty of piste-side powder in either of the bowls to the left and right of the lift, and it is a particularly good area for spring snow conditions.

The 20-minute cable-car ride in the summer across the Glacier du Géant to the start of the Vallée Blanche is one of the most spectacular in the world.

The Vallée Blanche is one of the longest off-piste runs in the world. Starting from the top of the Aiguille du Midi cable-car (3,842m/12,605ft) three-quarters of the way up Mont Blanc, it is also one of the busiest, with up to 2,500 skiers on a sunny day. Confident intermediates regularly tackle the long, gentle slopes and are rewarded with stunning glacier views, but guides are essential as there is always the possibility of encountering crevasses. There are also some wonderfully testing technical variants through the glaciers that can only be attempted by expert skiers with an experienced local guide.

One of Chamonix's greatest qualities is its location. Not only can you explore the ski areas that comprise Chamonix itself, but Italy is just 20 minutes' drive away through the Mont Blanc tunnel, with the resorts of Courmayeur, Cervinia and La Thuile all easily accessible. Back on the French side, there are plenty of characterful, small ski areas on the road to the glamorous Megève.

Chamonix is not renowned for its moun-tain restaurants, but you can eat very well in the town, with everything from traditional Savoie specialities (Le Chaudron) to Thai/ Swedish fusion (Munchie). Chamonix has a great atmosphere and there are over 30 bars and five clubs in town. The best are found near the train station (don't miss happy hour at the Chambre Neuf) and the best beer is brewed on site at the Microbrewery of Chamonix (MBC). Good-value hotels are plentiful but those in the know stay in the boutique hotel/members club, The Club-house. There is also a casino, bowling, swim-ming pool, ice rinks, cinema and both indoor- and ice-climbing.

# Paradiski (La Plagne and Les Arcs)

BY FELIX MILNS

Since the two resorts of La Plagne and Les Arcs rebranded as Paradiski in 2003, literally joining forces with the opening of the Vanoise Express (a cable car running across the valley between the two resorts), skier numbers have increased dramatically. Already popular high-profile resorts in their own right, the added mileage they are now able to offer has considerably enhanced their profile and put them firmly in the spotlight.

Before they joined forces, La Plagne and Les Arcs were dwarfed by Les Trois Vallées and Espace Killy. But thanks to the very impressive double-decker cable car that crosses the Ponturin gorge hundreds of feet below in just four minutes, they have joined the major league. They now offer 175 lifts servicing 425km (264 miles) of pistes, 239 marked trails, several glaciers and two of the most renowned 3,000-m (9,842-ft) plus peaks in the Alps; the Aiguille Rouge (3,226m/ 10,584ft) and Bellecôte (3,417m/11,210ft).

While famously appealing to piste-hungry intermediates searching for mile after mile of varied cruising, the two resorts now also offer a treasure trove of off-piste opportunities. Both are also excellent places to learn, making Paradiski – a little paradoxically – ideal for everyone from a skiing perspective. However, the statistics need to be put into perspective; despite the new cable-car, you still cannot ski between the two resorts and rather than circling around several key mountains, both resorts spread outwards alongside the flanks from the central point of the new lift. This means that, unless you are staying right by the lift and therefore on the fringes

**One of the world's first double-decker cable-cars, the Vanoise Express, takes only four minutes to cross between La Plagne and Les Arcs.**

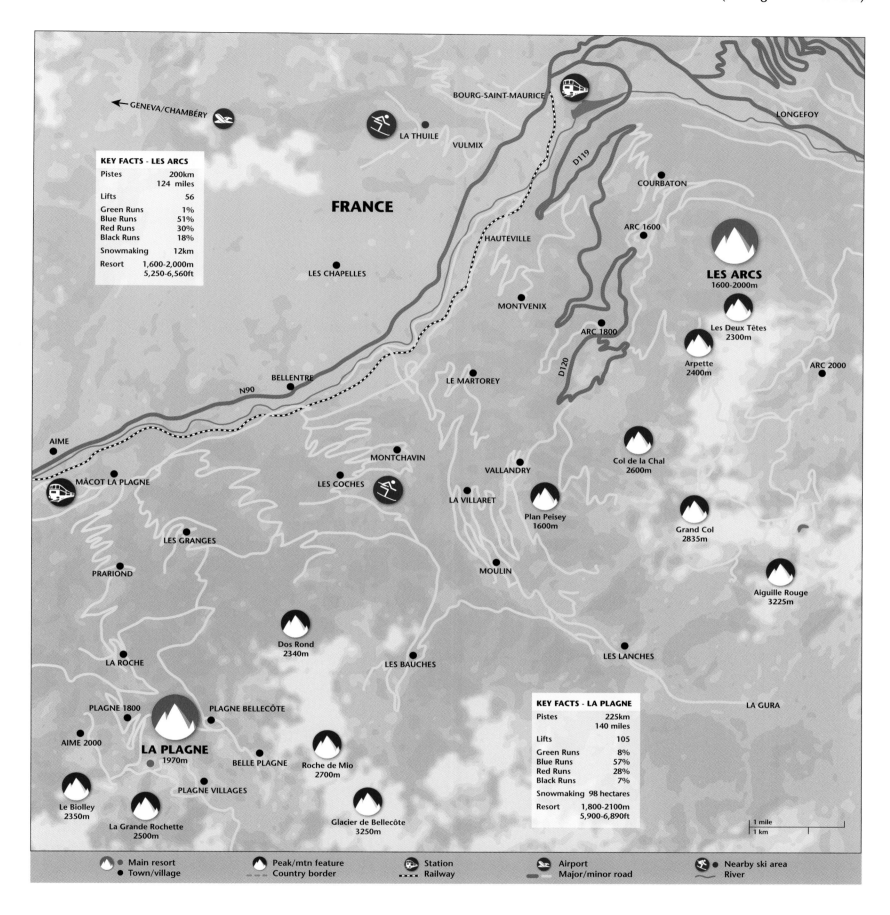

KEY FACTS - LES ARCS

| Pistes | 200km |
| --- | --- |
| | 124 miles |
| Lifts | 56 |
| Green Runs | 1% |
| Blue Runs | 51% |
| Red Runs | 30% |
| Black Runs | 18% |
| Snowmaking | 12km |
| Resort | 1,600-2,000m |
| | 5,250-6,560ft |

KEY FACTS - LA PLAGNE

| Pistes | 225km |
| --- | --- |
| | 140 miles |
| Lifts | 105 |
| Green Runs | 8% |
| Blue Runs | 57% |
| Red Runs | 28% |
| Black Runs | 7% |
| Snowmaking | 98 hectares |
| Resort | 1,800-2100m |
| | 5,900-6,890ft |

Map labels: GENEVA/CHAMBÉRY, BOURG-SAINT-MAURICE, LONGEFOY, LA THUILE, VULMIX, D119, COURBATON, ARC 1600, FRANCE, HAUTEVILLE, LES CHAPELLES, MONTVENIX, ARC 1800, LES ARCS 1600-2000m, Les Deux Têtes 2300m, Arpette 2400m, ARC 2000, D120, BELLENTRE, N90, LE MARTOREY, AIME, MONTCHAVIN, Col de la Chal 2600m, MÂCOT LA PLAGNE, LES COCHES, VALLANDRY, LA VILLARET, Plan Peisey 1600m, Grand Col 2835m, LES GRANGES, PRARIOND, MOULIN, Aiguille Rouge 3225m, Dos Rond 2340m, LA ROCHE, LES BAUCHES, LES LANCHES, LA GURA, PLAGNE 1800, PLAGNE BELLECÔTE, AIME 2000, LA PLAGNE 1970m, BELLE PLAGNE, Roche de Mio 2700m, PLAGNE VILLAGES, Le Biolley 2350m, La Grande Rochette 2500m, Glacier de Bellecôte 3250m

Legend:
- Main resort
- Town/village
- Peak/mtn feature
- Country border
- Station
- Railway
- Airport
- Major/minor road
- Nearby ski area
- River

1 mile / 1 km

of either resort, you will still probably choose to ski in just one of the two areas each day.

Staying on the fringes is not such a bad idea. A great deal of investment is going into these areas; all of the lower runs are covered by snow guns and, certainly in the case of Montchavin-Les Coches on the La Plagne side, these villages have the most alpine character. They are also markedly cheaper. For nightlife however, they are decidedly quieter, so are a good option for families. Apart from these lower villages, the major criticism of both resorts is their lack of charm and alpine character, a side effect of which is a lack of diversity in the après-ski scene.

Centrally located in the Tarentaise valley, La Plagne and Les Arcs also form part of the Savoie Olympic area, which means you have a day's free skiing in neighbouring Olympic resorts (including L'Espace Killy and Les Trois Vallées) with a week's pass.

## Les Arcs

High in the Upper Tarentaise Valley, Les Arcs is one of the more distinctive of the purpose-built French resorts. A relic of experimental 1970s architecture, you have to grudgingly admire the imaginative curves and stacks that make up the major resort centres. There are five main resort bases: the apartments of Arc 1600, the central hub of Arc 1800 and, behind the flank, Arc 2000 and the Intrawest-developed new resort of Arc 1950, re-defining the nature of purpose-built European resorts. Previously a cheaper fringe village, rapidly expanding Peisey-Vallandry now finds itself at the centre of the Paradiski ski area, and is now home to the biggest Club Med in mainland France. With the exception of Peisey-Vallandry, most of the accommodation is ski-in/ski-out.

On the mountain, Les Arcs is perhaps best known as home of the 'flying kilometre', where Lycra-clad skiers in aerodynamic helmets sport extra-long skis and a sharp tuck in their bid to become the fastest downhillers on earth. However, this is only one out of 200km (124 miles) of extremely well-proportioned, pisted terrain. Les Arcs is one of the world's best resorts for mixed-ability groups, with a good amount of suitable terrain for every level. From the lowest resort base of 1,200m (3,937ft), the ski area rises to 3,226m (10,584ft), the summit of the Aiguille Rouge, a jaw-dropping 2,026m (6,647ft) of vertical divided up into 104 runs and myriad areas of off-piste.

There are two major ski areas either side of the high dividing flank. Above 1800 is the western flank that stretches from 1650 over to Peisey-Vallandry, and behind is the wide bowl of Arc 2000, overlooked by the mighty Aiguille Rouge. The central part of this bowl is the site of the most gentle intermediate terrain in the resort and both progressing intermediates and confident beginners will enjoy the reds and blues running down from Col de la Chal (2,600m/8530ft) under the Plagnettes lift.

The most testing pistes in this valley run down from the top of Aiguille Rouge, though the cable-car is prone to closure during bad weather. This is no bad thing, however, as you would not want to be in this steep, exposed area in flat light and bad conditions. Generally speaking, the blacks and high-altitude reds in the resort are of a steep pitch and quickly develop moguls. The blacks of Robert-Blanc (next door to the 'flying kilometre' and nearly as steep), Varet and Génepi, all coming down the northwest face, are no exception. However, justifiably the most famous run in the resort is named after its highest point and drops down from the summit (via a narrow path) over 2,000m (6,562ft) of vertical to Le Pré. Black at the top and red below, this run has practically every aspect of terrain over 7km (4½ miles) of twists and turns. Confident intermediates should be fine.

Off the back of the mountain is some of the best off-piste in the French Alps. Classic descents such as Combe de l'Anchette drop down the back to Villaroger where there is some very pleasant tree-skiing – best attempted in late morning as it loses the sun in the afternoon – and is a good place to stop for lunch. Alternatively, dink between the north-facing slopes on the main face or take a line down under or to the left of the Grand Col chair, which also services an easier black and enjoyable red.

On the opposite side of the valley there are five points where you can cross over to the 1800 side. In general, the runs in the Arc 2000 valley get harder as you work your way east, culminating in the ferociously tight couloirs located skier's right of the black Comborcière. There is a good circuit dropping down to intermediate-friendly, tree-lined skiing of Arc 1600 from the top of this lift. Take the characterful winding red of Malgovert around the shoulder and do a

quick run on Les Deux Têtes before following the blue of the aptly-named Mont Blanc down to 1600. One of the Alps' most scenic runs, this route affords epic views of the Mont Blanc massif.

From here, the western flank stretches all the way across to Peisey-Vallandry. Particular areas of note include the scenic descents in 1600 of Cachette and Rouelles, a bumpy, scenic black recently re-classified from its previous red incarnation. The main snowpark is found mid-way along the flank between 1600 and 1800, and the best central reds are those serviced by the Vagere chair from the heart of 1800. Particular attention should be paid to Golf and Froide Fontaine.

Conversely, 1800 is also the best base for beginners as there is a fine network of blues and the beginners' slopes are of a high enough altitude generally to guarantee good conditions. Arc 1800 is the largest village, with, fittingly, 18,000 beds and the best nightlife. Check out the Red Hot Saloon followed by either Apocalypse or über-trendy Igloo Igloo.

Peisey-Vallandry also has some excellent tree-lined pistes and stern off-piste around the back of the Aiguille Grive/Rousse, accessed from the top of the Transarc cable car. You can join the bottom of it skier's left of the Grizzly chair for some truly absorbing terrain down past the mediaeval church to the village of Nancroix.

There is night-skiing until 7pm in 1600 and 1800 and until 9pm in 1950 and 2000 on Tuesdays and Thursdays, and three designated quiet ski areas given over entirely to beginners and families near the main resort areas. The lift system is generally good.

**The best tree-lined powder is found on the fringes of the resort above Peisey-Vallandry.**

### LES ARCS FIRSTS

*It is no surprise that Les Arcs finds itself at the forefront of public attention. It has always been a pioneering destination – European home of the snowboard, the first to use shorter skis for beginners and the first to build an integrated high-altitude golf course around the resort centre of Arc 1800 – and has become the first European site for an Intrawest development. Based on the successful model of Tremblant in eastern Canada, Arc 1950 has proved an immediate success. Apartments sold out before they were built and the range of family-focused, all-day entertainment is a welcome addition to the Alps, despite the slightly artificial and slick nature of the village.*

## La Plagne

Best known as an intermediate destination, La Plagne actually boasts more skiable terrain than the entire Espace Killy. Its 10,000ha (24,000 acres) comprise 225km (140 miles) of largely intermediate pistes, plus vast swathes of off-piste above and below the tree line. In keeping with Les Arcs, there is a great balance of snow-sure high-altitude runs and plenty of pistes down through the trees, guaranteeing skiing and definition even in bad weather and poor light – a virtue often overlooked but one that should never be undervalued.

La Plagne roughly translates as 'the plain', a very suitable name given the spread-out and rather gentle nature of the runs in the heart of the resort (86 per cent of the runs are blue and red). Indeed, early intermediates will be able to ski around the entire resort, and confident intermediates will enjoy the largely flattering but, frequently enough, challenging pistes. At this point, expert skiers may want to

*La Plagne may not be the best looking in terms of architecture, but no other resort boasts so much ski-in/ski-out accommodation.*

look elsewhere, but to do so would be an unfortunate error. For while most of the pistes favour intermediates there is a veritable embarrassment of unpisted terrain and the powder usually lasts longer here then elsewhere, as many expert skiers make the mistake of overlooking the resort. In fact, La Plagne's plethora of powder is one of the least-known attributes in the mountains.

Practically every aspect of all of the peaks in the valley can be skied, though many are off-piste, meaning that good snow conditions can always be found. The high-altitude reds and blacks are generally allowed to keep their bumps, and moguls also develop swiftly between the pistes. A classic example is the unpisted stretch between the bottom of the black Bellecôte runs and the base of Les

Crozats. Alternatively, stay right at the top of the glacier runs, take a five-minute hike and follow the ridge line down past the Pointe de Friolin to an immaculate haunch of powder and 2,000m (6,562ft) of vertical from the top of the Bellecôte Glacier (3,250m/10,663ft) down to Montchavin. The valley between Bellecôte and neighbouring Roche de Mio (2,700m/8,858ft) is often used for filming extreme ski videos.

The north face of the Bellecôte glacier has pitches of up to 60 degrees in places and is one of the truly all-time great alpine descents. There are over 20 established lines, ranging in difficulty from the hard to the near-impossible. This descent actually finishes on the fringes of Les Arcs, meaning that you can do a few runs here before coming back via the Vanoise Express.

Much of the skiable terrain is compromised by the forests, a swirling beard beneath the spread-out villages. While this remains purely

aesthetic to most visitors, to the advanced skier it is, quite literally, a playground. In good conditions there are many routes from the summits of L'Arpette (2,385m/7,825ft) and neighbouring Mont St Jacques (2,407m/ 7,897ft) all the way down another vertical drop of 1,600m (5,249ft) to the village of Macot (800m/2,625ft).

The Olympic bobsleigh course is a forest attraction open to all. Winding down through the trees along the main road below Plagne 1800, there are a few different ways to experience the bobsleigh rush. The best is the taxibob, where three passengers are driven by a professional pilot at speeds in excess of 100km/h (60mph).

There is also some excellent tree-lined piste skiing on the fringes of the resort (Plagne Montalbert and Montchavin-Les Coches) and these lower areas should not be overlooked, as altitude does not always equal character. The main ski area is quite spread out, but the

*Tall, snow-laden pines stand sentinel above one of the many gentle pistes used for teaching the next generation of skiers.*

bowl above Plagne Centre (which also offers night skiing) and the summit of Roche de Mio (2,700m/8,858ft), which is also the gateway to the Bellecôte glacier area, both have some particularly fine pistes.

## Champagny and Montchavin

Off the back of the main ski area is the sometimes overlooked south-facing Champagny flank. From this side you get a good view of the back of Courchevel across the valley. You can drop in from peaks stretching along from above Plagne Centre all the way over to the Bellecôte glacier, from where there are some excellent off-piste itineraries down to the village. The best pistes run down from the back of Les Verdons (2,500m/8,202ft) with Mont de la Guerre a mighty, long red.

Champagny is a charming little village with an excellent ice-climbing centre. Although not recommended for boisterous nightlife, it is a good, cheap and characterful family base for those wanting to concentrate largely on La Plagne. It is the furthest point in the resort from the Vanoise Express; in fact, from here it is quicker to get to Courchevel than to Les Arcs.

Historically La Plagne has received justifiable criticism for being a rather soulless collection of often ugly purpose-built villages, but there have been improvements here, too, and the charming lower alpine villages of Montchavin and Les Coches have been given a new lease of life as the gateway into Les Arcs. Centrally located Belle Plagne is the liveliest place to stay. It is not a place for the jet set, expensive shopping and boutique hotels, but in terms of convenience and reasonably priced mid-range accommodation, it is hard to think of a superior alternative.

# La Grave and Les Deux Alpes

### BY FRANCIS JOHNSTON

The spectacular Ecrins mountain range, south east of Grenoble, marks the stunningly scenic boundary between the northern and southern Alps and houses two of Europe's most noteworthy snowsports destinations: La Grave, a freeride-only station accorded almost mythical status by extreme snowsports enthusiasts; and Les Deux Alpes, home to Europe's largest skiable glacier and boasting one of the world's greatest on-piste verticals. Although not seamlessly linked, these two great ski areas can be combined on a single ski pass and converge at the summit of the Dôme de la Lauze, at 3,568m (11,706ft) the highest lift-accessible point in this region.

## La Grave

La Grave is a compact mountain community straddling the sole main road near the bleak and frequently snowbound Col du Lautaret, in France's Haute-Alpes *département*, not far from the Italian border. This remote alpine outpost is not really a ski resort at all and certainly doesn't have the extensive tourist infrastructure that you would expect from one, but, for its many aficionados, that is definitely one of La Grave's considerable charms. Thrusting directly above the village is the primal bulk of La Meije, one of the most impressive mountains in the Alps: unconquered until 1877, this was the last major peak in Europe to be climbed. It still presents a daunting challenge to modern mountaineers and draws as many alpinists as skiers to this otherwise unassuming village. The steep and challenging flanks of the massif are the prime attraction for skiers and snowboarders: the Vallons de la Meije ski area delivers a thigh-burning vertical drop of 2,150m (7,054ft) and ranks alongside Chamonix's Vallée Blanche as one of Europe's most emblematic off-piste descents. Following heated debate and strong resistance to any exploitation of this pristine environment (the cable-car base station was bombed shortly after opening in 1976), La Grave turned its back on modern ski resort development and decided instead to preserve the Vallons de la Meije as an exclusively off-piste ski area.

Access to these challenging slopes is by a two-stage gondola-style cable-car, based

**Not for the faint hearted: glacial big country towards La Grave's Vallons de Chancel route.**

a short stroll below the village. A massive middle pylon, supporting the lift cables on the first stage of the journey, serves as an intermediary station that is useful when the lower slopes are impassible, or simply for avoiding the long trek up to the base station from the valley floor following each descent. The second stage of the journey is provided by a twin of the lower cable-car, departing from a shared mid-station at 2,400m (7,874ft), accessible directly from the main slopes at mid-altitude. From the upper station at 3,200m (10,498ft), it's a short uphill trek to reach the first of two button lifts serving La Grave's only groomed runs: three short blue routes secured across the Glacier de la Girose. These surface lifts and accompanying pistes link to and from the summit of the Dôme de la Lauze, permitting crossover into the Les Deux Alpes' ski area and towards the serious off-piste routes towards St-Christophe-en-Oisans in the neighbouring Vénéon valley.

The descent to La Grave from this altitude passes through one of the most challenging lift-served ski areas in the Alps: the classic Vallons de la Meije route descends to the right of the cable-car line; to the left lies the even wilder Vallons de Chancel route. Both routes are unmarked and are testing off-piste descents that are suitable only for very fit advanced-ability all-mountain riders, ideally

accompanied by a qualified local mountain guide. This is not a 'resort' for novices, although the pisted blue runs on the glacier are manageable by early intermediates. Less experienced visitors and non-skiers can still share the buzz of this breathtaking environment by travelling as pedestrians on the cable-car. There are mountain restaurants located at both the mid and upper lift stations, easily accessible by all and providing wide-ranging vistas over this magnificent range.

Après-ski in La Grave is low-key and mostly revolves around a few beers, dinner and a convivial chat with like-minded off-

*Traditional alpine charm and a warm wecome is typical of the southern alps.*

piste enthusiasts and mountaineers, before turning in early to arise fresh for another full day tackling the demanding terrain of this unique alpine station. So demanding, in fact, that skiers perish here almost annually, especially in the network of couloirs, some of which are severely difficult. La Grave's slopes have claimed the lives of some of the world's most renowned extreme skiers; La Meije has a powerful beauty, but the seriousness of this environment cannot be understated.

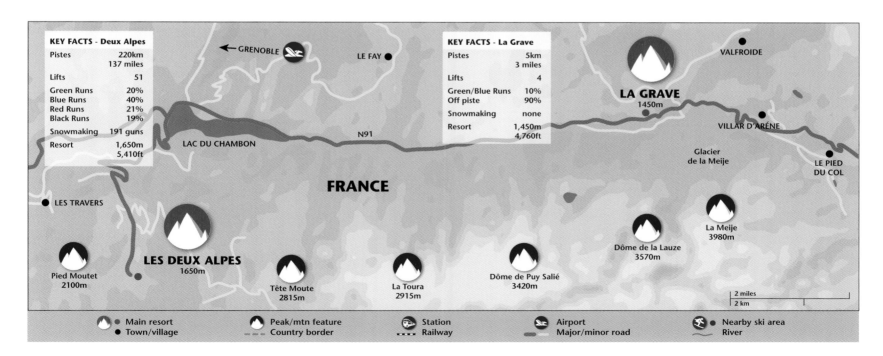

**KEY FACTS - Deux Alpes**

| Pistes | 220km |
| | 137 miles |
| Lifts | 51 |
| Green Runs | 20% |
| Blue Runs | 40% |
| Red Runs | 21% |
| Black Runs | 19% |
| Snowmaking | 191 guns |
| Resort | 1,650m |
| | 5,410ft |

**KEY FACTS - La Grave**

| Pistes | 5km |
| | 3 miles |
| Lifts | 4 |
| Green/Blue Runs | 10% |
| Off piste | 90% |
| Snowmaking | none |
| Resort | 1,450m |
| | 4,760ft |

← GRENOBLE

LE FAY

VALFROIDE

LA GRAVE
1450m

VILLAR D'ARÉNE

Glacier
de la Meije

LE PIED
DU COL

LAC DU CHAMBON

N91

**FRANCE**

LES TRAVERS

La Meije
3980m

Dôme de la Lauze
3570m

Dôme de Puy Salié
3420m

LES DEUX ALPES
1650m

Pied Moutet
2100m

Tête Moute
2815m

La Toura
2915m

| 2 miles |
| 2 km |

| ▲● Main resort | ▲● Peak/mtn feature | 🚉 Station | ✈● Airport | 🎿● Nearby ski area |
| ● Town/village | – – – Country border | ⊞⊞⊞ Railway | Major/minor road | River |

ABOVE: **The lower reaches of the Vallons de la Meije, approaching La Grave: if the descent doesn't finish off your thighs and knees, the hike up to the village will!**

BELOW: **Les Deux Alpes' fast eight-pack serving the glacial zone above the La Tours sector.**

## Les Deux Alpes

Although it shares the same lift-accessible summit as La Grave, Les Deux Alpes is very different from its wilderness-focused neighbour. This is a full-on mountain resort bristling with the facilities and infrastructure necessary for mass-market tourism. Les Deux Alpes occupies a wide linear col between the deep Romanche and Vénéon valleys in the picturesque Oisans area of the Isère *département*, amid an incredibly diverse landscape of sun-drenched meadows and glacial deserts, on the edge of the wildly beautiful Ecrins National Park.

The core ski area lies well above the magic 2,000-m (6,562-ft) mark and benefits from having Europe's largest skiable glacier, which guarantees a long and snow-sure season. In a reversal of the usual topography of ski resorts, the higher you go here the easier the slopes are. The expansive groomed trails on the glacier even have a dedicated beginners' zone. This uppermost glacial sector of year-round snow affords a truly breathtaking panorama across the roof of the Alps, and encompasses some of the highest peaks in Europe. The full descent from the summit to the lowest village slopes delivers a remarkable on-piste vertical of 2,220m (7,283ft), one of the greatest in the world. Advanced-ability visitors may find the gentle glacier slopes somewhat limiting, but this sector also provides access to the seriously challenging Vallons de la Meije freeride paradise at La Grave. Once a month, on full moon evenings (weather permitting), Les Deux Alpes keeps its glacier slopes and lifts open until sundown and offers dinner and entertainment at the nearby high-altitude restaurant complex. Competent riders are then able to experience the thrill of descending on-piste by torchlight, all the way down to Les Deux Alpes.

The station prides itself on being in the vanguard of new-school snowsports, boasting one of the biggest snowparks in the Alps plus an innovative range of exciting in-bounds freeride features: these include steep couloirs, cascading jumps and winding canyons. The main ski area is characterized by long, well-groomed cruising pistes, flowing down the long backbone of ridges from the glacier. Despite its quite narrow layout, this big domain has a respectably wide range of terrain, from enjoyably gentle snowfields and style-flattering cruises to difficult off-piste tours, and offers something for everyone – from nervous novices to hardcore thrill-seekers. A ski pass sharing agreement with Alpe d'Huez in the huge Grandes Rousses ski domain nearby, connected via an inexpensive twice-weekly bus service, also opens up a total of over 460km (286 miles) of available pistes – more than enough to keep even the most mileage-hungry visitor happy.

Les Deux Alpes is a large and vibrant town with a bustling and animated ambience. It offers a wide choice of accommodation and has a good selection of shops, restaurants, bars and late-night venues. The range of alternative activities and attractions is also fairly broad: mostly centred on high-adrenaline sports such as snowmobiling, quad-biking and paragliding but with plenty of tamer diversions too, such as ice skating, 10-pin bowling, an open-air heated swimming pool and an ice cave. Two delightful villages (Venosc and Mont-de-Lans) nestle in the valleys at opposite ends of the resort. These authentic mountain communities are connected by pedestrian-accessible lifts and offer an insight into the traditional regional character. Venosc (which cannot be reached on skis) features a charming artisans quarter, with local craft shops in a warren of ancient narrow streets, complementing the more cosmopolitan character of the main ski resort and consolidating Les Deux Alpes' claim to be one of the best all-round holiday destinations in this region.

**Big mountain freeride in La Grave's Vallons de la Meije.**

**FRANCE**

**GER**

**G E R**

Epinal

Colmar

Lahr

Ulm

Freiburg

SCHWARZWALD

Neckar

Rhine

Mulhouse

Memmingen

Weingarten

Kempten

Bodensee

Basel

Baden

Frauenfeld

Bregenz

Oberstdorf

Delemont

Zurich

St Gallen

Dornbirn

Feldkirch

**Lech & Zürs**

Zug

Luzern

**Vaduz**
**LIECHTENSTEIN**

**St Anton**

**Ischgl**

**Bern**

**S W I T Z E R L A N D**

Lac de Neuchâtel

J U R A

Fribourg

Thun

Brienz

Chur

**Davos &**
**Klosters**

Scuol

Interlaken

Finsteraarhorn

Zernez

Lausanne

**Gstaad**

**Jungfrau**
**Region**

**Andermatt**

Lac Léman

Montreux

Lenk

Engadin-
St Moritz

Thonon

Aigle

BERNERALPEN

ALPI LEPONTINE

Geneva

Sierre

Brig

Chiavenna

Sion

Locarno

Bellinzona

Tirano

Martigny

**Verbier**

L. di Como

Annecy

Chamonix

Mont Blanc

**Zermatt**

Lugano

Chambéry

Matterhorn

Monte Rosa

Como

L. Maggiore

Albertville

**Val d'Aosta**

Varese

Bergamo

Moûtiers

Biella

Brescia

Ticino

Milan

Adda

**Sestriere**

Turin

**I T A L Y**

Po

Oglio

Gap

Tanaro

Parma

Rhône

0   20   40   60   80   100 miles

0   50   100 kilometres

M A N Y

Augsburg

Landsberg

Lech

München

Inn

Waldkraiburg

Braunau

Donau

AUSTRIA
St Anton: p.80
Ischgl: p.84
Saalbach-Hinterglemm: p.86
Schladming: p.88
Bad Gastein: p.90
Lech & Zürs: p.94
Kitzbühel: p.96

Rosenheim

Salzach

Salzburg

Hallein

Bad Ischl

Gmunden

Garmisch-Partenkirchen

Reutte

Kufstein

Kitzbühel

A U S T R I A

Schladming

Radstadt

Bischofshofen

Kapfenberg

Leoben

Telfs

Inn

Schwaz

Innsbruck

Saalbach-Hinterglemm

andeck

Brenner

H O H E T A U E R

N I E D E R E T A U E R N

Knittelfeld

Sölden

Bad Gastein

Mur

Judenburg

Graz

Merano

Lienz

Sillian

Spittal

Klagenfurt

Villach

Drau

Wolfsberg

Drava

Selva
Gardena

Bolzano

Cortina
d'Ampezzo

Kranjska Gora

Kranj

Celje

Sava

Adige

A L P I  D O L O M I T I C H

J U L I J S K E A L

Madonna di
Campiglio

Trento

Belluno

Ljubljana

S L O V E N I A

L. di Garda

Udine

Piave

Nova Gorica

SLOVENIA
Kranjska Gora: p.78

Trieste

Kocevje

Vicenza

Venice

Golfo di
Venezia

Padova

Rijeka

Verona

Po

ITALY
Cortina d'Ampezzo: p.62
adonna di Campiglio: p.64
Selva Gardena: p.66
Val d'Aosta: p.68
Sestriere: p.74

panaro

Reno

KEY

Ski resort

National border

Airport

Main road

Main railway

C R O A T I A

Mountain High Maps® Copyright © 1993 Digital Wisdom®, Inc.

# ITALY

# Cortina D'Ampezzo

BY MINTY CLINCH

Cortina is pure Italian style, a handsome town in the Dolomites with views of stunning rock faces that glow pink and gold in the setting sun. You would think looking at them would make you long to ski among them, yet 70 per cent of Cortina's wealthy Italian visitors prefer to see and be seen without breaking sweat. Many are businessmen from Milan and Rome, the owners of luxurious chalets overlooking the town. If they go up the mountain, it is usually to bask on the terraces of some of Europe's most delectable mountain restaurants until it is time for lunch.

**Speed freaks love to take it straight down the fall line between majestic rocks in the higher reaches of the Cortina lift system.**

The town's main artery is the Corso Italia, a wide pedestrianized street dominated by the campanile. Its shops offer upmarket shopping in the form of oriental rugs, paintings, designer clothes and furs. The number of Italians who emerge at 5pm for their traditional evening stroll suggests that the shopkeepers make an excellent living.

The resort has three main ski areas: Socrepes, Tofana and Faloria-Cristallo. There are several outlying areas, none of them ski-in/ski-out and none accessed by lifts from the town centre. They are linked by an erratic and at times very crowded bus service (free for ski pass holders), but making the most of the region requires a car and the cunning to slide into the rare parking spaces before anyone else does.

Socrepes, accessed by the Roncato lift to the west of the town, is the largest area. It links at mid-mountain level with Tofana, which is reached by the Col Druscie cable car from a slightly more convenient base station near Cortina's ice rink. A second stage goes up Ra Valles, the highest slopes with the best natural snow in the resort. There is suitable

*Off the pistes, the top thrill is a blast down the Olympic bobsled run in a taxi bob that takes three guests and a professional driver – part of the Cortina Adrenalin Centre's winter programme, which also includes snow-rafting, snowshoeing and Crazy Sledge descents under a full moon.*

terrain for all levels, but particularly for beginners and anxious intermediates who can only gain confidence on the broad meadowlands between the mid stations on Socrepes and Tofana and the town. The greater challenge comes on the higher slopes, often on short but very steep shots, the perfect adrenalin prelude to a long lunch.

Faloria-Cristallo, to the east of Cortina, has the most dramatic scenery, famously captured in the 1993 film *Cliffhanger*, which starred Sylvester Stallone. The severest test comes on the upper slopes at Forcella Staunies, where steep mogul fields plunge down between towering rock walls. These require the right amount of snow – neither too little or too much – to open.

Of the smaller areas, it's worth devoting a day to Cinque Torri, which has a fine open bowl, and neighbouring Lagazuoi, characterised by swooping high-speed pistes accessed by an isolated two-stage cable-car on Passo Falzarego. In both cases, the rewards include spectacular rockscapes.

The German-speaking South Tyrol resorts that share the Dolomite Superski pass – probably the most extensive in the world, with 450 lifts accessing 1,220km (758 miles) of piste – look on sybaritic Cortina with a slight touch of envy. While they have been investing heavily in modern lifts, their all-Italian neighbour has been resting on its laurels since it staged the Winter Olympics in 1956. For Cortina, the issue seems to be: why spend money on improvements when skiing is not the main event?

However, the upgrading completed for the 2006 Olympics in Piedmont may herald a change of direction. In the Cristallo area, the Pardeon double chair has been replaced by a high-speed quad, while at Tofana, a six-seat express chair does the work of two old lifts, the Col Taron and the Pie Merlo. When it comes to snowmaking – a key requirement in a region where the gods don't always deliver – Cortina is at the top of the league, with 95 per cent of its slopes covered by cannons.

Cortina's hotels are worthy of their clientele. The Miramonti Majestic Grand represents five-star luxury on the outskirts of town, but foreigners may prefer the de la Poste or the Ancora, two centrally located 19th-century hotels run on traditional lines by their founding families for over a century. Their ornate styles, with the emphasis on decorative painted woodwork, are fairly interchangeable, with the Ancora scoring highly for comfort and cusine, while the de la Poste is famous for its terrace and its cosy panelled *stube*.

Eating at the top of the gastro range in the Michelin-starred Tivoli, which specializes in venison, or El Toula, a stylish hayloft conversion, may require a second mortgage, but many of Cortina's 80 restaurants are reasonably priced and authentically Italian. Changing fashion dictates which of the half dozen clubs that kick in after 11pm is flavour of the month.

Cortina's dramatic rockscape provides a stunning backdrop for piste skiing on a blue-sky day.

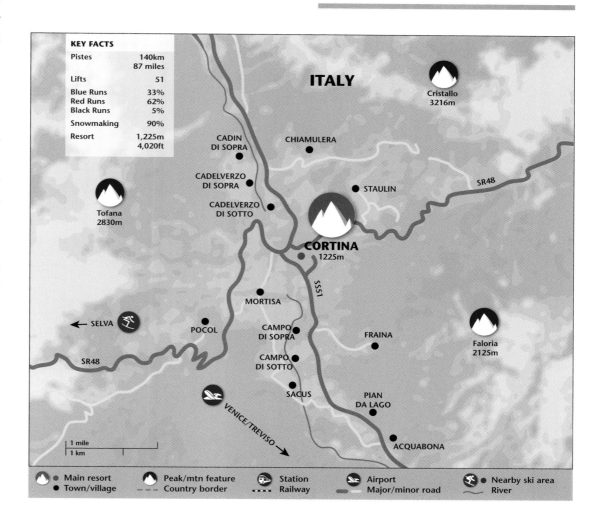

**KEY FACTS**

| | |
|---|---|
| Pistes | 140km |
| | 87 miles |
| Lifts | 51 |
| Blue Runs | 33% |
| Red Runs | 62% |
| Black Runs | 5% |
| Snowmaking | 90% |
| Resort | 1,225m |
| | 4,020ft |

ITALY

Cristallo 3216m

CADIN DI SOPRA

CHIAMULERA

CADELVERZO DI SOPRA

STAULIN

SR48

Tofana 2830m

CADELVERZO DI SOTTO

**CORTINA** 1225m

MORTISA

SSS1

SELVA

POCOL

CAMPO DI SOPRA

FRAINA

Faloria 2125m

CAMPO DI SOTTO

SR48

SACUS

PIAN DA LAGO

VENICE/TREVISO

ACQUABONA

1 mile
1 km

| | | | | | |
|---|---|---|---|---|---|
| ● Main resort | ▲ Peak/mtn feature | ⊙ Station | ✈ Airport | | ● Nearby ski area |
| ● Town/village | – – – Country border | ···· Railway | Major/minor road | | River |

# Madonna di Campiglio

BY ALF ALDERSON

If you like your skiing fun but not too challenging and want to sample some of the best that Italy has to offer in terms of alpine scenery and après-ski styling, you owe it to yourself to visit Madonna di Campiglio.

Beginners and intermediates will love the skiing here, and there's plenty of Italian pizzaz to go with it – wander around the pleasant town centre after a day on the slopes and you'll see enough fur and jewellery on display to grace a Parisian catwalk – you can be sure the owners have not been tearing up the slopes earlier in the day, rather idling over

On the bumps at Madonna di Campiglio, one of Italy's most exotic resorts.

coffee and cakes in a chi-chi café. However, while this kind of clientele may make the people-watching more colourful, they also have the unfortunate effect of helping push up prices, to the point that Madonna is definitely not the place for budget skiers.

Lift-accessed skiing in Madonna dates back to the installation of the resort's first chair-lift, in 1935. Needless to say, things are considerably more efficient and high-tech these days, but even so, quite serious lift queues develop at weekends and holidays, so try to visit in January or March for the best access to the slopes. Sunny days are common – so much so that snow conditions may not always be ideal, especially in early and late season.

Renowned for the impeccable quality of its piste grooming and the preponderance of beginner and intermediate runs, Madonna is the kind of place that will massage your ski ego at the same time as providing great pistes on which to develop your technique. It's also located beneath some wonderful mountains, particularly the Monte Spinale/Grostè area, above the tree line to the east of the town. The huge and impressive granite cliffs of Pietra Grande loom over the area, dwarfing the skiers below; the Graffer blue run, starting at the top of 2,504-m (8,215-ft) Grostè, links with other blues lower down the mountain to take you on a long, undemanding but exhilarating run all the way back into town.

Another great attraction of Madonna for intermediate skiers is the opportunity it provides to get out and explore on your skis. Beside the Monte Spinale/Grostè area, there are two other fine ski areas accessible from the town: 5-Laghi and Pradalago, both of which are the stuff of intermediate dreams, with plenty of long blue and red tree-lined cruisers. All three areas are linked at valley level, and from the latter two you can explore further afield in the attractive Marilleva and Folgarida areas, where yet again more long, wide cruisers provide fine open skiing down into blue-shadowed, tree-lined slopes. The slopes are a little short on classic mountain

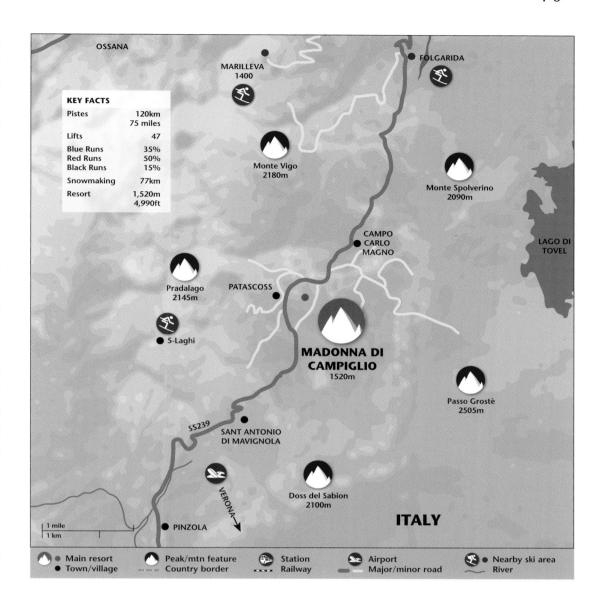

restaurants to refuel during all this exploration, but you can easily make up for that later in the day – a classic Madonna après-ski experience is to take a heated snowcat up to the mountain restaurants on Cascina Zeledria, Malga Boch or Malga Montagnoli.

Beginner skiers will find that Madonna offers a great introduction to the sport. Not only does it provide all the character and atmosphere you would expect of a classic alpine resort, it also has some excellent learner slopes, and within a couple of days on skis you'll find around half of Madonna's runs accessible to you, some several kilometres in length. Unlike many resorts, a novice skier in the first week can access the top levels of all lifts and find a way down that isn't too demanding. Indeed it's only when it comes to demanding skiing that Madonna doesn't really deliver. There are only five black runs,

and of these the only ones likely to offer any real excitement to expert skiers are the steep-but-short World Cup Canelone Miramonti just above town and the longer Spinale Diretissima on the opposite side of the valley.

But if the skiing doesn't wear you out, the legendary nightlife of Madonna will come close. The bars in town are busy immediately after the lifts close, and you can pretty much wander out of some bars at the end of a big session and hop straight on to the first lift of the day.

It may not be a bad idea to explore the town at some point during your stay – it is, after all, an integral part of what the place is all about – but save some strength for the slopes as well, for Madonna really is a delightful resort and presents a distillation of the best of Italian skiing for all but choosy expert skiers.

# Selva Gardena

BY ALF ALDERSON

Selva Gardena is set in one of the four valleys that make up the magnificent Sella Ronda ski circuit through the heart of the Dolomites, surely amongst the most beautiful mountains in the world. When the late afternoon sun turns these spectacular limestone spires and crags shades of rose, mauve, purple and pink, it's all too easy to stop skiing and spend time admiring the breathtaking free show.

When you eventually get back to your skiing, the Selva Gardena area and the vast array of slopes surrounding it will provide you with more terrain than you could hope to explore in a season, let alone a week or two. The Dolomiti Superski area, of which Selva Gardena is part, consists of an incredible 1,180km (733 miles) of pistes and 460 lifts – arguably the world's biggest (but not always linked) ski area – with wide, open cruiser runs leading to and from a selection of attractive villages and excellent restaurants (both in the villages and on the slopes).

The proliferation of relatively undemanding blue and red runs makes Selva Gardena an ideal and very popular destination for inter-mediate skiers (as the depressingly frequent lift queues will attest). The main attraction is the Sella Ronda ski tour, based on an ancient high-level route that crosses four mountain passes, involves 26km (16 miles) of lift-linked downhill and can be easily completed in a day. Most skiers will even have time to enjoy a relaxing lunch en route at one of several fine mountain restaurants.

Along the way you can ski, wine and dine in a style that you'd be hard pressed to match anywhere else in Europe. You'll schuss beneath vertiginous, finger-like peaks that were created 350 million years ago as trillions of dead organisms piled up on the floor of a Caribbean-warm ocean and were compressed into golden-yellow rock strata; through a region that still has its own language (Ladino); and across pistes that have been the training grounds for a rich lineage of Alpine skiing stars, such as Peter Runggaldier and Isolde Kostner. (The famed Val Gardena World Cup ski course is located here.) Try to do it in a clockwise direction for maximum skiing and minimum skating and poling. The Sella Ronda circuit is well signposted so you shouldn't get lost, but timing is still important because if you relax too much and find yourself a couple of lift rides away from home when everything has closed down you're in for an expensive taxi ride.

Beginners also have a good selection of slopes to cut their teeth on, and good ski schools to help them along the way. Because of the gentle nature of so many of the slopes even never-evers should be able to get around many of the mountains above Val Gardena and enjoy the lovely scenery within a few days of starting out.

Experienced skiers need to get themselves over to Arabba, where some seriously steep and challenging terrain can be accessed via the gondola and cable-car that rise up above the attractive little village, or onto the slopes of the mighty 3,342-m (10,964-ft) Marmolada. The skiing here isn't necessarily that challenging, but it's high, exposed and thrilling. Before you tackle the slopes, check out the museum on the upper slopes of Marmolada, which presents exhibits on World War I and the exploits of Italian and Austrian troops who fought in these mountains. There's also some outstanding off-piste skiing on Sass Pordoi above Canazei, but it's best tackled with a guide.

**Selva Gardena has world-class skiing and scenery, but it can get busy.**

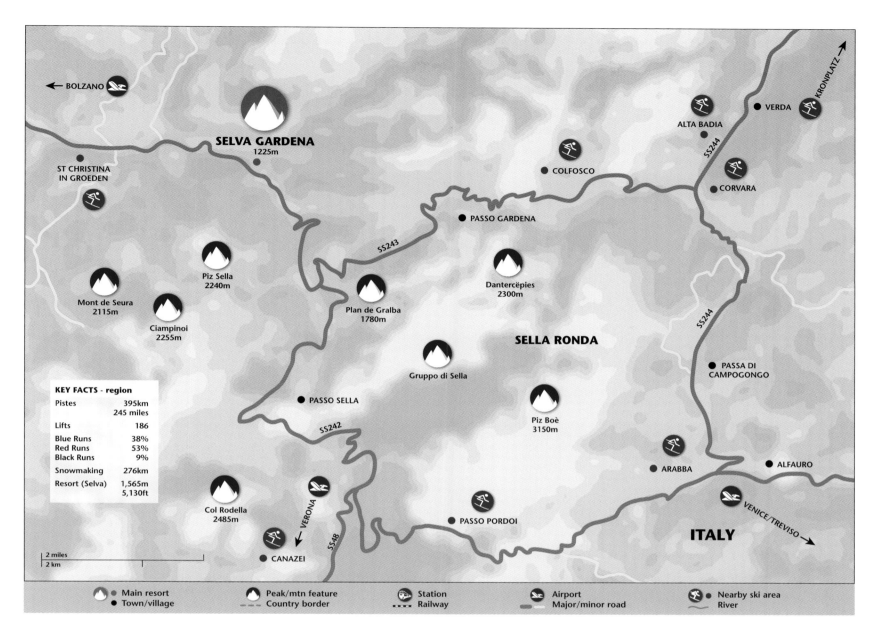

← BOLZANO

SELVA GARDENA
1225m

ST CHRISTINA
IN GROEDEN

KRONPLATZ →

VERDA

ALTA BADIA

CORVARA

COLFOSCO

PASSO GARDENA

SS243

SS244

Piz Sella
2240m

Dantercëpies
2300m

Mont de Seura
2115m

Ciampinoi
2255m

Plan de Gralba
1780m

SELLA RONDA

Gruppo di Sella

PASSA DI
CAMPOGONGO

SS244

**KEY FACTS - region**

| Pistes | 395km |
| | 245 miles |
| Lifts | 186 |
| Blue Runs | 38% |
| Red Runs | 53% |
| Black Runs | 9% |
| Snowmaking | 276km |
| Resort (Selva) | 1,565m |
| | 5,130ft |

PASSO SELLA

SS242

Piz Boè
3150m

ARABBA

ALFAURO

Col Rodella
2485m

VERONA

SS48

PASSO PORDOI

**ITALY**

VENICE/TREVISO →

CANAZEI

2 miles
2 km

● Main resort
● Town/village

Peak/mtn feature
--- Country border

Station
Railway

Airport
Major/minor road

Nearby ski area
River

## CULTURAL MIX

When you take time out from skiing to wander around Selva or any of the linked villages, you'll find a mix of cultures. Being so close to the Austrian border (in fact part of the area used to be in Austria until after World War I), Italian and Austrian culture, language and cuisine co-exist, along with the local Ladino culture.

Nightlife in the area tends to be rather low-key – this isn't really the place to visit if you're intent on partying – but with such a staggering amount of skiing to try it's probably best to save your energy to ski as much of the Dolomiti Superski area as you can.

Classic conditions allow the experts to show how it's done – but someone should have a word about those ski outfits!

# Val d'Aosta and Alagna

BY FELIX MILNS AND MINTY CLINCH

The Val d'Aosta is Italy's smallest and highest region, and has an average altitude of above 2,000m (6,562ft). Many of its most famous peaks surpass 4,000m (13,123ft), with Monte Bianco (Mont Blanc) heading the charge at a formidable 4,807m (15,771ft). Adding to the imperiousness are Monterosa (4,685m/15,371ft), the Matterhorn (4,478m/14,692ft) and Gran Paradiso (4,061m/13,323ft). It should come as no surprise, therefore, that the valley is Italy's premier skiing destination.

Headline resorts are the intermediate-friendly Cervinia, gourmet-friendly Courmayeur and the Monterosa ski area, still largely unknown to many, in spite of its high-quality skiing. The area comprises Gressoney, Champoluc and Alagna, the Italian three valleys and virtually unheard of outside Italy. Of the other resorts, La Thuile is also worth a mention.

Historically this steep-sided valley running east–west, abutting both France and Switzerland, was one of the main access points between northern and southern Europe. Hannibal came through here with his elephants in the third century BC and Napoleon followed in his tracks as he marched his armies across the Alps. Today, things are a little easier, with the Mont Blanc tunnel linking Italy with France and the Grand St Bernard tunnel through to Switzerland.

The Val d'Aosta's ski areas are richly diverse but all distinctly Italian in feel. Much store is placed on leisurely starts, long lunches and gentle afternoons, meaning that the slopes – particularly during the week – are comparatively quiet. Crucially, it is one of Europe's best destinations for heliskiing. If you're planning a tour of the resorts in the area, the Val d'Aosta ski pass covers all the resorts and offers excellent value for money.

**The views from the Courmayeur bubble stretch from Mont Blanc all the way down the Aosta valley – and they are spectacular.**

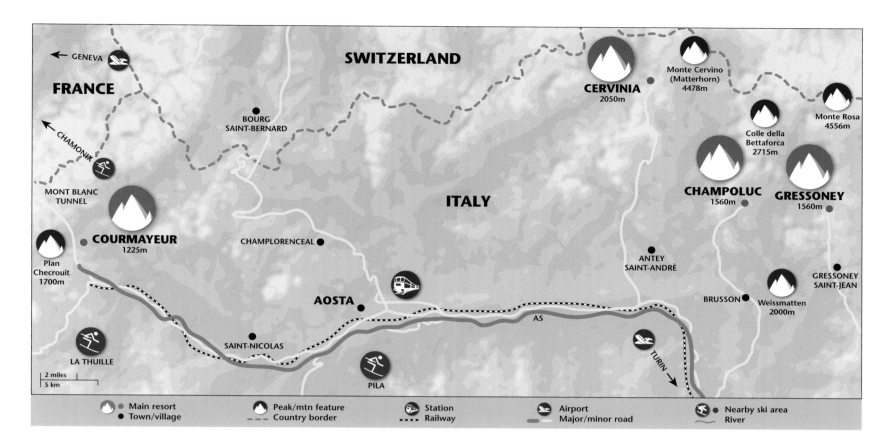

## Courmayeur

Located next to the Italian side of the Mont Blanc tunnel, Courmayeur is the first resort you come to from France and backs onto the reverse side of Mont Blanc from Chamonix. However, it could not be more different from its French neighbour. The main ski area is relatively small and remarkably, there are more mountain restaurants than lifts; the standard of food is, not surprisingly, excellent. Skiers certainly look the part, but generally there is really not much on the piste to test them. The relaxed approach is immediately apparent; even the instructors are more keen to show you the best hot chocolate on the mountain than to perfect your turns.

However, there is another side to Courmayeur, one that most visitors are probably unaware of. Three cable-cars from neighbouring Entrèves service the entirely separate ski area on the back of Monte Bianco; you have to be with an official guide to take the lifts which are not even

*There's no better feeling in the world than leaping into fresh powder; dusty clouds of snow releasing, tracking the backs of your skis.*

shown on the piste map. From the top you can take an alternative route down the Vallée Blanche from the Punta Helbronner (3,462m/11,358ft). This 24-km (15-mile) intermediate-friendly descent crosses into France and finishes in Chamonix. Sterner stuff borders the Toula glacier, where ropes are sometimes necessary.

Back in the main area, there are also three marvellous off-piste itineraries from the top of Cresta d'Arp (2,755m/9,038ft): the Dolonne channel; south through the Youla gorge; or a wide loop alongside the Miage glacier to Val Veny. Heliskiing is plentiful, with the glamorous attraction of the helicopter taking off from the middle of the ski area. Undisturbed powder also lurks in the Val Veny forests long after a snowfall.

On the 100-km (62-mile) piste network, there is not really much to challenge advanced skiers, nor enough to keep mileage-hungry intermediates happy for a week. However the groomed pistes are generally kept in excellent condition and it is worth coming for a weekend or a few days as part of a wider tour. The scenery is inspiring and the friendly and welcoming nature of the resort, plus the laid-back attitude and excellent mountain restaurants, make it one of the most characterful ski destinations.

The central Checrouit ski area has a well-groomed collection of reds best skied under the morning sun, with the antique cable-cars above really only worth queuing for the view and the off-piste as the short red is otherwise underwhelming. The most challenging runs are those serviced by the Bertolini chair, which conveniently leads you into the Val Veny section, which gets the sun, and the crowds, in the afternoon. There are also marvellous close-up views of Mont Blanc and the Grands Jorasses from here. If you are only skiing the main area, then it is worth hiring or storing your skis at the top of the first cable-car from the town as the blue path down to town rarely has good snow cover and finishes far from the lifts and the town centre.

The charming old stone-built village of Courmayeur comes alive at the end of the skiing day, with crowds of well-dressed visitors perusing the shops and bars along the Via Roma, the main street. The restaurants in town are equal to those on the mountain and some bars also offer free food with your drinks throughout the evening.

## Cervinia

Literally standing head and shoulders above the rest of Italy's ski resorts is the country's highest resort, Cervinia. The resort centre sits at 2,050m (6,726ft) on the southern side of one of the most emblematic of all alpine peaks: the famous Matterhorn – or Monte Cervino, as the Italians call it. The resort is named after the mountain, but this was not always the case. It was Mussolini, in fact, who decided that the original name of Breuil was not Italian enough for his vision of a fascistic, dominant and modern Italy. In 1934 he renamed it to bask in the reflected glory of the mighty mountain above, and built the first road up to the resort.

The highest peak in Cervinia itself is the Plateau Rosa (3,480m/11,417ft), and the ski area drops down to neighbouring Valtournenche (1524m/5,000ft). However, from this plateau you can drop straight into

the linked resort of Zermatt and take one lift up to the top of the Klein Matterhorn glacier (3,885m/12,746ft), giving a more stately 2,350m (7,708ft) of vertical. It is also from this point that you get the best views of the Matterhorn, as the southern aspect seen from Cervinia is not as bold and defined.

However, this resort should not really be looked at as a cheap backdoor into Zermatt. Most of Zermatt's supreme ski terrain lies on the other side of the valley and is difficult to get to on a day trip from Cervinia. That said, until 1997 the resorts were not even officially linked because of political disputes, and today's shared lift pass is a definite plus for both resorts. Cervinia guests should, at the very least, venture down to a couple of Zermatt's legendary mountain restaurants – just leave plenty of time to get back.

Most of the skiing at Cervinia takes place high above the tree line, in the large, open and sunny west-facing bowl on the southern side of the Matterhorn. In many ways, it is absolutely ideal for intermediates, particularly those lacking the confidence to deal with narrow, twisty switchback runs. It has one of the best snow records in the Alps and most of

the 200km (124 miles) of runs are long, easy reds and blues. In fact, many of the reds would probably be classified blues elsewhere. Ventina is a superb red from the top of Plateau Rosa to the village, and the run from the same point to the lower-altitude Valtournenche is an impressive 13km (8 miles) in length. Add in the Klein Matterhorn leg and you ski a top-to-bottom run of 22km (13½ miles).

Cervinia is also a good place for beginners; the nursery slopes are high and snow-sure, the level of instruction is excellent and all the ski instructors speak English. Add to this the favourable price comparisons with other high-altitude resorts in Europe and you soon see why this is such an appealing resort for progressing intermediates. Even strong beginners will be able to ski from the top of the mountain to the bottom by the end of their first week, guaranteeing a real sense of achievement and, more than likely, a lifetime addiction to skiing. Experts, however, are limited here, though there is some heliskiing available.

On a clear day, the vistas are truly spectacular, with views down the beautiful

*The Seggiovia Plan Maison chair-lifts take Cervinia's skiers into the middle of wide open intermediate terrain.*

valley of the Gran Paradiso National Park and, of course, of the Matterhorn itself. However, in flat light or high winds the resort can almost grind to a halt. The upper lifts are prone to closure and the lack of trees not only detracts on an aesthetic level but also means the ski area is exposed and suffers correspondingly. This exposed mountain can be somewhat bleak and cold in early season, but under the warmth of the late-season sun the slopes are high enough to remain snow, not slush, and there are few resorts that can offer such flattering intermediate skiing. The high altitude also normally guarantees a season lasting from October into May.

The centre of the resort is traffic-free and fairly charming, but surrounding it are large, amorphous apartment blocks and hotels. Make sure that your hotel offers a shuttle service to the base of the lift as otherwise this can be a soul-destroying breakfast hike up a steep, twisting road.

The working village of Champoluc has a life outside tourism that appeals to those who favour a rural lifestyle.

Alagna is the natural habitat for the adrenaline skier, as much for the variety of its extreme terrain as for its virgin powder.

## Monterosa

The Monterosa ski area is isolated, beautiful and remarkably untouched by time. For this, it can thank its relative inaccessibility on the sunny side of the Alps. Each of the three resorts has its own character: Champoluc is a no-nonsense village with a river running through it and local hotels and bars that offer a proper Italian welcome. Convenience is not a priority: there are two lift stations, but neither starts from the village centre. In Gressoney-La-Trinité, it's the same story, with an 800-m (2,625-ft) walk from the centre to the base station to go up to Stafal, a modern satellite development dead in the middle of the Monterosa spectrum. Gressoney-La-Trinité majors on rustic charm, with cobbled streets and an historic church, but remote Alagna, with its distinctive agricultural architecture – wooden farmhouses with integral hayracks – steals the show.

Settled in the 13th century by the wandering Walsers – originally from Germany – the region remains true to its mongrel origins. Locals speak German or French dialects as well as Italian, but don't expect English beyond the absolute basics. Each of the resorts lies at the head of a different valley, with a minimum two-hour drive from one to the other. On the mountain, it's a different picture. Until recently, the lifts linked up efficiently, but the infrastructure was antiquated, a situation that is turning around fast with the help of European Union funding.

The price demanded by Brussels was the total integration of Alagna, previously a powder outpost with no groomed connections with Gressoney. To the regret of its faithful off-piste army, the cable-car from the Pianalunga midstation to Passo dei Salati, the top of skiing at Gressoney, and the magnificent Olen red/black piste back towards

Alagna, opened in 2005. The payoff for obeying the EU came in the form of upgrading designed to reduce queues above Champoluc. In 2006, a high-speed quad replaced the twin veteran chairs between the Crest midstation and Ostafa, with a new eight-seat gondola to Colle Sarezza, a key link to the Gressoney Valley.

In an area dominated by the mightily impressive Monte Rosa Massif, the end-to-end trip from Champoluc to Alagna is 17km (10½ miles), with the slopes getting progressively more demanding the farther east you go. The Monterosa is not the most reassuring place to learn to ski, but if you must, Champoluc is the best base for beginners. The nursery slopes above Crest are user-

friendly, but progress is limited by the shortage of blue runs.

Intermediates should stay in Gressoney-La-Trinité or its more developed neighbour, Gressoney-St-Jean, the most efficient launch points for the extensive network of red runs that fan out from Stafal. It is sometimes claimed that the Monterosa piste map is the worst in Europe, and possibly in the world, but good signposting makes it easy to find your way around the mountain once you're on it. Grooming is excellent, so all you need to do is switch on cruise control and ski 'til you drop. Ready for a real high mountain adventure? Hire a guide, prepare a picnic and take a helicopter (always very affordable in Italy) to the shoulder of Monte Rosa (approx. 4,200m/13,780ft), the start of the long descent, initially on the glacier, to Gressoney. Depending on snow conditions, it may take several hours, but it is unforgettable.

In Alagna, one of Europe's most radical off-piste areas, you can forget the tame excursions on skins you're offered in other resorts: the local guides are keen to test their clients' nerves with roped sections down rocky couloirs, bridge crossings and demanding tracks through hummocky snowfields. Heliskiing is often spontaneous: in good weather, the chopper waits below Punta Indren for skiers who want to jump in and go.

The whole area is rich in mountain restaurants offering simple but delicious food, either plates of local sausage, ham and cheese with coarse bread, or pasta dishes. Don't miss the Rifugio Guglielmina, on the new Olen piste to Alagna, but still run by the family that built it in 1878: they offer exceptional polenta dishes, a wide choice of wine, even a room for the night, if required.

If you ski to the max, you may be too tired to go out in the evening, which may be an

**Where shall we go next? Skiers pause between the Champoluc and Gressoney ski zones while they decide which route to take.**

advantage as the nightlife is minimal throughout the region. Champoluc has a disco on Saturday nights in the hip Hotel California on the outskirts of the village. It also has a good selection of traditional hotels, notably the centrally located Castor, run with due respect for pub traditions by an Englishman who married into its Italian founding family, and the more luxurious Breithorn. The Jolanda Sport Hotel is the most convenient place to stay in Gressoney-La-Trinité, while the modern Monboso, at Stafal, is comfortable if soulless. In Alagna, the Bar Mirella has rooms to rent over the cake shop within moments of the cable-car station. Alternatives include the four-star Cristallo and the cavernous but engaging Monterosa.

# Sestriere and The Milky Way

BY FRANCIS JOHNSTON

Skiing first achieved significant popularity in the 1920s, when it became the winter leisure activity of choice amongst international high society. Established spa and mountaineering resorts such as St Moritz, Zermatt and Chamonix welcomed increasing numbers of glamorous visitors, as winter sports took centre stage for the *beau monde*. Wealthy Italians from Milan and Venice flocked to the slopes of chic Cortina d'Ampezzo in the Dolomites, while those from Turin travelled to nearby France and Switzerland. One of Turin's most respected public figures, Giovanni Agnelli, the politician and industrialist who founded the Fiat empire, decided to develop a world-class resort within easier reach of his home city. Sestriere, located just one hour's drive west of Turin, is the result of his vision. Ownership remained in the Agnelli family until the resort was sold following the Winter Olympics in 2006.

The wide Colle di Sestrières pass connects the upper Chisone and Susa valleys, close to the French border. Until the 1930s, this high col was an undeveloped area of summer meadows and Alpine wilderness, providing Agnelli with a blank canvas on which to create the first truly purpose-built ski resort in the Alps.

Cable-cars were installed; innovative cylindrical tower hotels were constructed, with helical ramped floors designed to ensure that all rooms had views and sunlight; and a luxury hotel was built in the style of a romantic chateau. On completion, Sestriere quickly became one of the most fashionable resorts in

Europe, attracting royalty, stage and sports celebrities and Hollywood movie stars. The resort also hosted important ski competitions, including the famous Kandahar Trophy races

The floodlit Olympic slalom course, viewed from Sestriere's Olympic village.

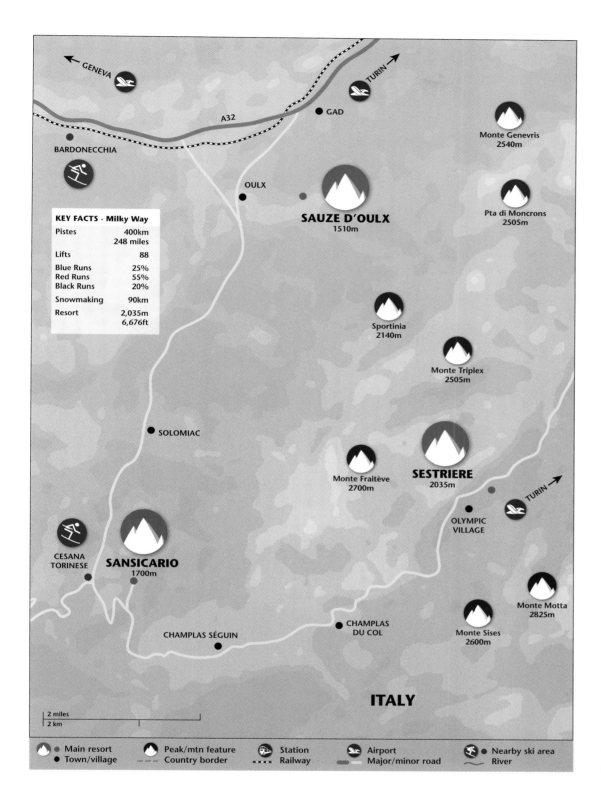

**KEY FACTS - Milky Way**

| | |
|---|---|
| Pistes | 400km |
| | 248 miles |
| Lifts | 88 |
| Blue Runs | 25% |
| Red Runs | 55% |
| Black Runs | 20% |
| Snowmaking | 90km |
| Resort | 2,035m |
| | 6,676ft |

2 miles
2 km

| | | | |
|---|---|---|---|
| Main resort | Peak/mtn feature | Station | Airport |
| Town/village | Country border | Railway | Major/minor road |

| |
|---|
| Nearby ski area |
| River |

The Olympic course finish area at Borgata, Sestriere; towards the gondola link with Sauze d'Oulx/Sansicario.

founded by the ski pioneers Sir Arnold Lunn and Hannes Schneider. FIS Alpine World Cup races are still regularly held here.

During the 1980s Sestriere became part of the huge Milky Way ski domain that straddles the Franco-Italian border, opening up 400km (248 miles) of lift-linked pistes. Despite this impressive expansion, even more extensive ski domains with more modern facilities and better-integrated links were also being developed at higher altitudes in the French Alps,

and Sestriere rapidly began to look dated in comparison. However, before terminal decline set in, Turin was selected as the host city for the 2006 Winter Olympics, and Sestriere was chosen to stage the blue-riband downhill events. Ski-lifts were upgraded, the snow-making network was expanded, new accommodation was built and existing facilities were given a makeover, marking the renaissance of Sestriere and thrusting it back into the international spotlight.

The core ski area covers two main sectors: Monte Sises, directly in front of the resort and Monte Motta/Monte Banchetta above the neighbouring village of Borgata. Monte Sises offers a small snow park and straightforward, fast red and black runs zooming down to the edge of the town, including the floodlit World Cup/Olympic slalom course. The gentlest town slopes are roomy beginners' zones, conveniently close to the resort centre and served by snack bars and canteen-

75

style restaurants. On-mountain catering is sparse, but generally fair in standard and reasonably atmospheric.

Long easy blue cruises extend to Borgata, where more extensive and varied terrain on exclusively red and black runs includes the World Cup/Olympic men's downhill course. A two-way gondola links Borgata to the Col Basset above Sauze d'Oulx, providing onward links to Sansicario and the other Milky Way resorts. Two epic red runs also allow on-piste links in the opposite direction back to Sestriere; unfortunately these face southeast and therefore often have insufficient snow cover.

Despite having an ice rink and good municipal sports facilities, Sestriere's off-slope

Sauze d'Oulx's attractive resort centre with views across the upper Susa Valley towards France.

attractions are limited, but there are a fair number of shops and cafés, several good restaurants, animated bars and two small nightclubs. Weekday evenings can be quiet, but the weekends still retain a lively flavour of the town's glory days when Turin's socialites pack the slopes, streets and nightspots to see and be seen. As well as being the region's most up-market resort, Sestriere is also the most reliably snow-sure and continues to offer the strongest all-round choice for keen skiers in this easily accessible corner of Italy.

## Sauze d'Oulx

Sauze d'Oulx rose to prominence in the 1980s as one of Europe's hotspots for young and lively British package tourists, who affectionately nicknamed the resort 'Suzy does it'. With animated and often raucous young Brits thronging its slopes and streets, the resort often felt like an English-speaking enclave.

Thankfully, the rowdiest crowds have been lured away by cheaper Eastern European resorts and, after hosting the 2006 Winter Olympics, this picturesque corner of northwestern Italy is taken a lot more seriously on the international snowsports scene. Suzy has mellowed with age, but she hasn't forgotten how to party.

The resort sits on a forested shelf overlooking the upper Susa Valley, facing an impressive skyline of major peaks marking the nearby border with France. The ski area lies at the northern extremity of the Milky Way (Via Lattea) ski domain, a 400-km (248-mile) circuit of lift-linked pistes covering five major Italian resorts plus the French resort of Montgenèvre. The village is quite spread out over the wooded hillside, but has an attractive pedestrian-friendly 'old town' at its core, packed with lively bars and restaurants. It is easy to escape the crowds, though, with

plenty of accommodation tucked away in secluded corners yet still close to the action.

Despite being strongly promoted for beginners, Sauze d'Oulx is actually best suited to keen intermediates. Novices will find the crowded beginners' zones limiting and the main pistes too challenging. The area is also quite fragmented and still relies heavily on old-fashioned steep draglifts; this is particularly frustrating for snowboarders, with just one fairly basic snow park at the far reaches of the ski area. The region has also recorded some notable snowfall droughts and key links are therefore prone to closure, although increased snowmaking equipment and first-rate piste grooming has done much to lessen the problem. That said, in good conditions Sauze d'Oulx offers some of the most enjoyable and attractive snowsports terrain in the Alps, with big mileage possible for adventurous intermediate/advanced ability visitors who can make the most out of the vast cross-border circuit. Mountain bars and restaurants are reasonably numerous and generally good value; most are atmospherically Italian and many have superb views.

## Sansicario

Sansicario was purpose-built at the heart of the Milky Way in the 1980s to exploit the slopes on the sheltered western flanks of Monte Fraiteve. Its low-rise apartment blocks, monorail and mall-style services centre make it feel like a university campus rather than a ski resort, but the peaceful pine-forested surroundings are undeniably pretty and offer some of the region's most enjoyable cruising.

Sansicario hosted the biathlon, bobsled and women's downhill events during the 2006 Winter Olympics; the signature piste is the Olympic course that swoops straight down to the foot of the resort. The gentlest snowfields directly in front of the central services area house an easily accessible beginners' zone, served by two chairlifts that provide smooth progression into the more testing main ski area. The majority of runs are red-graded and meander through the beautiful park-like terrain on long forest trails, the density of the trees creating the impression that the area is a lot bigger than it actually is.

The links towards Sauze d'Oulx and Sestriere are quite tough and are prone to

*Off-piste at the heart of the Milky Way. Descents are possible from Monte Fraitève towards Sestriere as illustrated, as well as Sauze d'Oulx and Sansicario.*

closure in rough weather and/or when snow is scarce. In the opposite direction, a more reliable gondola connects with a chairlift on the valley floor near Cesana towards the Monti della Luna ski area for Claviere and Montgenèvre, completing the Milky Way circuit. Although a car is not necessary to reach the other Milky Way resorts, visitors with their own transport can also easily plan days out to Serre Chevalier or Val Thorens.

Once the sun goes down, Sansicario's few hotels and handful of restaurants focus on convivial dinners and low-key post-prandial drinks, with just one small late-night venue. Sauze d'Oulx, on the other hand, moves seamlessly from the sound of schussing on snow to the clinking of ice in glasses and continues rocking until the early hours. There's something for everyone in this varied domain, with the welcoming flair of *bella Italia* providing a refreshing change from the sometimes overly serious French Alpine experience.

# SLOVENIA

# Kranjska Gora

BY MINTY CLINCH

Kranjska Gora, Slovenia's best-known ski centre, is a cheap and cheerful resort in the Julian range on the sunny southern side of the Alps. Slovenia was the first of the former Yugoslavian republics to get its independence following a 10-day war in 1991. This small country, with a population of two million, is adjusting to the European Union after becoming a member state in 2004. Slovenia is developing several resorts for the international market, but Kranjska Gora, close to the borders with Austria and Italy, is still the major player. Budget-minded skiers will appreciate Slovenia's prices, although these may rise when the country adopts the euro in 2007.

Kranjska Gora is a bizarre, indifferently planned combination of old and new. The modern tourist hotels are geared towards package tourists – chiefly British and Dutch. The hotels are clustered at the bottom of the slopes, unfortunately cutting off easy access to the 300-year-old farming village, with its cobbled streets, traditional taverns and unassuming B&Bs. Curiously, there are no

on-mountain restaurants or bars, so skiers have to return to base whenever they want a break.

The mountain has relatively old-fashioned lifts, mostly T-bars backed up by slow chairs, including a single that is a genuine museum piece. As it is a 45-m (164-ft) walk across the road via the rental shop to the slopes, there is no more convenient place to learn to ski, and the ski school is geared to teaching 'never-evers' in fluent English.

The area is heavily wooded, but the trees on the lower part of the mountain have been

cut down to create a wide integrated nursery area, served by half-a-dozen parallel lifts. Two chairs go up to Vitranc, but serve only to look at the view as there is no piste down to Podkoren 1, the second of Kranjska Gora's three linked areas and the top venue for skiing. It has icy World Cup slalom and giant slalom tracks, accessed by three lifts, including a new chair. Advanced skiers will soon exhaust the potential, but intermediates will find them intimidatingly steep.

Further round the mountain, a long, flat schuss leads to a small network of easy blue

**Party time on Kranjska Gora's gentle slopes as locals get kitted out for a blast from the past.**

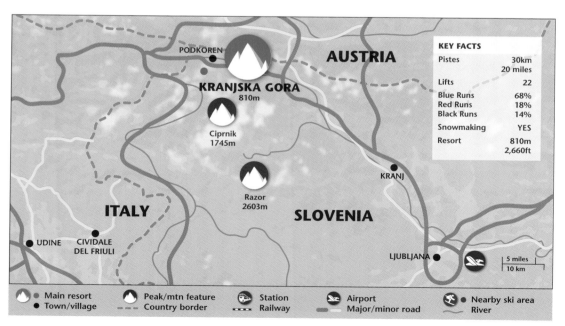

| KEY FACTS | |
|---|---|
| Pistes | 30km |
| | 20 miles |
| Lifts | 22 |
| Blue Runs | 68% |
| Red Runs | 18% |
| Black Runs | 14% |
| Snowmaking | YES |
| Resort | 810m |
| | 2,660ft |

PODKOREN

AUSTRIA

KRANJSKA GORA
810m

Ciprnik
1745m

KRANJ

Razor
2603m

ITALY

SLOVENIA

UDINE     CIVIDALE
DEL FRIULI

LJUBLJANA

5 miles
10 km

| | Main resort | | Peak/mtn feature | | Station | | Airport | | Nearby ski area |
|---|---|---|---|---|---|---|---|---|---|
| | Town/village | --- | Country border | | Railway | | Major/minor road | | River |

runs on Podkoren II. Going there creates a mild sense of adventure, but the terrain is otherwise uninteresting. Beginners may find enough challenges in Kranjska Gora to last a week, but there is nothing much to keep intermediates or experts amused for more than a day.

Bled, an hour's drive away, is an attractive spa town overlooked by a fortress and featuring a lovely 17th-century church on an island in the lake. It has its own modest slopes, but it's worth driving for a further 30 minutes to Mount Vogel, in the Bohinj basin. Accessed by gondola, Mount Vogel feels much more like a real ski resort, with runs for all standards cut through the woods and a number of attractive taverns with terraces and mountain fare. When snow conditions are right, which they rarely are, the long run back to base eliminates the irritation of downloading.

Back in Kranjska Gora, the night is yet young. The Kompass and the Larix hotels are popular with families, but the smartest choice in the four-star bracket is the renovated Grand Hotel Prisank, with a terrace overlooking an ice rink and a Manhattan cocktail bar with pool tables. Although many visitors are locked into half-board packages, often with free wine or beer at dinner, there are some appealing restaurants of the converted-barn variety in the old village. The cuisine, a mixture of Austrian and Italian, with the emphasis on homemade soup, game and pasta, is often unexpectedly good. The casino is as learner-friendly as the slopes, with croupiers taking a much more relaxed attitude to people trying to grasp the basics of blackjack than would be the case elsewhere. Alternatively, a late-night pub crawl would take in a varied selection of bars. Slovenia has good Lasko beer and home-grown red wine, plus a rewarding line in blueberry and other fruit schnapps.

**A picture postcard view of a traditional Slovenian village dominated by a church spire in the shadow of the magnificent Julian Alps.**

# AUSTRIA

# St Anton BY MINTY CLINCH

Whether you see it as a small town or a large village, St Anton is a top-class resort, with magnificent terrain, both on- and off-piste, matched by a relentless party spirit. The building of the railway under the Arlberg Pass in the early years of the 20th century allowed an isolated farming community to expand its horizons into tourism. Skiing arrived between the world wars, taking off in the 1930s with the opening of a groundbreaking cable car to Galzig. Hannes Schneider, the son of a local cheese maker, enhanced St Anton's reputation by founding the celebrated Arlberg Ski School, promoting a technique that was copied throughout the skiing world. In 1928, he started the Arlberg Kandahar downhill race with Britain's ski pioneer, Sir Arnold Lunn.

### St Christoph and Stuben

St Anton has two linked resorts: St Christoph, high on the Arlberg Pass, and Stuben, on the other side of it. St Christoph is famous for the Hospiz, originally a 13th-century monastery which provided a very welcome refuge for travellers, especially during winter storms in

what was then a remote and hostile area. Although it has burned down and been rebuilt several times over the centuries, the Hospiz has survived, although today it is run as a megabucks five-star hotel. Appropriately, it dominates a hamlet geared towards affluent visitors who shun noisy nightlife.

Stuben is quieter still, a pretty village with a yesteryear feel and a number of affordable family-run hotels.

Until 2001, Nasserein, a kilometre down the valley, was a poor relation, but it achieved total integration when the new fast gondola to Gampen was installed for the World

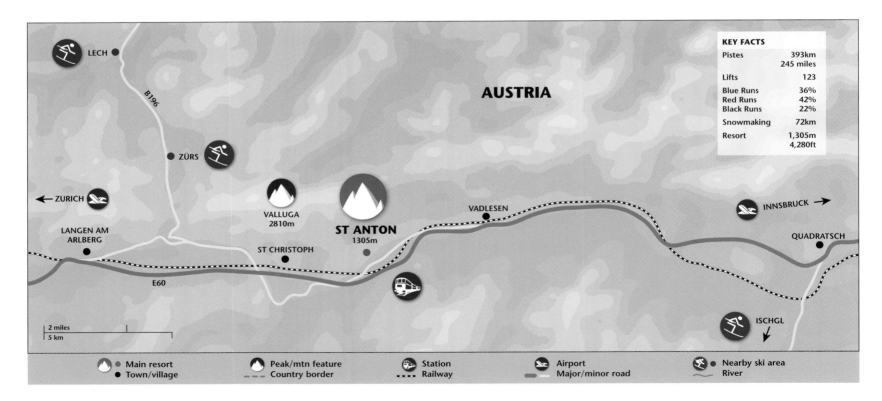

| KEY FACTS | |
|---|---|
| Pistes | 393km |
| | 245 miles |
| Lifts | 123 |
| Blue Runs | 36% |
| Red Runs | 42% |
| Black Runs | 22% |
| Snowmaking | 72km |
| Resort | 1,305m |
| | 4,280ft |

LECH

B196

AUSTRIA

ZÜRS

ZURICH

INNSBRUCK

VALLUGA 2810m

ST ANTON 1305m

VADLESEN

QUADRATSCH

LANGEN AM ARLBERG

ST CHRISTOPH

E60

ISCHGL

2 miles
5 km

Main resort • • Town/village
Peak/mtn feature — — Country border
Station ···· Railway
Airport — Major/minor road
Nearby ski area ≈ River

*In the 20th century, St Anton was a railway town, bisected by the main line from Zürich to Vienna. Cars and pedestrians waited at the level crossing while express trains blasted through the town centre. For regular visitors, it was all part of the character of the place, but for locals, it was an ongoing annoyance. Hosting the World Championships in 2001 finally secured the funding to put the railway underground on the outskirts of the town, with a new station that provides almost as easy access as before.*

*Shifting the railway freed up prime land between the large hotels on the pedestrianized main street and the lift area at the base of the mountain. Fears that it would be handed over to developers have proved groundless: the old station is now a restaurant and the tracks have given way to open space, attractively land-scaped around a pond that becomes a skating and eis stock (Austrian curling) rink in winter. The well.com centre may not be to everyone's architectural taste, but there is plenty of enthusiasm for its swimming pools, saunas and fitness rooms.*

**A typically steep powder slope in the heart of the Arlberg ski area. On a snowboard or skis, this is as good as off-piste skiing gets.**

Championships. Prices are still lower, but the facilities have been upgraded and its status is rising steadily.

St Anton is dominated by the mighty Valluga, often mysterious under swirling cloud. The main ski area spreads across the predominantly south-facing slopes below it, with two main access points – to the Valluga Grat and Kapall – from the same base area a couple of minutes' walk from the town centre. Although it has resort-level nursery slopes, beginners and timid skiers may find it hard to progress on St Anton's demanding slopes: blue runs would be red and red ones black in less ambitious resorts. Adventurous

intermediates love the chance to cruise and improve, but it is advanced and expert skiers, especially those who enjoy off-piste, who benefit most from St Anton's magnificent terrain.

For most people, the Valluga Grat, 160m (525ft) below the summit, is the top of the skiing. On a sunny day, the tiny cable-car to the peak opens up superb views of the Arlberg, but only those accompanied by a guide are allowed to take their skis to the peak. This is the start of the off-piste run over the back to Zürs, gentle for the most part but with a few steep turns above rocks at the outset, which could make falling dangerous in

icy conditions. Inevitably, confident fit skiers hike up and go down on their own, but the resort is keen not to encourage the masses by making it too easy.

Likewise, it is unwilling to take the legal responsibility for patrolling the wonderful bowls below the Valluga Grat, a cop-out it effected by regrading the Schindler Kar and the Mattun as ski routes, described as 'extreme' and 'tackled only at the skier's own risk', rather than the black runs they used to be. As a result, there is only one official descent from the Valluga Grat: the massively enjoyable 10.2-km (6¼-mile) red/blue piste via the Ulmer Hutte – well worth a scenic

Confidence is the key to a perfectly balanced powder descent on St Anton's upper slopes.

pitstop – and the tunnel under the road at Rauz to Stuben.

Looking for that magic combination of challenging terrain and deep, light powder? Stuben's north-facing slopes are the best bet, although the freeze factor on its two venerably sedate chairs is a deterrent, especially in windy weather. Historically St Anton suffered from serious queues, a problem the high-speed quads installed before the World Championships almost eliminated, but even in peak holiday periods, no one ever waits in line in Stuben. The downside is that the existing lifts are unlikely to be replaced in a hurry.

Nevertheless, off-piste enthusiasts will need to ride them, not only for the runs on the Stuben side, but for the possibility of more radical adventures over the back, either by walking up and skiing down to Langen or,

with less effort, into the lovely Verwall valley. The northwest-facing slopes in the Rendl area, a few hundred metres from the centre of St Anton on the other side of the main road, offer further rewarding off-piste options on snow that lasts longer than it does in the main area.

In the interests of safety and route finding, guides are required for many of these descents: the Arlberg Ski School can no longer claim cutting-edge technical expertise but, like its competitor, the St Anton Ski School (under the same ownership), it has plenty of qualified mountain guides. For a more personal touch, try Piste to Powder, a small school run by Graham Austick, born in Newcastle in the UK but living in St Anton for the past 17 years.

St Anton is markedly more cosmopolitan than rival Austrian resorts, thanks partly to its global 'must ski' reputation and partly to the Australians who came to work as lift attendants in the 1960s and stayed to open busi-

nesses that are still running today. The most enduring is the Krazy Kangaruh, a legendry après-ski bar just off the main run from the Galzig area to the town. Nowadays it is rivalled by the Mooserwirt, a more Teutonic bar on the other side of the piste. When the lifts close, both are crowded with adrenalized skiers downing steins of beer and dancing on the tables in their boots to the all-embracing oompah music. The ski back to town is a snow cannon slalom, short but often performed imperfectly. No worries, mate: if you're too inebriated by 8pm, when both bars think about closing, you can take a taxi home.

Night-lifers should stay in the pedestrian zone, a short street crowded with good hotels – the Schwarzer Adler, the Alte Post and the Post are the traditionals, but the Sport, a brash newcomer, has outstripped its rivals for hospitality and the quality of its food. Alternatively, there are bed-and-breakfast places to suit all budgets, invariably sparkling clean, although non-German speakers will have to do their deals in sign language in the absence of a common tongue. Less stressfully, the excellent tourist office at the end of the pedestrian zone will make the bookings for you.

Where you go after dinner depends on generation and inclination. The Funky Chicken, with a 'funky margarita hour' starting at 11pm, is the youth choice. Slightly older players might prefer the more intimate Platzl or the characterful Underground, both Australian owned (as is the Funky Chicken) and both with live music. Post midnight means the Postkeller disco or the Raj-themed Kandahar. Owned by an Englishman, it is all things to all party animals, with Thai food for dinner, live music until 2am and progressive dance music until the last customer leaves, usually between 6 and 7am. By then, it's surely bedtime.

The lights go on in St Anton at dusk. The onion-domed church dominates the clustered hotels and bar, with the nursery slopes in the background.

# Ischgl

BY MINTY CLINCH

In the 21st century, Ischgl has reinvented itself as Austria's leading party resort, with Germans as its core clientele, but backed up by a growing international presence. The start and finish of the season are marked by high profile on-mountain concerts, each headed up by a famous name – for example Deep Purple, The Corrs, Alanis Morisette and Lionel Richie. On a day-to-day basis, the village rocks from 4pm, when girls in abbreviated dirndls dance on the bar outside the Hotel Elisabeth at the base of the mountain, setting the tone for nights that end at dawn.

Like many Austrian resorts, Ischgl started as a remote farming community grouped around a church set on a low hill. Further up the Paznaun Valley, Galtür provides a gateway to the majestic Silvretta range, known for top-level ski touring since Ernest Hemingway joined the pioneers over two winters in the 1920s. Today, Ischgl's landmark church stands above a maze of hotels, mostly opulent four-stars targeted at the owners of ranked BMWs and Mercedes with German plates parked on the other side of the main road for the duration of their holidays. With space at a premium, the buildings are crowded together rather too closely for comfort. The upside is that walking is easy, both on the pedestrianized main streets and the covered moving walkways and escalators that protect visitors in bad weather.

Ischgl may be conspicuously rich, but it is also a serious resort, widely considered the second best in Austria (after St Anton). In recent years, it has invested €120 million in improvements, much of it in replacing its infamous long drag lifts with sleek modern chairs, many of them with hoods. It has welcomed snowboarders from the outset and now claims the largest funpark in Europe and possibly in the world, a 400-m (1,312-ft) facility above Idalp with a quarterpipe, a boardercross course and some impressively challenging jumps.

**Legendary nightlife? After a hard day on the slopes, visitors switch on for fine dining and late night clubbing in one of Austria's liveliest resorts.**

Ischgl shares a lift system and a lift pass with Samnaun, a duty-free outpost in a lost corner of Switzerland. Guests make a habit of skiing over for a Swiss rösti lunch, filling their empty backpacks with cheap booze and clinking their way back to base via the Pendelbahn, the first ever double-decker cable-car.

## The skiing

Wherever you stay in Ischgl, access to the mountain is easy. The Silvretta and Fimba gondolas take skiers straight up to Idalp, the flat sunny midstation plateau where students of the ski school usually meet, while the Pardatschgrat gondola goes a little higher. Idalp is the focus of the upper mountain lift system, with rapid connections to skiing at the top of Palinkopf, Greitspitz and Idjoch.

Most of the terrain is for intermediate cruising, perfect for building confidence or racking up kilometres on wide, impeccably prepared red pistes. One of the most rewarding – and the emptiest – is the sweeping descent from Palinkopf to Gampenalp on the Fimbatal edge of the ski area. Palinkopf is also the launch point for the fine fast track run down to Samnaun. Inneres Viderjoch, in the same area, is the start of Ischgl's most demanding advanced pistes, with two options, both potentially rocky in parts, down to Bodenalp.

From a beginner's point of view, Ischgl has two main drawbacks: there are no resort-level nursery slopes, so they have to go up to Idalp to learn, and there is no remotely easy way back to base. All the home runs are graded red, but they turn into racetracks when the lifts close at 4pm as skiers of all standards compete for space on narrow, icy trails, often heading up the sides to escape disaster.

Small wonder perhaps that the survivors start on their après-ski programme within metres of the finish. When they tire of the Elisabeth's dancing girls – which can take some time – many head for Niki's Stadl, named for its owner, a self-appointed DJ and comedian who entertains his public in his

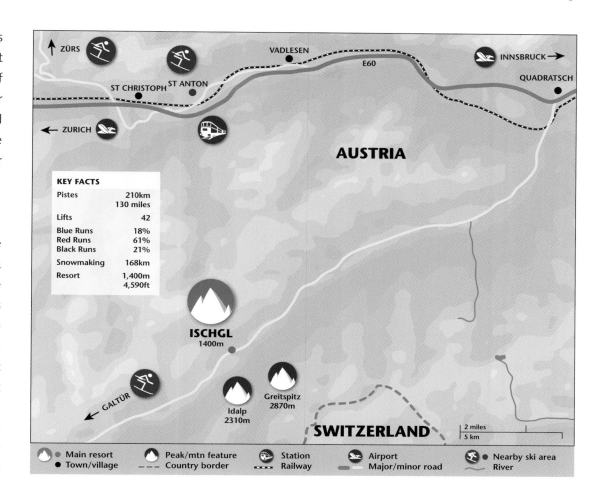

| KEY FACTS | |
|---|---|
| Pistes | 210km |
| | 130 miles |
| Lifts | 42 |
| Blue Runs | 18% |
| Red Runs | 61% |
| Black Runs | 21% |
| Snowmaking | 168km |
| Resort | 1,400m |
| | 4,590ft |

large two-level bar. This is one of several places targeted specifically at après-ski, which is promoted in Ischgl as an activity in its own right.

The best restaurant in town is the Tofana Royal Paznaunstube, which has a celebrity chef in the kitchen and jackets and ties in the dining room. Almost anywhere else is much cheaper, with places offering either traditional Austrian fare, served in massive portions, or international menus of the pizza, burgers and steak variety.

When the après-ski bars start to wilt, the late-nighters kick in. The Guxa cigar lounge, featuring deep sofas and offering expertly shaken cocktails, is the antidote to pubs with loud, and in some cases, live music. The frenzy increases after midnight, with up to 1,200 people crowding into the Trofana Arena to dance under cutting-edge laser lights, but there are cooler discos, notably Pacha, which also has branches in London and Ibiza. It is under the same roof as Coyote Ugly, Ischgl's lap-dancing club, which closes at 6am.

An expert twin-tip skier makes the most of the terrain on the slopes above Ischgl.

# Saalbach-Hinterglemm

BY ARNIE WILSON

The most visited location in Austria after Vienna, these villages – almost joined at the hip – provide intermediate skiers and upwards with one of the finest and best connected ski circuits in the Alps. And for those who like to burn the candle at both ends, there is one of Austria's liveliest party circuits too – liable to exhaust any energy salvaged from the slopes. Skiing and partying are certainly not mutually exclusive in Saalbach-Hinterglemm.

The actual village centres – both traffic-free – are 4km (2½miles) apart. Saalbach, a traditional mountain village long before skiing became popular, nestles in the narrower part of the valley, with an impressive mountain backdrop for the chalet-style hotels and their carved wooden balconies. The yellow steeple of the old church towers above the rooftops, and a small torrent gushes through the town.

The Glemmtal Valley floor broadens considerably just 1.6km (1 mile) up the road at the village of Hinterglemm. Here, the hotels are larger and the more sedate village fans out over a wider area – but it's no less central to the main ski crossroads of the valley than Saalbach.

The 'ski circus' is set in a huge, sunny, bowl-shaped valley on wide-open slopes, with skiing on both sides so that you can follow the sun. With picturesque peaks lining the whole valley, the scenery is exceptional, particularly the views right the way across the Kitzbüheler Alps. There's mile after mile of linked runs, some through the trees, some wide-open, and little that's extremely difficult – there is really no part of the ski circus that is off-limits to the intermediate with the possible exception (depending on how icy it is) of the runs under the Schattberg X-press and Zwölferkogel Nord gondolas. However, even experts determined to put as many miles under their skis as possible can find themselves hard-pressed to cover the area from one end to the other in a single day – never mind stopping along the way to enjoy a tasty long lunch!

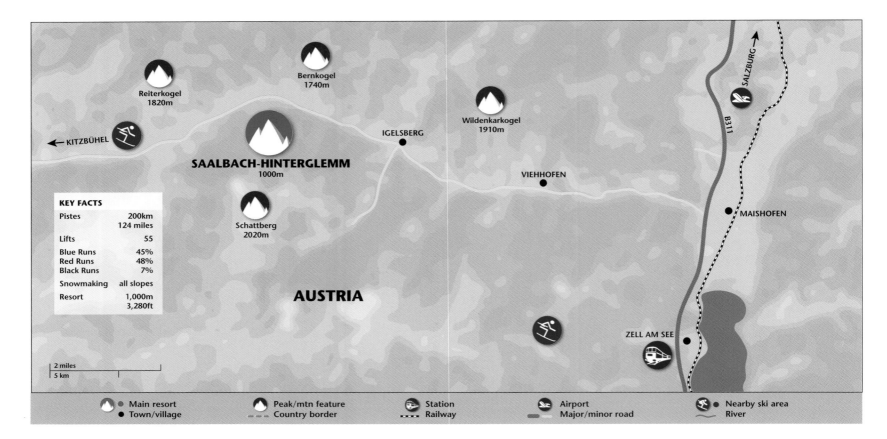

KEY FACTS

| | |
|---|---|
| Pistes | 200km |
| | 124 miles |
| Lifts | 55 |
| Blue Runs | 45% |
| Red Runs | 48% |
| Black Runs | 7% |
| Snowmaking | all slopes |
| Resort | 1,000m |
| | 3,280ft |

Saalbach and its close neighbour Hinterglemm form a dynamic duo of resorts which are the gateway to one of the Alps' classic ski circuits.

The northern sector of the circuit, above Saalbach, has the easier slopes, and it's not obligatory to complete the tour – you can simply hop on a ski bus when you get tired. You can also short-circuit the route by crossing the valley at Hinterglemm to pick up the homeward-bound runs. Either way, before the week is over, intermediates are likely to have made considerable progress, and be able to move up a gear to the more demanding runs. There are some 40 mountain restaurants to keep them refreshed on their travels.

Depending on how much progress you are making, try not to miss some good skiing en route – if you're preoccupied with getting to the finishing post you risk missing some wonderful roller-coaster runs, especially during the early part of the tour on Reiterkogel, Hasenauer Köpfl and Reichkendlkopf. Two in particular provide sheer joy to anyone prepared to take their foot off the brake and relish the ride: Sunliner (run 36) and Bachabfahrt (33) are well worth interrupting the flow of the circuit for.

At the end of what should have been an exhilarating day, if you're heading home to Saalbach, there's a choice between the long black run from Schattberg Ost – often icy and mogulled – or the more mellow Limberg-Jausern run, at just under 8km (5 miles) the longest in the resort, which meanders down to Vorderglemm en route.

Save a day, if possible, for a side trip to Leogang. Leogang is not part of the circuit, but at some stage during your visit it is well worth skiing the fast cruising trails from the top of the Asitz gondola all the way down to this pretty little village in the neighbouring valley. You start with a sweeping red run, then there's a choice of blue, red or black all

the way down, with an impressive vertical drop of more than 922m (3,000ft). Leogang, dubbed 'the longest village in Europe', also has 40km (25 miles) of cross-country tracks.

Saalbach-Hinterglemm specializes in catering for snow-users of all persuasions. As well as 12km (7½miles) of specially marked snowboard runs and dedicated 'carving zones' for boarders and skiers, there are snowboard parks, halfpipes, 'carving fun' parks, dedicated mogul areas where you can enjoy 'hot rides' over the bumps, and a permanent race course where you can test yourself against

the clock from the Unterschwarzach lift at Hinterglemm. Fun parks are groomed daily by professional snowpark 'shapers'.

Saalbach-Hinterglemm is one of the most celebrated party resorts in the Alps. The festivities start as early as 3:30pm when skiers remove their skis as the dancing begins. Skiers can choose from 65 restaurants. Alternative activities to skiing include curling, ice-hockey, skating, tobogganing, sleigh-rides, paragliding, plus a ski museum, and sauna/solarium facilities. Excursions to Kitzbühel and Salzburg can be organized.

Following the sun: on a blue-sky day, skiers who embark on the round trip of the Saalbach-Hinterglemm circuit can stay in the warmth for most of the tour.

# Schladming

BY ARNIE WILSON

The picturesque and historic town of Schladming is an ancient mining community at the heart of the Schladming-Dachstein-Tauern Region, between the precipitous limestone ranges of the Dachstein Massif and the prehistoric rocks of the Schladminger Tauern. Parts of the old town are said to date back to 1322. The slopes comprise a vast area, with four principal mountains, plus several smaller areas and the Dachstein glacier: Schladming-Rohrmoos, Pichl-Reiteralm; Ramsau, Haus, Gröbminger Land, Naturpark Sölktäler, Vitaldörfer Öblarn and Niederöblarn, Donnersbachwald and the Bergregion Grimming.

**Schladming is part of the Ski amadé region – the country's biggest collection of resorts.**

In turn, Schladming's slopes are part of the gigantic Ski amadé region, which brings together 860km (540 miles) of skiing served by some 270 lifts on one lift ticket. To put it another way, that's 25 resorts in five different ski regions, each region an extensive arena in its own right, all based around Salzburg, Mozart's birthplace (hence the 'amadé' connection). In general, the resorts are ideal for families, with long, uncrowded slopes, friendly ski schools and charming mountain restaurants.

Many of the Austrian ski team went to Schladming's celebrated Handelsschule ski academy, and for many years Schladming (once a favourie local haunt of Arnold Schwarzenegger, who was born nearby) was a regular early-season location on the World Cup circuit. Indeed it was here in 1973, when the first World Cup race was held on the icy and treacherous Planai downhill course in front of 25,000 spectators, that a young skier celebrated his first success on the tour. A star was born that day as Franz Klammer, wearing bib number 16, beat the Swiss favourites to win the first of his 25 World Cup downhills. These days Schladming is better

known for its exciting floodlit World Cup slalom nights in January.

But in spite of these challenges, most of the skiing here is an intermediates' playground – an attractive prospect for most skiers, except perhaps for beginners, for whom the layout is a little awkward, and the beginner slopes difficult to get to. The skiing includes some of the longest uninterrupted runs in Austria; for example, the 4.6-km (2¾mile) FIS run or the 7.7km (almost 5 mile) Hochwurzen Valley descent.

The 'local' slopes stretch from Hauser Kaibling, above Haus, to Planai, Hochwurzen and Reiteralm. Also included on the pass is glacier skiing at Dachstein, above Ramsau. American visitors, often more accustomed to single-mountain resorts, love it here. As one said: 'If you get tired of one mountain, just move on to the next.'

### HISTORY OF SCHLADMING

*Schladming's picturesque medieval town and extensive ski arena is scattered along the southern side of a long, attractive valley. Its history dates back more than 600 years, when the town was known for its rich silver, lead and copper ore deposits. Miner and peasant revolts in 1525 burned the town to the ground – and this inevitably led to a decline in the mining industry!*

## Four mountains

Schladming's four linked mountains are each served by a gondola (the Haus slopes can be reached by cable-car, too). The obvious mountain to start exploring is Planai (1,894m/6,214ft), the nearest to town, and dominated – as is much of Schladming's skiing – by red runs. There are good nursery slopes near the top. But unless they are experienced enough to cope with the runs down to the Planai West chair-lift link which, rather spookily, goes through a tunnel as it takes skiers to the outer base area of Hochwurzen, complete beginners will prefer the Rohrmoos plateau. This old mining area is a bus ride away for skiers based in Schladming.

Fundamentally the skiing is similar throughout the resort: fairly long, fairly steep gladed runs. There is considerable satisfaction to be had from travelling under your own steam from one area to another, and the broad scope of the skiing means that the slopes are usually relatively uncrowded.

The area has three halfpipes, a new board-ercross run and an excellent terrain park. There's a halfpipe in the middle of the Planai area, and another at the top of the gondola at Reiteralm. But pride of place goes to the huge halfpipe in the snowpark further along the valley at the top of Galsterbergalm. There are also almost 306km (190 miles) of cross-country trails in the region. Other skiing alternatives include snow-shoeing, a 7-km (4¼-mile) toboggan run (floodlit at night) from the top of the Hochwurzen gondola, skating, curling, hot-air ballooning, para-gliding and sleigh rides, usually combined with a restaurant visit. At a more down to earth level, there are also 30km (19 miles) of winter walking paths. Don't miss the picturesque town centre, with its tea rooms. Day trip excursions to Salzburg can be arranged.

**The warm glow of Austria's celebrated *gemütlichkeit* or welcome, at the Winteridylle in Hockwurzen.**

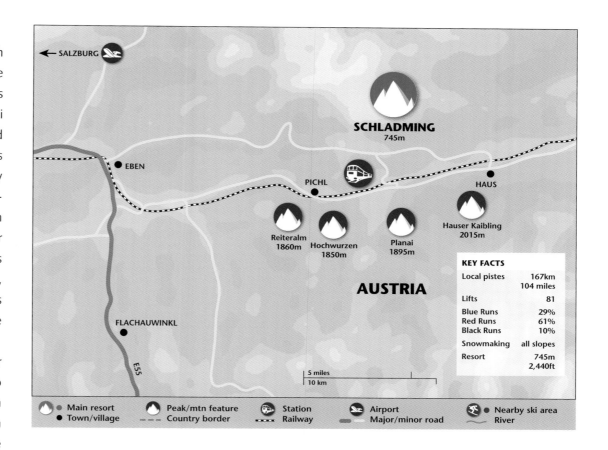

| KEY FACTS | |
|---|---|
| Local pistes | 167km |
| | 104 miles |
| Lifts | 81 |
| Blue Runs | 29% |
| Red Runs | 61% |
| Black Runs | 10% |
| Snowmaking | all slopes |
| Resort | 745m |
| | 2,440ft |

Main resort · Town/village · Peak/mtn feature · Country border · Station · Railway · Airport · Major/minor road · Nearby ski area · River

# Bad Gastein

BY ARNIE WILSON

It was gold and therapeutic hot springs, rather than skiing, that first made the Gasteinertal famous. According to legend, in the seventh century, high in Austria's Hohe Tauern mountains, two hunters chasing a wounded stag close to a fast-flowing river found the animal standing in a steaming pool, nursing its injuries. The hunters had discovered the Gasteiner hot springs. If they could have bottled it they might have made a fortune – the waters are said to promote cell growth and help disorders such as rheumatism, arthritis, poor circulation, diabetes, gout, bad gums, tuberculosis, asthma, respiratory disorders, premature ageing and even impotence.

The 'cure' is still very much available, and was given a boost some 50 years ago when miners in search of gold claimed to have gained relief from their rheumatic complaints while working inside the Radhausberg mountain near Böckstein. Although the mines eventually closed, health tourists started taking the 2.4-km (1½-mile) train ride inside the mountain to the abandoned mine workings and the Gastein Healing Gallery, where temperatures hover at around 32°C (90°F) and you can relax in a sort of glorified natural Turkish bath.

At around the same time, in 1950 – in rather lower temperatures – local residents threw caution to a bitter wind, wrapped themselves warmly against the elements and braved a violent snowstorm to cluster around an exciting innovation at the base of the Stubnerkogel, the mountain that overlooks the picturesque Salzburgerland spa town of Bad Gastein. One of Austria's earliest cable-cars was about to make its debut. It would change the community forever.

At the top, the blizzard obscured the magnificent view of Austria's highest peak, the Grossglockner (3,798m/12,461ft) but there would be plenty of opportunities to see that later. Bad Gastein, famed for its healing waters, would soon become equally celebrated for its extensive ski slopes, and miles of quite easy, but enjoyable, off-piste.

## The Gasteinertal

The Gasteinertal (Gastein Valley), is the longest side valley of the Hohe Tauern range. It borders the Grossarl and Rauris valleys and, in the south, the province of Carinthia. The ski network is complex, but well worth the journey, with four ski areas to explore: the pretty village of Dorfgastein, with its own ski area centred around the Kreuzkogel, at 2,027m (6,650ft), is the lowest. Dorfgastein (830m/2723ft), is linked with Grossarl in the next valley, but not with the other Gastein Valley resorts. Although Bad Hofgastein (860m/2,821ft) is linked with the brightest star in the valley, Bad Gastein (1,080m/ 3,543ft), Bad Gastein itself is not linked with its own satellite area, Graukogel, which has some of the most challenging skiing.

There turns out to be unexpectedly good skiing at Dorfgastein and Grossarl, too, but many visitors ignore this area as they rush

A true boarder's paradise: so much snow – and so many places to go in the four-resort valley.

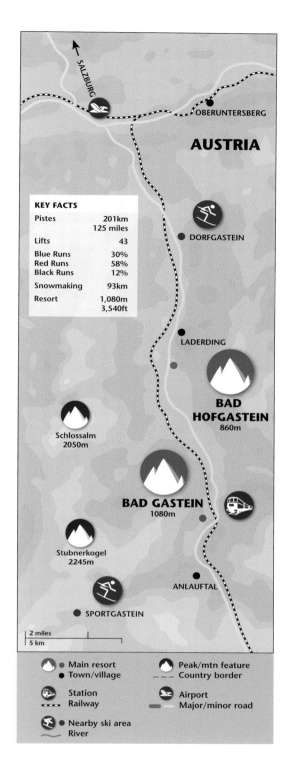

**KEY FACTS**

| | |
|---|---|
| Pistes | 201km |
| | 125 miles |
| Lifts | 43 |
| Blue Runs | 30% |
| Red Runs | 58% |
| Black Runs | 12% |
| Snowmaking | 93km |
| Resort | 1,080m |
| | 3,540ft |

SALZBURG

OBERUNTERSBERG

**AUSTRIA**

DORFGASTEIN

LADERDING

**BAD
HOFGASTEIN**
860m

Schlossalm
2050m

**BAD GASTEIN**
1080m

Stubnerkogel
2245m

ANLAUFTAL

SPORTGASTEIN

2 miles
5 km

● Main resort ● Peak/mtn feature
● Town/village --- Country border
Station ✈ Airport
Railway Major/minor road
Nearby ski area
River

past on their way to the linked ski areas of the two spa towns of Badhof Gastein and Bad Gastein. You can't blame them. If you include the unusually extensive and accessible off-piste areas on Bad Gastein's Stubnerkogel (2,245m/7,365ft) and Bad Hofgastein's Schlossalm (2,050m/6,725ft) there's more than enough skiing and boarding to last a week or more. The longest run, from the

The ultimate for two off-piste enthusiasts as they execute near perfect figures of eight in virgin snow.

Just one of the many ski locations in the Gasteinertal: the Angertal Valley provides easy skiing as well as good snowshoe hiking. The descent from Stubnerkogl is the longest in the region.

Stubnerkogl to Angertal, is 8km (5 miles), with the Schlossalm to Hohe Scharte Nord a very close second. There are also some long runs on- and off-piste on the Graukogel. The Stubnerkogl has four faces, but only two are regularly skied. The other two are off-piste. Much of the Schlossalm's considerable off-piste is easily accessible, and not difficult to ski. It also offers some delightful, wide, sunny runs – many suitable for novices – on a large plateau. One magnificent descent, off the beaten track down the north slope of Bad Hofgastein's Hohe Scharte, stretches for almost 8km (5 miles).

## Bad Gastein

Bad Gastein is the most celebrated and historic of the valley's communities. The once internationally famous spa town springs up dramatically from the banks of a gorge, where a semi-frozen waterfall plunges into the River Ache, cascading past colourful buildings, which include a Baroque town hall, casino and tall and venerable *belle époque*

hotels painted in the Imperial yellow of Vienna's Schönbrunn Palace. It was once described as being "like a piece of 19th-century Vienna or Salzburg dumped onto the steep mountainsides of the Hohe Tauern Alps".

Each day some 105 kilolitres (23 million gallons) of hot water bubble up from 17 natural springs and are piped into Bad Gastein's main hotels, including some in neighbouring Bad Hofgastein. Over the centuries, kings, emperors, princes, heads of state, composers, church leaders and other international 'celebrities' have been attracted by the healing properties of the hot springs. However, the skiing is the big attraction these days.

Because of the need to bus or drive between some of the resorts, it makes sense to aim for one area at a time. The obvious principal targets are the main linked areas of Bad Gastein and Bad Hofgastein.

## Sportgastein

Somewhat isolated at the far end of the valley, a 25-minute bus ride beyond the spa towns, is Sportgastein (1,600m/5,250ft), a high-altitude area with good snow and some of the best off-piste skiing in the valley. Sportgastein has runs reaching 2,686m (8,813ft) on the Kreuzkogel. The slopes are

close to a once-important mining village, which in the Middles Ages supplied as much as 10 per cent of the world's gold and silver. With broad, wide-open, above-tree-line slopes, and good off-piste opportunities, Sportgastein comes into its own in lean snow years, when its high altitude makes good conditions a near-certainty. The 'ski route north', an 8-km (5-mile) run from the top stage of the Goldbergbahn, finishes near the Gastein Healing Gallery, where you can catch the ski bus shuttle to the bottom station. There's also a magnificent off-piste run down a wide, open valley and then through the trees all the way to Heilstollen.

The resort is, however, disarmingly honest about how unpleasant Sportgastein can become 'when the wind blows too hard over the top of the Alps', which can mean the gondola has to stop running. Skiers and snowboarders are warned: 'Sportgastein is definitely a fair-weather skiing area. We've tried skiing there in windy and misty weather, and we don't recommend it!'

You can be sure of a hot bath afterwards: one very pleasant way of recovering from such exertions is to immerse yourself in open-air pools, where you can swim outside in the cold night air but maintain body heat in temperatures of around 24°C (75°F) as you lie and look at the stars and the odd aircraft or satellite passing in the night. If you're ever going to indulge in spa treatments, now's the time. There are indoor and outdoor pools galore.

Other activities include cross-country skiing on 90km (56 miles) of trails, ice skating, ice-climbing, curling, scenic walking (there are some 100km/62 miles of winter hiking trails), snowshoe hiking in the Angertal valley, the Hohe Tauern National Park and the Fulseck area (Dorfgastein), tobogganing and sleigh rides.

Activities that don't involve snow or spas include indoor tennis, squash, golf, horse-riding, parapenting and even gliding. It's worth making the effort to drive (or bus) the 3km (1.8 miles) to eat at the Hotel Grüner Baum, a magnificent hunting lodge established in 1831 by Archduke John. The local valley is now a national park and the lodge and its village have been transformed into a luxury hotel.

The Gastein Valley is an integral part of the vast Ski amadé alliance, Austria's largest ski 'association', with more than 854km (534 miles) of slopes and 270 lifts available in 30 resorts on the same ticket. These include Schladming (Arnold Schwarzenegger country) and Flachau (the home of the great downhill racer Hermann Maier).

RIGHT: **Tomorrow's champions: the Gastein Valley provides perfect slopes for young racers to hone their skills.**

BELOW: **Earning their turns: where there's no lift, there's a way, as skiers and snowboarders hike up in search of fresh powder.**

# Lech and Zürs

BY FELIX MILNS

Undeniably Austria's most exclusive resort, Lech pretty much sets the standard for five-star hotel service in the Alps. Along with neighbouring Zürs and the high-altitude satellite resort of Oberlech, there are six large five-star hotels here, acting as a powerful magnet to the wallets of wealthy German and Austrian aristocracy.

By no means is it a resort exclusively for royalty, however; like many up-market resorts, the large majority of visitors are your average skiing groups of friends or families. It is no more expensive than any of the other top European resorts. Part of the Arlberg ski area, which includes neighbouring St Anton, its skiing and snow reliability are both excellent, offering primarily uncrowded intermediate slopes as a counterweight to the more extreme terrain of St Anton, best for more expert skiers.

Unlike its boisterous and exuberant neighbour, Lech has a refined feel, with elegant couples as likely to be strolling along the river with coiffured dogs as carrying a pair of skis. The hotel culture is really dominant, with little chalet or apartment accommodation available. The hotels are generally of an excellent standard and the hotel experience is as crucial as the skiing to get the real flavour of the resort. In contrast to other high-profile 'jet-set' destinations, Lech does not feature arcades of up-market shops; the real luxury of the resort stems from its pretty alpine architecture, setting and atmosphere and the warm, individual touch of the family-run hotels.

## Zürs

There are three main resort centres, of which Zürs is the highest, at 1,716m (5,629ft). There is not much of a village here, just a collection of high-end hotels built along the busy road, and good skiing links both sides of the valley. One advantage is that it is the nearest of the resorts to Alpe Rauz, which is linked by a free bus service and gives you access into the St Anton ski area. Don't be put off just because you cannot ski directly between the two areas; the buses are quite efficient, apart from peak hours in high season when they can make you weep periodically. On those occasions, plan ahead and pre-order a taxi.

FACING PAGE: **Fireworks explode in the skies above Lech, casting an eerie beauty over this up-market resort.**

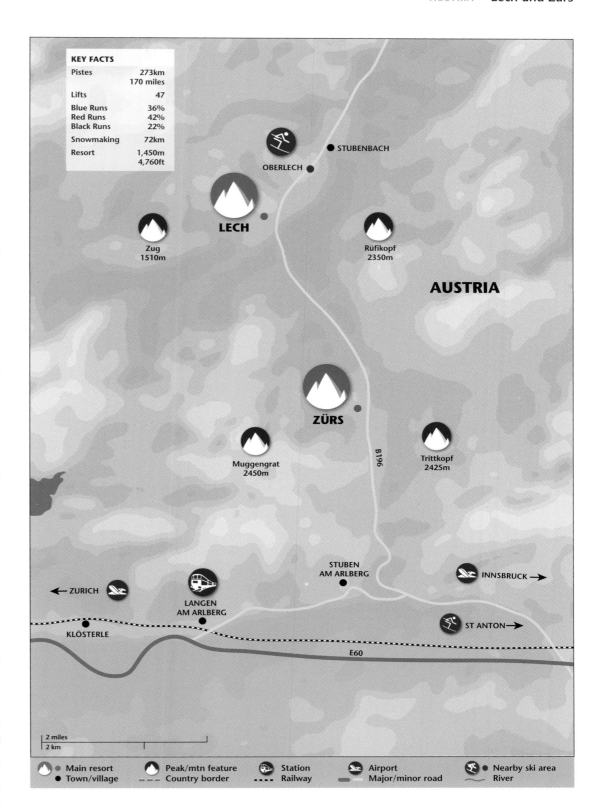

**KEY FACTS**

| Pistes | 273km |
| | 170 miles |
| Lifts | 47 |
| Blue Runs | 36% |
| Red Runs | 42% |
| Black Runs | 22% |
| Snowmaking | 72km |
| Resort | 1,450m |
| | 4,760ft |

2 miles
2 km

| ● Main resort | ● Peak/mtn feature | Station | Airport | ● Nearby ski area |
| ● Town/village | --- Country border | •••• Railway | Major/minor road | River |

## Lech

The bus service also runs between Zürs and Lech, further down the valley at 1,450m (4,757ft), and the recognized centre. Most of the hotels are located along the river and main street (which can, unfortunately, become clogged with traffic, especially at weekends), with the base station of the Rufikopf cable-car right in the centre. The other cable-car from the centre is actually the pedestrian link to car-free Oberlech, up at 1,660m (5,446ft), which runs until 1am. Guests staying in one of the select few four-star ski-in/ski-out hotels leave their cars in Lech and make their way out by cable-car while their luggage is transported through a network of tunnels underground. In bad weather, guests find their way down there too. The late-night lift works well, as Lech is the centre of a lively après-ski scene.

Cheaper accommodation can be found further up the valley at the small hamlet called Zug, which links into the Oberlech ski area via a two-person chair.

Lech is high enough to almost guarantee the charming scene of banks of snow piled high through the village and along the river. Despite getting a lot of sun, the snow record in the valley is extremely good, making it an excellent place in good weather, especially after a fresh snowfall when there is abundant off-piste. Lech normally gets double the amount of snow that neighbouring St Anton does which, in turn, still has an excellent snow record. The downside to this altitude is that when the weather closes in there are very few trees to offer any definition so the whole valley can be quite desolate and unforgiving.

When the sun is shining, though, the three main mountains that comprise the skiing area offer some of the best intermediate cruising in the mountains and will rarely be compro-

mised by an abundance of skiers. The lift system is consistently improving, and many of the new chairs now have heated seats. The main collection of slopes are found on the Oberlech sector and are largely well-pisted reds and blues perfect for motorway cruising.

Unusually, the piste map also marks out off-piste trails (look for the red and black dotted lines and do not get them confused with marked runs as they are rarely groomed so can quickly develop bumps), of which there is a preponderance in this sector. Most are accessed by the top of the eight-person Steinmahder chair. To get the full benefit of the off-piste in this area, it is worth hiring a guide as there is much more beyond the marked trails with short climbs opening up unspoiled bowls of fresh powder. Many of the itineraries get so thoroughly skied that they come to resemble pistes and adventurous intermediates should not be

afraid to give them a go, particularly 48, which is a beautiful winding route down to the village of Zug.

Those wishing to ski a circuit rather than stick to one area need to work in a clockwise direction from this sector across to the west-facing slopes of Trittkopf via the Rufikopf cable-car, the long flank above Zürs as, unfortunately, there are no lifts between the two to allow you to navigate in an opposite direction. The reds here are some of the best runs in the area.

Across the valley, several four-person chairs ascend the east-facing slopes from where you can head up to Muggengrat, at 2,450m (8,038ft) the highest point in the Zürs sector, which services a very pleasant blue underneath the lift and a testing red, and lots of off-piste heading back to town. Alternatively,

**The views over town are more often than not decorated with fresh dollops of pure white snow.**

*A dairy-farming village since 1300, and marooned in a high mountain valley, the village took its name from the River Lech, which in turn comes from* licca, *an ancient and rather apt word for stone-water. It was not until the building of the Flexen Road at the beginning of the 20th century that the valley became known to the rest of the Arlberg – let alone the wider world. Shortly afterwards skiing was introduced, and the ski school was founded in 1925, with the first lifts built shortly before World War II.*

continue the circuit back round to Lech via the Madloch chair, from where you can follow an itinerary either back to Lech or drop down to Zug and back up the Oberlech.

Some of the best off-piste skiing is, paradoxically, in the Zürs valley but only accessible from St Anton, and only with a guide. This is the epic descent from the top of the Valluga (2,811m/9,222ft), through a wonderfully deserted valley back round into the Trittkopf sector.

Apart from the buses, queues are never really an issue, as Lech is one of a few resorts to limit the amount of passes it sells to keep the numbers on the slopes at around 14,000 (give or take the visitors to and from St Anton), a laudable policy with positive implications on the mountains and one in clear contrast to the busy main routes of St Anton. Also covered on the ski pass are the Sonnenkopf slopes, which are again linked by a free bus service and most definitely worth a visit. Similarly quiet, they make a wonderful day trip with picturesque tree-lined skiing, rolling switchback pistes and some seriously undervalued off-piste runs.

Stuben and St Christoph, the nearest fringes of St Anton, can be done in a few hours without having to commit to a full day's expedition. Both these areas have a typical Arlberg mix of good pistes and almost limitless off-piste terrain. Ski schools are generally good, but it is important to book ahead in peak periods as many instructors have regular private clients.

Most of the après-ski centres on the hotel bars and discos, from the afternoon hotspot of the champagne bar of the hotel Montana (in Oberlech) to almost any of Lech's hotel discos. Similarly, most of the

Head off-piste and drop down through the trees before a leisurely lunch in Lech.

restaurants are situated in the hotels and are better than those found on the mountain, which, surprisingly, are nowhere near the high standard set by St Anton.

# Kitzbühel

BY FELIX MILNS

It is perhaps ironic that the resort most closely associated with one of the steepest and most toe-curling of all downhills is actually best suited to intermediates. The downhill run, known throughout the season as the Streif (a largely unpisted red that begins below the very top of the near-vertical downhill start and has a path to cut out the rest of the severe pitch) is one of only a handful of really testing pistes. However, there are not many other Alpine resorts so rooted in the history of skiing and dripping with alpine charm.

Kitzbühel has long been a romantic Tyrolean favourite. The old town is a delightful old settlement resplendent with colourful frescoes on the exteriors of buildings, cobbled streets and iconic churches, all dating back to medieval times. Despite the trappings of tradition, the town is chic and cosmopolitan, managing to marry a modern outlook seductively with its historical heritage. Many

people fall in love with, and in, Kitzbühel – it's easy to see why.

The one factor most likely to stand in the way of this love affair is the resort's low altitude. The resort sits at an altitude of 760m (2,493ft) – practically the valley floor in many other Alpine ski areas – and the slopes top out at 2,000m (6,562ft). While the upper slopes are relatively snow-sure, the runs down to the

resort can be quite bare during the early and late season. However, there has been massive recent investment in artificial snowmaking, and the resort now has commendable snow guns, directed largely at the lower runs.

**In good conditions, skiing the powder through the trees off the back of the Hahnenkamm is one of skiing's top experiences.**

Kitzbühel's ski area is extensive, with 160km (99 miles) of pistes, and in good conditions this is actually one of the most beautiful intermediate alpine settings. The low altitude means that most of the skiing is through the trees, and the views from the summits are particularly scenic.

Most of the skiing takes place on and from the Hahnenkamm, southwest of the town centre. Fortunately most of the runs face northeast or northwest, meaning they hold their snow well. The most famous run of all is of course the World Cup downhill. Held in mid-January each year, this is an excellent time to be in the resort. Bands belt out oom-pah tunes in town and cowbells create the music of the mountains, while lederhosen are the leather pants of choice. The atmosphere in the bars, clubs and casino is electric when the World Cup circus rolls into town. The run itself is normally closed early season and, depending on snow conditions, opens to the public after the race weekend. It starts at the top of the gondola and drops 860m (2,822ft), finishing on the very outskirts of the town.

Off the back of the summit is the largest of the ski areas, running between the Hahnenkamm peak (1,710m/5,610ft) and Pengelstein (1,935m/6,348ft). Between the two is the large Ehrenbachgraben bowl, with a variety of short slopes coming down from all sides. Here is where most of the steep and bumpy runs and off-piste are found among pleasant intermediate terrain.

A longer run is the picturesque, winding blue down to Klausen from Ehrenbachhöhe (1,800m/5,906ft), boasting 1,000m (3,280ft) of vertical. Also down this flank are the runs dropping down to neighbouring Kirchberg (850m/2,789ft), another picturesque Austrian village that shares its slopes with Kitzbühel. There are also some fabulous off-piste itineraries that you can follow off the back of the Hahnenkamm, but a guide is recommended.

The top of Pengelstein is also the start of the renowned Ski Safari, a charming circuit of pistes leading from the Hahnenkamm area and circling the other main ski area

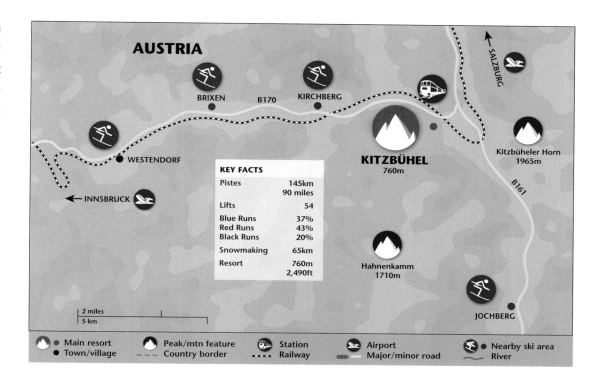

| KEY FACTS | |
|---|---|
| Pistes | 145km |
| | 90 miles |
| Lifts | 54 |
| Blue Runs | 37% |
| Red Runs | 43% |
| Black Runs | 20% |
| Snowmaking | 65km |
| Resort | 760m |
| | 2,490ft |

comprising the slopes above Jochberg and Pass Thurn. It is easy not to get lost; just follow the elephant signs around a gentle circuit of blues and cruisy reds along the east-facing slopes. Progressing intermediates should be fine. Until 2005 there was no return gondola-link from Jochberg to the top of Pengelstein, but the new lift thankfully now replaces what could sometimes be a lengthy walk and wait for a bus. The runs in this far sector are generally scenic and reasonably gentle, with a vertical drop of 1,075m (3,527ft) from the summit of Zweitausender (2,000m/6,562ft) down to Jochberg at 925m (3,035ft).

The same is true for the Kitzbüheler Horn (1,965m/6,447ft), which rises up across town from the Hahnenkamm. Most of the skiing is in the sunny, south-facing Trattalm Bowl and offers very pleasant cruising. Skier's left of the Horn is the relatively new off-piste sector of Bichlalm. A snowcat service offers further off-piste adventures up to the top of Stuckkogel (1,860m/6,102ft), a welcome innovation that recognizes the growing numbers of people who want to ski unpisted terrain.

The charm of the town spills over into the mountain restaurants, and there is more than enough here to go around. There are over 40 of a generally high standard, and these suitably encourage a rather relaxed approach.

The resort is larger than it first appears, with more modern developments mushrooming around the walled centre. While these do detract from Kitzbühel's chocolate-box charm, these accommodation centres also allow a younger crowd to bolster the celebrated après-ski scene at far cheaper rates than the hotels in the centre. While many people choose to stay in the town, it is worth bearing in mind that most experienced skiers prefer to be near the Hahnenkamm gondola (southwest of the centre), though both major lifts are within walking distance of the centre.

The focus of the après-ski scene is in the heart of the town at a British/Austrian bar called the Londoner. Live music, happy hours and rambunctious behaviour is the order of the day. Brass Monkeys is a recent addition very much in the Kitzbühel spirit and there are many other bars and small clubs. There is a dress code for the casino.

Kitzbühel is also an excellent resort for non-skiing activities, with good shopping, fantastic cafés and cake shops, as well as easy day trips to Salzburg and Innsbruck. It is deservedly one of the most famous resorts in the Alps, but booking far ahead early or late season can be a risk. You are better advised to go for mid-season or to book late when you know the snow conditions are good.

# SWITZERLAND

# Zermatt

BY ARNIE WILSON

The Matterhorn lured the first inhabitants to this idyllic alpine valley – yet at first scared them away from any thoughts of scaling its magnificent peak. Europe's celebrated mountain has the same extraordinary power today over visitors who just stand in awe beneath it. It's as if some colossal deity is standing at the head of the valley, and indeed the world's love affair with Zermatt involves something close to worship for this iconic granite monolith.

When the British climber Edward Whymper made his historic but disastrous first ascent of this bewitching mountain almost a century and a half ago, Zermatt was a tiny mountain village, with wooden huts supported by stone slabs (to keep the mice and rats out) and sleepy lanes and alleys – some of which exist to this day in the back streets of 'old' Zermatt. It was a prime location for alpinists during the golden age of climbing, and still is, to some extent, although that classic era has long since been overshadowed, at least in winter, by Zermatt's emergence as one of the world's most highly rated ski destinations.

The celebrated car-free Valais village (you have to park your car a little down the valley at Täsch and catch a train or taxi into town) is perched on either side of a river at 1,620m (5,315ft) in the scenic Matter Valley in the southwest of Switzerland. For once the word 'idyllic' really does apply: Zermatt is almost surrounded by a seriously impressive landscape of mountains and glaciers, and from the higher slopes you begin to feast your eyes on some of the highlights of an extraordinary panorama of 4,000m (13,123ft) peaks. There are 38 of them in the region – not all visible at the same time, or even at all, even from Zermatt's highest slopes.

**The unmistakable Matterhorn and the world-famous mountain community of Zermatt.**

## THE MATTERHORN

*Whether skier or walker, you are unlikely to tire of the ever-changing profile of the Matterhorn – the emblem of Zermatt, and probably the most photographed mountain in the world. Yet although the 4,478-m (14,691ft) peak seems to tower above the resort, majestic and fascinating in every light, it is far from being the highest mountain in the region. However, its silhouette is unique, in spite of which everybody seems to want a copy! All around the world there are ski areas anxious to claim a look-alike – or at least name their highest 'hill' after it. (The closest 'look-alike' is probably Canada's Mount Assiniboine, on the skyline across the British Columbia border at Sunshine Village, Alberta.)*

## Lie of the land

For first-time visitors, the resort layout can be a little overwhelming, if not confusing. There are three main skiing areas, and – at the time of writing – the various lift companies' marketing people have made the faintly absurd decision to re-brand them as 'paradises'. Hence the Sunnegga area – gateway to the sunniest slopes, furthest from the Matterhorn (but with some of the best views of it) on the other side of the valley – has been designated 'Sunnega Paradise'. Furi, at the far end of the village, is the gateway to the region on the Matterhorn side of the valley: the Trockener Steg link to the confusingly named Matterhorn 'Glacier Paradise' (which is in fact on the Matterhorn's much less-imposing little sister, the Klein Matterhorn), the Theodulpass, close to the Italian border, and the Schwarzsee 'Paradise', the closest slopes to the foot of the Matterhorn. Even the 'International' ski region comprising Zermatt and its Italian neighbour across the border at Cervinia (where the Matterhorn is known as Monte Cervino) was remarketed as the 'Matterhorn Ski Paradise'.

Zermatt's altitude and climate allow the ski season to extend until the beginning of May. And on the glacier, Zermatt has snow year-round on what is claimed to be the highest

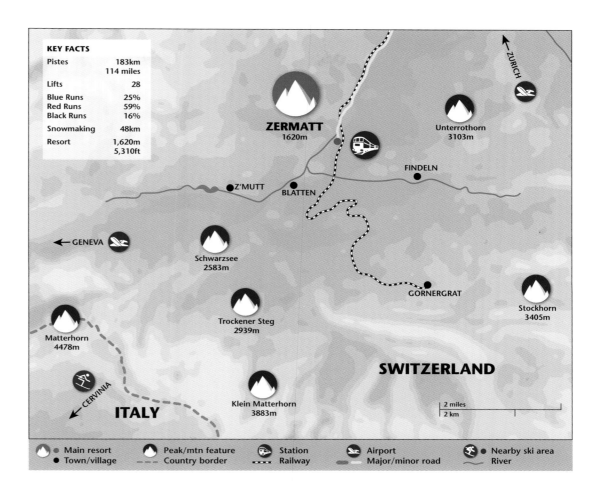

**KEY FACTS**

| | |
|---|---|
| Pistes | 183km |
| | 114 miles |
| Lifts | 28 |
| Blue Runs | 25% |
| Red Runs | 59% |
| Black Runs | 16% |
| Snowmaking | 48km |
| Resort | 1,620m |
| | 5,310ft |

ZERMATT 1620m
Unterrothorn 3103m
FINDELN
Z'MUTT
BLATTEN
GENEVA
Schwarzsee 2583m
GORNERGRAT
Stockhorn 3405m
Trockener Steg 2939m
Matterhorn 4478m
SWITZERLAND
CERVINIA
ITALY
Klein Matterhorn 3883m
2 miles / 2 km

Main resort · Town/village — Peak/mtn feature ---- Country border — Station Railway — Airport Major/minor road — Nearby ski area River

summer ski area in the Alps. More than half of Zermatt's pistes now either have snow-making facilities or are on the glacier.

A slower, but attractive up-hill transport alternative on the Sunnegga side of the valley is the Gornergrat Railway, which went into service more than 100 years ago as the first electric-track railway in Switzerland. This takes skiers, snowboarders and non-skiing sightseers to a small, but magnificently situated, plateau at Gornergrat (3,089m/ 10,164ft), the most popular high-level view-point in the resort, surrounded by 4,000m (13,123ft) peaks. The top station was completely renovated in 2005–6. Oddly, the Gornergrat – in spite of having some of the most stunning scenery in the region – has not been designated a 'paradise'. The reason for this is that the Gornergrat Railway, which operates the transport system here, is not from the same stable as the other lift companies, and its own marketing department has opted not to join in the 'paradise fest'.

The Sunnegga Alpen Metro funicular is the gateway to some of Zermatt's easier and

## MOUNTAIN FARE

*Zermatt's mountain restaurants are legendary. There are supposed to be some three dozen in all, scattered in all directions. It's difficult to count them all, though, let alone visit them, and they epitomize the main gastronomic difference between skiing in the Alps and in the Rockies. Zermatt's excellent mountain fare – accompanied by more than a touch of chic ambience – is rarely found in the USA. However, some American resorts have opened bijou mountain restaurants in an attempt to counter criticism of their mountain culture in which lunch is seen simply as a pit-stop to refuel.*

*But they are unlikely to rival the likes of Chez Vrony at Findeln, an area where many other good mountain restaurants are located. Or even some of the restaurants across the Italian border, when, on a sunny day, skiers and snowboarders find it hard to resist zooming down to Cervinia for a bowl of pasta.*

sunnier slopes at Blauherd (2,571m/8,435ft), as well as the more challenging runs higher up at Rothorn (3,103m/10,180ft), Hohtälli (3,286m/10,780ft) and Stockhorn (3,405m/ 11,171ft).

From the large, but quaint hotel at the top of the Gornergrat – the Kulm, with its landmark observatory domes, and its sunny terrace overlooking the Gorner Glacier – train passengers, including skiers and boarders, can marvel at one of the greatest mountain panoramas in Europe. Monte Rosa, at 4,634m (15,203ft) second in the Alps only to Mont Blanc in altitude, stands alongside Lyskamm, the twin peaks of Castor and Pollux, Breithorn and the Klein Matterhorn, where Europe's highest cable-car takes skiers and boarders to the Italian border, from where they can make their way down to Cervinia in the Aosta Valley.

From the Gornergrat there is an assortment of mainly gentle blue runs going down to Riffelberg, where the hotel was the location for some of the most powerful scenes in

the 1969 film version of D. H. Lawrence's *Women in Love*.

In recent years, there have been some extensive improvements to the lift system. A major new 'combination' lift, replacing the old gondola linking Sunnegga with Blauherd, opened in the winter of 2005–06, with eight-person gondolas alternating with six-person chairs. And a new eight-seat gondola was due to go into operation in the winter of 2006–07 between Furl and Riffelbereg.

Above Gornergrat and Blauherd, the runs from Stockhorn (including the celebrated descent to Triftji from Rote Nase – an exhilarating challenge in fresh powder or moguls) and from the Rothorn are more difficult. From Blauherd back down to Sunnegga, however, the terrain opens out into easy cruising.

## Other ski areas

Furi, at the far end of the village, is the gateway to Zermatt's other areas – the Trockener Steg link to the Klein Matterhorn and Theodulpass, close to the Italian border, and

*Zermatt's popular Gornergrat, with the recently refurbished Kulm hotel. Sightseers make the journey up here on the cog railway to enjoy the panorama.*

Schwarzsee, closest to the foot of the Matterhorn. It takes a long time to get there from the village, but the final section of the journey up to the Klein Matterhorn (or Matterhorn 'glacier paradise') is dramatic: the cable-car soars above steep glacial terrain to 3,885m (12,746ft). With the combined skipass, tourists have full use of the Matterhorn Ski Paradise international ski area, which connects Zermatt with Cervinia.

Those skiing into Italy have the possibility of a long run down, not only to Cervinia, but onward to the picturesque village of Valtournenche. Depending on which guidebook you read, this is a distance of at least 20km (12 miles). Collectively the Swiss and Italian slopes claim more than 300km (186 miles) of pistes. (This used to be higher until 2005, when, according to Zermatt, their Italian counterparts made a more serious attempt at measuring the mileage of their slopes and discovered a serious shortfall). There's certainly no doubt, however, about the breathtaking scenery right the way across the border between Switzerland and Italy.

Some of Zermatt's most challenging skiing is encountered below Schwarzsee, on the way back to Zermatt via Furri. These include Furgg-Furi, Aroleid, Tiefbach and Momatt, but intermediates can take the Weisse Perle, a roller-coaster red, as an alternative route. This gives skiers and boarders the opportunity to visit some of the mountain restaurants for which Zermatt is so justly famous, including Farmerhaus, Furi, Simi's, Zum See (arguably the best in the resort) and Blatten, famous both for its food and après ski.

Snowparks and fun parks, toboggan runs, snowshoe walking tours and 45km (28 miles) of prepared winter-hiking paths provide an alternative for non-skiers or skiers who feel like a day off from the slopes. During the summer, up on the Theodul glacier, Zermatt has as much as 24km (15 miles) of skiable trails, a halfpipe and nine ski-lifts open for most of the day.

The village of Zermatt has grown dramatically since its humble early days, but traffic is limited to electrically-powered trolleys, buses and horse-drawn carriages. A handful of classic hotels help lend Zermatt an air of high-living and up-market ambience: the Mont Cervin, with its spa and pool, and Zermatterhoff are the showpiece hotels. Not far behind is the Monte Rosa, from where Whymper and his ill-starred party set out to climb the Matterhorn on that fateful July day in 1865. Up on the mountain, close to the Gornergrat Railway route to Riffelberg, is the recently transformed luxury Riffelalp Resort and spa.

Zermatt is, without question, one of the great and most charismatic winter sports resorts of the world – yet provides blissful holidays for those who never go near the slopes.

**There's no escaping it: almost wherever you ski or snowboard in Zermatt, the Matterhorn – in one shape or form or another – will be watching over you.**

# Engadin-St Moritz

BY LESLIE WOIT

Thank heaven for Johannes Badrutt. It was 150 years ago that the first pre-jet set winter guests arrived in St Moritz, thanks to the enterprising hotelier's wager that they would enjoy sunshine – even in the middle of winter. The first wintersports visitors did what countless others have continued to do since: enjoy the stunning Engadine Mountains as an ideal backdrop for their fancy furs and mountain games. The name St Moritz – now trademarked as a brand – was well on its way to becoming the *ne plus ultra* for stylish skiers and discriminating aristocrats alike.

They were on to a good thing. In St Moritz there is much to keep even the non-titled amused, provided you can bear to leave your elegant hotel or feel sufficiently well dressed to do so – more than half the resort's hotels are in the four- and five-star categories. Its 1,828-m (6,000-ft) high, south-facing position in the southeastern corner of the Swiss Alps makes both snow and sun safe bets, and the long season runs from November to April.

The best position from which to access both the sporting amusements and the nightlife is from St Moritz Dorf, the main town, which is dotted with jewellery shops, cafés and almost all the accommodation options. Its smaller neighbour, St Moritz Bad, is home to the five-star Kempinski Hotel, though off the beaten track in terms of any significant nightlife.

Of course, beneath the glare of their much-boasted 322 annual days of sunshine, there is a goldmine of skiing and boarding. With 350km (217 miles) of pistes in nine different areas, the full Engadin area encompasses Switzerland's largest winter sports region. And the pistes are as well groomed as their patrons.

Engadin-St Moritz does for intermediates what Coco Chanel did for women – it makes them look fabulous. Nearly 90 per cent of the runs are graded beginner or intermediate – that's 315km (196 miles) of wide-open feel-good factor. Should the feeling ever get too good, some 37 mountain restaurants ensure you're never far from a *chaise longue* on which to rest your beautiful body.

## Corviglia

The Corviglia area, including Piz Nair and Marguns, is the largest single skiing area. A funicular paves the way to more than 20 other lifts above St Moritz Dorf, stretching to 3,057m (10,029ft) above sea level, well above tree line and ideal for cruising. From here you can cover miles, many on the sunny side of the south- and east-facing valley.

On the opposite side of the valley, reachable by a free bus, 14 lifts serve the Corvatsch Furtschellas skiing areas. The Corvatsch towers over the valley floor, and

**Postcard-perfect grooming make St Moritz the ultimate poseur's paradise.**

## TIME OFF FROM SKIING

*Apart from skiing and boarding, a winter-long calendar of esoteric activities to both watch and partake in are on offer, including bob-sleigh with passenger rides, the derring-do Cresta Run for skeleton toboggans, skikjöring (being towed on skis by a horse) and other horse races, greyhound races, a Gourmet Festival, Snow & Symphony, cricket and polo tournaments as well as winter golf, curling, 180km (112 miles) of cross-country trails and the 12,000-person strong Engadin Cross Country Ski Marathon.*

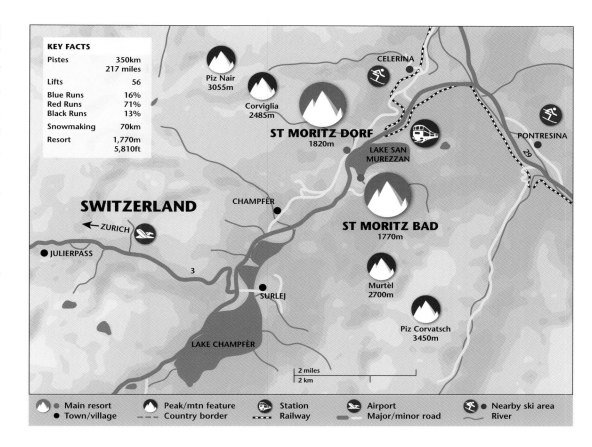

KEY FACTS

| Pistes | 350km |
| | 217 miles |
| Lifts | 56 |
| Blue Runs | 16% |
| Red Runs | 71% |
| Black Runs | 13% |
| Snowmaking | 70km |
| Resort | 1,770m |
| | 5,810ft |

Main resort — Town/village — Peak/mtn feature — Country border — Station — Railway — Airport — Major/minor road — Nearby ski area — River

some good black runs provide a challenge. A lovely 9-km (6-mile) long descent from Corvatsch via the Hahnen Lake leads back down to St Moritz. Further up the valley, you can connect with neighbouring Furtschellas-Sils, which also has both intermediate and expert terrain. At Corvatsch, every Friday is a party on snow from 7pm–2am, held on Switzerland's longest floodlit ski slope, with bars open for dancing and hot Pflaumi Schlumis – heavily spiked coffee with whipped cream.

### Diavolezza Bernina

About a 20-minute shuttle away from St Moritz Dorf across valley is the other main area of Diavolezza Bernina, above the neighbouring resort of Pontresina – an impressive glacier reached via a 125-person cable-car. Don't miss the 10-km (6-mile) off-piste glacier run from Diavolezza down to Morteratsch. A second 80-person cable-car goes up to the Piz Lagalb, where there are some steep and challenging runs.

From high mountains to high culture, Engadin-St Moritz is a classic Alpine destination. Here the most discriminating tastes are met with matter-of-fact professionalism. But there are also country and western nights at the Muli and beautiful walks on the lake. Watching brave, crazy men negotiate the bone-crushing Cresta Run is worth the price of admission. After 150 years of welcoming every breed of wintersports enthusiast to their home, St Moritz has become an icon of mountain elegance. Thank goodnes Johannes was a betting man.

LEFT: **The frozen lake is within a furlong of many glitzy hotels.**

BELOW: **Aside from skiing, high-adrenaline pursuits, such as the bob-sleigh, abound.**

# Gstaad

BY ARNIE WILSON

Gstaad's name is famous throughout the world, but charm, glitz, world-class restaurants and more than a touch of snobbery – rather than superlative skiing – are the principal reasons for its celebrity status. However, there are more challenging slopes nearby. And few winter resorts enjoy such an international cachet: when Americans feel like a change from Aspen or Sun Valley and head for Europe, Gstaad will be high on their list of 'must-ski' resorts. They come not just for the glamour of the resort itself, but for the diversity offered by the Gstaad lift pass. Once purchased, this really is a ticket to ride, with a litany of resorts available to skiers and boarders with both stamina and wanderlust. And yet variety, rather than serious challenge, is in general what they will find.

This chic and very up-market resort, at 1,050m (3,444ft), is a place you used to hear a lot about in skiing circles, but not so much today. For years it was the winter playground of the rich and the royal – and still is, to a certain extent – but the resort has a couple of drawbacks as a ski area: it's on the low side (although the lift ticket includes skiing on the glacier at Diablerets), and it relies on neighbouring resorts, particularly Rougemont, for its more interesting slopes. Its own runs are somewhat tame and fairly limited. Fortunately, apart from Rougemont, Gstaad skiers can enjoy the slopes at the charming old village of Saanen, as well as nearby Schönried and Saanenmoser. They're not all linked, however, and you'll need transport to get around. There's a bus service between the ski areas, and the Montreux-Oberland-Bernois (MOB) railway visits most of them.

The village of Gstaad itself has managed to preserve its genuine wooden chalets, albeit some rebuilt after a disastrous fire in 1898. And the centre is no longer packed with Range Rovers, Bentleys, Mercedes and Ferraris now that there's a huge underpass: after the lifts have closed, pedestrians can now wander through the attractive, traffic-free centre, dotted with boutiques, chalets

and hotels, pausing to shop or visit the numerous tea-rooms.

Standing out among the many high-class hotels (most at least three-star) is the celebrated Palace, a landmark that dominates the resort like a fairy-tale castle. For those who can afford it, the Palace – expensive, turreted and looking down almost haughtily on the

village – is the *ne plus ultra*. Once known as 'Switzerland's biggest family boarding house', it gradually evolved into one of the finest holiday destinations in the Alps. Gstaad is also the location for the exclusive Eagle Club, formed half a century ago as a glorified and extremely expensive social dining and drinking club on top of the Wasserngrat.

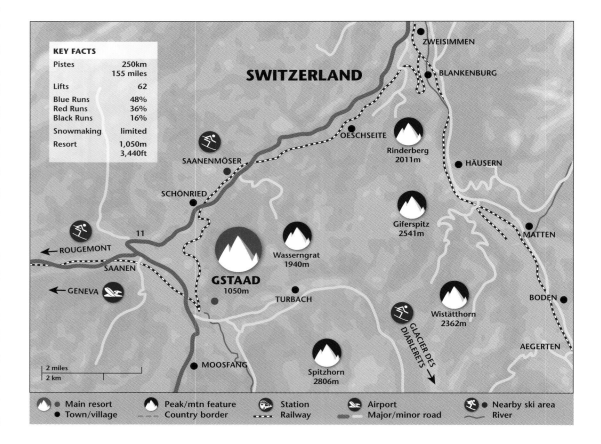

**KEY FACTS**

| | |
|---|---|
| Pistes | 250km |
| | 155 miles |
| Lifts | 62 |
| Blue Runs | 48% |
| Red Runs | 36% |
| Black Runs | 16% |
| Snowmaking | limited |
| Resort | 1,050m |
| | 3,440ft |

There are three mountains in Gstaad's own backyard – the Eggli (the easiest), Wispile and the Wasserngrat (the most difficult). But 10 resorts can be explored on the Ski Gstaad lift ticket, stretching right across the French and German-speaking border (sometimes affectionately known as the 'rösti' border) across some of Switzerland's most spectacular scenery. (On a clear day from some of the higher slopes, you can see the Eiger.) These range from the quaint, unspoilt village of Chateau-d'Oex, just 'up the road' from trendy Montreux, all the way to Zweisimmen and St Stephan, incorporating 69 lifts serving more than 258km (160 miles) of pistes. Needless to say, there is no shortage of mountain restaurants along the way.

There is an arrangement by which you can use your six-day lift pass to ski in Adelboden and Lenk, as well as Leysin and Villars in the Alpes Vaudoises. There are many off-piste opportunities: the key to Gstaad's most exciting skiing is a mountain called Videmanette, reached by a gondola that climbs steeply out of the Rougemont base area. This brings you to a dramatic location on a balcony very close to the summit, at 2,285m (7,497ft), where there are really spectacular views and the opportunity to ski the excellent 8-km (5 miles) run down to Rougemont or surge down the slopes returning to Gstaad.

Another highlight is the black 'Tiger' run (vertical drop 890m/2,919ft) on the Wasserngrat. One of the most challenging runs in the area, this should only be attempted by strong skiers and snowboarders, preferably with a guide.

The après-ski scene is quite lively, but a touch restrained, although there are discos, and some nightspots have live music. It's well worth watching an ice hockey game if you have the opportunity.

For snowboarders, there are terrain parks at Hornberg, above Saanenmoser, Rinderberg

*The celebrated Swiss resort of Gstaad: what it lacks in ski challenges it makes up for with its traditional charm and ambience.*

above Zweisimmen and one on the Eggli, above Gstaad. Another is to be found on the Diablerets glacier.

Gstaad has an indoor pool to which skiers receive free admission, with their lift pass, up to 6pm. There are exceptionally good toboggan tracks: the Eggli-Grund and the Chinnetritt-Gsteig runs are both 6km (4 miles) long. There's a tennis centre, and other activities include badminton, squash, table-tennis, ice-skating, curling, snow-carting, snowshoeing, ice-climbing, sleigh rides, bowling, billiards, horse-riding and 50km (31 miles) of winter walking paths. It's well worth taking the Montreux-Oberland-Bernois railway (MOB) down to explore the lakeside at Montreux. And Chateau d'Oex is famous for its hot-air ballooning, if not its skiing.

# Verbier

BY LESLIE WOIT

From the jet set with girls to the twin sets with pearls, Verbier lures the devoted like a siren in a storm. This is one of the most celebrated resorts of the Alps, renowned as much for its broad expanses of powder-laden off-piste as for its hospitable chalet culture and legendary nightlife.

Verbier is in the heart of the Swiss Alps, just 258km (160 miles) from Geneva, near the Italian border. At an altitude of 1,500m (4,921ft) on a sunny southwesterly shelf above the valley floor, the village is dominated by a plethora of chalets. Its 12,000-visitor bed base ensures a wide choice of chalets and apartments, though it has fewer hotels than other resorts of similar size.

Come with energy for the main event. The Four Valleys connects the pistes of Verbier, La Tzoumaz, Nendaz, Veysonnaz and Val de Bagnes/Entremont, comprising one of the world's largest ski areas and certainly one of the most exciting. In addition to 410km (255 miles) of marked pistes served by 95 lifts, the off-piste terrain is renowned for its gnarly steeps and hike-to accessibility. With an area that stretches northwest of Verbier to Nendaz, Thyon and Veysonnaz in the west, through the central Savoleyres and Mont-Fort areas, and out to distant edges almost as far as Sion, there isn't a ski bum or extreme ski filmmaker alive who wouldn't quite happily while away a season here.

Built in 1983, the Mont-Fort gondola was key to joining up the vast terrain of the Four Valleys. At 3,330m (10,925ft), it's the highest point in the region; from here you can spy as

RIGHT: **En-route to the spectacular Mont-Fort which tops out at 3,330m (10,930ft).**

far as the Matterhorn and Mont Blanc – at 4,807m (15,771ft) the highest peak in western Europe. The Mont-Fort Glacier ensures the snow will be as ready as you.

However, beginners' options are somewhat limited here. There are some nice underused slopes at Savoleyres, and also a good long blue on the opposite valley face at Bruson. A few other gentle runs are located close to the village at Medran. Once comfortable in the red-run department, more choice awaits. All around Attelas and La Chaux are some good wide pistes, and intermediates will be keen to ride the 150-person Jumbo and the Tortin cablecars to reach the giddy heights beneath Mont-Fort itself. From the Tortin area, you can continue on to Nendaz and Thyon. Be aware both of other skiers (pistes can be notoriously busy) and of the time; it can be a long day's journey into night if you have to ski back from one side of the area to another. Signage has been known to be an issue; and although things have improved, this is one resort where you don't want to be caught without a map.

But it's in the advanced and off-the-map categories that Verbier really delivers. Tortin or off the back of Mont-Fort are classic off-piste runs that can be steep and deep in powder or in bumps. Ski routes like Col des Mines off Lac des Vaux or Vallon d'Arbi onto Savoleyres are ungroomed free-for-alls. And with a guide – critical to get the best

from such a large area safely – short hikes to well-known off-piste runs like Stairway to Heaven and Rock Garden truly are other worldly, but get skied out fast on a powder morning. If you're into cliff jumps, Lac des Vaux delivers the cliffbands and couloirs, as well as an audience (passing overhead on the chairlifts). So if you're up for something more involved than an edge-of-the-piste adventure, and want to take advantage of a Garden of Eden of delights – even heliskiing – meet your guide, pack your shovel, turn your transceiver to 'transmit' and go. Verbier flies the flag for endless vertical and unalloyed pleasure.

Verbier's off-piste attracts powder enthusiasts from around the world.

## Off the slopes

The pleasure principle operates 24 hours a day. More than 60 bars and restaurants are dedicated to keeping you fed, watered and mingling. But nightlife here is no bargain – buying a bottle at the Farm Club can set you back more than 200 SF – but you're likely to be mixing your tonic with royalty and their hangers-on. Low-key hangouts like Pub Mont-Fort and Fer à Cheval do fast food and pints at ski-bum prices. King's is a dark sultry room with good music and cocktails. When

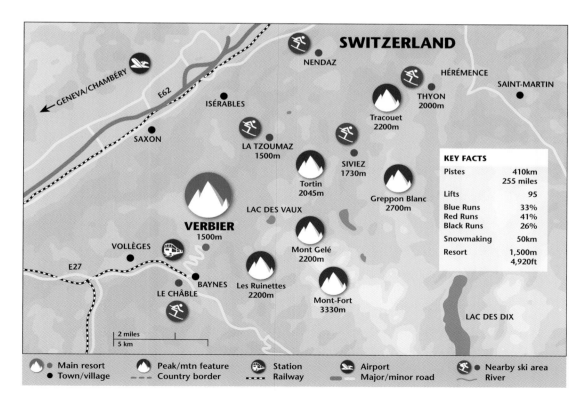

**KEY FACTS**

| Pistes | 410km |
| | 255 miles |
| Lifts | 95 |
| Blue Runs | 33% |
| Red Runs | 41% |
| Black Runs | 26% |
| Snowmaking | 50km |
| Resort | 1,500m |
| | 4,920ft |

your night ends at 3 or 4am, lunch comes around even quicker. Unlike Zermatt, its big-mountain neighbour, Verbier is not known for mountain restaurants. A few, such as Chez Dany, Cabane Mont-Fort and Marmotte, are charming and atmospheric. The new Chalet Carlsberg at La Combe has 80 seats inside and 80 seats on the terrace, with table service and a snowbar.

Eating in town is a suitably cheesy affair. For the requisite *raclette* and fondue, Aux Vieux Verbier is a cozy corner with lovely local Valais wines. The Michelin-starred Rosalp is rather stiff, but if you're looking to splash out the Chalet d'Adrien Hotel has five-star dining with chic design.

Boarders will be happy here, not only because of the natural halfpipes and almost no drag lifts, but also the big snowpark. The 1936 Neipark, located at La Chaux, is a playground of tables, gaps, double-hips, rails and more. Some of the best boarders and skiers congregate for annual free-ride competitions like the Verbier Ride and Verbier Xtreme.

For advanced or keen intermediate skiers and boarders who revel in off-piste, Verbier is a top pick, and its late-night action makes it ideal for party animals. Here you can easily combine both for that most glamorous of big mountain holidays.

As both a summer and winter resort, Verbier's facilities are wide-ranging. Cross-country skiing is available both in town and up on the mountain on a 5-km (3-mile) high alpine circuit at Ruinettes-La Chaux. You can also take to the skies amid the area's fantastic conditions for hang-gliding, or stick to terra firma on well-maintained winter walking paths and showshoeing trails, or go sledging on a thrilling 10-km (6-mile) track at Savoleyres-Tzoumas. The sports centre offers an indoor swimming pool, curling, covered ice-skating rink, sauna, Turkish bath, solarium and squash courts.

**The Four Valleys offer extensive off-piste terrain, best explored with a guide.**

ABOVE: **In a party town like Verbier you have to relax sometimes.**

RIGHT: **There is enough off-piste terrain in the Four Valleys that surround Verbier to live nine lives and never jump the same cliff twice.**

## RESORT UPGRADES

*In the past decade Verbier has been upgrading continually. One recent innovation is a funky 'combo' lift, a so-called 'chondola'. The La Chaux Express combines an eight-seat gondola and a six-seat chairlift from Les Ruinettes to La Chaux via Fontanays. Visitors can buy a half-day ticket to cover a morning's skiing, rather than the typical afternoon – handy for a Saturday departure. Night skiing is available on selected nights, as is moonlight skiing in Nendaz, Thyon and Veysonnaz.*

# Davos and Klosters

BY ALF ALDERSON

Davos and Klosters are neighbouring resorts in Switzerland's Grisons region, with long histories dating back to the very beginning of skiing in the Alps in the 1880s. Sir Arthur Conan Doyle further popularised the area by writing about his ski adventures here in 1894, and there then followed an invasion of well-heeled British winter sports enthusiasts, which to some extent has continued to this day, with Klosters in particular being well known as a favourite haunt of Britain's Prince of Wales.

Davos and Klosters regularly have superb off-piste conditions.

Indeed, in 1988, the Prince was almost swept away by an avalanche whilst skiing near the Gotschnawang (or 'Wang'), one of a number of more interesting runs that connect the two resorts, and his equerry, Major Hugh Lyndsey, was tragically killed.

Since the accident, the run has been regraded as an 'itinerary' rather than a marked piste, and is rarely open because of continuing avalanche danger. But the alternative, Drostobel, is actually more technical and difficult – though much less avalanche prone.

The popularity of the two resorts is well justified, with some 370km (230 miles) of well-maintained pistes which are particularly good for intermediate and advanced skiers, magnificent mountain scenery, an efficient lift and transport system (including trains) – and the options of hectic nightlife in the busy conference town of Davos or an altogether quieter and more genteel experience in Klosters, which is essentially no more than a pretty alpine farming village.

## Parsenn

On the slopes you're spoilt for choice, with several different ski areas to choose from. The biggest and most popular is the Parsenn, with upwards of a hundred pistes and long, exhausting runs which, snow conditions permitting, will take you down to Serneus and Küblis, some 12km (8 miles) and 2,000 vertical metres (6,560ft) away.

The Parsenn area, which is at the heart of the skiing in Davos-Klosters, can be accessed from both resorts (although queues can be a problem): head for the Weissflujoch, just beneath the summit of 2,844-m (9,329-ft) Weissfluhgipfel for a superb range of wide, open blue and red runs which will flatter your technique, whilst stronger skiers can continue on a couple of black options all the way back down to Davos Dorf at 1,560m (5,117ft). For quieter slopes, simply head away from Parsenn to the outlying areas, which are inevitably less busy.

It's intermediate skiers who will enjoy the upper slopes of both resorts most, since these are criss-crossed almost entirely by blue or red runs, some over 10km (6 miles) long – try, for instance, the long runs down to the village of Saas, an engrossing 12-km (7-mile) thigh-burner from Weissfluhgipfel to Küblis, or the delightful cruiser from the top of the Madrisa down to Klosters Dorf.

The resorts' lower slopes are invariably steeper and thus tend to be laced with black runs, which in poor conditions can suffer from ice. However, when the snow is good, advanced skiers can enjoy warming up on the intermediate terrain above before moving on to a wide range of exciting runs, which vary from Meierhofel Tälli on the Parsenn ski area to several fine tree runs and the challenging bumps above Davos Dorf.

Options for beginners are somewhat more limited, although by no means so few as to rule this area out as a ski option. The open and easy slopes at Bolgen and Bünda in Davos Platz and Davos Dorf are a good bet, as are the gentle beginner slopes of Madrisa above Klosters.

If you're looking to venture off-piste, Davos-Klosters is a great area to be in. From easy little adventures in the powder on either side of the groomed runs to quite serious backcountry expeditions such as the circuit from the Madrisa to Gargellen at the head of

Austria's Montafon Valley, or the exciting back-country terrain off the back of the Rinerhorn area, there are plenty of options. Snowboarders in particular will find some exciting slopes in another autonomous area on the Jakobshorn – like the Rinerhorn, just a short train ride away. And the separate but lift-linked Pischa area, across the valley from the main resort, has reinvented itself as one of the largest freeriding regions in Europe.

When the skiing is over, Davos is the place to head for if you want more action – although not the prettiest of towns, many bars are open until the early hours. Over in Klosters things are considerably quieter. The dining there, however, is worth checking out, in particular at Michelin-starred Hotel Walserhof – but be sure to book your table several days in advance.

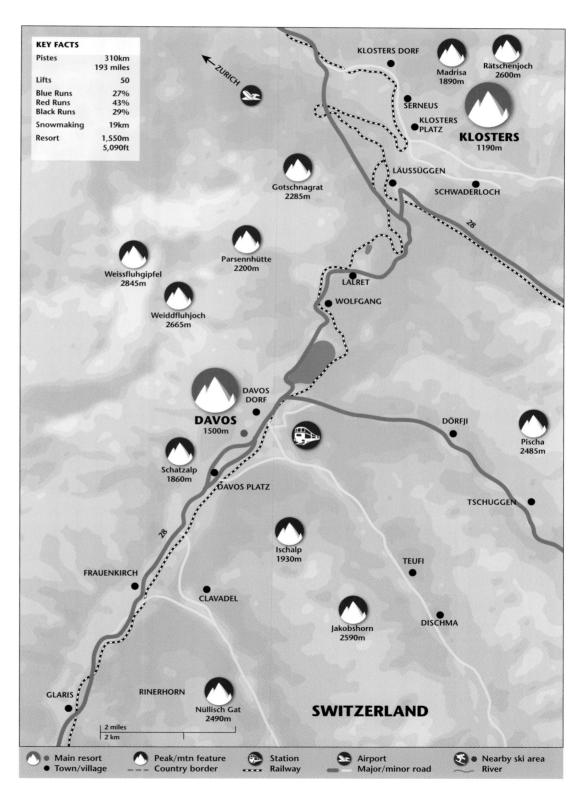

**KEY FACTS**

| | |
|---|---|
| Pistes | 310km |
| | 193 miles |
| Lifts | 50 |
| Blue Runs | 27% |
| Red Runs | 43% |
| Black Runs | 29% |
| Snowmaking | 19km |
| Resort | 1,550m |
| | 5,090ft |

← ZURICH

KLOSTERS DORF

Madrisa
1890m

Rätschenjoch
2600m

SERNEUS

KLOSTERS
PLATZ

KLOSTERS
1190m

Gotschnagrat
2285m

LÄUSSÜGGEN

SCHWADERLOCH

28

Parsennhütte
2200m

Weissfluhgipfel
2845m

LALRET

WOLFGANG

Weiddfluhjoch
2665m

DAVOS
DORF

DÖRFJI

DAVOS
1500m

Pischa
2485m

Schatzalp
1860m

DAVOS PLATZ

TSCHUGGEN

28

Ischalp
1930m

TEUFI

FRAUENKIRCH

CLAVADEL

Jakobshorn
2590m

DISCHMA

GLARIS

RINERHORN

Nüllisch Gat
2490m

**SWITZERLAND**

2 miles
2 km

| | | |
|---|---|---|
| Main resort | Peak/mtn feature | Station |
| Town/village | Country border | Railway |
| | | Airport |
| | | Major/minor road |
| | | Nearby ski area |
| | | River |

# Jungfrau Region

BY ALF ALDERSON

My favourite memory of skiing the Jungfrau region is of a snowy day late in January when a friend and I decided to race the train from Kleine Scheidegg Station beneath the North Face of the Eiger down the easy Mettlen run to the station at Brandegg. As it happened we were so far ahead of the little mountain locomotive that we had time for a beer at the station café before we heard the whistle forewarning of the train's arrival. But that was beside the point, for where else can you 'race' on your skis against a train beneath some of the most dramatic mountains in the world? It is little things like these – fun skiing, tremendous scenery, and fascinating history and mountain culture – that make skiing the Jungfrau region such a memorable experience.

The region consists of a mighty wall of peaks that rise boldly and uncompromisingly above the ant-like humans at play on their lower slopes. The Wetterhorn, Schreckhorn, and Jungfrau all top out at over 4,000m (13,123ft), and the infamous Eiger stops just 30m (98ft) short of this magical threshold.

Indeed, the whole place has a magical feel to it, even before you reach the slopes. The pretty villages of Grindelwald and Wengen, along with Mürren, high on the opposite side of the Lauterbrunnen valley, which make up the Jungfrau region (and whose slopes are accessed through the Jungfrau Top Ski pass

which covers each resort) are typically Swiss, and have scarcely changed since the British ski pioneer Henry Lunn brought the first 'package' skiers here in the early 1900s. His son Sir Arnold Lunn founded the Kandahar Ski Club in Mürren in 1922, and in 1928 he was responsible, along with the Ski Club of Great Britain, for organizing the infamous Inferno Downhill, the oldest surviving downhill ski race in the world.

Wengen and Mürren have direct access to the pistes from their centres, while Grindelwald sits beneath its ski slopes, which can be reached either by lift or train. Beginners are best catered for at Wengen and Grindelwald – Wengen has a beginners' park at Kleine Scheidegg and convenient nursery slopes in the centre of the village, along with a well-respected ski school, while Grindelwald's ski school is at the top end of the village; once you get beyond complete beginner stage, it offers some great confidence-building blue runs directly above. Mürren has two small beginner areas, but they're not as extensive, nor quite as well laid-out as those of the neighbouring resorts.

The infamous Inferno Downhill, the world's oldest ski race.

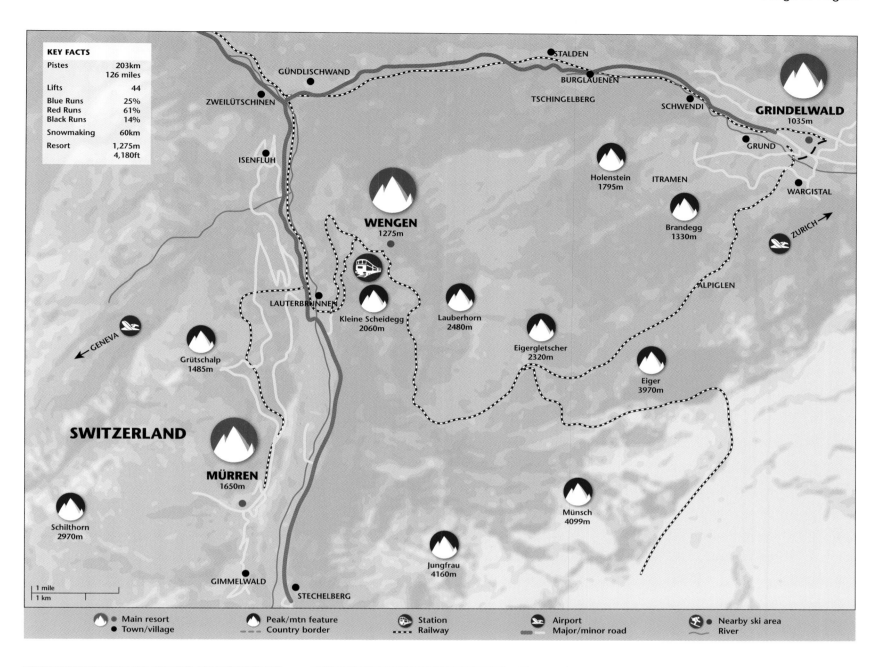

**KEY FACTS**

| Pistes | 203km |
| | 126 miles |
| Lifts | 44 |
| Blue Runs | 25% |
| Red Runs | 61% |
| Black Runs | 14% |
| Snowmaking | 60km |
| Resort | 1,275m |
| | 4,180ft |

Main resort • Peak/mtn feature • Station • Airport • Nearby ski area
Town/village — Country border ··· Railway — Major/minor road River

## MOUNTAIN RAILWAY

Despite the forbidding nature of these mountains, the region is connected by a historic and picturesque mountain railway, built in the 1880s, which accesses both the resorts and the ski slopes. With a top station of 3,454m (11,332ft) on the Jungfraujoch, this is the highest railway line in Europe. All can be reached by train from Interlaken, which in turn has connections to all the major Swiss cities and airports: it really is worth trying to come here by train for the marvellous scenery (and Swiss efficiency) that you encounter en route.

All aboard! The delightful mountain railway climbs to an incredible 3,454m (11,332ft).

ABOVE: **The Jungfrau region has plenty of undemanding skiing set amidst tremendous mountain scenery.**

side of the valley; in Mürren, the runs from Schiltgrat and Birg are well worth checking out. The three resorts are a delight for intermediates to explore via an eclectic combination of skis, lifts and railway.

Advanced skiers will probably enjoy Mürren the most, although the two other resorts offer plenty of top options – and don't forget that the combination of lift and rail links means it's easy to ski all three resorts on the same day. In Mürren you have to do the world famous Kandahar, of course, while the steeps at the top of the Schilthorn offer some interesting challenges; Grindelwald has the entertainingly steep black Chapf in the First area, which leads all the way back into the town; and Wengen has the alarmingly named Oh God along with the Blackrock on the Eiger glacier; the steep Männlichen, which plummets down towards Grund; and its own World Cup downhill race course, the Lauberhorn, which, at recreational speed at least, is more of an endurance test than a seriously difficult run (although there are a couple of tricky, steep sections).

Needless to say, in an area of such dramatic mountains there is also some dramatic off-piste skiing to be found. If you're not too adventurous you'll find plenty of enjoyment on the ungroomed powder alongside many pisted runs, along with some lovely glades at lower elevations, while more demanding off-piste options include the White Hare, dramatically situated beneath the Eigerwand, the powder-rich Blumental above Mürren and the lovely Hidden Valley, which starts from the top of the Maulerhubel. It makes good sense to employ the services of a mountain guide and Grindelwald's Bergsteigerzentrum is one of the oldest and most respected guiding companies in the world.

What makes a visit to the Jungfrau region so memorable is the experience of skiing amid such awesome landscapes and scenery. It's possible for an adventurous intermediate to start off literally beneath the North Face of the Eiger, swoop down the wide open slopes that follow the course of the famous

## Grindelwald and Mürren

For intermediates, Grindelwald and Mürren are the best bets, with an extensive selection of enjoyable, long blue and red runs on the slopes in both resorts. From Grindelwald the top spots are the train-accessed Kleine Scheidegg area beneath the awesome Eigerwand and the First area on the opposite

Lauberhorn ski race, pass through deep forest and finish the run among the picturesque streets of Wengen in the course of a few kilometres, and not many more minutes, taking in the very essence of what skiing in the Alps is all about.

And the fun on the snow isn't restricted just to skiing – one bit of traditional alpine tomfoolery to indulge in at some point during your stay is the traditional 4-km (2½-mile) toboggan descent down Wengernalp to Wengen. You'll be sharing the slopes with everyone from toddlers to pensioners, but even so it can get surprisingly competitive at times.

When the skiing is over, tradition continues in the form of activities such as curling and ice hockey on the rinks in Wengen. The town is otherwise pretty quiet after dark, although you can get a further taste of local culture in the form of cheese fondue and Alphorn-blowing contests. Grindelwald is somewhat busier, although more so immediately after the lifts close than later in the evening. Later on, the action moves to hotel bars such as the Cava in the Derby and the Chälli Bar in the Hotel Kreuz and Post, although the best late-night action is usually in the Mescalero or the Plaza Club. There are also some good, if rather muted, dining options, among them the Derby-Bahnhof and the opulent Hotel Regina opposite the rail terminus.

Mürren is the best option for après-ski action, although it's mainly restricted to peak season, when lively choices include the busy Tächi Bar in the Hotel Eiger, or the discos in the Blumental and the Anfi Palace.

All is not perfect, however – snow cover can be unreliable, especially at the beginning of the season, and links between ski areas are often slow. And in July 2006, a massive chunk of rock and ice from the peak of the Eiger collapsed after warnings from scientists about rock loosened by melting glacial ice. More than 20 million cubic feet of stone thundered down from the Eiger's east face onto the lower Grindelwald glacier and into the valley below. The rockfall continued for more than 15 minutes, but no-one was injured and no buildings were hit. Nonetheless, if you want to ski in an awesome alpine environment, surrounded by a palpable atmosphere of ski history and tradition, there are few places to match the Jungfrau region.

**Spectacular mountains and pretty alpine villages are the leitmotif of the Jungfrau region.**

# Andermatt

BY ARNIE WILSON

Andermatt, at 1,444m (4,738ft) in the beautiful Ursern Valley, is the gateway to some magnificent skiing – particularly touring and other off-piste terrain. Situated on the approaches to the St Gotthard pass into Italy, the resort is also close to the junction of three other Alpine passes: the Furka, Susten and Oberalp.

Enigmatic, beautiful and challenging, this picturesque resort has the added mystique of being almost isolated in winter. In its heyday, it was bustling with tourists, but once traffic was re-routed through the road tunnel in 1980, Andermatt suddenly seemed remote. All this has brought a touch of the ghost town to this once thriving tourist destination. A pretty ghost town, nonetheless – apart from the rather bleak Swiss army barracks – and the après-ski can be quite lively in a few bars. The fact that the sun pays only a fleeting visit to the cobblestoned village, dotted with wooden buildings, adds to the imagery.

The railway reached here as long ago as 1882, and traditionally many skiers arrive by rail, having put their cars on the train. Chamois can often be seen wandering on the roof of the tunnel between Andermatt and Göschenen. It provides a useful walkway for them during snowy winters. Skiers with a current lift pass can use the trains for free to get around the area.

Until the new millennium, what kept Andermatt going economically was the presence of the Swiss army, which gradually took over the area – for the training of alpine troops – according to the terms of an unwritten 'agreement' that it would help finance the resort's development if tourism were put on a low-key footing. Andermatt then became the semi-secret retreat of a small, dedicated, off-piste *cognoscenti*. But in recent years the military has dramatically scaled down its operations here. Although Andermatt is still used to train mountain specialists, the army's presence has dwindled dramatically, and the area is being looked at afresh by potential developers.

Because it's a little run-down, the lifts aren't exactly the most high-tech and efficient, but Andermatt still maintains its picturesque charm. And because it has slipped behind other resorts, it feels delightfully uncrowded.

## Gemsstock, Gütsch and Winterhorn

There are three separate, unlinked areas. Far and away the most important is the celebrated Gemsstock (2,965m/9,728ft), which lures 'serious' skiers – tourers and other off-piste specialists – to the resort. The Gemsstock is not really a place for beginners or inexperienced skiers, who would be far better off on the other two mountains: Gütsch (2,345m/7,694ft) or the Winterhorn (2,460m/8,071ft) above the neighbouring village of Hospental, which are linked by shuttle bus.

There is only one way up Andermatt's magnificent Gemsstock: the two-stage cable-car. From the top there are various ways down, none of them easy and some suffi-

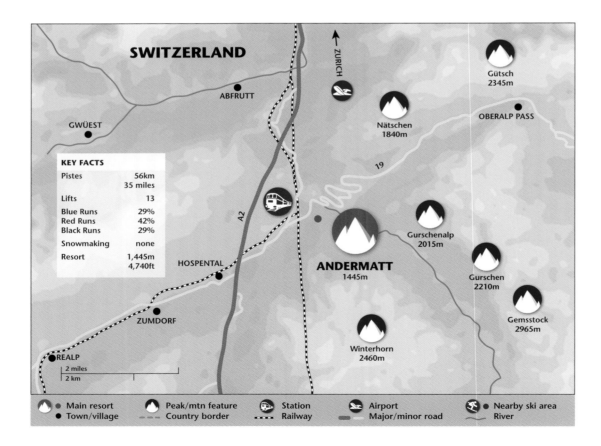

**KEY FACTS**

| Pistes | 56km / 35 miles |
|---|---|
| Lifts | 13 |
| Blue Runs | 29% |
| Red Runs | 42% |
| Black Runs | 29% |
| Snowmaking | none |
| Resort | 1,445m / 4,740ft |

Map labels: SWITZERLAND, ZURICH, ABFRUTT, GWÜEST, Gütsch 2345m, OBERALP PASS, Nätschen 1840m, 19, A2, HOSPENTAL, ANDERMATT 1445m, Gurschenalp 2015m, Gurschen 2210m, ZUMDORF, Gemsstock 2965m, REALP, Winterhorn 2460m, 2 miles, 2 km

Legend: Main resort ● Town/village | Peak/mtn feature ▲ Country border | Station ▬ Railway | Airport ✈ Major/minor road | Nearby ski area ⛷ River

ciently tricky to require a guide. One route takes you all the way down to Hospental. From the top of the slopes, there are views of three other cantons – Graubünden, Ticino and Valais. The most interesting part of the mountain is formed by two vast bowls that dominate the front face of the Gemsstock: just over 750m (2,500ft) of classic off-piste terrain. Top to bottom, the vertical drop to Andermatt is 1,500m (just under 5,000ft).

Apart from these easily accessible powder-fields, Andermatt is the gateway to a number of ski-touring routes in which skiers trek far from the lifts, spending the night in Alpine refuges. The easier – and sunnier – skiing (especially at Nätschren) is on the Gütsch, a mountain that reaches 2,344m (7,68ft) with a fairly gentle blue meandering all the way from top to bottom. There are gentler slopes too at nearby Hospental and a tiny area at Realp. There's a superpipe and rail park near the cable-car midstation on the Gemsstock.

**The two faces of the legendary resort of Andermatt: ABOVE, challenging off-piste on the extensive slopes of the mighty Gemsstock, fabled for its hard-core slopes,** and, BELOW, **rather easier skiing for a young novice in the capable care of a Swiss ski instructor – not quite ready for the Gemsstock adventure.**

119

# GERMANY

# Garmisch-Partenkirchen

BY ARNIE WILSON

Like its less famous German counterpart, Oberstdorf, the slopes of Garmisch-Partenkirchen are linked with those across the border in Austria. The immediate area is sometimes known as the Tiroler Zugspitz Arena. The whole region – which includes the surrounding German villages of Ohlstadt, Eschenloe, Farchant and the Austrian ski resort of Oberau and its neighbours – is known as Zugspitzland.

The celebrated Zugspitze (2,962m/9,781ft), which stands out magnificently among its fellows in the Wettersteingebirge and Ammergauer mountain ranges, is also shared by both countries. Germany's highest mountain provides the country's only glacier skiing:

beneath the German side of this iconic peak are the picturesque and historic twin towns of Garmisch and Partenkirchen.

Both towns are architecturally alluring, with many buildings featuring *luftelmalerei* frescoes, and are today joined as one, but

Partenkirchen pre-dates its companion by many centuries. It was a Roman settlement, while Garmisch's roots are 'merely' medieval. It was Adolf Hitler who decreed that the two towns should join forces in time for the historic 1936 Winter Olympics – the first to include alpine skiing. The Olympic stadium, complete with the original observation towers, has changed little since the war.

Garmisch-Partenkirchen's local skiing is divided into four sections – five, if you count the Wank area, which has no lifts. And in a sense, there is yet another: a little slice of America right here in the Alps. At the end of World War II, the US Army built a recreation centre here, and GIs who could ski – or wanted to learn – were in their element. It is an association that lingers to this day. Back home, the Americans tried to bring a flavour of the Bavarian and Austrian Alps to the Rockies in resorts like Sun Valley, Vail and Jackson Hole. But they continue to visit the 'real thing' at Garmisch in their thousands; a private ski hill and T-bar is still reserved for the exclusive use of US Army and NATO forces.

Garmisch-Partenkirchen's high-altitude glacier runs, well above the tree line on the

**Skiing off-piste in Klein Kanada (Little Canada) on the mighty Zugspitze.**

Zugspitze, are handy for early-season visits. There are breathtaking views from here right across the Alps – not just into neighbouring Austria, but across to Italy and Switzerland too. On the Austrian side, there are resorts at Ehrwald, Lermoos, Berwang/Namlos, Bichlbach, Biberwier, and Heiterwang am See (the Tiroler Zugspitz Arena).

Although it takes time to reach the glacier, it has become popular with snowboarders, and features a 140-m (460-ft) superpipe and a fun park. There are also some easy runs for novices among the 16km (10 miles) of fairly undemanding runs, although the Hausberg area has the best nursery slopes.

Altogether there are some 58km (36 miles) of groomed runs scattered around the resort's different ski areas, and a total of 257km (160 miles) in the region. The so-called 'classic' area combines the slopes of Alpspitze, Kreuzeck (where the early local pioneers first skied between the wars) and Hausberg. Wank overlooks Partenkirchen, but has no marked runs or lifts. Those who wish to ski here need to hike up.

But Garmisch-Partenkirchen's reputation is based on its World Cup races, a permanent fixture in the sporting calendar. Although the TV cameras linger on the majestic summit of Germany's most famous mountain, the World Cup races are held lower down on the wooded slopes. The celebrated Kandahar and Olympia downhill runs were cut between Hausberg and Kreuzeck.

## Reaching Zugspitze

There are three ways to reach the Zugspitze slopes: from Garmisch, there is a choice between cable-car and cog railway. The railway route ends with a short cable-car ride, which takes you to the very top of the Zugpspitze. From the summit, after allowing time to admire the breathtaking view, you take another cable-car down to the slopes on the Zugspitze Platt. (Don't try to ski down – it's almost impossibly steep!) On the Austrian side, the glacier can also be reached from the Tyrolean resort of Ehrwald.

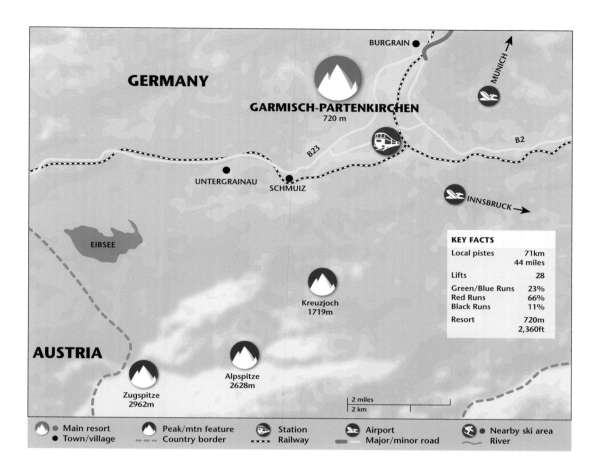

KEY FACTS

| Local pistes | 71km |
| | 44 miles |
| Lifts | 28 |
| Green/Blue Runs | 23% |
| Red Runs | 66% |
| Black Runs | 11% |
| Resort | 720m |
| | 2,360ft |

Most skiers and snowboarders start their day by making for the summit station of the Alpspitz cable-car at 2,050m (6,726 ft). From here they can reach the slopes at Osterfelder and Längenfelder moving on to the Kreuzeck area, with its fast, 15-person gondola.

The Eckbauer, the smallest ski area in the resort, is a 3-km (2-mile) intermediate run down to the Olympia Ski stadium, where the traditional New Year's ski jumping competition is held.

Apart from skiing, Garmisch offers ice skating, ice hockey, curling, sleigh riding, tobogganing, climbing and hiking. If you have the nerve, the dramatic mountains also lend themselves to excellent hang-gliding and parapenting. The twin towns are a natural focus for a vibrant après-ski culture, and also provide a rich diet of cultural events, including theatre, concerts, museums, as well as many examples of the now-obligatory 'wellness' spa ingredient.

Non-skiers or boarders will also be in their element here: the twin towns provide a magnificent holiday experience even if you never carve a single turn.

Big air: local racers climb a few extra vertical feet as they survey the vast extent of the German and Austrian Alps on Garmisch-Partenkirchen's high-altitude border.

# Oberstdorf

BY ARNIE WILSON

This impressive Bavarian resort is one of those ski areas that has somehow escaped the attentions of the international skiing set and never really become fashionable outside Germany – possibly because of its traditional role as an important centre for Nordic skiing and as a spa resort. It has an extensive cross-country network of more than 80km (50 miles), and is renowned for its ski jumping, hosting an annual tournament.

The entire Nordic skiing area was either rebuilt or renovated for the World Championships in February 2005. And yet the resort – which is linked, bizarrely, with a part of Austria completely surrounded by German territory (and thus separated from the rest of Austria) – is worthy of far wider recognition as an alpine ski resort. Because of this strange set-up, the ski area is known as the Zwei-Länder (Two Countries) ski region and supports no fewer than 11 ski and snowboard schools. Oberstdorf itself is a substantial ski area, and provides more than adequate skiing for a week's holiday. The addition of Austria's Kleinwalsertal adds all kinds of permutations.

Oberstdorf is perched at 813m (2667ft) in the Allgäu region of Bavaria, the most southerly winter sports region in Germany. It is a large, busy but attractive town, enjoying the scenic benefits of its location in Germany's highest valley. At the heart of the town is a pedestrian precinct with a wide selection of shops and hotels, and an impressive spa (Vital-Therme Oberstdorf) and swimming pool complex.

## Three zones

The community has three ski areas, all linked by a shuttle bus service. The biggest, Fellhorn/Kanzelwand, crosses the Austrian border, is located 8km (5 miles) from the town centre on the Fellhorn (2,037m/ 6,683ft), and is linked with Riezlern (1,086m/ 3,563ft) at the end of the Kleinwalsertal Valley. The long and meandering Kanzelwand run to Riezlern enables reasonably experienced skiers and snowboarders to wander down to Austria, perhaps for lunch or a drink, before returning to Oberstdorf. Although Riezlern marks the end of the Zwei-Länder ski arena, there are three other Austrian ski areas further along the valley: Hirschegg, Mittelberg and Baad. So an enterprising Oberstdorf visitor with transport could tick off a handful of resorts.

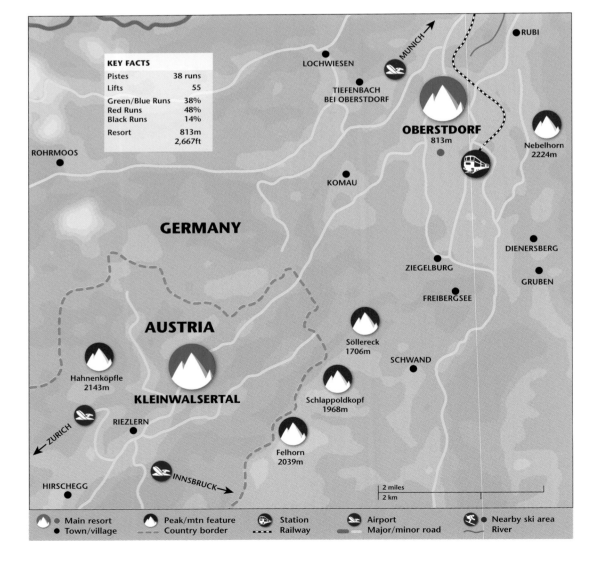

**KEY FACTS**

| | |
| --- | --- |
| Pistes | 38 runs |
| Lifts | 55 |
| Green/Blue Runs | 38% |
| Red Runs | 48% |
| Black Runs | 14% |
| Resort | 813m 2,667ft |

Oberstdorf's second largest ski area – and the most convenient to get to – is on the Nebelhorn (Misty Mountain), a 2,224-m (7,297ft) peak reached by cable-car from the town centre. The Nebelhorn is Oberstdorf's original ski area, and has the highest and most challenging slopes. The cable-car has three stages, but less experienced skiers and boarders should think twice before taking the final section to reach the top, where most of the runs are either black or red. When the mountain is not living up to its 'misty' name, the views from the top are outstanding: it is said that you can see 400 peaks between the Zugspitze (the mountain overlooking Garmisch-Partenkirchen, Germany's most famous ski area) and Switzerland. But the Nebelhorn has limited skiing for beginners, except for a few runs from the top of the first section of the cable-car. And although the upper slopes of the Nebelhorn are particularly off the menu for inexperienced skiers, there are good off-piste and ski-touring opportunities and wonderfully long runs all the way to the valley floor.

The resort's third area – in many ways the most delightful, particularly for families – is on the Schönblick, reached by the Söllereckbahn gondola. The Söllerek area has the smallest vertical drop of the three, but families and lower intermediates thrive here. The runs are mainly gladed and sunny, and the pistes served by the Höllwies draglift (the longest in Germany) are a delight. There is a children's 'fun area' at the bottom gondola station. Some families spend their entire week there.

Most of the Oberstdorf slopes are suitable for snowboarders, and there's a snow park with a bordercross trail and a 'Fun Park' with snow tubing at Seealpe, on the lower section of the Nebelhorn. There's also a snow park below the midstation on the Fellhorn. Oberstdorf has an unusually good scattering of mountain restaurants – 27 in all – but after hours the town comes into its own. With 22 bars and bistros and 150 restaurants, visitors are never going to run out of options. Skiing alternatives include a bowling alley, sports centre, gym, indoor and outdoor heated pools, saunas and solariums, curling, and three ice rinks. Visitors can also try hang-gliding, paragliding or hiking on almost 145km (90 miles) of walking trails. There's snowshoe hiking too, along with two toboggan runs, each almost 3km (2 miles) in length. Oberstdorf surely deserves wider recognition.

**Oberstdorf, the most southerly winter sports region in Germany, attracts world-class Nordic skiers and shares its downhill slopes with Austria's Kleinwalsertal.**

**KEY**

⛰ Ski resort
⛰ Peak
    National border
✈ Airport
    Main road
- - - Main railway
    Local railway

**NORWAY**

NORWEGIAN

SEA

Vilhelmina

Namsos

Åre   Offerdal

Kristiansund   Trondheim   Ostersund

Oppdal

Ålesund   Sunndalsøra   Røros

Dombås

Galdhøpiggen   Särna

Sande   Trysil

Hemsedal   Lillehammer   Sälen

Voss   Fagernes   Höljes

Bergen   Myrdal   Gjøvik   Hamar

Gä

Borlänge   Falun

Västerdalälv

Haugesund   Drammen   Oslo

Dalen   Västerås

Stavanger   Fredrikstad   Karlstad   Örebro

Larvik

Egersund

Arendal   Vänern

Kristiansand   Vättern   Linköping

*Skagerrak*   Västervik

Göteborg   Boras   Jönköping   Västervik

**DENMARK**

Ålborg   *Kattegat*

**NORTH**

**SEA**   Växjö

Århus   Halmstad   Kalmar

Helsingborg   Karlskro

Esbjerg   Copenhagen

Malmö   *Bornholm*

NORWAY

SWEDEN

Scale:
0   100   200   300   400 *miles*
0   250   500 *kilometres*

# SWEDEN

# Åre

BY ARNIE WILSON

Åre, the host of the 2007 World Alpine Ski Championships, is Scandinavia's biggest single resort. It straggles along a big frozen lake, Lake Åresjön, together with the neighbouring resort of Duved, a cosy little mountain village with good skiing just a few kilometres away, and linked by bus.

It takes about 60 minutes to drive here from the nearest airport at Östersund, or you can take the high-speed ski train link from Stockholm, which takes five and a half hours. It was the arrival of the railway, in the 1880s, which brought the first tourists to the area, eventually paving the way for winter visitors and skiers. In fact, the resort's first restaurant was opened in the railway station, by the stationmaster and his wife.

Åre is divided into four areas – Duved, Tegefjäll, Åre and Åre Björnen (the Bear) – with more than 100 trails served by a variety of 40 lifts – including Sweden's only cable-car and a funicular, a six-seater lift in Duved, another in Åre, and a gondola. There is just as much variety on the slopes – plenty of easy skiing, but challenging terrain too, including two World Cup downhill courses, two natural ravines and three snowparks.

Duved has some of the best skiing: plentiful wide-open slopes with plenty of space for carving. The modern Linbanan chair takes skiers and snowboarders to the top of the mountain, and from here you can move across to Tegefjäll, where the emphasis is on family skiing. There's a gentle nursery slope for young children and a fun park for more experienced youngsters, who can also try the skiercross trail or off-piste skiing in the forest. Åre Björnen, too, is a village that specializes in families: slopes, lifts and restaurants are all within easy reach. All the Björnen lifts are linked to the main Åre lift network. Children under eight wearing a helmet ski for free.

## Off-piste

Åre's off-piste is plentiful and varied. One highlight is the extensive and gnarly Susabäckravinen area, much favoured by freeriders and snowboarders. Two ravines – the Western Ravine and Eastern Ravine – eventually merge, and end up in the same valley. The western version is a deep cleft leading down from around 1,005m (3,300ft) almost all the way to the valley. The upper part is steep and prone to avalanches. Lower down, it gets bumpy and unpredictable as skiers and boarders negotiate woods and a stream that is usually buried deep under the snow, but here and there the water has washed away the snow from below. This can make it tricky to ski, with the danger of falling through holes in the snow into the stream. The Eastern Ravine, which starts in a steep bowl beneath a big cornice, is no less challenging.

From Åre's so-called 'high area', you can also hitch a ride behind a snowmobile (weather permitting) to the very top of

With plenty of off-piste plus its celebrated natural ravines, the slopes at Åre provide challenges that match most ski areas in the Alps.

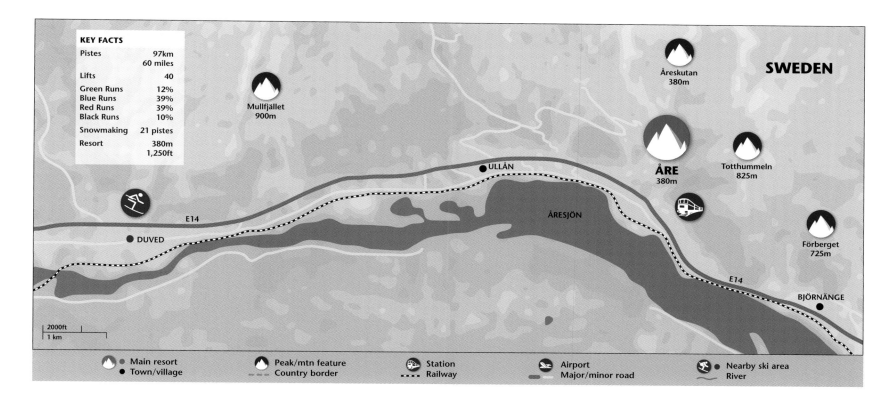

**KEY FACTS**

| Pistes | 97km |
| | 60 miles |
| Lifts | 40 |
| Green Runs | 12% |
| Blue Runs | 39% |
| Red Runs | 39% |
| Black Runs | 10% |
| Snowmaking | 21 pistes |
| Resort | 380m |
| | 1,250ft |

| | | | |
|---|---|---|---|
| Main resort Town/village | Peak/mtn feature Country border | Station Railway | Airport Major/minor road | Nearby ski area River |

Åreskutan, the principal mountain. This will give you a vertical drop of some 1,040m (3,412ft).

Spread across Åre's lift network are five quarterpipes, a halfpipe, a boarder-cross course and two fun parks. The main park is at Bräcke in Åre, with black, red and green 'snowparkpistes' and a halfpipe. At the smaller parks, Duved has a red and a green line, or run, and in Åre Björnen just a green run. There's a 'snow-cross' slope in Tegefjäll.

Åre village is delightful – a real picture-postcard scene, with traditional wooden buildings painted in typical Swedish brick-red and yellow. Away from the slopes, the characterful main square, where a dozen or more restaurants have sprung up, is the focal point. It's inherently cosy, but when the weather turns bitter there's usually a blazing open fire in the square to help keep the chill out.

After hours, Åre's nightlife is notoriously vibrant. The village has a variety of discotheques, numerous bars, ski lodges and other nightspots. Piles of ski boots outside any bar announce the commencement of Sweden's favourite alpine pastime: dancing to live bands. From late December (when it gets dark around 3pm!) until mid-March, by which

time the evenings have become lighter than 'mainland' Europe, there's night skiing four days a week. Of the many excellent restaurants, one is worth singling out because of its intriguing history: the Villa Tottebo is an old hunting lodge moved in its entirety from the slopes to the town centre. You'll probably need to book.

Among many other winter adventures on offer are safaris by snowmobile, huskies or reindeer, horse-riding, ice-climbing, para-gliding and tobogganing down to Åre's

village square. The Åre region is also the centre for some magnificent cross-country opportunities, with almost 306km (190 miles) of trails, some of them floodlit. Heliskiing at Snasahögarna is also possible. In 2000, the resort held its first gay ski festival and introduced 'snowfering' – wind-surfing on snow on the frozen lake.

*Åre, Sweden's biggest single ski resort, with four ski areas, started as a railway town which brought tourists here in the 1880s.*

# Sälen

BY ARNIE WILSON

Sälen has lent its name to what is technically Sweden's biggest ski region. Between the town of the same name and an assortment of nearby ski areas lie the resorts of Lindvallen, linked with the smaller resort of Högfjället (*fjället* means 'mountain'), and two linked resorts close by – Tandådalen (sounds like 'tender darling') and Hundfjället, linked by shuttle bus. Other local resorts include Stöten and Kläppen. The main resorts lie along the crest of a long mountain escarpment, with flattish skiing at the top of the plateau, and the majority of interesting runs descending more steeply down to the valley floor. Most of the skiing is ideal for families and intermediates, and children even have their own piste maps.

But it's not all plain sailing. There are plenty of black runs scattered through the region, including such pistes as Adam, Pernilla, Stina and Kent. The off-piste skiing between Eva and Ville in Lindvallen, and in Väggen at Hundfjället, also demand considerable experi-ence. The toughest skiing is the steep off-piste Wall between Hundfjället (Dog Mountain) and Tandådalen – said to be one of the steepest slopes in Sweden.

Although Sälen is the name of the ski 'area' you may well find you never visit the town during your visit to the slopes of the four main component resorts. The area is extremely popular with families, although the lift connection between the small ski area of Högfjället and Lindvallen is lengthy and flat. So is the long lift between Tandådalen and

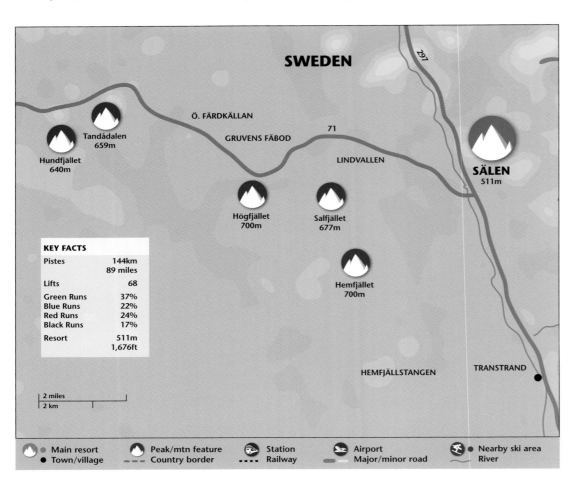

**KEY FACTS**

| Pistes | 144km |
| | 89 miles |
| Lifts | 68 |
| Green Runs | 37% |
| Blue Runs | 22% |
| Red Runs | 24% |
| Black Runs | 17% |
| Resort | 511m |
| | 1,676ft |

● Main resort ▲ Peak/mtn feature ▭ Station ✈ Airport ▭ Nearby ski area
● Town/village --- Country border ▭ Railway ▭ Major/minor road ～ River

## CHILDREN'S ACTIVITIES

*The ski-through children's parks are among the best of their kind in the world. The longest, in Hundfjället, is exceptional: Trollskogen (Enchanted Forest) features 400 trolls in a variety of groups, complete with sound effects, along a winding forest trail through the forest. To appreciate some of the trolls, you really need to take your skis off: there's a church where a 'wedding' takes place every seven minutes, an entire classroom of schoolchildren and their teacher, and even an outside loo with a grumpy old troll entrenched on the seat. You have to ski the run several times, searching in the trees, behind stones or in tiny timber-framed houses, to discover even half of these rough-hewn char-acters. There are also various children's activi-ties, including 'Viking adventures', night trips to Snögubbeborg and Trollskogen and treasure hunts. If you've got the nerve, you can even ski the Enchanted Forest at night, when 'only the grooming machine drivers are awake'.*

Hundfjället. But there are regular free ski buses between the two resort clusters.

Sweden's wide-open, uncluttered landscapes of forests, lakes and mountains have more in common with the wilderness areas of North America than with the Alps. Although some British visitors believe it's going to be cold and dark, the reverse is often the case, especially from late February onwards. By March it's light until 8:30pm. Although the resorts are not as high as those in the Alps, they get plenty of snow because they're further north, but skiers don't have any altitude problems. As the Swedes love to tell the visitor, 'the only thing here that will take your breath away is the view'.

The run at the top of Gustavbacken is said to be visited by more skiers than any other in Sweden. Every year Lindvallen, which has the biggest children's and beginners' area, builds what it claims is the world's biggest snowman at the top of Gustavbacken. At the heart of the ski area, he's a useful landmark to help you find your way around Lindvallen as well as the Sälenstugan and Högfjället slopes.

There are nine snowparks spread through the Sälen region. At Lindvallen (home of the world's first ski-in/ski-out McDonald's), the two funparks have been given a 'dream concept', with new, 'easy' lines to encourage beginners alongside the more advanced lines and jumps for experts. There's also a special fun park for young children. At Tandådalen, the White Magic dreampark has a variety of lines for all levels, a 'Black Magic Crossland' (a skier and boardercross slope with jumps, curves, table-tops and rollers) and a World Cup halfpipe. The children's fun park has a special skiercross run.

The Sälen region is famous for its cross-country skiing, with some 100km (62 miles) of tracks. Sälen's Vasaloppet race, when up to 15,000 competitors ski to the lakeside town of Mora, 90km (56 miles) away, is the oldest, largest and arguably the longest ski race in the world. Dog sledging, ice carting, snowmobile safaris, ice-skating, paragliding, bowling, ice climbing and paintballing are also available.

**ABOVE:** Hundfjället, aka 'Dog Mountain', may be flat at the top, but the steeper sections provide some of the most challenging skiing in Sälen.

**BELOW:** The start at Sälen's strength-sapping Vasaloppet cross-country race. 15,000 competitors take part in the world's oldest, largest and probably longest ski race.

# NORWAY

# Hemsedal BY ARNIE WILSON

Hemsedal, in the heart of the 'Winterland' region between Oslo and Bergen, is one of Norway's biggest and best ski areas. It's a go-ahead resort with a fast, modern lift system, including an eight-seat chair, the highest lift-served slopes in the country and extensive beginner and intermediate terrain.

For those in the know, there is also some challenging off-piste. Hemsedal claims the best back-country area in Scandinavia – along with Narvik and Åreskutan (Åre's main mountain, in Sweden) – but most visitors, even regular returnees, have little idea that it exists. However, if they do attempt it, they are strongly advised to take a guide. Many 'promising' backcountry runs are surprisingly dangerous, ending up in very steep and dangerous ravines, sheer cliffs or tight tree areas. There is plenty of scope for errors, which could easily be fatal.

Hemsedal's highest slopes on Hamaren Peak (1,444m/4,738ft), such as Fjelløypa, Superbreidalen and Hallinghovdløypa, tend to be wide open and easier to negotiate than the steeper, more challenging runs through the trees on the lower slopes above the base area, like Hjallerløypa, Tottenløypa and Skråstigen. The resort's second mountain, the pointed peak of Røgjin (1,370m/4,495ft) – dubbed 'Lille (little) Matterhorn' by the locals – has two exhilarating runs where skiers and snowboarders can often escape the herd and simply hurtle back down a steep bowl towards the base. One is an easy blue, the other quite a fierce red. The backside of the mountain is known locally as 'Katmandu'. From the Roni lift one can access the in-bounds off-piste area known locally as 'Rubber Forest'.

Of the four classic off-piste runs in Hemsedal, Reidarskaret, a moderately serious challenge on the backside of Totten mountain (at 1,497m/4,911ft, the highest skiable peak), is perhaps the best compromise for an experienced off-piste enthusiast. From the summit, which, after a long T-bar ride, offers its own gentle 'in bounds' skiing towards mid-mountain, there are superb views across to the Skogshorn peaks on the other side of the valley. The chute down the back is steep, but manageable. You need a guide to ensure you keep right of a huge cliff you could easily fall off if you were skiing alone in the forest. You also need transport back to Hemsedal from the eventual destination back down in the valley.

Of the other three off-piste classics, Katmandu is the steepest and most dangerous, and involves a 45-minute walk to the 'Radio Hut'; Lille Matterhorn is on the

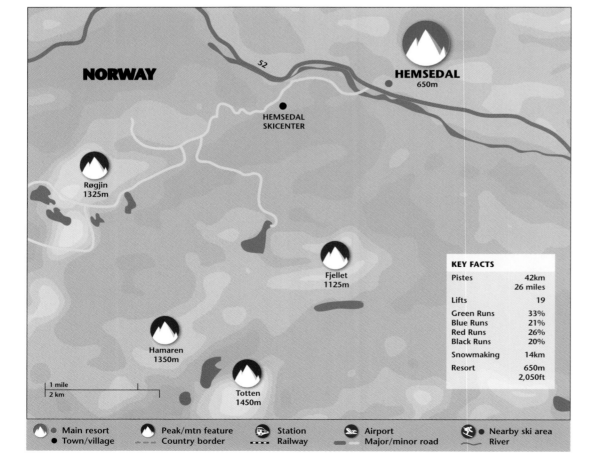

NORWAY

S2

HEMSEDAL
650m

HEMSEDAL
SKICENTER

Røgjin
1325m

Fjellet
1125m

Hamaren
1350m

Totten
1450m

1 mile
2 km

| KEY FACTS | |
|---|---|
| Pistes | 42km |
| | 26 miles |
| Lifts | 19 |
| Green Runs | 33% |
| Blue Runs | 21% |
| Red Runs | 26% |
| Black Runs | 20% |
| Snowmaking | 14km |
| Resort | 650m |
| | 2,050ft |

| | | | | | | |
|---|---|---|---|---|---|---|
| ▲● | Main resort | ▲ | Peak/mtn feature | 🚉 | Station | |
| ● | Town/village | --- | Country border | ▪▪▪ | Railway | |
| ✈ | Airport | | | ⛷● | Nearby ski area | |
| | Major/minor road | | | 〰 | River | |

frontside of Røgjin, and brings you back to the Hotel Skarsnuten, the focal point of the rapidly growing mountain village; and Mortenskaret, on the east side of Røgjin mountain – also the easiest of the four – brings you out on one of the Roni pistes.

But it's what is on-piste and in resort that most skiers are concerned with and Hemsedal is definitely a ski area where progress is on the march. There are plans for the base area to be moved, and further expansion will include new runs and lifts.

The resort also has a big snowboard park, floodlit at night, with two halfpipes and a self-timing course, plus a smaller park for beginners. The focal point of the rapidly growing mountain village and its self-catering apartments is the ski-in/ski-out Skarsnuten hotel, which has its own lift connecting it with the main slopes and superb views across the valley. The Hemsedal Resort Fjell-Landsby, just 50m (164ft) from the lifts, has 261 rooms, a piano bar, nightclub, three bars, three restaurants, its own ski hire shop, a bowling alley, an indoor golf practice centre and live entertainment.

But many people still stay in the original village (a mile or so away by bus or car) where the après-ski is vibrant, particularly at weekends. At Garasjen (an old bus garage) skiers and snowboarders who can't find space in the bar simply take their drinks into the street. Those inside are so cramped that it's difficult to find space to drink.

## OTHER ACTIVITIES

*Apart from skiing, there's horse-drawn sleigh riding, dog sledding, snowmobiling and swimming. Hemsedal is celebrated for its ice-wall climbing on frozen waterfalls. The most famous, Hydnefossen, has a 160-m (525-ft) vertical drop. There are another 20 frozen waterfalls in the area. (Water is quite a theme here – Hemsila is the name of the river flowing through Hemsedal.) There's also a phenomenal amount of cross-country skiing available – more than 225km (140 miles) – in the area.*

RIGHT: Hemsedal's slopes are sufficiently rewarding for many skiers to keep going after dark. The resort has night skiing from **Tuesday** through to **Friday**.

BELOW: The mountain village has gradually taken over from the old town as the focal point of the ski area. Self-catering apartments – with access to their own connecting ski-lift – dot the lower mountain.

# Oppdal

BY ARNIE WILSON

Oppdal is way up in the Trøndelag region of central Norway, at a crossroads between Trondheim and the west coast – quite a way further north than other Norwegian ski areas. This gives the resort, which opened in 1952, something of a geographical disadvantage compared with most of the country's other top-flight resorts. It's perhaps ironic that one of the main reasons for Oppdal's qualities as one of Scandinavia's finest ski resorts is also the reason for its relative obscurity on the world skiing map. Its location – about as far north as the southern tip of Iceland – brings with it plenty of snow, and a long season, but makes it a little far-flung to attract the mass market. Most visiting skiers are from Denmark, Finland and Germany.

The town of Oppdal, population around 6,500, is surrounded by majestic mountains. Locals look out of their windows into the Dovrefjell National Park and the Trollheimen Mountain Plateau. During the winter months their ski area is usually buried snugly in a reassuringly deep blanket of snow. Most of the broad and sweeping slopes are above the tree line, and there's some wonderful ski-where-you-like wilderness skiing.

Oppdal's remoteness is a double-edged sword. It has open valleys, excellent fishing, clean air and what's said to be Norway's cleanest drinking water. It is also reputed to be Norway's largest ski area. But although Oppdal's symbol is a red sun, the climate can

**Once skiers are free of the forested lower slopes at Oppdal, they can access a vast area of above-the-tree-line powderfields.**

be harsh, even by Norwegian standards. The resort stages an annual ice festival, and snow falls as late as the end of May.

Oppdal is located 120km (75 miles) from Trondheim, Norway's third city, and 420km (261 miles) from Oslo. There are four areas, all linked at the top of their respective lifts. Stölen, with skiing up to 1,280m (4,199ft) at Aurhøa, has a good mix of trails, and some extensive snowboarding terrain off the Storsleppet run. Hovden is more for experts, with some challengingly steep runs like Bjørndalsløypa (one of the runs that's floodlit for night skiing) and skiing as high as 1,125m (3,691ft), where you'll find some of the most outstanding scenery. Vangslia, with some of the highest skiing, also features a good mix of terrain, with some expert trails, including a World Cup run and a good snowboarding area. Yet the emphasis here is on family skiing: there's a magic carpet lift, a toboggan run and a snow terrain park. Tucked in between the other areas is Ådalen, with some of the sunnier slopes. It's possible to hike up to Blåøret, at 160m (525ft), but there are no lifts to get you there.

Altogether the area has 16 lifts, including two quad chairs, and 28 runs with a total of 55km (34 miles) of groomed runs. Beginners

Apart from the occasional tree to give you some sort of definition, skiers and snowboarders at Oppdal are used to an unbroken sea of whiteness.

are well catered for, and there's also a wealth of intermediate skiing. The resort has a big snowboard and terrain park (off run 22, at Hovden), with three lines: black, red and blue. There are two halfpipes, a big jump, whales, rails, fun boxes, corners, quarterpipes and a self-timing course. An express chair operates next to the park. As is common throughout Norway, children under seven years old ski for free when using a helmet and accompanied by an adult.

## Off the slopes

Oppdal also has excellent cross-country, with 100km (62 miles) of tracks. Other exciting winter activities include snowshoeing, ice climbing, ice fishing, tandem hang-gliding, sleigh rides and curling. Oppdal's extensive, wide-open slopes are ideal for kitewing manoeuvres. The kitewing had its origins in ice-windsurfing in Scandinavia in the 1980s. When extreme sports started to become popular, young snowboarders and extreme skiers experimented with a 'wing' that was something of a cross between a windsurfer and hang-glider, and found they could execute exhilarating jumps and tricks using just wind power and gravity. Jumps on ice of up to 290m (951ft) at about 2–3m (6½–10ft) in the air have been achieved in Norway.

Another claim to fame is the ancient burial ground at Vang, just over a mile from the centre of Oppdal, with 750 graves dating from the Iron Age – the largest site of its kind in Norway. Amongst artefacts found here have been items of jewellery originating in Britain – evidence, perhaps, of British trade with the Vikings (although possibly stolen by Viking raiders). Either way it is proof of an early 'relationship' with the British that persists to this day: skiers from the UK have long had an affinity with the mountains of Norway.

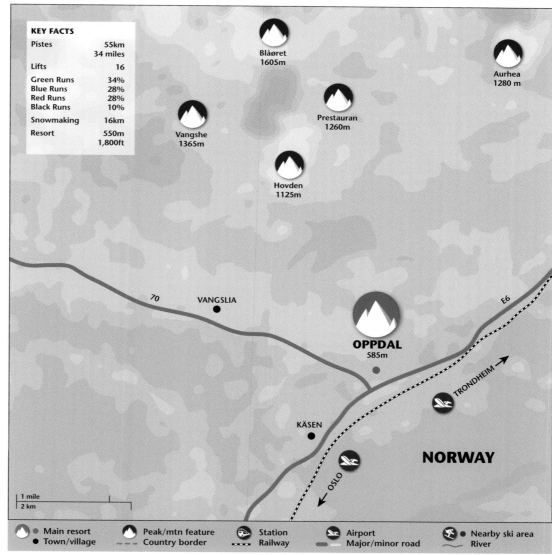

| KEY FACTS | |
|---|---|
| Pistes | 55km |
| | 34 miles |
| Lifts | 16 |
| Green Runs | 34% |
| Blue Runs | 28% |
| Red Runs | 28% |
| Black Runs | 10% |
| Snowmaking | 16km |
| Resort | 550m |
| | 1,800ft |

Blåøret
1605m

Aurhea
1280 m

Vangshe
1365m

Prestauran
1260m

Hovden
1125m

70   VANGSLIA

E6

OPPDAL
585m

TRONDHEIM →

KÄSEN

NORWAY

OSLO

1 mile
2 km

● Main resort ● Town/village    ▲ Peak/mtn feature --- Country border    Station ···· Railway    Airport Major/minor road    ● Nearby ski area River

# Lillehammer
BY MINTY CLINCH

Lillehammer, a small unpretentious town at the northern end of Lake Myosa, is Norway's oldest downhill ski destination. As is customary in a place where cross-country races routinely attract thousands of entries, the whole area is a network of trails, many of them dual-track to cater for both traditional and skating techniques.

Lillehammer itself has 18km (12 miles) of floodlit trails where locals sweat it out on skis after work on the long winter evenings.

The most convenient alpine slopes are at Hafjell and Sjusjøen, 15km (9 miles) and 22km (14 miles) from the town centre, respectively, while the most difficult are at Kvitfjell, some 50km (31 miles) to the north. When Lillehammer hosted the 1994 Winter Olympics, Hafjell staged the slalom and giant slalom races, but Kvitfjell was developed specifically for the downhill and the super G.

## Hafjell

Hafjell (the town's original ski hill) is the largest area, a compact, user-friendly resort with all the runs funnelling back to a simple base station equipped with a hotel, apartments, restaurant and rental shop. It is also possible to stay near the top of the mountain at Gaiestova, or, if you prefer an even more remote location, at the Nordseter Fjellstue, an isolated inn connected with Hafjell by a well-used hilltop telemark trail.

The slopes are fairly undemanding, but extensive snowmaking and grooming guarantee good conditions throughout the winter. Beginners, whether on alpine or telemark skis, should be able to tackle most of the terrain within a week, and intermediates will enjoy the feel-good factor that comes with effortless progress on sweeping pistes. Experts in search of steep challenges or mogul fields will exhaust the possibilities fairly quickly.

## Sjusjeon

The same is true of Sjusjeon, until recently a pretty forested area marked by up-market second homes and criss-crossed with Nordic

trails, including a 5km (3 mile) stretch with artificial snow that ensures a start in early November. In 2003, the Sjusjoen Ski Centre opened as a family facility, with two chair-lifts,

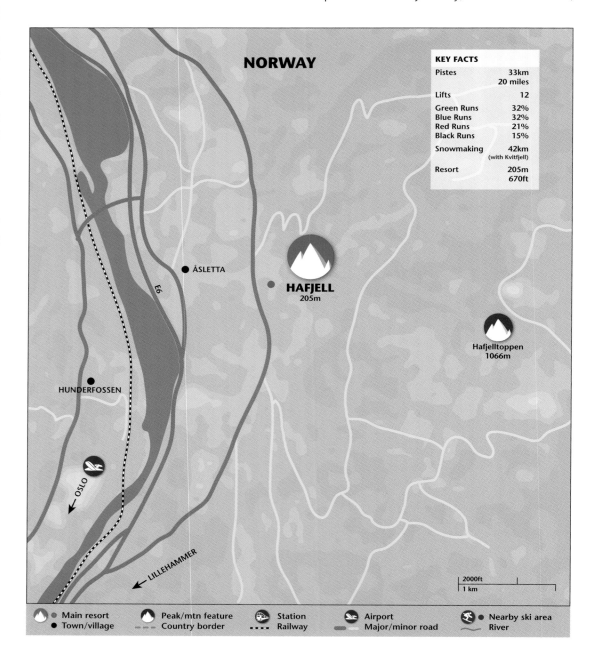

**NORWAY**

| KEY FACTS | |
|---|---|
| Pistes | 33km |
| | 20 miles |
| Lifts | 12 |
| Green Runs | 32% |
| Blue Runs | 32% |
| Red Runs | 21% |
| Black Runs | 15% |
| Snowmaking | 42km |
| | (with Kvitfjell) |
| Resort | 205m |
| | 670ft |

ÅSLETTA

**HAFJELL**
205m

Hafjelltoppen
1066m

E6

OSLO

HUNDERFOSSEN

LILLEHAMMER

2000ft
1 km

| | Main resort | | Peak/mtn feature | | Station | | Airport | | Nearby ski area |
|---|---|---|---|---|---|---|---|---|---|
| | Town/village | | Country border | | Railway | | Major/minor road | | River |

one drag and a free children's lift for the nursery slope and play area. The vertical is a tiny 250m (820ft), exhausted in moments by any competent skier, but there is no more relaxing place for first-timers to learn the basics.

## Kvitfjell

Kvitfjell is equally compact, but its character is completely different. Two chairlifts access the top of the hill and the start of the two harrowingly steep black pistes that were used for the Olympics. The main one is a rare treble-black diamond, a genuine grading for a descent of polished ice that seems uncomfortably close to vertical at times. Professional racers are trained to handle super-slick, so much so that they actually prefer it, but recreational skiers, even those of a standard to cope with most black pistes with ease, tend to ski down the edges where there is enough loose snow to provide a modicum of grip. The motto is, don't attempt Kvitfjell's Number One piste unless you've got the guts to look down the barrel and survive.

No matter, there are alternatives in the shape of a lesser black loop (2) and a long top to bottom red cruiser (3). The top of the mountain also has a single blue run (7) and a mini network of greens (5 and 9) but these end at the midstation, leaving cautious intermediates with no alternative but to download.

In the Olympic era, Kvitfjell was a simple base station, but it is now a resort in its own right, following 21st century investment in lodges, apartments and two hotels: the Kvitfjell, a popular family choice, and the GudbrandsGard, with swimming pool, spa and disco.

Those who thrive on speed who make it to the bottom of the downhill may be ready for the Olympic bobsleigh and luge track at Hunderfossen. The main event, a four-man descent with an experienced pilot authorized to go at 120kmph (75mph), is a genuine white-knuckle ride, with the risk of whiplash, especially for the person at the back. Less intrepid visitors may prefer the unpiloted five-man rubber raft which doesn't exceed

80kmph (50mph). Activity alternatives include sleigh rides, snowmobiling and dog sledding at Hafjell and Sjusjøen, plus a moose safari that can be booked in Lillehammer.

Although most foreigners prefer the ski-in/ski-out facilities in the resorts, Lillehammer has its own attractions, including a popular traffic-free main shopping street and a choice of museums.

### CULTURE – NORWEIGAN-STYLE

*The open-air exhibition at Maihaugen takes visitors through 500 years of Norwegian history, with the emphasis on housing, folk art and craft workshops. The Norwegian Road Museum and the Rock Blasting Museum give insights into transport in a cold climate, while the Olympic Museum covers the Games, both in summer and winter, since the start of the modern era in 1896.*

BELOW: **A lone skier floats effortlessly through champagne powder in search of the most rewarding route through the all-embracing forest.**

ABOVE: **The view over the town from the top of the 90-m (295-ft) ski jump built for the Lillehammer Olympics in 1994 inspires white knuckle terror.**

# VOSS

BY ALF ALDERSON

It certainly adds to the experience of a ski holiday if your destination is exactly what you'd expect from a traditional ski resort – quaint and attractive, and surrounded by majestic mountains, snow-draped forests and frozen lakes – and Voss fits very nicely into that niche. Add an historic old timber-built hotel, like the town's famous Fleischer's Inn, and you pretty well have the perfect little Scandinavian ski resort.

Perhaps the only downside to all this is that you can't ski into the town. However, you access the slopes via a lovely old red cable-car from just above the town's railway station, then take either a slow, relaxing and lovingly maintained little single chair-lift or a faster T-bar (Scandinavians seem to have an inordinate fondness for surface lifts, and five out of the 10 ski lifts at Voss are drags), with ever more expansive views opening out as you gain altitude.

This relaxed approach epitomizes skiing in Voss – no one seems to rush anywhere, everyone is friendly and polite and even the

mountains seem welcoming in a way that the savage crags and precipices of somewhere like Chamonix never do.

The big whaleback mountains that make up Voss' relatively small ski area are mostly above the tree line and are perfect for beginners and intermediates, rarely being so steep as to cause panic. The trail down Horgaletten is a perfect example of that rare combination where good and indifferent skiers can both start and finish at the same point on a run, with various detours on the way down, to accommodate their individual skill levels.

Beginners – children in particular – will especially benefit from the good ski schools and the impeccable English spoken by the affable local instructors. But it's lower-level intermediates who are best catered for, with a good range of blue and red runs which start above the tree line before meandering down through the trees of the lower slopes. More experienced skiers need to explore a little to make the most of Voss, but that's easy – just head off the side of the groomed runs and you'll find a good range of more challenging terrain. The long blacks from the summit of Horgaletten and Hanguren are enough to get anyone's legs screaming for a break; indeed, the former is used for downhill races, the latter for FIS giant slaloms.

Despite its low altitude, Voss still has just under 914m (3,000ft) of vertical, and the modest altitude and rolling mountains are

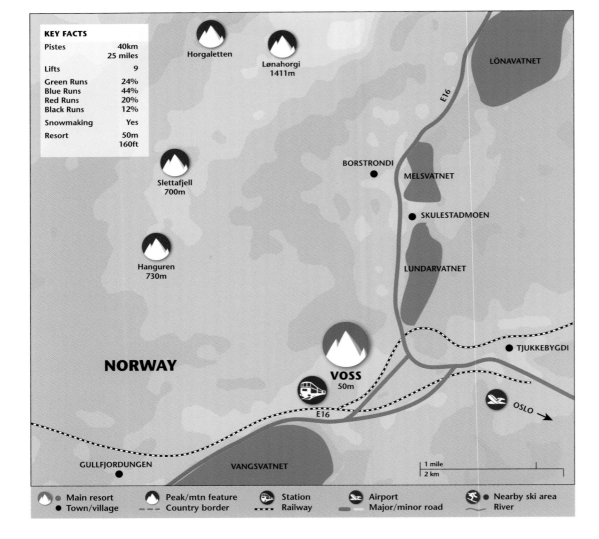

**KEY FACTS**

| | |
|---|---|
| Pistes | 40km / 25 miles |
| Lifts | 9 |
| Green Runs | 24% |
| Blue Runs | 44% |
| Red Runs | 20% |
| Black Runs | 12% |
| Snowmaking | Yes |
| Resort | 50m / 160ft |

Horgaletten
Lønahorgi 1411m
LØNAVATNET
E16
BORSTRONDI
MELSVATNET
Slettafjell 700m
SKULESTADMOEN
Hanguren 730m
LUNDARVATNET
NORWAY
TJUKKEBYGDI
VOSS 50m
OSLO →
E16
GULLFJORDUNGEN
VANGSVATNET

1 mile
2 km

Main resort / Town/village — Country border
Peak/mtn feature
Station •••• Railway
Airport — Major/minor road
Nearby ski area River

ABOVE: **Although mainly an intermediate resort, there is still some good off-piste action to be had at Voss.**

more Scottish than Alpine in character. Britons have always been among the most numerous of the foreign skiers in Voss, and have been coming here for almost a century.

Voss has recently invested heavily in snow cannon after a series of poor winters, and these cover so much of the area that snow is now virtually guaranteed. The region also has a very long season, with skiing starting as early as the beginning of November in some years, going onto Easter in others, and lift queues rare outside of holiday periods. Mid-winter temperatures can be very cold, and, because of the latitude, daylight hours are limited. Conversely, by April it's light well into the evening. Calm, sunny high-pressure conditions are common.

The relatively limited amount of skiable area here means that anyone who can move reasonably quickly around the slopes can dis-cover most of what Voss has to offer in a day or two. But there are plenty of other options if you start to feel you are exhausting the downhill possibilities, particularly cross-coun-try skiing, since this is the home of the sport.

### FLÅMSBANA RAILWAY

*It's worth taking time out from skiing to enjoy the journey on the Flåmsbana railway down to the shores of Sognefjord, the world's longest fjord – a really enjoyable daytrip from Voss. From the centre of Voss, a short train ride brings you to Myrdal, where you transfer to a lovely little engine for the ride to Sognefjord. The line takes you almost 914m (3,000ft) and 20km (12 miles) down a rail line that clings to the side of glacier-carved chasms, and burrows through black-cragged mountains and snow-plastered peaks before arriving on the shores of Sognefjord. There are few better or more spec-tacular ways to give your legs a break from the rigours of the slopes, and after your long down-hill on rails you'll be all the more ready for some more long downhills on skis.*

RIGHT: **Telemark skiing is big in Voss – Norway is, after all, the home of the sport.**

# Trysil

BY ARNIE WILSON

For a resort that is little known outside Scandinavia, Trysil is surprisingly big. It has more terrain than Hemsedal, though without Hemsedal's off-piste. It is close to the Swedish border – 30km (19 miles) away – offering the possibility of a contrasting two-centre holiday for skiing and snowboarding with the Swedish resort of Sälen. Trysilfjellet (Trysil Mountain) offers the best part of 360 degrees of mountain – all linked, so you can follow the sun (if there is one) all day if you wish. Gladed slopes, with long, satisfying boulevard skiing girdle the lower slopes, while the upper half of the mountain is treeless and a little flat at the top. It's almost as if two rather different mountains have been fused into one.

Trysil was the home of one of the world's original slalom clubs. The wooded lower slopes alone, with their three base areas, have enough trails to keep most skiers happy for several days. The upper mountain, like a huge cream topping above the tree line, has another big selection of runs. These include 'Run 75', the steepest in the resort (at least

the first section, which is a briefly daunting 45 degrees). Quite why it's called 75 is a mystery – there are 'only' 64 runs all told in the whole resort. But even that will give you a clue about how extensive the skiing is. More lifts and slopes are being added.

Trysil prides itself on the fact that blue and black runs often run side by side, enabling people of all ages and abilities to keep close together. You really can burn the candle at both ends here: twice a week, from mid-February, there's brisk early-morning skiing on freshly-groomed cruising runs at Høgegga (some of the best skiing on the mountain) – a breakfast-and-ski package for keen skiers and boarders who don't mind an early and often cold start. The skiing quickly warms them up; with no-one else to get in the way, it's exhilarating to be able to speed down the long, beautifully groomed runs through the trees long before the slopes officially open to the public. And two evenings a week there's night skiing, either at Trysil Turistsenter or Trysil Høyfjellssenter

During the day, don't be surprised to find little pockets of picnickers lining some of the less wind-blown slopes. Slopeside snacks are

**Skiers and snowboarders at Trysil make for the lifts at the start of the day – no doubt pausing at one of the base area cafés for a quick breakfast.**

a big thing in Norway. Skiers pack picnics in their knapsacks – including a good few miniature bottles of *akvavit* – and during the early afternoon duly halt their skiing to enjoy it. The main ingredient is often something their Swedish neighbours would call *surströmming*, a delicacy made from fermented Baltic herring, and loosely translated as 'stinking fish'. It sounds horrible, and smells worse, but it tastes wonderful – as long as you don't breathe in through your nose. There are also four barbecue sites on the mountain. The Norwegians like to bring their own lunches up the mountain, and this is possibly the only ski nation where hotels permit skiers to help themselves to extra food at breakfast to take on the piste with them.

The town of Trysil, which has been described as Scandinavia's 'southernmost wilderness with town status', is 2km (1¼ miles) from the slopes. Most skiers and snowboarders stay at the ski village (Trysil Turistssenter), also the location for the snow-park, which has everything from easy to difficult jumps, as well as rails, boxes and a halfpipe. There's a smaller park further up in the mountainside.

Trysil is highly rated by snowboarders, especially its novice terrain. That's true for beginner skiers too. The resort has invested heavily in improving its children's facilities,

Skiers who prefer to keep going rather than join the exuberant après-ski can night-ski two evenings a week.

and the Children's Adventure Centre includes a mini snowboarding park, crèche, and dedicated lifts and pistes. Children under eight ski free with a helmet.

There are 100km (62 miles) of cross-country tracks, 3km (1¾miles) of which are floodlit. Other activities include dogsledding, sleigh rides using Nordlandshest horses (an old Norwegian breed) and bowling. There's a lively après-ski scene, but, as one wit put it, Trysil may have too many T-bars and not enough bars.

## LOCATION

*Trysil is 160km (99 miles) from Oslo's Gardermoen International Airport (and 210km/130 miles from Oslo itself). From Oslo it's a 2½–3 hour drive: take the E6 highway to Rv 3 north and then Rv 25 east into the mountains. Buses leave eight times daily, taking you right to the centre of Trysil. Elverum (11km/7 miles) is the closest railway station – linked with Trysil by the Trysilekspressen shuttle bus, which also travels in both directions eight times a day. The town of Trysil is some way from the slopes (2km/c1¼ miles) and most people stay at the ski village (Turistssenteret) or the other base areas.*

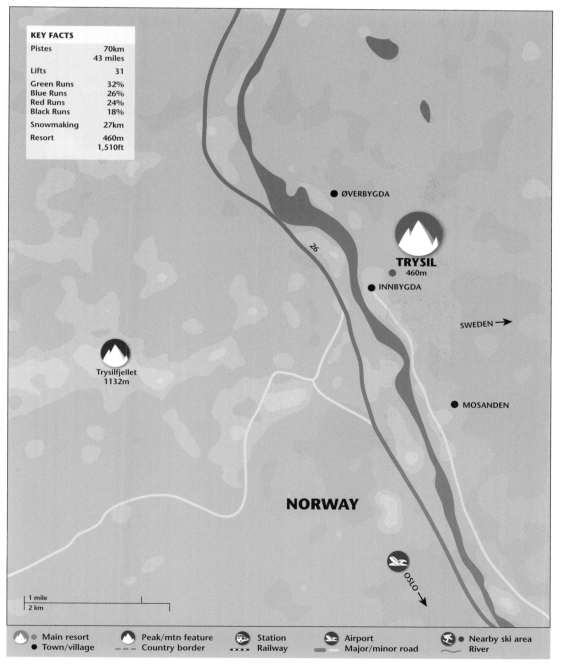

| KEY FACTS | |
|---|---|
| Pistes | 70km |
| | 43 miles |
| Lifts | 31 |
| Green Runs | 32% |
| Blue Runs | 26% |
| Red Runs | 24% |
| Black Runs | 18% |
| Snowmaking | 27km |
| Resort | 460m |
| | 1,510ft |

ØVERBYGDA

26

**TRYSIL**
460m

INNBYGDA

SWEDEN →

Trysilfjellet
1132m

MOSANDEN

**NORWAY**

OSLO →

1 mile
2 km

| | | | |
|---|---|---|---|
| Main resort | Peak/mtn feature | Station | Airport | Nearby ski area |
| Town/village | Country border | Railway | Major/minor road | River |

## KEY

- **Ski resort**
- **National border**
- **Airport**
- **Main road**
- **Main railway**
- **Local railway**

## ROMANIA
**Poiana Brasov: p.144**

## BULGARIA
**Borovets : p.142**

Dnestr

**UKRAINE**

**MOLDOVA**

Prut

■ **Chisinau**

• Odessa

• Cluj-Napoca

**CARPATHIANS**

**MUNTII APUSENI**

Tîrgu Mures

• Alba

Sibiu

**CARPATII MERIDIONALI**

**Poiana Brasov**

• Ploesti

Galati •

**ROMANIA**

• Tirgu-Jiu

**Bucharest**

• Craiova

Danube

**BLACK**

**SEA**

Mikhaylovgrad

Pleven •

Varna •

**BULGARIA**

Burgas •

Sofiya

**STARA PLANINA**

Kyustendil

**Borovets**

Plovdiv

Maritsa

• Blagoevgrad

Istanbul •

**IA**

Mountain High Maps® Copyright © 1993 Digital Wisdom®, Inc.

0   50   100   150   200 miles

0   125   250 kilometres

# BULGARIA

# Borovets

BY ARNIE WILSON

The phrase 'cheap and cheerful' could almost have been invented to describe skiing in Bulgaria. And Borovets, just an hour or so (72km/45 miles) from the capital, Sofia, is perhaps the most cheerful of all. The resort, in the Rila Mountains, sits snugly in thick pine forests at 1,390m (4,559ft) at the foot of Mount Musala (2,935m/9,627ft), the highest peak in the Balkan peninsula. It is Bulgaria's oldest and – until the recent emergence of its big rival Bansko – was its most important ski area.

Rudimentary skiing started here long before the first lifts – as long ago as the dawn of the 20th century, when the area was known principally as a hunting region. (The village was originally the site of a hunting lodge for the then Bulgarian royal family.) Now there are plans to give it a 21st-century upgrade, with a $125–$175 million programme to make it 'a modern European resort'. The make-over, which will double the size of the resort, will include additional trails to the existing 20 or so runs (25 miles/40.5km) of pistes) and a vital link between the two main ski areas. At the time of writing, you either access Yastrebets and the three high-altitude upper lifts in the Markoudjika area (including the disconcertingly named Avalanche run which is actually quite benign) via the resort's ageing gondola, (built about a quarter of a century ago), or take the four-person chair to

**Chalet city: wooden cabins of every description line the pedestrianised main street of the Borovets ski village, providing bars, shops and restaurants.**

Martinovi Baraki, where long, steep and quite challenging runs are cut through the pine forest. This area is also the location for some good night skiing. It is important to link these two areas because the way things are, so many skiers and snowboarders are keen to get as high on the mountain as possible at the beginning of the day – and can only do so by using the gondola – that huge queues can build up there after breakfast when the ski schools and their clients assemble. Some visitors, faced with such long delays to get on to the upper slopes opt instead for the quad chair, and ski the Martinovi Baraki area until the queues have died down.

There's a good mix of steep and gentler terrain (the resort has twice hosted World Cup races), and some exciting off-piste potential (much of the mountainside is dotted with nicely spread-out stunted pine trees – ideal for easy tree-skiing) and adequate nursery slopes at the Martinovi Baraki base area. Even low-cost heliskiing is possible. Borovets has a colourful village centre, with attractive chalets serving as souvenir shops, bars and restaurants lining a narrow, partly traffic-free street close to the lifts. In stark contrast, many of the major hotels are inspired by the genre of purpose-built architecture common in modern French resorts. With such a strong Turkish influence on Bulgaria's history (the Turks ruled here for centuries), it comes as no surprise that there's a touch of the orient about the culture, not least in the choice of music in the marketplace, and in the local cuisine. There are so many bars and restaurants (almost 30) that you will have plenty of options all week. Like Bulgarian resorts in general, Borovets is very popular with budget-conscious skiers – especially now that Andorra has made a major attempt to go up-market. Visitors experience a great variety of lively après-ski, colourful folk-lore traditions and hearty dishes for their money. By the end of their week, they will often find that no matter how much shopping, eating and drinking they may have accomplished, they'll have had difficulty in spending their Leva (the

local currency). Drinks which would cost a small fortune in a chic nightclub in the French Alps are surprisingly cheap in Bulgaria, and many bars and nightclubs even offer you a free drink with every one you actually buy. Popular excursions include visits to the celebrated Rila monastery, a 'world monument of culture' and of course the capital, Sofia.

There are some 200 ski instructors. Most of them – sometimes performing miracles on ancient skis – are friendly and speak good English. The Bulgarians are skilful with languages, and they're often adept at understanding Russian and Macedonian too: the languages are similar, although Russians and Macedonian visitors find it much more difficult to understand Bulgarian than the other way round. The one word of Bulgarian you might find useful is *nazdrave!* – cheers!

**Enjoying fresh snow at Martinovi Baraki, overlooking modern hotels which resemble the French architecural style common in the Alps during the 1960s and 70s.**

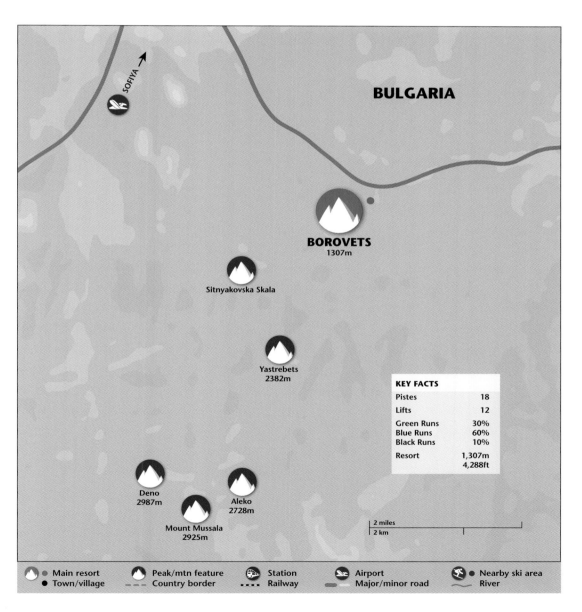

**BULGARIA**

**BOROVETS**
1307m

Sitnyakovska Skala

Yastrebets
2382m

| KEY FACTS | |
|---|---|
| Pistes | 18 |
| Lifts | 12 |
| Green Runs | 30% |
| Blue Runs | 60% |
| Black Runs | 10% |
| Resort | 1,307m |
| | 4,288ft |

Deno
2987m

Aleko
2728m

Mount Mussala
2925m

2 miles
2 km

| | Main resort | | Peak/mtn feature | | Station | | Airport | | Nearby ski area |
|---|---|---|---|---|---|---|---|---|---|
| ● | Town/village | - - - | Country border | ▪▪▪▪ | Railway | | Major/minor road | ～ | River |

# ROMANIA

# Poiana Brasov

BY ARNIE WILSON

Romania – so called because it was once an important province of the Roman empire – has an intriguingly eclectic location – bordered to the north and east by Moldavia and Ukraine, to the south by Bulgaria, to the southwest by Serbia, and to the west by Hungary. The purpose-built resort of Poiana Brasov, Romania's only major ski area, is where the Transylvanian Alps meet the Carpathian Mountains, and the picturesque old medieval city of Brasov – some 13km (8 miles) below - is 'surrounded like a halo' by peaks.

With only 14km (9 miles) of skiing, the resort is definitely on the small side, but there's a surprising amount of good terrain. Probably not enough, however, to keep a really strong skier engrossed for more than a day or two, let alone a full week. The compensation is that this may be some of the cheapest skiing in Europe. The cost of drinks, for example, is a fraction of what you would pay in the Alps. Accommodation, at least in the main hotels, is surprisingly comfortable for a country only now really emerging from years of deprivation, especially in the grim Ceausescu years,

which finally ended in 1989. One bizarre throwback to the old institutionalized days of communism is that the instructors assume that everyone is a beginner until proved otherwise. Many visitors are, in fact – this is a good place in which to learn to ski. But if you have booked an instructor to show you round the mountain rather than to learn the basics from, it's very likely that he or she, in spite of speaking more than adequate English, will insist on testing your skills on the nursery slopes before even letting you near a T-bar, let alone allowing you anywhere near the

lifts which take you to the highest slopes on Mount Postavaru. (In mainstream Alpine resorts, of course, one is used to doing a warm-up run so that the instructor or guide can take a look at your level of skiing, but at least this is normally undertaken on a sensible lower-intermediate run and involves the use of a lift!) Having established that perhaps you do actually know at least the rudiments of skiing, you will then be allowed up to the summit of Mount Postavaru, reached by a choice of two fairly ancient cable-cars and a gondola. They serve a handful of easy green and blue runs, as well as some more-demanding terrain, which seems to be marked red or black (intermediate or expert) according to the width of the pistes rather than the gradient.

The local countryside is reminiscent of New England (even bears are plentiful) – hence the decision to make the film *Cold Mountain* here, about the American Civil war. With Romania's low cost of living, all the production costs – including the extras' wages – were considerably lower than would have been the case in the US. While in Hollywood mode, it is perhaps worth mentioning that Bran Castle, a spectacular edifice near Brasov known as Dracula's Castle, was

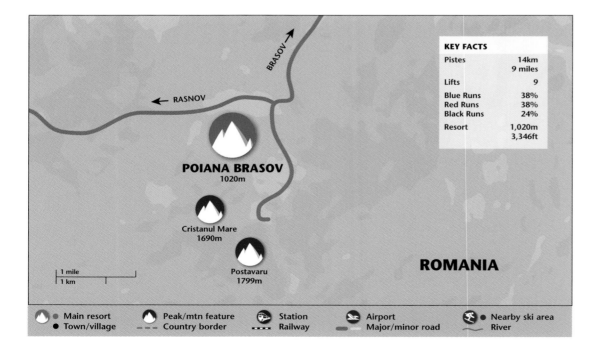

| KEY FACTS | |
|---|---|
| Pistes | 14km |
| | 9 miles |
| Lifts | 9 |
| Blue Runs | 38% |
| Red Runs | 38% |
| Black Runs | 24% |
| Resort | 1,020m |
| | 3,346ft |

probably only used by Vlad the Impaler (the 'real' Dracula, a version of Draculea or Draculya, meaning the devil's son) on the odd night or two in the 13th century. It was Bram Stoker's fanciful book, published centuries later in 1897, which spread the Dracula myth across Europe. Brutal he certainly was, impaling would-be Turkish and Saxon invaders, as well as thieves and other criminals on sharp stakes, but the vampire myth was embroidered if not invented by Stoker. Needless to say the tales of Dracula and Transylvania have helped attract tourists as well as skiers, some of whom might not have bothered to come all this way if it hadn't been for the fascinating local history. Transylvania belonged to Hungary from the 11th century

until 1918. It was only finally restored to Romania in 1947.

The city of Brasov, with its pubs and cellar bars, is well worth exploring – especially as the skiing will not keep you busy all week. Alternative resort activities include paint-balling (one wonders how Vlad the Impaler might have viewed this latter-day sport), and a visit to a folkloric evening in a Romanian yurt, complete with gypsy dancing, spicy sausage starters washed down with hot brandy, and a main course of steak – later discovered to be wild bear. A side trip to Peles Palace, near Sinaia (where there is an even smaller ski area) is well worth the experience. This fascinating and richly decorated Renaissance castle was built for Romania's

first monarch, King Karel, a German prince who accepted the throne in 1877.

There is a market at the foot of Dracula's Castle (also well worth a visit, whether Dracula stayed there or not) with countless rather gruesome Dracula souvenirs, including the almost inevitable Vampire label red wines. I haven't yet dared to open the bottle of 1999 Vampire Cabernet Sauvignon I purchased – with some reservations – for less than $4. I feel the deep red liquid needs to mature for a little longer.

**Before you are allowed anywhere near Poiana Brasov's cable cars or gondola, you may have to demonstrate to your instructor that you can actually ski!**

# Donovaly

BY NICK DALTON

Donovaly is nestled in a beautiful spot in the Carpathian Mountains between the Low Tatra and Big Fatra ranges, near the historic towns of Banská Bystrica and Ruĺomberok. It's a region where the past is never far away – with little farms, caves to visit and mineral springs to laze in – but Donovaly, the biggest of the country's more than two dozen ski areas, is pushing into the future. There are modern lifts, notably the Telemix chondola – part chair, part gondola – which takes skiers up Nová Hol'a, newly developed across the E77 road from the original Záhradište area. There may be only 18 lifts serving 18 runs on 11km (7 miles) of piste, but that's good by Slovak standards.

Donovaly is a rambling, welcoming little mountain community with much original architecture. So wild and tucked away was it, that in World War II this was one of the centres of partisan resistance. The ski area is one of two that comes under the Park Snow banner – the other is Vysoké Tatry-Šrbské Pleso, with a similar amount of skiing but only five lifts, by the pretty Štrbské Lake in the High Tatras. Donovaly has a new hands-free lift pass.

Like many East European ski areas, the naming of runs isn't something that seems to be a priority. Suffice to say the Záhradište area is mostly blue, big open runs that are excellent for beginners and low intermediates. The main lift is the four-man Buly Express, but four long drags back it up to get you to different spots. This is where many of the lessons take place and, as such, can't be faulted.

The other side of the road – negotiated by a couple of quaint wooden bridges, although a lift connection is imminent – is what makes Donovaly the envy of other Slovak ski areas. The chondola takes you up to 1,361m (4,410ft) at the top of Nová Hol'a for some stunning views and a selection of weaving reds, the longest of which claims to be 2.2km (1½ miles) long with a vertical of 447m (1,466ft). Snowmaking covers a number of runs. There's some off-piste that is usually in good condition.

The friendly ski school boasts that all their instructors speak at least one foreign language, including English. The ski kindergarten teaches youngsters from the age of four with fairy-tale fun and carnivals; younger children can get private lessons.

The terrain is nicely rolling for snowboarders, and there are some rails and jumps in the Bulldog Club. There's also cross-country, with a selection of tracks disappearing into the forest, one 20km (12 miles) long.

As for other activities, paragliding is popular – flights with instructors are much cheaper than the main European resorts. There's also dog-sledding, bowling, skating and snowrafting (speeding down the slopes on a rubber raft), plus night skiing most evenings.

## Restaurants and hotels

By day, there are several small places to eat on the slopes. In the evening there are a handful of restaurants to choose from, the main one being the barn-like Koliba Goral, which serves hearty local food and hosts local folk music. The menu is big and boisterous eastern style, with more than a few influ-

Dog-sledding is just one of the many activities you can take part in in Donovaly.

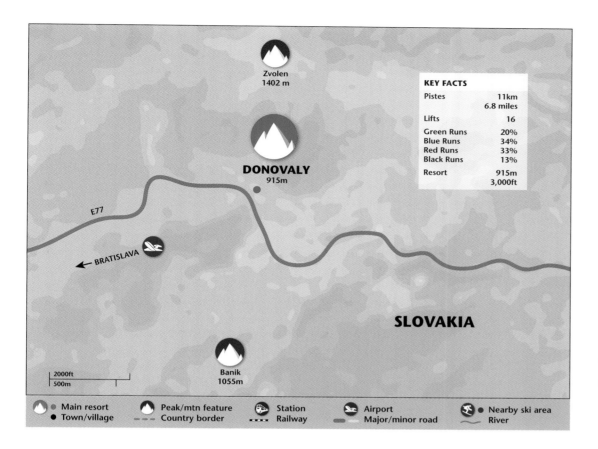

Zvolen
1402 m

DONOVALY
915m

E77

← BRATISLAVA

SLOVAKIA

2000ft
500m

Banik
1055m

| KEY FACTS | |
|---|---|
| Pistes | 11km |
| | 6.8 miles |
| Lifts | 16 |
| Green Runs | 20% |
| Blue Runs | 34% |
| Red Runs | 33% |
| Black Runs | 13% |
| Resort | 915m |
| | 3,000ft |

●▲● Main resort    ▲● Peak/mtn feature    🚉 Station    ✈ Airport    Nearby ski area
● Town/village    – – – Country border    ▪▪▪ Railway    Major/minor road    River

ABOVE: **Snowboarding is well catered for with good, easy terrain and rails to ride in the Bulldog Club.**

BELOW: **The six-seat chairs of the Telemix chondola on Nová Hol'a combine with eight-person gondola carriages.**

ences from Slovakia's Austrian, Hungarian and German neighbours. There are dumplings, pork and sauerkraut, with some dishes involving all three. You're unlikely to get through your holiday without trying *bryndzové halušky* (potato dumplings with sheep's cheese, topped with bacon).

There are a number of places to stay. Perhaps best is the 4-star Sporthotel, with several restaurants, and an impressive spa and pool. Another favourite is the Hotel Donovaly, a big, modern but traditional place on the edge of the woods near the Nová Hol'a lifts. It has a restaurant as well as a bar and disco. At both hotel restaurants you'll find a modern take on traditional specialities.

There are pensions scattered within walking distance of the slopes, as well as apartments. Of the latter the most impressive is woody, attractive Greehhill, which sleeps 14 in something like chalet-style, with self-catering kitchen and adjoining restaurant. Nightlife can be jolly in hotel bars and discos where local favourites *borovicka* (a type of gin) and *slivovica* (plum brandy) are in ready supply.

If you fancy an excursion there are buses to Banská Bystrica, around 20 minutes away,

as well as several other towns where you'll find museums, ice caves, 13th-century wooden churches and thermal spas.

Donovaly might not be the biggest of areas but it makes for a great winter holiday.

CHUKCHI SEA

*Pt. Barrow*
●Barrow

BEAUFORT

SEA

*Victoria Island*

*St. Lawrence Island*

*Yukon*

*Porcupine*

B E R I N G

SEA

**ALASKA (USA)**

●Fairbanks

▲Mt. McKinley

*Great Bear Lake*

*Mackenzie*

MCKENZIE MOUNTAINS

●Anchorage

▲Mt. Logan

*Great Slave Lake*

*Kodiak Island*

GULF OF

ALASKA

Juneau●

*Peace*

C A N A

**ALASKA: p.180**

**Prince Rupert**●

●Edmonton

*N. Saskatchewan*

●Saskatoon

QUEEN
CHARLOTTE
ISLANDS

●Winnipe

R

O

C

●Calgary

*S. Saskatchewan*

K

Vancouver●

P A C I F I C   O C E A N

*Cape Flattery*

●Seattle

Olympia●

*Mt. Rainier*▲

**WASHINGTON**

**MONTANA**

*Missouri*

**NORTH DAKOTA**

●Bismarck

Salem●

CASCADE RANGE

M

O

U

●Helena

Y

**SOUTH**

●Pierr

**DAKOTA**

**OREGON**

●Boise

**IDAHO**

**WYOMING**

**UNITED STA**

N

T

**NEBRASK**

●Cheyenne

*Cape Mendocino*

SIERRA NEVADA

*Great Salt Lake*

**NEVADA**

●Carson City

Salt Lake City●

A

I

●Denver

Sacramento●

**UTAH**

*Colorado*

**COLORADO**

**KAN.**

San Francisco●

▲Mt. Whitney

**CALIFORNIA**

Las Vegas●

N

S

*Canadian*

C

*Pt. Arguello*

Los Angeles●

**ARIZONA**

Santa Fe●

**NEW MEXICO**

San Diego●

●Phoenix

*Baja California*

GULF OF CALIFORNIA

**CALIFORNIA/NEW MEXICO/COLORADO/ WYOMING/IDAHO/MONTANA: p.181**

●El Paso

M E X I C O

●Chihuahua

*Punta Eugenia*

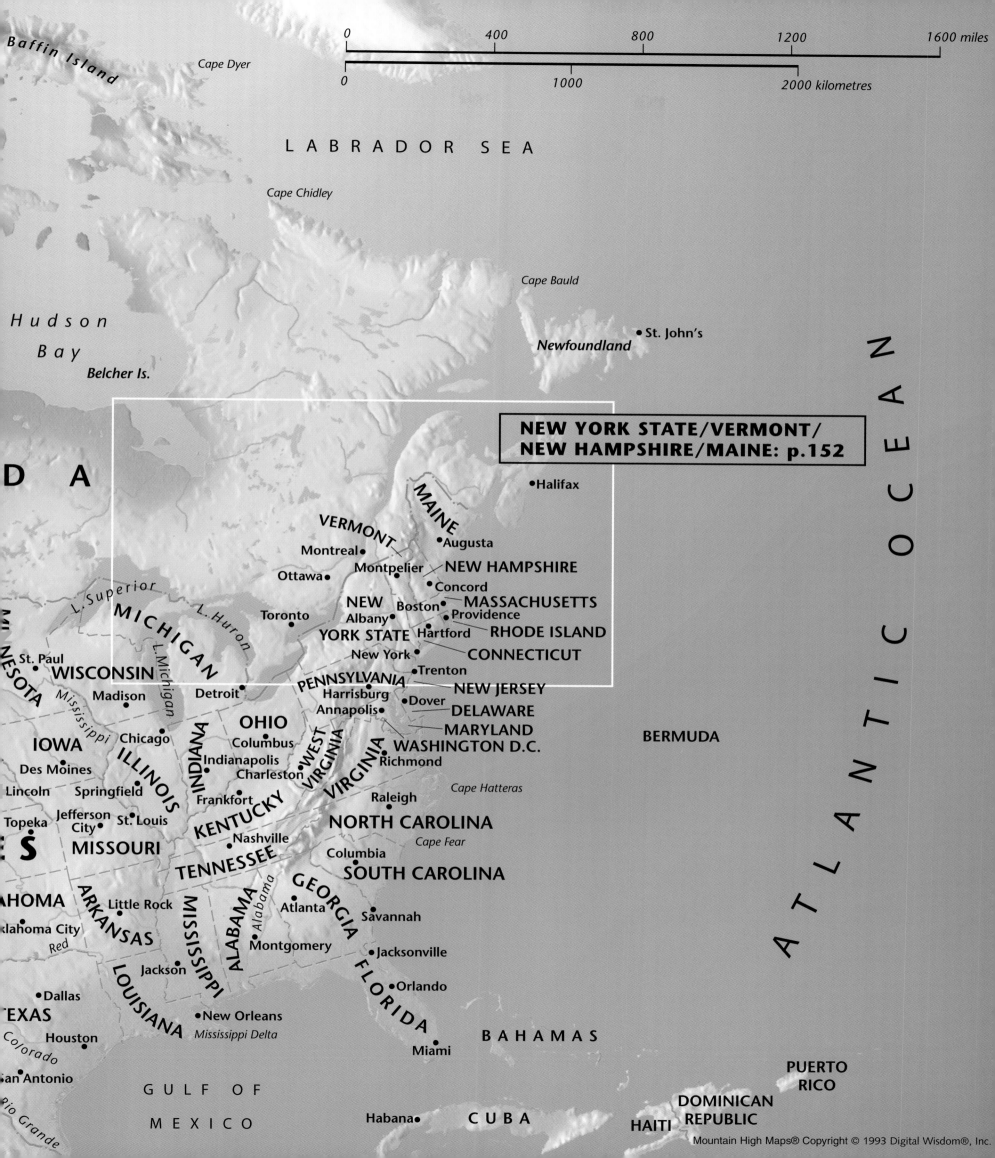

0        400            800            1200          1600 miles

0            1000                    2000 kilometres

**Baffin Island**

Cape Dyer

**LABRADOR SEA**

Cape Chidley

Cape Bauld

*Hudson*
*Bay*

•St. John's

*Newfoundland*

Belcher Is.

**NEW YORK STATE/VERMONT/**
**NEW HAMPSHIRE/MAINE: p.152**

D A

•Halifax

**MAINE**

**VERMONT**

•Augusta

Montreal•

•Montpelier        **NEW HAMPSHIRE**

Ottawa•

•Concord

**NEW**      Boston•    **MASSACHUSETTS**

Toronto•    Albany•    •Providence

**YORK STATE**    Hartford•    **RHODE ISLAND**

**MICHIGAN**    L. Huron    New York•    **CONNECTICUT**

*L. Superior*

**WISCONSIN**

St. Paul    •Trenton

•    L. Michigan    **PENNSYLVANIA**    **NEW JERSEY**

Madison•    Detroit•    Harrisburg•    •Dover

NESOTA    *Mississippi*    Annapolis•    **DELAWARE**

**OHIO**    **MARYLAND**    **BERMUDA**

**IOWA**    Chicago•    Columbus•    **WASHINGTON D.C.**

**INDIANA**    **WEST**    •Richmond

Des Moines•    Indianapolis•    **VIRGINIA**

Lincoln•    Springfield•    Charleston•    **VIRGINIA**    *Cape Hatteras*

Topeka•    Jefferson    Frankfort•    Raleigh•    **NORTH CAROLINA**

•    City•    St. Louis•    **KENTUCKY**

**MISSOURI**    Nashville•    Columbia•    *Cape Fear*

**S**    **TENNESSEE**    **SOUTH CAROLINA**

HOMA    Little Rock•    **GEORGIA**

**ARKANSAS**    **MISSISSIPPI**    Atlanta•

lahoma City•    *Alabama*    Savannah•

**ALABAMA**

Red    **LOUISIANA**    Montgomery•    •Jacksonville

**FLORIDA**

Jackson•    **ATLANTIC OCEAN**

•Dallas    •Orlando

EXAS    •New Orleans    **BAHAMAS**

Houston•    *Mississippi Delta*

*Colorado*    Miami•    **PUERTO**

n Antonio•    **GULF OF**    **RICO**

*Rio Grande*    **MEXICO**    Habana•    **CUBA**    **DOMINICAN**

**HAITI**    **REPUBLIC**

# UNITED STATES

BY LESLIE WOIT

Have a nice day. Yes, it's a tired cliché, but when it comes to your ski holiday in America, it's also a welcome truth. Customer service is fundamentally an American invention. Mapped onto its natural resources – big mountains, dependable snowfall and good ole American ingenuity – you've got yourself a ski destination and a half.

From the beginner who receives a learn-to-ski-or-your-money-back guarantee, to the 'ski mom' who appreciates the tissue box in the lift line corral, to the family that takes advantage of free mountain tours, America is the land of plenty, with loads to do and ski.

To start with, almost every resort these days offers free guided tours several times a day. This is an ideal way to familiarize yourself with the mountain. Trails are labelled green (beginner), blue (intermediate) and black diamond and double black diamond for expert and really expert. Grooming is a science taken seriously, and some runs will be half groomed and half moguls, for variety.

And variety is the name of the game. The US Rockies stretch from the Canadian border down nearly to Mexico. In parts, the air can feel catwalk thin; though rounded and less dramatic than their Canadian counterparts, Colorado peaks reach more than 4,260m (14,000ft). Once adjusted, you'll find skiing in the trees makes for good visibility, and fleets of grooming machines work their night-magic like nowhere else. From the Rockies of

Colorado, Wyoming, Montana and Idaho to Utah's Wasatch and Mammoth's Sierra Nevadas, the variety among these resorts – let alone those in the remaining western states – is immense. Live out your Wild West fantasy in Jackson Hole or Steamboat, join the jet-set in Aspen, or have a black-and-white movie moment in Sun Valley. The states, and the distances between them, are large, but some areas lend themselves well to multi-resort excursions. Within about an hour of Salt Lake City, Utah, are more than half a dozen ski areas including Snowbird and the Olympic-host resort of Park City, justifiably famous for their deep and light powder snow. So too do the resorts dotted around the shores of Lake Tahoe, including Squaw, Heavenly and Kirkwood – make a sunny and scenic menu – all within a short drive of each other.

LEFT: **Resorts on the east coast, such as Smugglers' Notch, offer spectacular panoramas and the plentiful snow will keep skiers and boarders of all levels happy.**

BELOW: **The well-manicured slopes of Crested Butte make everyone look and feel like heroes. Not to be forgotten, the light-as-air powder does the same.**

Far across the flat expanse of Middle America, to the east, lies America's second major mountainous spine, the 2,414-km (1,500-mile) long Appalachians. Until the late 18th century, the Appalachians formed a natural border between settlers and Indians; today they are home to New England's surprisingly extensive network of resorts. No one would claim that Vermont, Maine, New Hampshire or New York can compete with their high and mighty western cousins, but as Robert Pirsig, author of *Zen and the Art of Motorcycle Maintenance*, rightly observed: 'It's the sides of the mountain that sustain life, not the top'.

With high-speed lifts, good grooming, clever snowmaking and excellent family facilities, eastern resorts are making their mark – even among international markets like Canada and the UK. With the notable exception of the towns of Stowe and Lake Placid, most are purpose-built resorts that are short on atmosphere but long on enjoyable add-ons like snowshoeing, snowmobiling, tubing, and cross-country skiing. Mountains can

range from over 914m (3,000ft) of vertical and 200 trails at Killington, the largest, to 50 trails and 10 lifts at Loon, New Hampshire, one of many small and friendly family resorts.

American après-ski culture runs the gamut from first-class spas and dog-sled rides to margaritas and nachos – and everything in between. It would be rare to encounter the raucousness of the renowned Austrian resorts anywhere on this relatively puritanical continent – but that doesn't mean you can't find a drink, even in Utah. America is renowned, of course, for its fast food, but you'll also find an ethnic diversity – served more slowly – that makes dinner an international culinary event. Good or bad, there is a certain consistency in many resorts here. From Starbucks in one to a Marriott hotel in others, the corporate ownership of many big-name destinations brings with it a uniformity some find appealing, and others can find repetitive. Still, when your latté is delivered with a smile and the ski valet has laid out your warm dry boots in the morning, it's tough not to do exactly as they say. Have a nice day, indeed.

ABOVE: **Snowbird's legendary tram is a one-way ticket to the lightest snow on earth. All aboard for the ride of your life.**

BELOW: **Welcome to Alyeska, Alaska. You've come a long way but the rewards of their big-mountain skiing and boarding make every mile worth it.**

RIGHT: **Aspen has everything going for it, including good looks. It's been attracting thrill-seekers and beautiful people for more than half a century.**

Mountain High Maps® Copyright © 1993 Digital Wisdom®, Inc.

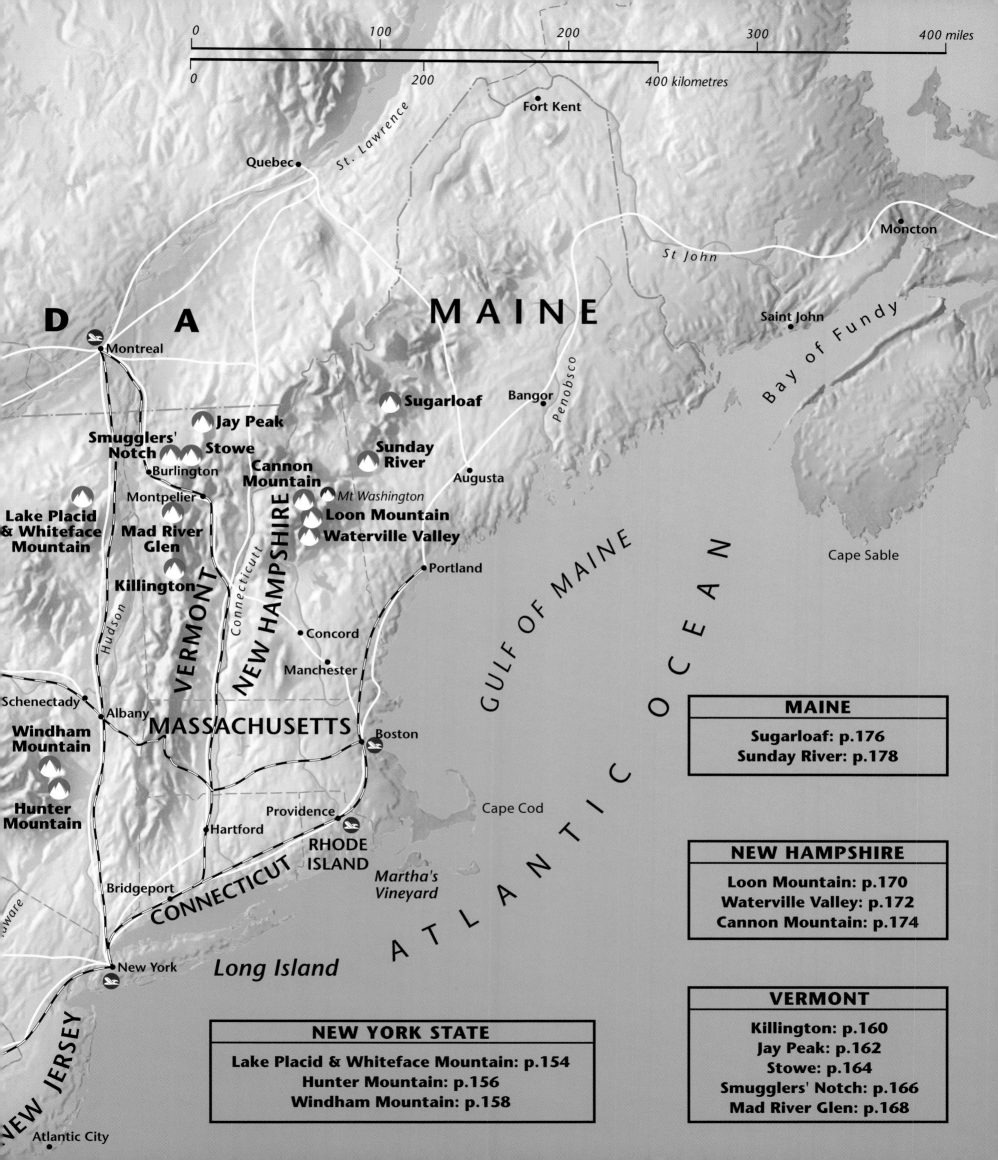

Fort Kent

Quebec

St. Lawrence

D A

MAINE

Moncton

St John

Montreal

Saint John

Bay of Fundy

Sugarloaf

Bangor

Penobsco

Jay Peak

Smugglers'
Notch

Stowe

Burlington

Cannon
Mountain

Sunday
River

Augusta

Montpelier

Mt Washington

Lake Placid
& Whiteface
Mountain

Mad River
Glen

Loon Mountain

Waterville Valley

Cape Sable

Killington

VERMONT

NEW HAMPSHIRE

Connecticutt

Portland

GULF OF MAINE

Concord

Hudson

Manchester

Schenectady

Albany

MASSACHUSETTS

Boston

Windham
Mountain

ATLANTIC OCEAN

Hunter
Mountain

Providence

Hartford

RHODE
ISLAND

Cape Cod

Bridgeport

CONNECTICUT

Martha's
Vineyard

NEW YORK

Long Island

A T L A N T I C

NEW JERSEY

Atlantic City

Delaware

# NEW YORK STATE

# Lake Placid (Whiteface Mountain)

BY ALF ALDERSON

As a ski resort Lake Placid is small and relatively unknown outside the USA, yet it has an impeccable winter sports pedigree. Not only does its ski hill, Whiteface Mountain, boast the biggest vertical drop east of the Rockies, the town has also hosted the Winter Olympics twice (in 1932 and 1980), and consequently has all the infrastructure to go with it along with an attractive downtown area.

This means that, besides simply skiing, you can go bobsledding at the Olympic bobsled course 11km (7 miles) out of town; you can stop off on the way and take the elevator 26 storeys to the top of the Olympic ski jump where Eddie the Eagle made his first attempt to fly; back in town you can skate on the rink where in 1980 Eric Heiden won five gold medals and the irritatingly over-hyped US hockey team also won gold; or you can simply wander around the absorbing Olympic Museum, funky bars, coffee shops and bookstores of downtown Lake Placid, which, in its winter coat looks like the setting for the remake of *White Christmas*.

## The mountain

And then, of course, there's the skiing. Some 14km (9 miles) from town, the 1,483-m (4,867-ft) Whiteface Mountain rises above the forests and lakes of the Adirondack Mountains. You can follow in the footsteps – or should that be ski tracks? – of Olympians on the 1980 Olympic Downhill course, or seriously test your off-piste skills by hiking out to the very challenging steep tree runs of the Slides. And for those not intent on

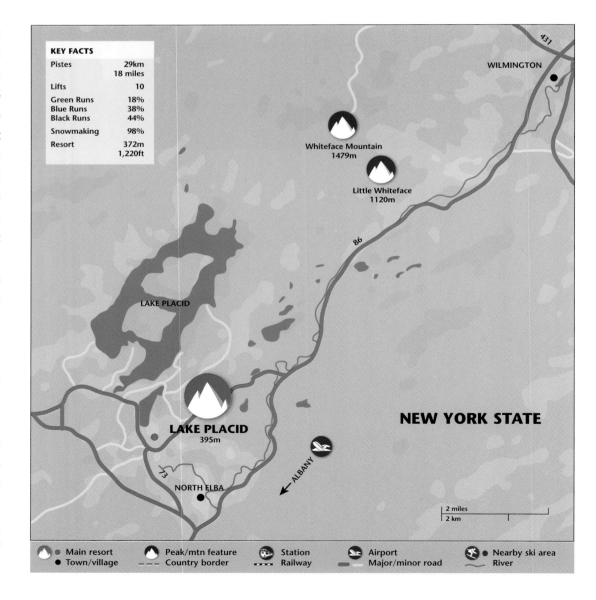

**KEY FACTS**

| | |
|---|---|
| Pistes | 29km |
| | 18 miles |
| Lifts | 10 |
| Green Runs | 18% |
| Blue Runs | 38% |
| Black Runs | 44% |
| Snowmaking | 98% |
| Resort | 372m |
| | 1,220ft |

WILMINGTON

Whiteface Mountain
1479m

Little Whiteface
1120m

86

LAKE PLACID

**NEW YORK STATE**

**LAKE PLACID**
395m

ALBANY

73

NORTH ELBA

2 miles
2 km

| | | | | | | | | |
|---|---|---|---|---|---|---|---|---|
| ● | Main resort | | Peak/mtn feature | | Station | | Airport | |
| ● | Town/village | - - - | Country border | ▪▪▪▪ | Railway | | Major/minor road | |
| | | | | | | | ● | Nearby ski area |
| | | | | | | | | River |

**With the biggest vertical drop east of the Rockies, the slopes of Whiteface Mountain shouldn't be underestimated.**

pushing themselves to extremes there's a more than adequate selection of blue runs on Whiteface and the somewhat lower Little Whiteface (1,120m/3,676ft). Hop off at the top of Little Whiteface, for instance, take a break to enjoy the panorama, then drop down the mountain on Excelsior or Northway, which, like most runs here, start off quite steeply then ease off on the lower half of the mountain.

An obvious feature of the resort is the snow cannons, and a massive 97 per cent of Whiteface can be covered by their output. There's a good reason for deploying the cannons; with heavy traffic (and the sometimes bone-numbingly cold weather) the pistes can become incredibly hard and icy. The snow machines help to alleviate the worst of this, and, if you head towards the

snow machines as you ski downslope, you can drift through extensive patches of ankle-deep fluff. It may be far removed from a natural mountain environment, but it's good fun all the same!

On the lower half of the mountain, beginners have their own quiet areas set aside where they can get to grips with the basics on some pleasant easy tree-lined slopes before heading up the summit of Little Whiteface – its bigger brother's upper slopes are really out of bounds for anyone below intermediate level.

## The resort

As befits a former Olympic city, there are lots of other activities besides skiing (and bobsledding). These include cross-country skiing, skating, snowboarding, snowshoeing and tobogganing.

Although bluebird days are by no means uncommon, Lake Placid is notorious for high winds and bitter cold. You need to be well

wrapped up to ski here – that said, spring can offer great skiing without the intense cold.

At day's end, Lake Placid provides an excellent array of après-ski options, from bustling and unpretentious bars and other low-key options, to the opulent Mirror Lake Inn. If you're really looking to splash out, try the gorgeous Lake Placid Lodge – as long as you don't mind paying around $400 per night for the cheapest rooms and up to $12,000 for a bottle of wine – yes, really!

Lake Placid and its mountain are a long way from the Alps, or the Rockies, come to that, but a little variety in your ski life is character-building. Who knows? You might just catch the place after a fresh fall of powder (it's not an irregular occurrence), in which case you'll be struggling to take in all that Lake Placid has to offer.

# Hunter Mountain

BY ARNIE WILSON

Hunter Mountain Ski Bowl is the most famous and popular resort in a state that, to many people's surprise, has more ski areas than any other in the USA. It's also the biggest, brashest and busiest. New York State has 45 resorts – almost twice as many as Colorado – although the size of these East-coast ski areas cannot compare with those in the Rockies. Hunter is the closest 'big mountain' to metropolitan New York, and the main destination for large numbers of skiers and snowboarders from the 'Big Apple' who traditionally head for the 'sleeping giant' (a touch of marketing hype), located a 193-km (120-mile) drive away, mainly along Route 87, the state 'Thruway' into the northern Catskills. Hunter's slogan is 'creating mountain memories, one smile at a time'.

Rather like Sun Valley, across the other side of the country in Idaho, Hunter launched itself with the help of cohorts of Hollywood film stars. When it opened in 1959, it was backed by a number of figures from the entertainment industry, including Paul Newman and Christopher Plummer, and among the guests were Oscar Hammerstein and the actor Laurence Harvey.

Hunter has something of a mixed reputation. It has dedicated itself recently to providing family skiing, and the Catskill ambience is markedly different from the culture of New York City from which it draws the majority of its visitors. Some city visitors are astonished to find that many folks in the mountains don't even bother to lock their front doors. Hunter, though, has also been described as a 'human zoo' – a microcosm of New York, with all the appropriate hustle, bustle and hassle. Hunter dedicates some of its 53 trails to well-known New York City areas and streets like Madison Square, Central Park, 7th Avenue and Broadway.

'It was a unique idea', said the owners, 'a ski resort that would bring the flavour and the life of metropolitan New York to all. A ski resort which would remind people why New York was the Empire State and Broadway was the Big Apple.'

In the past, a little of New York's drug culture rubbed off too, particularly at weekends when exotic substances were sometimes marketed on the lifts. Unfortunately, many years ago, one guest was famously shot dead by another at Heartbreak Hotel in Hunter Village. However, it would be wrong to paint an unpleasant picture. After all, this is the venue for the East Coast Police Winter Games! And the local chamber of commerce also likes to remind visitors of the words of the writer Hervey Voge: 'The mountains will always be there. The trick is to make sure you are too.'

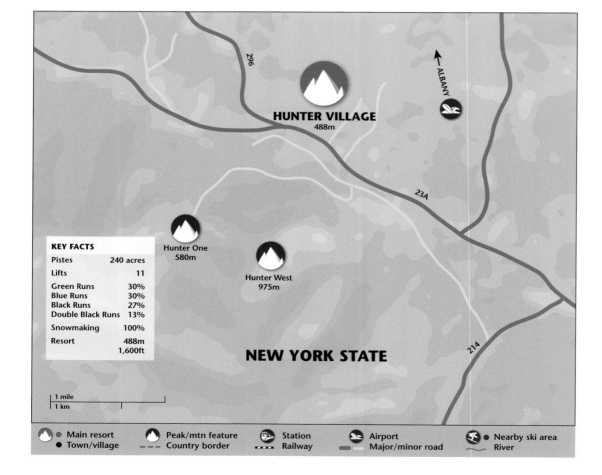

**KEY FACTS**

| Pistes | 240 acres |
|---|---|
| Lifts | 11 |
| Green Runs | 30% |
| Blue Runs | 30% |
| Black Runs | 27% |
| Double Black Runs | 13% |
| Snowmaking | 100% |
| Resort | 488m |
| | 1,600ft |

HUNTER VILLAGE
488m

Hunter One
580m

Hunter West
975m

NEW YORK STATE

1 mile
1 km

Main resort • Town/village — Peak/mtn feature · Country border — Station · Railway — Airport · Major/minor road — Nearby ski area · River

## Great skiing

The reason so many Manhattan skiers come here is because the skiing is challenging and extensive. A high proportion of the runs – 43 per cent – are designated 'advanced'. Hunter also has some of the most efficient snowmaking in the US, although its self-awarded sobriquet of 'the snowmaking capitol (sic) of the world' is perhaps over-enthusiastic.

Hunter has three mountain faces, served by 11 lifts, with some 56km (35 miles) of trails and a vertical drop of 488m (1,600ft). Hunter One has mainly easy runs, while Hunter West and Hunter Mountain itself offer some of the steeper options; for example, Annapurna, which is graded a double-black diamond. There's a two-trail terrain park complete with a halfpipe and jib-park, and a snow-tubing park with three tows and 12 chutes. Hunter West is where good skiers – and skiers who think they're good – go in order to return to the big city with tales of derring-do. The innocent-sounding Clair's Way turns out to be too tough for many. As one visitor said: 'Clair's is the most kick-ass run anywhere around – you could ski it all day and not get bored. Tired yes, but not bored.' People tend to ski it too fast, and a slip here can mean a long plunge. The resort's steepest mogul run, K27, is another major challenge.

A new learning centre has enhanced Hunter's claim to be 'a great place to learn to ski, snowtube, snowshoe and/or snowboard'. There are no fewer than 13 mountain restaurants (including a bistro called Van Winkle's) – far more than you would expect out west in a Rocky Mountain resort. And these days there is on-slope accommodation, too – at the recently opened Kaatskill Mountain Club, complete with spa and fitness centre – to 'eliminate the need to pile everyone into the car after a day on the mountain'. This makes all the difference. Few people would want to rush home to New York City while there is snow to be skied and mountain air to be breathed. Besides, it's a big enough ski area to need two or three days to explore it properly.

ABOVE: **From skate-boarding to snowboarding: swapping the streets of New York for the snowy steeps of the state's biggest ski area.**

BELOW: **Seeing the trails from the trees: Hunter Mountain Ski Bowl has three mountain faces with slopes to engross all levels.**

# Windham Mountain

BY ARNIE WILSON

The town of Windham is located along the banks of the Batavia Kill River, in upstate New York's Catskills region. It features some delightful colonial and Victorian architecture and eclectic restaurants that echo the best of Manhattan. Windham Mountain was opened by private investors in 1960 as Cave Mountain Ski Area. It was once described as 'a private club for city escapees'. In 2005 it was sold to a consortium of local skiers and investors.

Windham provides a fascinating contrast with its neighbour, Hunter Mountain (see pages 156–57), less than half an hour away. Whereas Hunter is bustling, busy and vibrant in a very New York City way, Windham is quieter (except when the snow guns are blitzing the slopes during the night), smoother, more restrained, more discreet and more private. There is little crossover between the two resorts, which, in a way, rather resembles the contrast between the neighbouring Utah resorts of Deer Valley and Park City Mountain Resort – right down to the valet parking. And

there are definitely more helmets per acre at the much-more-macho Hunter than Windham, regardless of the relative terrain.

'We are very different from Hunter', says Kirt Zimmer, Windham's sales and marketing chief, 'yet the yin-yang works well for both. Inevitably, people end up feeling more comfortable at one resort or the other and I'm glad the Catskills can offer more than one experience. Even though Windham is 'upscale', that doesn't make it dull.'

Families – often second-home owners – seem to thrive here. The resort even has a

'Family of the Year' campaign. Families trekking here from New York City are the first to appreciate the area's rural charms: an article in America's *Ski* magazine talks of 'urban warriors who hack their way through city-traffic snarls to emerge, gasping with relief, on Interstate 87, the main artery connecting zippy downstate to supposedly sleepy upstate'. For those without second homes, the resort owns and operates the Winwood Inn, on Main Street in town.

The skiing takes place on the north face of Cave Mountain, in the Northern Catskill Mountains' High Peaks. The vertical drop of 488m (1,600ft) is one of the highest in the Catskills. There's a total of 42 trails (set in 99ha/245 skiable acres), of which eight runs are open for night skiing on Thursdays through to Sundays. Much of the skiing is enhanced by stands of birch, maple, oak, beech and several varieties of pine. There is one delightful stand of white birch that mountain-lovers find 'almost mesmerizing'. This is 'East Coast' skiing at its best.

One really unusual aspect of Windham's skiing is that just about every run begins with the letter W, from Wanderer (a green run, with stirring views of the surrounding countryside) and Why Not (black diamond) to Way to Go (green) and Wonderfully Wicked

**A quiet day at Windham Mountain. Unlike its bustling neighbour Hunter, Windham's slopes are usually less crowded, adding a little serenity to the scene.**

(black diamond). Waltz, Whisper and Wrangler are blues. Double-black diamond trails include The Wall, Upper Wipeout and Upper Wolverine. The longest is Wraparound, 4km (2¼ miles) and the most curiously named Wheelchair (whose upper section is also a double black).

No one seems quite sure how this run got its name, but it's not a bad-taste joke suggesting that if you come unstuck here you might get badly hurt. Indeed, Kirt Zimmer points out that Windham is home to the Adaptive Sports Foundation, one of the largest programmes for skiers and riders with disabilities in the country. 'For many years they were located in our base lodge', he says, 'but they recently built a gorgeous 743m² (8,000ft²) building slightly uphill from our lodge. We built a new trail and lift to connect the two. Many families come here specifically because they have a family member with a disability, and this programme accommodates that need.'

Beginners tend to gravitate to the skiers' right of the area, while advanced skiers and riders prefer the steep cruising to their left. There are three parks, all open to skiers and boarders: The Park is located on Warm Up, the Jib Park on Lower White Way, and the Pipe Park en route to the 183-m (600-ft) long halfpipe is on Wilbur. There's also snow-tubing at the Mountain Top Adventure Park, with 12 lanes, three lifts and a base lodge, with night-tubing on Thursdays, Fridays and weekends.

With advance reservations, guests can ski the mountain with a guide for one hour before the lifts open on Saturdays, Sundays and holiday mornings – and on weekday powder days.

Visitors regard Windham as challenging for a relatively small mountain. One of the resort's more interesting enthusiasts is James Niehues, who has designed many of America's ski area trail maps – and as many as 120 worldwide. While working on Windham Mountain's map, he said: 'I am surprised by the scope of your mountain, and have noted

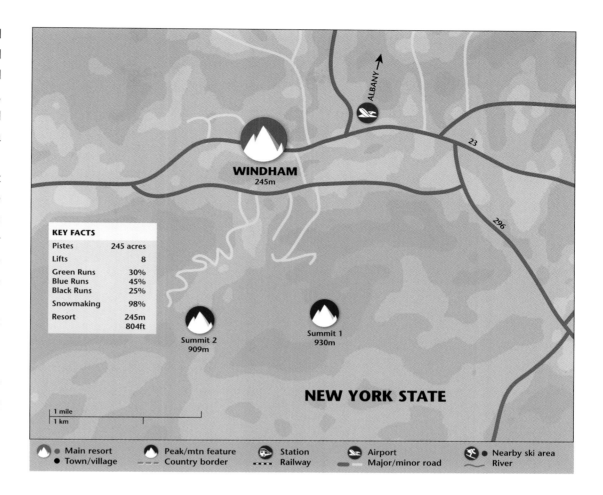

| KEY FACTS | |
|---|---|
| Pistes | 245 acres |
| Lifts | 8 |
| Green Runs | 30% |
| Blue Runs | 45% |
| Black Runs | 25% |
| Snowmaking | 98% |
| Resort | 245m 804ft |

the many facets that would offer the skier quite a variety of skiing. These, he said, include 'multi-faced slopes' and the 'vast width from one side to the other'. He should know.

Windham is a family-friendly resort. The Children's Learning Center offers classes and lessons for children aged 4–12, no matter what their skill level.

# VERMONT

# Killington

BY PEGGY SHINN

Ski resorts in the eastern United States do not come any larger than Killington Resort in central Vermont. With seven mountains and six base areas sprawling 18km (11 miles) across the Green Mountain Range, the resort is like a multi-screen cinema with everything from family matinées to extreme ski flicks on the marquee. Since it opened in 1958, Killington has strived to be all things to all people, an everyman's – and everywoman's – mountain. And mostly, it succeeds. If it has a flaw, it's the lack of a really central village.

Located on the snowy slopes beneath Vermont's second-highest peak, Killington has become the superlative ski experience in the eastern United States. It has the most trails in the east (200), the largest vertical drop 957m (3,050ft), the highest lift-served terrain (1,293m/4,241ft) and the longest and steepest trail in the east – the 366-m (1,200-ft)

Outer Limits. Killington's real draw, however, is that everyone – from diehard locals who would sooner miss a couple hours of work than even one faceshot of fresh powder, to families who drive from Boston or New York so their little ones can learn to ski – can find terrain to suit their ability.

Beginners and intermediates are happiest on the slopes of Snowshed and Rams Head. The Snowshed chairlift is a quick walk from the 200-room Killington Grand Resort Hotel. With its gentle sweeping intermediate runs – including a beginners' terrain park – and a Magic Carpet lift at the base, Rams Head is Family Central. Experts head to Killington Peak and Bear Mountain for double-black-diamond plunges and thickly forested glades. Bear Mountain is also home to several terrain parks, the superpipe and the famed Outer Limits trail. On sunny days, the deck at Bear's base lodge feels like a beach party, with a beer-drinking crowd happily, yet ruthlessly, hooting and hollering at skiers pounding down Outer Limit's moguled plunge.

Sunrise Mountain, next to Bear, is like a private ski club serving the only true ski-in/ski-out condominiums at Killington. Skye Peak and Snowdon peaks, reached from the Killington Base Lodge, have everything –

**VERMONT**

● SHERBURNE

← RUTLAND

PICO
1209m

Ramshead
670m

Snowdon Peak
1095m

BOSTON →

Bear Mountain
1005m

**KILLINGTON**
670m

**KEY FACTS**

| Pistes | 1,209 acres |
| Lifts | 33 |
| Green Runs | 26% |
| Blue Runs | 36% |
| Black Runs | 38% |
| Snowmaking | 775 acres |
| Resort | 670m |
| | 2,200ft |

2 miles
2 km

| | | | | |
|---|---|---|---|---|
| ● Main resort | ▲ Peak/mtn feature | Station | Airport | Nearby ski area |
| ● Town/village | --- Country border | ···· Railway | Major/minor road | River |

from the see-and-be-seen Superstar trail to the perfect-pitch Cruise Control. Physically separated from Killington (about 10 minutes drive by car), Pico Mountain is Killington Unplugged, a laid-back, less crowded ski area that's great for families.

Six of Killington's seven mountains are linked, but navigating this expanse of terrain can be challenging. At day's end, more than one skier has ended up at one base area while family and friends wait at another. Careful reading of trail signs can prevent such missteps. Another frustrating aspect of the resort is its advertised vertical drop: 957m (3,050ft), the most in the eastern US. However, only about 457m (1,500ft) can be counted as 'working' vertical. To ski the entire 957m (3,050ft) requires taking multiple lifts or meandering down a beginner run to the 'true' base at the little-used Skyeship Gondola Station on US Route 4.

The young and restless come to Killington for more than the skiing, though. When the lifts close, the action moves to the many watering holes along the Access Road, where pints of locally brewed Long Trail Ale and free chicken wings fuel the après-ski scene. As evening turns to night, those with enough energy to ski by day and dance by night move to the Wobbly Barn or Pickle Barrel, two nightspots that attract big-name bands. Long after midnight, the last few stumble home to catch a few hours of sleep before the lifts open again. From Halloween to Easter (and even later), Killington's Access Road hops with more nightlife than some major cities.

And this leads to what Killington is perhaps best known for: its long season. Thanks to a vast snowmaking operation, the resort often opens as early as October and closes in May. For those who can't wait for winter, who want to carve turns down ribbons of white framed by fall foliage, and then still haven't had enough come spring, making the season's last turns on the slushy moguls of Superstar, Killington isn't all things – it's the only thing.

**The Killington basin receives on average 635cm (20¾ft) of natural snow every winter. Most slopes are groomed, but skiers can still find fresh powder the day after a storm.**

# Jay Peak

BY LESLIE WOIT

This low-lying Vermont classic, situated 11km (7 miles) south of the Canadian border, has been defying the conventions of eastern seaboard skiing for 50 years. In 1955, a few locals and a parish priest gave birth to Jay Peak. If they were wishing for snow, their prayers were answered.

The mountain's unique location and geographical features make it subject to wondrous lake effect and orographic lift – science-speak for when moisture, temperature and terrain combine beautifully to make snow – lots of it. Be it climatic circumstance or divine intervention, Jay is blessed with more of the white stuff – often in powder form – than anywhere else in the region; its 889cm (350 inches) a year is twice as much as some Vermont resorts. It also features more than 610m (2,000ft) of vertical, an impressive system of glades and chutes, and the only aerial tram in New England. There you have it: east meets west at Jay Peak.

If the snow feels west coast, the landscape that surrounds it is pure east. Rural Vermont is a tapestry of winding scenic roads, pleasant wooded valleys, and brightly painted farmhouses selling homemade cheese and maple syrup. From Montreal, the journey to Jay is 1.5 hours; from Burlington, Vermont, it's a little over an hour. The country roads twist and curve rather more than you might expect, and, perhaps since Vermont bans billboards, its road signs are unusually discreet in sympathy. They are pretty, but it is also pretty easy to get lost.

Once there, however, you are free to roam 76 pistes, four terrain parks and, most obligingly, the 40ha (100 acres) of ungroomed and often powder-laden glades for which Jay is famous. In a state that has more cows than

**A freak of nature: Jay's powder position is unique on the East Coast.**

humans, finding room to move at Jay is as easy as finding steak on the menu. Though the area is small by Colorado standards, the network of glades is large enough so that you can often ski from top to bottom without seeing another person. It's even wild enough to warrant a backcountry 'policy': you are free to explore all the glades within the Jay Peak boundary, but make sure you have a partner and the necessary skills to do so safely.

At Jay's highest point, the top of the tram (cable-car) reveals a 360-degree panorama of four US states, and Canada to the north. From this peak leads the lovely scenic intermediate run, Vermonter, and the area's longest trail, the 5-km (3-mile) Ullr's Dream. Across terrain that blankets two peaks, challenging runs like the black-diamond groomers The Jet and Upper River Quai are mixed among steep glades like Timbuktu, at the very perimeter edge of the area accessed by the triple chair.

Though Jay is known for its steep chutes, beginners need not fear the deep abyss. Gentle glades are available too, like Moon Walk Woods, a wide, easy, treed area near the base of the tram. For those attempting their very first turns, The Zone is Jay Peak's dedicated learning area; it includes four lifts serving 11 trails and introductory glades. Two beginner terrain parks, the Grom Park and Rail Garden, are also located in The Zone, just off the Interstate trail on Tramside.

So whether novice or expert looking for an appropriate on-slope challenge, Jay can tick your box any day. Come night, life is quiet and centres around a few beers and a burger at the simple Jay Hotel or perhaps the Scrabble board in your townhouse or chalet. Ski-in/ski-out accommodation in the compact resort offers many new luxury chalets with fireplace, whirlpool and sauna. It really only gets busy here at weekends and holidays when folks from nearby Montreal and US cities roll into town in search of fresh snow.

Less than an hour's drive south of Jay are a handful of other resorts, including Stowe (see

pages 164–165) and Smugglers' Notch (see pages 166–167), making the area ideal for a multi-stop tour, though Jay's unique assortment of hard-to-believe-powder and glades make it tough to beat after a storm. And when that happens, and you awake to find a couple of feet of fresh snow on your car roof

*Take in the awe-inspiring views of four American states and Canada.*

in the morning, you may have to remind yourself that you're in Vermont. Just remember to pack your own road map – the road signs barely give the secret away.

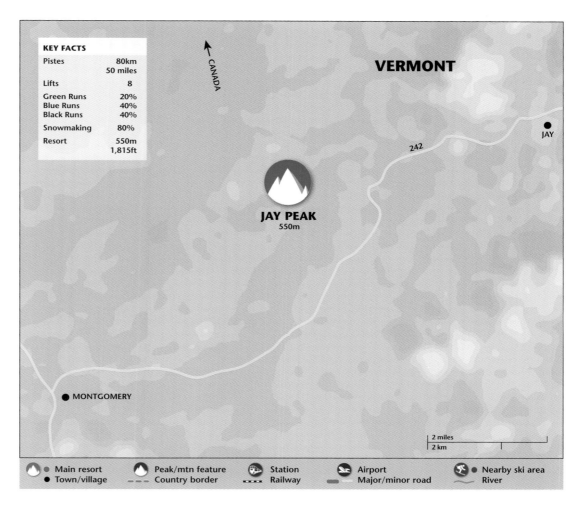

| KEY FACTS | |
|---|---|
| Pistes | 80km |
| | 50 miles |
| Lifts | 8 |
| Green Runs | 20% |
| Blue Runs | 40% |
| Black Runs | 40% |
| Snowmaking | 80% |
| Resort | 550m |
| | 1,815ft |

CANADA

VERMONT

JAY

242

**JAY PEAK**
550m

MONTGOMERY

2 miles
2 km

| | | | |
|---|---|---|---|
| Main resort | Peak/mtn feature | Station | Nearby ski area |
| Town/village | Country border | Railway | Airport Major/minor road | River |

# Stowe

BY LESLIE WOIT

It's everyone's idea of a New England picture postcard: candy-coloured clapboard houses, a church spire reaching for the sky and Vermont's highest peak, Mount Mansfield, lovingly quilted with runs for all levels of skier and boarders.

Not just another cute face, this small town packs a punch when it comes to top-to-bottom runs that cover the gamut from groomers to bumps to nicely spaced glades. In 1937, the first lift – a rope tow powered by a Cadillac engine – ran 304m (1,000ft) up the Toll House Slope, and a lift ticket cost 50 cents. Since then, Stowe has developed into a sophisticated resort town that appeals to skiers and non-skiers alike. It boasts the longest average runs in the East and an impressive 80 per cent of the terrain is covered by snowmaking. More than 4,000 people now call it home.

A little haven in the hills, Stowe is chock-full of intriguing craft shops and art galleries begging to be browsed. Some 70 shops stand shoulder to shoulder with 40 restaurants – including many award-winning ones – making it a happening yet decidedly mellow place to eat, drink and play in the great outdoors. It's the kind of place that's custom-made for sleigh rides and long romps in the woods, preferably with a handsome dog if possible.

Should you require a bit more hands-on attention, several luxury hotels are home to decadent spas. The Stoweflake and the Green Mountain Inn offer two of the best.

## Twin peaks

Located 15 minutes outside the town, two separate mountains, connected by a free shuttle bus, offer two quite different experiences. The largest is Mount Mansfield, served by five lifts and peppered with terrain that will make your ski socks damp in anticipation. Stowe is rightly proud of what they call the Front Four. A quadruple cluster of double-black diamond steeps that divide the cool cats from the scaredy ones – from 34 degrees on

**Ski under the stars on the slopes of Mount Mansfield. Ride the gondola above the lighted slopes and ski down the Perry Merrill and Gondolier trails.**

**The prettiest postcard you can sleep in first and send in the morning. The town of Stowe is one charming photo opportunity.**

Starr, to Goat's moguls that kick, to National's wide and big bumps, and more than 1,524m (5,000ft) of part groomed, part wildness on Lift Line – these are some of the East's most testing trails. There are also a bevy of nicely groomed intermediate trails. On the far southern edge is the area's longest trail, Toll Run, 6km (4 miles) of smooth green that will treat beginners – and the rest – to a scenic cruise.

For novice skiers and riders, Spruce Peak – on the opposing side of the valley – provides nearly an entire mountain full of sedate skiing and boarding, with three new lifts installed in the recent years. Learners will be gently tended at Little Spruce, a mercifully short few steps in ski boots from the Spruce Base Lodge. Once warmed up, they can progress easily to adjacent Big Spruce. Across the two mountain areas are 48 runs, totalling 63km (39 miles), which, if you ski them all, will earn you a certificate to verify the feat.

Many other outdoor activities vie for attention at Stowe. Off the beaten path, one of the hottest trends is to set out into the quiet wilderness on 5km (3 miles) of snowshoe trails. Stowe also has 35km (22 miles) of groomed and 40km (25 miles) of backcountry trails for cross-country skiers. There's also ice-fishing, as well as night skiing several evenings each week.

## SPRUCE PEAK

*More plans are afoot. Currently under construction, Spruce Peak at Stowe is a new slopeside village with a hotel, chalets and condos, a golf course, pool and spa, and a new ski-lift. This new ski-in/ski-out development will shift some of the accommodation opportunities away from the current town hub, making both skiing and après-ski on the mountain possible. Of the many diversions on offer, the most lip-licking one is a visit to nearby Ben & Jerry's Ice Cream Factory. Free for children 12 and under, and only $2 for adults, a dip into the place that brought Phish Food® to the world is entirely justified. And there's no lack of ways in Stowe to burn off the calories afterwards.*

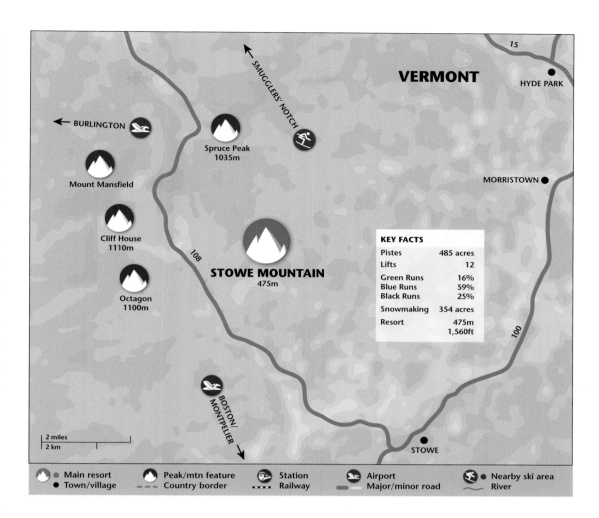

| KEY FACTS | |
|---|---|
| Pistes | 485 acres |
| Lifts | 12 |
| Green Runs | 16% |
| Blue Runs | 59% |
| Black Runs | 25% |
| Snowmaking | 354 acres |
| Resort | 475m |
| | 1,560ft |

Main resort · Town/village — Peak/mtn feature · — — Country border — Station ···· Railway — Airport — Major/minor road — Nearby ski area · ⌇ River

Few queues mean open-treed runs are yours for the taking.

# Smugglers' Notch

BY ARNIE WILSON

Smugglers' Notch – aka 'Smuggs' – got its name when President Thomas Jefferson pushed the Embargo Acts of 1807 and 1808 through Congress, forbidding export trade with Britain. Settlers in Vermont, the Green Mountain State, protested. The remoteness, encircling forests and seeming impassability of the Long Trail made the area ideal for illicit trade. The 'Notch' refers to the pass wedged between neighbouring Stowe's Mt. Mansfield (the highest peak in Vermont) and Sterling Mountain, an only slightly less imposing neighbour. (Smugglers' Notch Resort and its pedestrianized village are located in wide meadows below the Notch).

Skiing Red Fox Glades on Madonna Mountain at Smugglers' Notch.

More than a century later, in 1920, the Notch was again used for smuggling when Congress passed the 18th Amendment to the Constitution prohibiting the manufacture and sale of alcoholic beverages. But the thirsty New Englanders missed their moonshine, and found the Notch a ready way to get their liquor from Canada. Local caves and caverns were used to store it.

Much more recently, Smugglers' Notch had yet another clever idea: to distinguish itself from the many other ski areas in Vermont. It decided to go all out in its attempts to appeal to families. The result is 'America's Number One Family Resort', a happy sort of place with sufficient children's programmes to keep an army of children contented, enabling parents to enjoy the skiing (and the après-ski, too).

But it would certainly be a mistake to assume that the Smugglers' Notch family ambience excludes challenges on its three linked mountains, which share 78 trails and enjoy northern Vermont's biggest vertical drop (796m/2,610ft). Indeed, this was brought home when the resort reminded visitors that 'family is not synonymous with wimpy'. And when you hear that The Black

Hole, a 'steeper-than-hell' trail on Madonna Mountain ('ski it if you dare!') is the only triple-black-diamond run in the east, you get the message. As one skier commented when the run opened: 'Just for families? This mountain will whip any expert into shape, guaranteed!'

There is a wealth of other off-piste skiing, particularly in the woods, some of which should only be attempted in the company of someone with local knowledge: the unwary backcountry skier can be confronted by dangerous cliff bands and ledges.

Snowboarders have plenty to challenge them, too. There's a 107-m (350-ft) halfpipe, and the Birch Run terrain park is peppered with hits, rolls and spines. And for the uninitiated, there's a 'night school' for boarders at the curiously named Sir Henry's Learning and Fun Park.

Smugglers' claims to guarantee that each member of the family will learn to ski or snowboard, or will improve their technique – regardless of ability level – or the entire lesson portion of that person's vacation package will be refunded.

Of the three linked peaks, Madonna, at 1,110m (3,640ft) is the highest and most challenging, with steep, double-fall line runs, ledges and some excellent glade skiing, including the legendary Doctor Dempsey's,

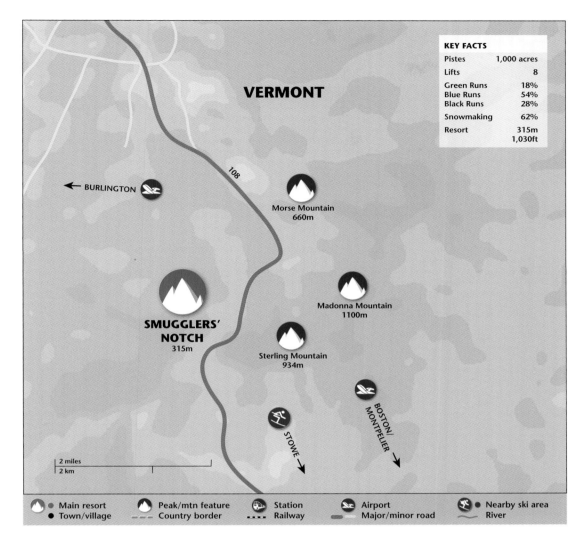

VERMONT

BURLINGTON

108

Morse Mountain
660m

Madonna Mountain
1100m

SMUGGLERS'
NOTCH
315m

Sterling Mountain
934m

STOWE

BOSTON/
MONTPELIER

2 miles
2 km

Main resort ● Town/village    Peak/mtn feature --- Country border    Station ⋯ Railway    Airport ▬ Major/minor road    Nearby ski area River

named after one of the resort's founders. From the top there are magnificent views across the Champlain Valley, the Worcester Range, neighbouring Mount Mansfield and some of Stowe's trails. In past years Smuggs and Stowe have been officially linked. The cognoscenti can still find their way on skis from one to the other but there is no reciprocal lift pass.

Sterling Mountain is predominantly for intermediates, and Morse Mountain, directly above the resort village, is the best place for beginners and young families. The Morse Highlands area has five out-of-the-way trails with a dedicated lift and base lodge. It is also the location for the Jib and Jump Park.

Altogether, the ski terrain covers 125ha (310 acres) of marked trails and glades, with an additional 283ha (700 acres) of terrain accessible in between, giving a total of 405ha (1,000 acres), claimed to be the largest ski area in Vermont.

## Family fun

Family attractions include the Treasures Child Care Center, which accommodates up to 85 children daily, and 'Kids' Night Out', which offers parents an evening alone while their children enjoy 'dinner and fun' with the Treasures staff. Some parents escape to the Birch Room restaurant upstairs at the Hearth and Candle – just about the only place in the whole resort where children are neither seen nor heard: it is for adults only to enjoy a bit of rest and relaxtion.

The resort has a bewildering selection of family activities: a Discovery Dynamos Ski Camp, Adventure Rangers Ski or Snowboard Camps, a Notch Squad Ski or Snowboard Camp, and Mountain Explorers Ski or Snowboard Instruction. Evening events include Nightspiker volleyball, The FunZone, tube sliding, and a 'Glowbal Dance Party'. An 'Outer Limits at the Yurt' for older teens and 'Teen Alley' for 13–15-year-olds are

*New England gets its fair share of fresh powder, opening up acres of excellent tree skiing. 'Smuggs' boasts the only triple-black-diamond run in the east.*

open daily. A 'family-fun venue' and adult entertainment are offered nightly. Events for parents and children range from a Bingo Blast, Showtime Theatre and an Old Time Tube Sliding Party, to a Torchlight Parade and Fireworks.

Prohibition Park, 1km (⅔ mile) long, is one of the biggest parks in Vermont. It has multiple hits for intermediate and expert riders, including table tops, hips, spines and a 107-m (350-ft) Superpipe. Other terrain parks for those graduating to 'big air' include one for intermediates and the Jibs and Jumps Park for beginners. Two hectares (5 acres) on Morse Mountain make up the Learning and Fun Park. Other available activities include cross-country, snow-shoeing, Nordic walking, snowmobiling and dogsledding.

# Mad River Glen

BY ARNIE WILSON

Mad River Glen is one of a kind. Even the name, with skiing on Stark Mountain, simply adds to this Vermont resort's mystique as New England's most intriguing cult resort. The skiing is rough, tough, in your face and pretty much as nature intended. Mad River is a relic, and anxious to stay that way. 'Ski it if you can' is its slogan.

The ski area was once owned and run by the indomitable Betsy Pratt, a pipe-puffing widow rarely seen out of her navy-blue parka, who these days runs the Inn at Mad River Barn. Once described as 'one of the most stubborn, most opinionated, most exasperating, most in-love-with-the-mountains people I have

In your face – literally! 'Ski it if you can' is this cult resort's slogan. The slopes at Mad River Glen are raw, wild and exhilarating.

ever met', she quit in 1995, but her resolute personality explains a lot about the continuing ethos of the resort: gnarly, funky, retro, no-holds barred. Cissies need not apply.

## Paradise et al

While many resorts in the US have gone the corporate way, with state-of-the-art high-speed quads dotting their mountains, Mad River, a co-operative venture, has stubbornly – and refreshingly – anchored itself in the past. Some of the terrain, particularly in the trees at Paradise (purgatory for some!) at the top of the mountain, is seat-of-the-pants stuff, where young blades test themselves on steep, gnarly rough-and-tumble slopes in the woods. Paradise epitomizes Mad River's

terrain – and attitude. 'Many ski resorts would demand that you hire a guide to lead you down this hidden gem' advises the ski area. 'At Mad River, if you can find Paradise, you are welcome to enjoy it. But beware! A snow serpent lurks here – and has been known to tempt many a hapless skier into an early descent into hell.' Jumping 1.5 m (5ft) over a frozen waterfall in the upper reaches is an option, but although it's difficult to find other ways down, this 'mean-looking, jagged agglomeration of rock one storey high, encased in a 30-cm (1-ft) thick layer of ice' can just about be avoided, although it stretches across much of Paradise. The terrain below is populated with white birches and choppy bumps – a difficult landing. The easier

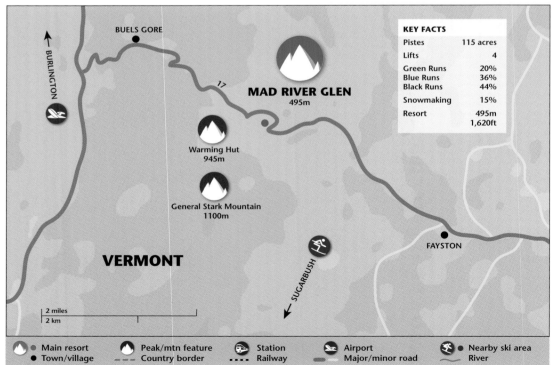

BUELS GORE

17

**MAD RIVER GLEN**
495m

BURLINGTON

Warming Hut
945m

General Stark Mountain
1100m

**VERMONT**

SUGARBUSH

FAYSTON

| KEY FACTS | |
|---|---|
| Pistes | 115 acres |
| Lifts | 4 |
| Green Runs | 20% |
| Blue Runs | 36% |
| Black Runs | 44% |
| Snowmaking | 15% |
| Resort | 495m |
| | 1,620ft |

2 miles
2 km

| | Main resort | | Peak/mtn feature | | Station | | Airport | | Nearby ski area |
|---|---|---|---|---|---|---|---|---|---|
| | Town/village | | Country border | | Railway | | Major/minor road | | River |

route is called 'the ladies' tee', but if you take it you won't receive a 'Ski It If You Can' bumper sticker, or have any bragging rights.

Another tough run, The Chute, can be found on the way down from the Ski Patrol HQ at Stark's Nest. 'Do or die bumps' warns the resort – 'in front of a highly opinionated audience!' There are easy runs too, of course: many are to be found in 'Birdland' – including Duck, Lark, Loon, Robin and Wren.

## Glades

Only a few of the mountain's gladed runs – favourites like Lynx, Paradise and Gazelle Glades – show up on the trail map. There is tree skiing (woods skiing might be a more accurate description) all over the mountain, from the upper Single to Birdland, but the mountain leaves it up to the skiers to find it for themselves. 'We believe that tree skiing should be an exciting adventure that involves some exploration and effort', explains the marketing director Eric Friedman. 'When there are trail signs pointing to a glade, the experience loses some of that excitement. There is nothing quite like stumbling across an untracked descent.'

It is important to stress that the Mad River Glen Ski Patrol does not patrol the woods, and skiers must enter and exit them via an open trail. The resort asks visitors not to ski in the woods after 3pm ('we don't want to look for you in the dark!') and to ski with at least two other people: in case of a mishap, one person can get help and one can stay with the injured skier.

The deliberate lack of sophistication is what many visitors find refreshing here. The fact that Mad River clings (metaphorically) to a single chair as its main artery up the mountain is indicative of its old-fashioned philosophy. The resort first cranked up its now famous chair on 11 December 1948. Almost 60 years on, it's still a single, and such an icon that, although it is being renovated, it remains a single chair. Yet there is one major surprise: a ski area where you might imagine snowboarders would be in their

Hard-core skiers in Vermont are keen to remind visitors that Mad River Glen is 'not a resort'. This is skiing as nature intended.

element is the only resort in the east that bans them. The occasional snowboarder does sneak in the back way and 'streak', prompting cries of 'snowboarder on the hill!' Typically, the lone invader will do a 'straight shot' and ride straight out of the ski area again, doubtless to brag to his friends that 'no damn ski resort is gonna keep me out'. Intriguingly, snowboarding *was* allowed briefly in the late 1980s, but banned again in the winter of 1991.

Again, it was an edict from Betsy Pratt that helps the ban live on. 'Snowboarding on a ski mountain is like playing croquet on the 18th green', she once said. 'You can do it, but I don't think it's appropriate.' She had a similar take on snowmaking. 'I hate man-made snow', she would say. 'If you want snowmaking, go ski somewhere else.' In fact, the resort

was an early pioneer of snowmaking – but only to cover 15 per cent of the mountain, as obtaining a good supply of water is a problem.

Roland Palmedo, the resort's original founder, envisioned a ski area where 'sport, not profit would be the overriding concern'. Palmedo believed that 'a ski area is not just a place of business or a mountain amusement park. It is a winter community whose members are dedicated to the enjoyment of the sport.' Nonetheless, the gung-ho, no-nonsense attitude towards the skiing here has paid off. Mad River makes a profit most years. The area's shares, once $1,500, were $1,750 apiece at the latest count.

# NEW HAMPSHIRE

# Loon Mountain

BY ARNIE WILSON

Like its sister resort, Waterville Valley, Loon Mountain epitomizes all that is good about 'east coast' skiing. It's a charming, friendly place with a variety of interesting slopes and a tangible feel-good ambience. The name refers not to a kamikaze skier, but the magnificent white-speckled black waterfowl (aka the noble Great Northern Diver) once reputed to nest by a large pond on the summit.

Loon, which likes to call itself 'Gravity's Playground', prides itself on both its picturesque setting in the White Mountain National Forest and its New England hospitality. The resort was founded by Sherman Adams, a former logger, Governor of New Hampshire and aide to President Dwight D. Eisenhower. Adams, an outdoorsman for 25 years, was the so-called 'walking boss', snowshoeing from one logging camp to another all winter long. And when it was time to name Loon's trails, Adams used evocative logging terms such as Picaroon, Cant Dog, Snubber, Scaler, Skidder – and, of course, Walking Boss, the name of one of Loon's finest runs.

Loon Mountain is located a few miles east of Lincoln, at the foot of the Kancamaugus Highway, on United States Forest Service land, surrounded by Loon Village below. A delightful and unusual attraction is the narrow gauge, wood-burning train that shuttles skiers between the two base lodges.

Although accommodation is available in slopeside condominiums, mountain homes and a hotel, the nearby towns of Lincoln and North Woodstock offer more than 13,000 rooms, as well as dining, outlet shopping and entertainment.

There are currently 46 mainly intermediate downhill runs, along with five skiable glades, and 12 more trails under development. The longest run is 3.6km (2¼ miles), with a vertical drop of 640m (2,100ft). The trail network offers a good variety of slopes – many user-friendly, some less friendly, and they're relatively uncrowded too, because when Loon has sold around 6,000 tickets, no more skiers or boarders are allowed on the mountain. And if you express dissatisfaction with your day before 11am you'll be given a voucher to ski or board for free during your next visit. Loon has 35km (22 miles) of cross-country skiing and snowshoeing tracks, too. Night-tubing is also a popular activity.

North Peak, served by the recently installed Express Quad, has Loon's highest skiing, and accesses the celebrated Walking Boss trail as well as other long, cruising runs. With a healthy vertical drop, most of Loon's more challenging slopes are at the top of the

Taking a break from Loon Mountain's "enjoyable intermediate terrain" at Camp III.

mountain, where the North Peak triple chair deposits the more adventurous skiers and riders. From here they have a choice between two steep black runs, Upper Walking Boss and Upper Flume, or the mellower alternative, Sunset.

Much of the rest of the mountain is devoted to enjoyable intermediate terrain. The quickest way to reach it is to take the four-passenger gondola to Summit Lodge, which is also a useful fast-track route to North Peak. From the top, beware of taking the trails to the right unless you are prepared for some testing terrain: East Basin, located between the Summit Lodge and Camp III, provides Loon's steepest trails, some with tricky double fall-lines. These include Triple Trouble, Big Dipper, Angel Street, Skidder and Basin Street.

Skier's left from Summit Lodge brings you to the more benign side of the mountain, with any number of intermediate trails, including the upper sections of the exhilarating Flying Fox trail, Picked Rock and Speakeasy. There is even a beginner's run all the way down Bear Claw to the bottom of the mountain. 'Never-evers' can move onto the Kissin' Cousin double-chair at the Governor Adams Base Lodge, and try their luck on Snubber and Sarsaparilla.

Loon Mountain is also pressing ahead with its expansion westwards into South Peak Resort, part of an expansion programme that will include four new lifts and 12 new trails. The first stage is due for completion in the winter of 2007–08.

Loon has several terrain parks, where the resort strives to live up to its 'never the same ride twice' philosophy. 'Loon's park curators and groomers are always dreaming up new hits, tricks, jumps, banks and gates', says the resort. Loon Mountain Park (LMP), between Picaroon and Picked Rock trails, is 1,097m (3,600ft) in length, and is Loon's signature park, with a 'super-dialled' superpipe, U-box, Battleship box, S-Rail, A-Frame Box and a large Wall Ride. It's accessible from the Gondola, Kancamagus quad chair and the Seven Brothers triple chair. The recently

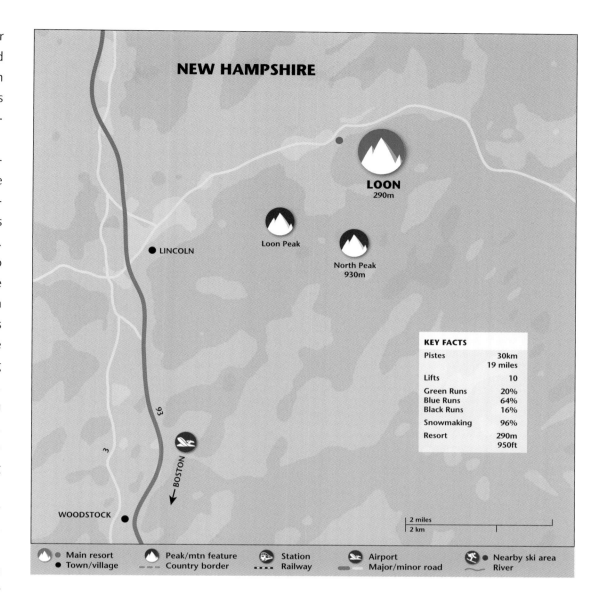

| KEY FACTS | |
|---|---|
| Pistes | 30km |
| | 19 miles |
| Lifts | 10 |
| Green Runs | 20% |
| Blue Runs | 64% |
| Black Runs | 16% |
| Snowmaking | 96% |
| Resort | 290m |
| | 950ft |

installed Burton Progression Park, featuring rails and funboxes and 'Stop and Drop Zones', is on Loon's Little Sister trail. A smaller park on the Northstar trail is designed to help riders learn terrain park skills. The Northstar Park includes a minipipe, hips, rollers, table-tops and step-downs, plus smaller versions of LMP's rails and boxes. There's a 122-m (400-ft) halfpipe near the base of the Gondola.

Children aged five and under ski or board free, and there are reductions for older children. Loon Mountain's Children's Center organizes children's lessons, including the Kinder Bear Camp, Adventure camp and Ski Mite Workshop. The centre includes a day-care area, nursery and rental shop for skiers aged three to six.

Loon has a maximum of 6,000 skiers on mountains which include five skiable glades and 46 downhill trails – with another 12 being added.

# Waterville Valley

BY ARNIE WILSON

The mountains of New Hampshire are hauntingly beautiful in a way that is totally different from the Rockies. There is something quite magical, even mysterious, about the misty woods of the east, and local skiers, who've been enjoying these mountains for some 75 years, are fiercely proud of their winter inheritance. Waterville Valley's catchphrase is 'Altitude without the Attitude'. It's difficult to escape slogans here: one of New Hampshire's is 'Our landscape is unspoiled – our visitors are anything but', while another proclaims: 'The state too great to abbreviate!'

Waterville Valley, 18km (11 miles) from Interstate 93 at the end of Route 49, officially opened for lift-served skiing in 1966, but locals had been hiking up since before World War II. At just over 1,219m (4,000ft), Mount Tecumseh has a 616-m (2,020-ft) vertical drop and 52 tree-lined trails, with 100 per cent snowmaking, along with some excellent gladed skiing. The longest run is 5km (3 miles). Waterville Valley has been host to 13 World Cup alpine ski events since 1969, including the World Cup Finals in 1991. There are 11 lifts, including a high-speed quad that whisks skiers to the mountain-top in just seven minutes.

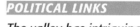

**POLITICAL LINKS**

*The valley has intriguing political links: in 1918, President Woodrow Wilson designated the White Mountains a US National Forest: 9,307ha (23,000 acres) of forest surrounding the valley were purchased by the US Government and became part of White Mountain National Forest. Today, some of those public lands are Waterville Valley's ski slopes.*

*When President Franklin D. Roosevelt announced a plan to create a Civilian Conservative Corps to alleviate unemployment and 'perform useful work on government land', the Waterville Valley Association recruited Nathaniel Goodrich to draw up plans for a ski area on Mount Tecumseh. He said: 'Anyone who could get to the top and down again on skis would get a tremendous kick out of it, if it were not so difficult that it was exhausting and dangerous.'*

**'Unspoiled landscape – spoiled visitors'. A skier cruises effortlessly down one of the resort's wide-open glades.**

## Around the trails

The first trails carved up the side of Mount Tecumseh were made-over logging roads. After Goodrich's observations about how challenging the mountain was, the first trail – Sel's Choice, a black diamond run named after Sel Hannah, who plotted its course – was built on the easier side of the peak. Scramble, Express, Main Street and Treeline, the trails at the top of the ski area, accessed from the High Country double chair, are fairly gentle blues, with inspirational views of the surrounding countryside.

But when you get down to the upper mid-mountain 'Schwendi Hutte', you need to keep your wits about you and decide whether to bear right towards part of the mountain with some tough terrain, or ski left towards easier trails. By bearing right, you have the choice between more blue runs, such as Oblivion and No Grit, and some sterner stuff: Ciao and Gemma are both single blacks, while True Grit is a double-black worthy of John Wayne-style gung-ho. If you want to take no risks, turn left at the 'Schwendi Hutte', and head for unequivocally blue runs like Tangent, Periphery and Tippecanoe. White Caps, another blue, is also an option, but spits you out into more difficult terrain in The Chute or Upper Sel's Choice.

Mirroring Upper Sel on the other side of the White Peak Express Quad is a trail called Bobby's. It's a run everyone wants to say they have accomplished. Traditionally, Waterville Valley is where the Kennedy clan used to ski, and this mogul run is named after Robert Kennedy, the assassinated former US Attorney General and younger brother of President John F. Kennedy. Bobby Kennedy, a friend of the resort's founder, Tom Corcoran, was a regular visitor, and this was one of his favourite trails. Upper Bobby's is a fairly easy blue, but it turns a little nasty when it becomes Lower Bobby's – a double-black diamond gladed run.

Waterville Valley has four terrain parks: the 2.75-ha (7-acre) Exhibition Park, with jumps, rails and boxes; the beginners' Little Slammer

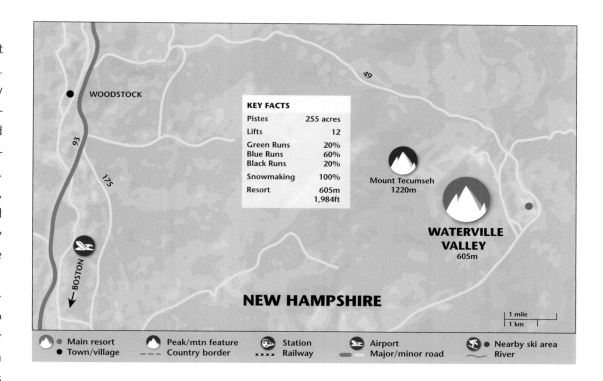

| KEY FACTS | |
|---|---|
| Pistes | 255 acres |
| Lifts | 12 |
| Green Runs | 20% |
| Blue Runs | 60% |
| Black Runs | 20% |
| Snowmaking | 100% |
| Resort | 605m 1,984ft |

WOODSTOCK

Mount Tecumseh 1220m

WATERVILLE VALLEY 605m

NEW HAMPSHIRE

1 mile
1 km

● Main resort
● Town/village

Peak/mtn feature
Country border

Station
Railway

Airport
Major/minor road

● Nearby ski area
River

Mini Park on Lower Periphery, with mini jumps, rails and boxes; the Boardercross Park located on Psyched, with 0.81ha (2 acres) of banked turns and rollers; and the celebrated Boneyard.

The 'Wicked Ditch of the East' is said to be New Hampshire's 'biggest and baddest pipe'. In recent years, Waterville has been experimenting with what it calls 'Wicked Venture Zones', introducing skiers and snowboarders of all ages to a variety of terrain challenges. 'WV' zones are situated throughout the mountain and allow visitors to progress through stations of varying difficulty. Small, medium and large features are available for bumps and glades. Certified instructors rotate through the zones to offer complementary advice at each zone.

There are also 105km (65 miles) of cross-country trails, and snowshoeing is becoming ever more popular too. Fundamentally, says the resort's management, Waterville Valley is a user-friendly mountain, 'with all the bells and whistles for families'.

**No end in sight – and none wanted. With 105km (65 miles) of cross-country trails, Waterville Valley provides a treat for downhill skiers who might want to take a day off from the slopes and try Nordic skiing.**

# Cannon Mountain ARNIE WILSON

Cannon Mountain is the toughest, bleakest and most challenging ski area in New Hampshire, a 'true skier's mountain' with classic narrow and twisty New England trails. Bode Miller, America's most powerful and successful skier so far this century, grew up in Franconia, 6.4km (4 miles) away, and learned to ski on Cannon's rugged, windswept terrain, where skiing can sometimes literally be 'a blast'. Surmounting this fierce reputation for challenging terrain – some wide open, some through forests of pine – may well help explain Miller's skiing strengths.

Cannon, designated a New Hampshire State Park, has the state's biggest vertical drop: 654m (2,146ft). The mountain's north-facing slopes tower above Echo Lake and Franconia Notch State Park, and there are no beginner slopes on the upper mountain. This is just as well, as even visiting intermediates and above can find Cannon daunting as local skiers jet past them down slopes that can often be icy.

One of the few state-owned ski areas in the United States, Cannon was built, like Waterville Valley, just before World War II by workers from the Civilian Conservation Corps. Cannon takes its name from a series of boulders which, when viewed from the foot of the mountain, are said to resemble an antique cannon. The first run cut, in 1933, was the Richard Taft slalom, said to be America's first race trail. Other early runs included Cannon, Ravine and Hardscrabble.

## A first

Cannon was the first ski area in the country with an aerial tramway (cable-car) – a rarity in the USA. The original tramway, which cost $250,000 when it was built in 1938, was replaced in 1980 at a cost of $4.7 million. One of the old cabins is now used as the entrance

**Down from the heights: Cannon's upper mountain can be bleak above the tree line, but pine forests offer some shelter from icy blasts on the lower slopes.**

to the New England Ski Museum, which features an extensive collection of historical ski equipment, clothing, film, photographs, literature and artwork. The new cable-car takes up to 80 people to the top of Cannon Mountain (1,280m/4,200ft) in eight minutes, affording impressive views of the neighbouring White Mountain National Forest. Well over six million people have travelled on the resort's trams. In addition, there are five lifts serving the 40 trails, plus glades. The longest run is 3.7km (2¼ miles). Cannon also has almost 64km (40 miles) of cross-country ski trails.

The village of Franconia, once home to the poet Robert Frost before it became famous for its links with Bode Miller, has some accommodation, but there is much more choice in the considerably larger town of Lincoln a few minutes' drive further south.

On the main mountain, most of the blue runs are down the middle, while the black diamond trails tend to launch themselves down the ski area perimeters. Cannon's most challenging slopes include the steep parallel Avalanche, Paulie's Folly and Zoomer trails, three of the so-called 'front five' runs, which you can see from the road. In recent years, aware that its reputation is a little daunting, the resort has opened more and more intermediate and beginner trails to try to strike a better balance.

Cannon has made great strides in trying to cater for families and beginners. It has expanded its Brookside area, which includes nine beginner and intermediate trails, including green trails like Deer Run, Bear Paw and Coyote Crossing, as well as Turkey Trot, Moose Alley and Rabbit Path, all gentle blues. On the main mountain, close to the lower section of the Peabody Express Quad chair and the Eagle Cliff chair, there are family runs like Gremlin and Toss Up, along with easy blues like Easy Link and Vista Way. Families have been enjoying Cannon for years – since 1938, in fact, when the resort opened, and there are many families with three or four generations of Cannon skiers.

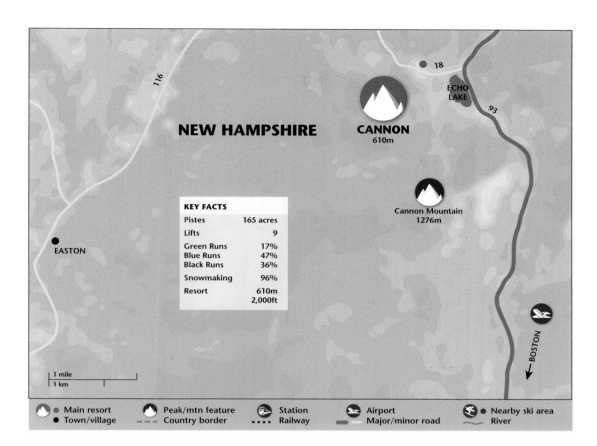

**NEW HAMPSHIRE**

**CANNON**
610m

**Cannon Mountain**
1276m

ECHO LAKE

EASTON

18

116

93

BOSTON

**KEY FACTS**

| | |
|---|---|
| Pistes | 165 acres |
| Lifts | 9 |
| Green Runs | 17% |
| Blue Runs | 47% |
| Black Runs | 36% |
| Snowmaking | 96% |
| Resort | 610m 2,000ft |

1 mile
1 km

| | |
|---|---|
| ● Main resort | |
| ● Town/village | |
| Peak/mtn feature | |
| – – – Country border | |
| Station | |
| ···· Railway | |
| Airport | |
| Major/minor road | |
| ● Nearby ski area | |
| River | |

## THE OLD MAN OF THE MOUNTAIN

*Cannon was originally known as Profile Mountain because of its famous landmark, The Old Man of the Mountain – New Hampshire's state symbol for many decades, which also appears on the state's licence plate and state quarter coin. Also known as 'the great stone face', the feature was a series of five granite cliff ledges which, when viewed from a certain angle, appeared to be the jagged profile of a face. The face, or 'profile', 366m (1,200ft) above Profile Lake, was 12m (40ft) tall and 7.6m (25ft) wide, and could be seen for many miles. Despite sustained attempts to preserve it, including the use of cables and spikes for most of the last century, the formation collapsed in May 2003 – finally broken up by centuries of wind, snow and rain, as well as freezing and thawing cycles.*

*There was so much sadness over the destruction of this treasured rock formation that people left flowers at the base of the cliffs, and some state legislators sought to change New Hampshire's state flag to include the profile. There were even suggestions that the Old Man should be replaced with a plastic replica, but the idea came to nothing.*

**Cannon Mountain was the first ski area in the US to build a tram (cable-car), which served the resort for 42 years until it was replaced in 1980. The modern version transports 80 skiers to the top of the mountain in under 10 minutes.**

# Sugarloaf BY HILARY NANGLE

Sugarloaf is a New England icon, a near-perfect triangle with ribbons of trails that cascade from its bald, 1,291m (4,237ft) summit. Thanks to the only above-the-tree-line, lift-serviced skiing in the eastern United States, the 'Loaf provides a taste of western terrain with a New England accent.

The treeless Snowfields is one distinguishing aspect of the northwestern Maine resort. Another is the 860-m (2,820-ft) vertical that permits a continuous top-to-bottom descent. All ability levels can descend from the summit after enjoying the head-swivelling views, which on a clear day range from Mount Washington, the East's tallest peak, to Mount Katahdin, Maine's highest one. Those adept at discerning other trail-lined peaks might spot nearby Saddleback Mountain (45 minutes away by road) or the 'Loaf's sister resort of Sunday River (about two hours by road). After taking in the views, beginners can ease their way down Timberline; intermediates can cruise the 6-km (3½ mile) Tote Road, and experts can fight gravity on White Nitro, where the slope literally falls from beneath one's skis.

Expert appeal is another thing that sets Sugarloaf apart. Locals say the path to Olympic gold goes down the famed Narrow Gauge, the only trail in the East that is FIS-approved for all four World Cup disciplines. That's validated by Carrabassett Valley Academy, the private school at the base of the mountain, where Bode Miller trained. While Sugarloaf has more than its fair share of buffed steeps, it's the ungroomed slopes

Sugarloaf's renowned for its lift-serviced snowfields, but below the treeless summit, ribbons of trails cascade through evergreens, birches and hardwoods.

and woods that tantalize bona fide experts. Skidder, another playground for CVA athletes, is a monstrous mogul run with few escape hatches. Winter's Way and Bubble Cuffer are human pinball machines, littered with natural obstacles that force skiers to ricochet from one mogul to the next. Sugarloaf's boundary-to-boundary policy opens the heavily wooded areas between trails to those who prefer snaking through the trees. Some glades are on the trail map, others can be found by following tracks into the woods. Hucksters preen and show in the enormous competition halfpipe and terrain park at the mountain's base; those still mastering the moves have other parks and easier glades for practice.

While Sugarloaf's expert terrain is legendary, the resort's 133 trails and glades mean there's plenty for everyone to experience. Intermediates do laps on the Super Quad, alternating runs on a triumvirate of corduroy cruisers – Tote Road, King's Landing and Hayburner. Even beginners have their own playground, and among the gentle trails served by the Whiffletree express quad are a few runs designated just for children. It's on these that the resort's mascots – Blueberry Bear, Amos Moose, Pierre the Lumberjack and Lemon the Yellow-nosed vole – often appear.

## The trails

In 1952, the appropriately named Amos Winter cut the mountain's first ski trails. While many older trails have been widened in the intervening years, most retain the ebb and flow of classic New England design. Names reflect the region's lumbering heritage: for example, Sluice (a chute that sent logs into a river), Widow Maker (a branch hung up in a tree) and Tote Road (a logging road).

Sugarloaf's remote location serves as both its biggest drawback and greatest asset. Getting here requires negotiating two-lane roads that weave through countryside dotted with tiny villages and wiggle through mountains. The reward, though, is uncrowded slopes. Seldom does the mountain feel really

**Sugarloaf's summit provides the only above-treeline, lift-serviced skiing in New England. From the open summit, trails for all abilities descend to the base village.**

busy, even during the annual Reggae Fest in mid-April, when live bands play outdoors. Even then, glades and less-utilized lifts deliver plenty of elbow room, and, this being Maine, it's a laidback crowd; pushing and shoving are rare.

Once here, a small base village provides everything necessary for a good vacation: a choice in restaurants and accommodation, a few bars and brewpubs, a good coffee shop and a handful of other shops. The compact size means the action is concentrated, so it's easy to find a spot that feels comfortable.

Speaking of comfort, Sugarloaf can be mind-numbingly cold, but that's ideal for snowmaking, which covers 94 per cent of the terrain and helps guarantee a mid-November opening. Natural snow falls most heavily in February, March and April, ensuring premium spring conditions. Spring is one big party, from the sun-worshippers soaking in the rays at the base to the T-shirt and shorts-clad skiers squeezing out as many runs as they can before the lifts close in late April.

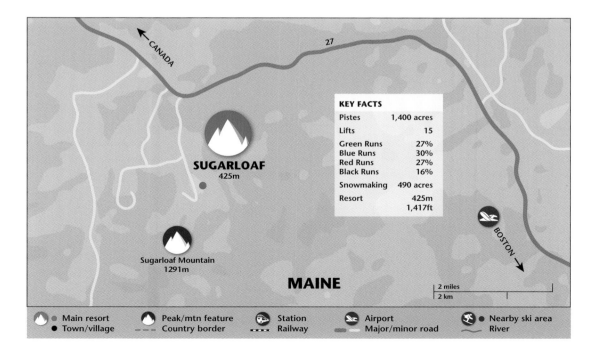

KEY FACTS

| Pistes | 1,400 acres |
| --- | --- |
| Lifts | 15 |
| Green Runs | 27% |
| Blue Runs | 30% |
| Red Runs | 27% |
| Black Runs | 16% |
| Snowmaking | 490 acres |
| Resort | 425m |
| | 1,417ft |

SUGARLOAF
425m

Sugarloaf Mountain
1291m

MAINE

2 miles
2 km

Main resort • Town/village — Peak/mtn feature - - - Country border — Station ···· Railway — Airport Major/minor road — Nearby ski area • River

# MAINE

# Sunday River

BY HILARY NANGLE

Perfect snow, and plenty of it, has earned Sunday River a blue-chip reputation among skiers. Between the 1970s and the 1990s, the then-owner Les Otten built the proverbial mountain out of a molehill, converting a small western Maine day area into one of the largest resorts in the eastern United States. He did so by investing heavily in snowmaking and grooming, expanding terrain and adding high-speed lifts. The result: a resort renowned for reliable skiing from its mid-November opening until its close, which can be as late as 1 May.

**Contributing to Sunday River's popularity are plentiful slopeside accommodation, a powerful snowmaking system and meticulous grooming.**

Sunday River sprawls across eight consecutive peaks, stretching 5km (3 miles) from White Cap to Jordan Bowl, and including Locke Mountain, Barker Mountain, Spruce Peak, North Peak, Aurora Peak and Oz. This massive resort is tucked in the folds of the Mahoosuc Range, where New Hampshire's White Mountains spill into Maine. Nearby are a couple of small areas, and about an hour's drive west is the resort-laden Mount Washington Valley (Wildcat, Attitash, Cranmore and Black Mountains), a cradle of eastern skiing.

While Mount Washington Valley's resorts are heavily into history, Sunday River is about the here-and-now. The River's powerful snowmaking system blankets 92 percent of the terrain. Its equally impressive grooming fleet massages that snow and any crud into corduroy. The resort recovers quickly from thaws or ice storms; that's important in a region where the weather can be finicky.

Sunday River is anchored by three base lodges and two hotels, with a wide range of restaurant options. Most skier services

are concentrated at South Ridge, the resort's biggest and busiest facility. Lacing the various parts together are 128 trails, 18 lifts, the on-mountain North Peak Lodge and a skier shuttle bus.

Most trails are wide boulevards cut for ease of snowmaking, grooming and taking advantage of the fall line. That's especially true for White Cap, on the southern end of the resort. White Heat, billed as the steepest, widest and longest trail in the East, is must-ski terrain for anyone who wants to score bragging rights at the office. The neighbouring trails of Shock Wave and Obsession aren't for the faint of heart or weak of quad either, and the glades in between deserve their double-black rating.

Moving across the resort, Locke and Barker – the resort's original peaks – and Spruce are all heavy on intermediate and expert trails, a mix of bump runs and cruisers. North Peak is primarily gentle terrain. Aurora, off-the-beaten-track, with a handful of trails and glades, is a great place to head right after a storm as few skiers find their way there until mid-morning. A half-dozen fall-line trails and glades spill down Oz, a rather isolated peak favoured by less-flashy experts for its challenging terrain and less busy lifts. Just beyond Oz is Jordan Bowl, prized for its long,

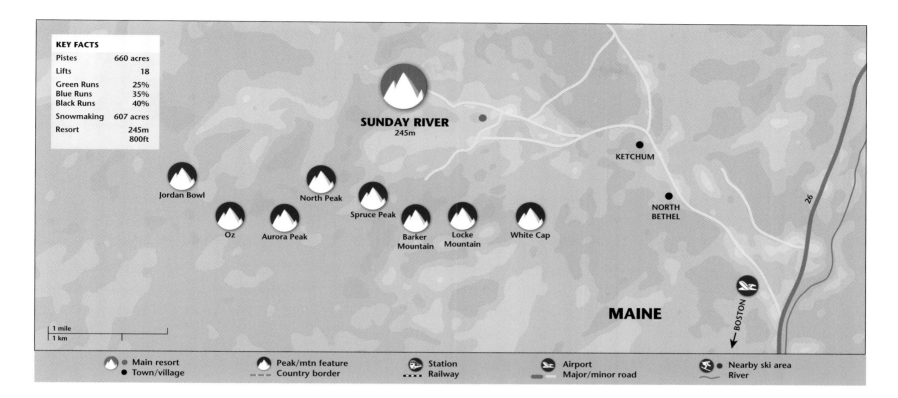

**KEY FACTS**

| Pistes | 660 acres |
|---|---|
| Lifts | 18 |
| Green Runs | 25% |
| Blue Runs | 35% |
| Black Runs | 40% |
| Snowmaking | 607 acres |
| Resort | 245m |
| | 800ft |

SUNDAY RIVER
245m

KETCHUM

Jordan Bowl

North Peak

NORTH
BETHEL

Oz

Aurora Peak

Spruce Peak

Barker
Mountain

Locke
Mountain

White Cap

MAINE

26

BOSTON

1 mile
1 km

Main resort
Town/village

Peak/mtn feature
Country border

Station
Railway

Airport
Major/minor road

Nearby ski area
River

undulating, groomed trails such as Excaliber and Rogue Angel – favourites for intermediates – and Lollapalooza, a seemingly endless beginner trail.

## Getting your bearings

Skiing at Sunday River requires constant decisions, from which base area to begin at to which peaks to ski. Its sheer size can be a bit disconcerting for first-time visitors, but it doesn't take long to get the hang of the place, although a trail map is a necessity. Moving from peak to peak can be frustrating, as sometimes it might seem as if you're spending the better part of your ski day trying to get somewhere via horizontal moves rather than actually getting in serious vertical. Another troublesome aspect is the frequent trail merges. Those peak-to-peak connector trails often bisect fall-line runs.

Although Sunday River lacks a true centre, it has plentiful lodging, most of it slopeside, and a handful of restaurants. Nightlife is spread out among the bars and restaurants on the access road, but the families that favour the resort usually stick to the numerous outdoor heated pools or the Nite Cap Fun Center, with a lit tubing park, skating rink and indoor arcade.

For a more typical New England experience, the lovely old town of Bethel, just 10km (6 miles) down the road, has classic inns and romantic B&Bs as well as excellent dining choices and a bit of nightlife. The free Mountain Explorer shuttle bus connects the town with the resort.

Undulating, quad-achingly long trails ripple down from the summits of Sunday River's eight peaks. Thanks to its huge snowmaking system and meticulous grooming, the 'Rivah' usually enjoys prime conditions.

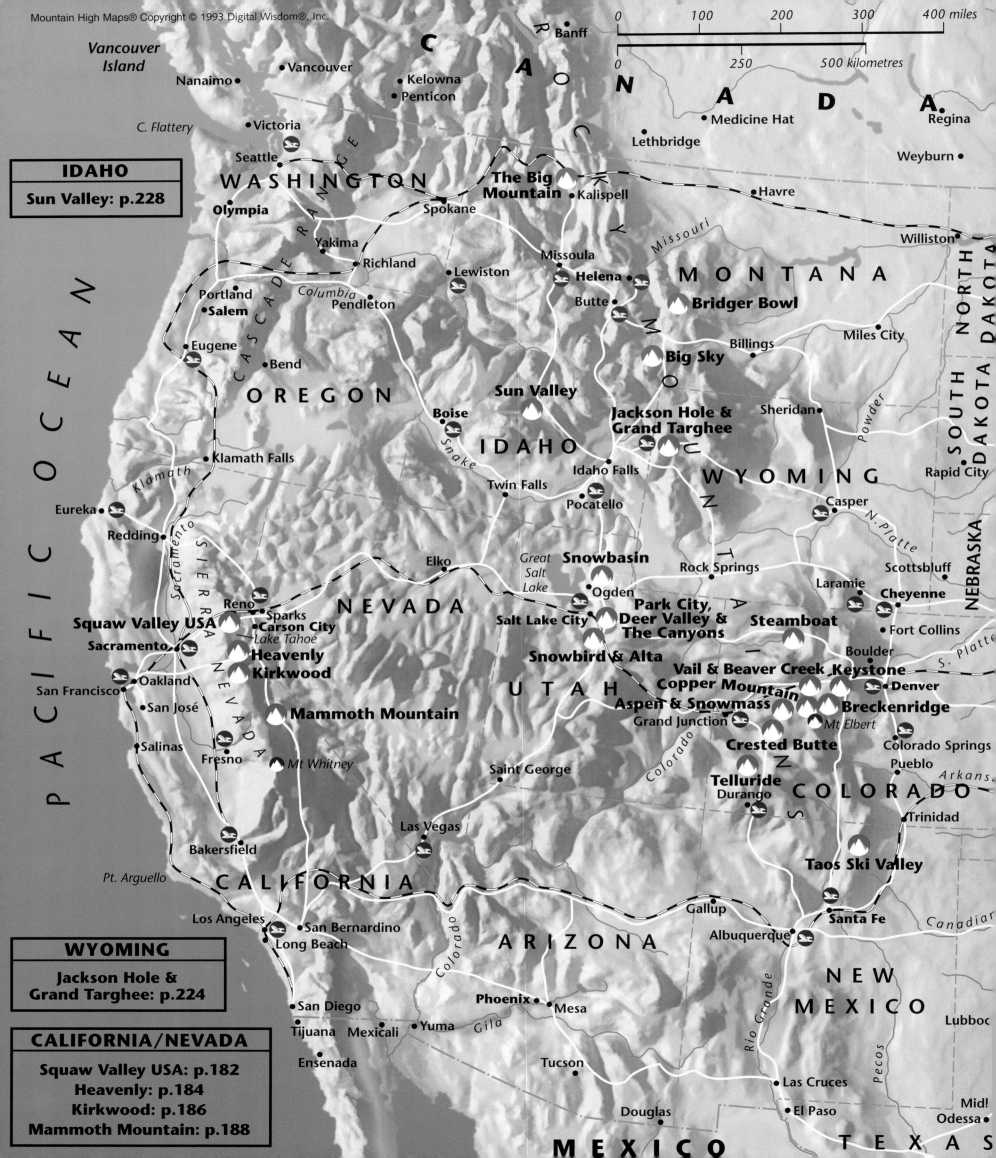

Mountain High Maps® Copyright © 1993 Digital Wisdom®, Inc.

**CANADA**

**U.S.A.**

*Vancouver Island*

*C. Flattery*

**WASHINGTON**

**OREGON**

**IDAHO**

**NEVADA**

**CALIFORNIA**

**UTAH**

**MONTANA**

**WYOMING**

**COLORADO**

**ARIZONA**

**NEW MEXICO**

**MEXICO**

**TEXAS**

**SOUTH DAKOTA**

**NORTH DAKOTA**

**NEBRASKA**

P A C I F I C   O C E A N

*Pt. Arguello*

*Lake Tahoe*

*Great Salt Lake*

*Mt Whitney*

*Mt Elbert*

*Columbia*

*Snake*

*Missouri*

*Klamath*

*Sacramento*

*Colorado*

*Rio Grande*

*Gila*

*Pecos*

*Powder*

*N. Platte*

*S. Platte*

*Arkans.*

*Canadian*

CASCADE RANGE

SIERRA NEVADA

ROCKY MOUNTAINS

Banff
Vancouver
Nanaimo
Kelowna
Penticon
Victoria
Seattle
Olympia
Yakima
Richland
Portland
Salem
Eugene
Bend
Spokane
Pendleton
Lewiston
Missoula
Helena
Butte
**Bridger Bowl**
**Big Sky**
Billings
Miles City
Medicine Hat
Lethbridge
Havre
Williston
Weyburn
Regina
**The Big Mountain**
Kalispell
**Sun Valley**
Boise
Twin Falls
Idaho Falls
Pocatello
**Jackson Hole & Grand Targhee**
Sheridan
Rapid City
Casper
Elko
**Snowbasin**
Ogden
Rock Springs
Laramie
Cheyenne
Scottsbluff
Fort Collins
Eureka
Redding
Reno
Sparks
Carson City
**Squaw Valley USA**
Sacramento
**Heavenly**
**Kirkwood**
San Francisco
Oakland
San José
Salinas
Fresno
**Mammoth Mountain**
Klamath Falls
Salt Lake City
**Park City, Deer Valley & The Canyons**
**Snowbird & Alta**
**Steamboat**
Boulder
**Vail & Beaver Creek**
**Keystone**
**Copper Mountain**
**Aspen & Snowmass**
**Breckenridge**
Denver
Grand Junction
**Crested Butte**
Colorado Springs
Pueblo
Saint George
**Telluride**
Durango
**Taos Ski Valley**
Las Vegas
Bakersfield
Los Angeles
San Bernardino
Long Beach
San Diego
Tijuana
Mexicali
Yuma
Ensenada
Gallup
**Santa Fe**
Albuquerque
Phoenix
Mesa
Tucson
Douglas
Las Cruces
El Paso
Trinidad
Lubbock
Odessa
Mid!

0   100   200   300   400 miles

0   250   500 kilometres

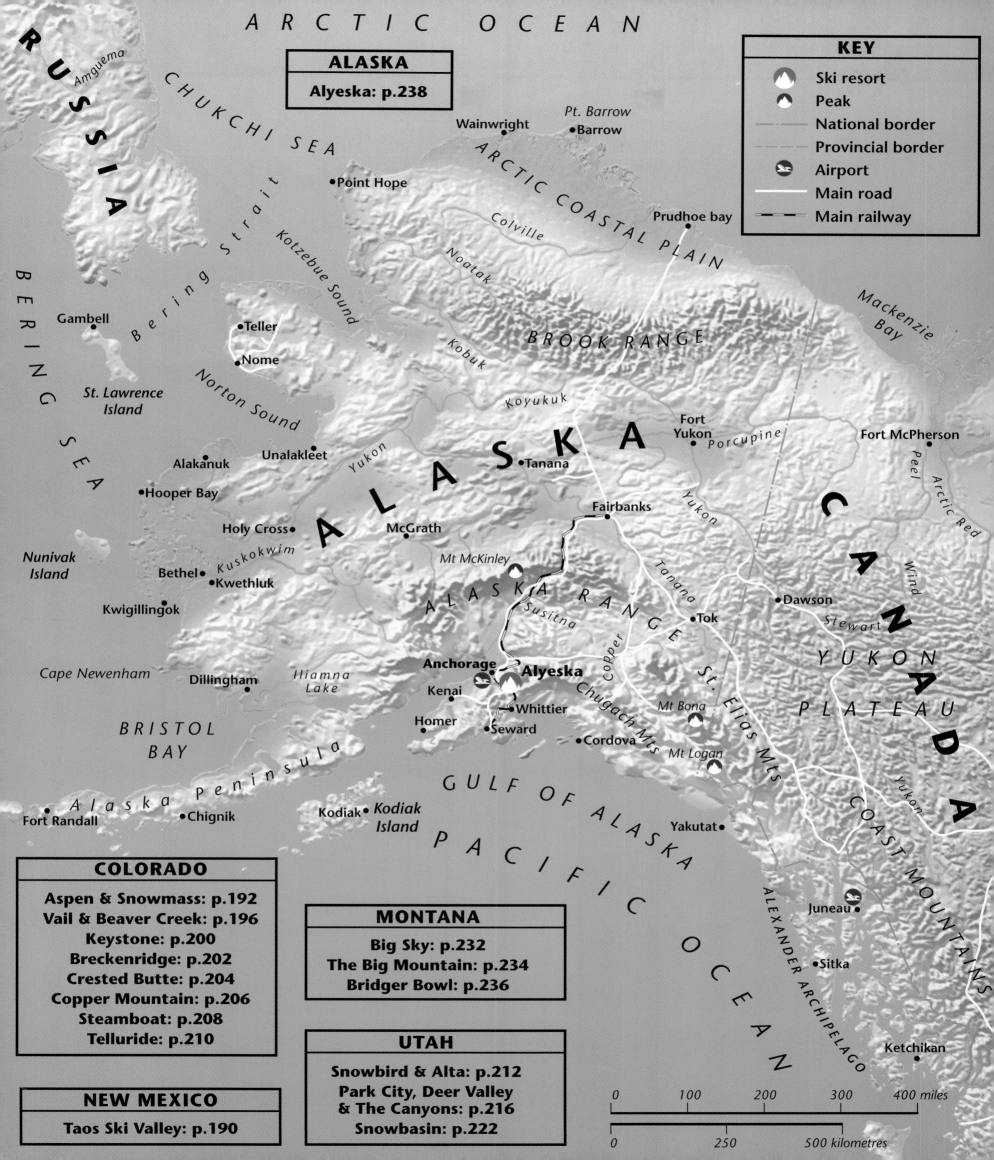

ARCTIC OCEAN

RUSSIA

*Amguema*

CHUKCHI SEA

*Bering Strait*

*Kotzebue Sound*

**ALASKA**

**Alyeska: p.238**

Wainwright  •  *Pt. Barrow*  • Barrow

• Point Hope

ARCTIC COASTAL PLAIN

*Colville*

Prudhoe bay •

**KEY**

Ski resort

Peak

National border

Provincial border

Airport

Main road

Main railway

*Mackenzie Bay*

• Gambell

BERING SEA

*St. Lawrence Island*

*Norton Sound*

• Teller

• Nome

*Noatak*

*Kobuk*

BROOK RANGE

Fort Yukon •

*Porcupine*

Fort McPherson •

*Peel*

*Arctic Red*

*Koyukuk*

*Yukon*

Fairbanks •

Dawson •

*Stewart*

*Wind*

• Unalakleet

Alakanuk •

• Hooper Bay

*Yukon*

ALASKA

Tanana •

*Yukon*

CANADA

• Holy Cross

McGrath •

*Kuskokwim*

*Nunivak Island*

Bethel •

• Kwethluk

*Mt McKinley*

ALASKA RANGE

*Susitna*

*Tanana*

*Tanana*

• Tok

YUKON PLATEAU

Kwigillingok •

*Iliamna Lake*

Dillingham •

Anchorage

Kenai •

Alyeska

Whittier •

*Chugach Mts*

*Copper*

Mt Bona

*St. Elias Mts*

Homer •

Seward •

• Cordova

Mt Logan

*Cape Newenham*

BRISTOL BAY

*Alaska Peninsula*

Fort Randall •

*Alaska*  • Chignik

• Kodiak  *Kodiak Island*

GULF OF ALASKA

PACIFIC OCEAN

Yakutat •

*ALEXANDER ARCHIPELAGO*

COAST MOUNTAINS

*Yukon*

Juneau •

• Sitka

• Ketchikan

**COLORADO**

**Aspen & Snowmass: p.192**
**Vail & Beaver Creek: p.196**
**Keystone: p.200**
**Breckenridge: p.202**
**Crested Butte: p.204**
**Copper Mountain: p.206**
**Steamboat: p.208**
**Telluride: p.210**

**MONTANA**

**Big Sky: p.232**
**The Big Mountain: p.234**
**Bridger Bowl: p.236**

**UTAH**

**Snowbird & Alta: p.212**
**Park City, Deer Valley & The Canyons: p.216**
**Snowbasin: p.222**

**NEW MEXICO**

**Taos Ski Valley: p.190**

0   100   200   300   400 miles

0   250   500 kilometres

# CALIFORNIA

# Squaw Valley USA

BY ARNIE WILSON

Squaw Valley USA (it likes – even insists – on incorporating 'USA' in its name) is perhaps the most dramatic and challenging of the Lake Tahoe resorts spanning the California–Nevada border. With its Olympic history (long ago but still glamorous) and extensive slopes, it is certainly a major force to be reckoned with.

With 1,619ha (4,000 acres) of virtually 'ski where you like' terrain spanning six peaks, together with 16 open bowls, 170 runs, 34 lifts (including North America's only Funitel gondola system and an aerial cable-car or tram) and a vertical drop of 869m (2,850ft), Squaw Valley is vast for an American resort. There are few named trails as such, just an almost endless array of big, wide-open bowls, bump runs and gullies, described by a

colleague as 'a hundred different chutes, cliffs, steep bumps and hairball rock bands – most of them open to the public'. What it lacks, perhaps, is charm.

Although the resort has quite a fierce reputation – thanks to areas such as the daunting Palisades Chutes – the rest of Squaw Peak (2,712m/8,900ft), like Emigrant Peak (2,651m/8,700ft) is, by and large, quite benign. Broken Arrow (2,444m/8,020ft) has something for everyone, while Snow King (2,301m/7,550ft) and Granite Chief (2,758m/9,050ft) are more challenging. So is KT-22 (2,499m/8,200ft), so-called because

when the original founder's wife, Sandy Poulsen, hiked up in the 1940s, she was unable to emulate the untroubled descent of her ski champion husband, Wayne, and ended up struggling down with the help of 22 kick turns. (KT-22's celebrated mogul run, The West Face, was re-named as Jonny Moseley's run after he took the gold medal for freestyle moguls in the 1998 Winter Olympics at Nagano, Japan.)

Sandy Poulsen would have been less troubled by what are today the resort's main nursery slopes, which are located, unusually, on top of Emigrant Peak. This provides a long

**Few American resorts have trams (cable-cars), but Squaw Valley's takes 150 skiers and snowboarders on a spectacular ride to High Camp at 2,499m (8,200 feet).**

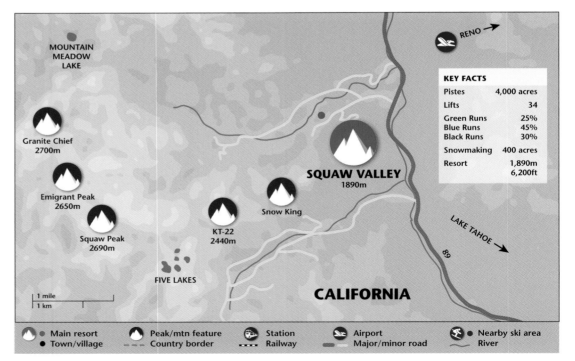

| KEY FACTS | |
|---|---|
| Pistes | 4,000 acres |
| Lifts | 34 |
| Green Runs | 25% |
| Blue Runs | 45% |
| Black Runs | 30% |
| Snowmaking | 400 acres |
| Resort | 1,890m |
| | 6,200ft |

MOUNTAIN MEADOW LAKE

RENO →

Granite Chief 2700m

Emigrant Peak 2650m

Squaw Peak 2690m

KT-22 2440m

Snow King

SQUAW VALLEY 1890m

LAKE TAHOE →

89

FIVE LAKES

CALIFORNIA

1 mile
1 km

● Main resort
● Town/village

Peak/mtn feature
Country border

Station
Railway

Airport
Major/minor road

● Nearby ski area
River

run of well over 4.75km (3 miles) all the way down to the base area. This is also the site of the Squaw Kids Children's Center, with its own dedicated rope tow, magic carpet and ski hill.

At High Camp, the centre of the resort's upper-mountain activity, and accessed by the High Camp cable-car, guests can take a spin on the ice at the Olympic Ice Pavilion, try the pool at the Swimming Lagoon and Spa, which opens in mid-March, a trip back in time at the Olympic Museum, and dine at one of four upper mountain restaurants. 'Only at Squaw Valley USA', claims the resort, 'can guests combine a great day on the slopes with a dip in a mountain-top swimming pool and a soak in a giant slopeside Jacuzzi.'

There are three terrain parks: Belmont (for novices), Central Park at Riviera ('Riv') for 'more advanced park rats' where night-riding is popular, and the Ford Mainline Park, as well as a Family Fun Park. Parents and children can warm up in Belmont Park on more gentle jumps, and progress (if they wish) to the 91-m (300-ft) Riviera Halfpipe (with 3.5m/ 12-ft-high walls). Advanced skiers and snow-

Squaw Valley has few marked runs as such. Instead skiers and snowboarders can pretty much ski where they want in a winter playground in the Sierra Nevada.

boarders can test their skills on the 5.5-m (18½-ft) walls of the 168-m (550-ft) Mainline SuperPipe. The Riviera and Mainline Parks have a wide variety of tabletop jumps, rails, fun boxes, volcanoes and a boardercross course.

Squaw Valley's snowtubing arena has a dedicated lift, and features wide-open boulevards of sliding terrain with rolls, banks, and berms, plus fast and slow lanes to accommodate tubers of all speeds and sizes. Other options include an Olympic-sized Ice Pavilion, an indoor climbing wall, snowshoeing, sleigh rides and dog sledding. The Olympic Winter Games Museum features a variety of historic memorabilia and photographs, including Alex Cushing's original bid for the games, course layouts, event results, newspaper articles and a video presentation. There are 18km (11 miles) of cross-country trails, snowshoeing, and sleigh rides in the valley.

### HISTORY OF SQUAW VALLEY

*Legend has it that Squaw Valley was discovered as long ago as AD500 by the Washoe Indians. In the 1860s, rumours of rich silver deposits brought prospectors flocking to the valley, but nothing was found. The area finally hit the jackpot when it was selected for the 1960 Winter Olympics, in spite of what could have been described at the time as a somewhat flimsy infrastructure.*

*There is no doubting its late co-founder Alex Cushing's chutzpah in offering his embryonic resort as an Olympic venue: when he suggested it, the resort had only a couple of lifts. However, he got away with it, and never really looked back. The opening ceremony, in 1960, was orchestrated by Walt Disney: 2,000 pigeons were released above Squaw's magnificent peaks, followed by a brilliant display of fireworks and balloons. The music was provided by 52 school bands, 2,645 voices and 1,285 instruments, and 800 athletes from 30 nations competed for medals.*

# Heavenly

BY ARNIE WILSON

Heavenly is a bizarre mix of Monte Carlo-style casinos, alpine peaks, a magnificent lake, and 24-hour nightlife. Lake Tahoe, one of the highest and largest alpine waterways in the world, was described by Mark Twain as: 'A noble sheet of blue water, lifted 6,300 feet above the level of the sea, and walled in by a rim of snow-clad peaks – brilliantly photographed upon its still surface.' Almost 0.5km (⅓ mile) deep in places, it is split across the border of two states – two thirds in California, the other third in Nevada.

The ski area started life as Heavenly Valley in 1955, with the Norwegian Olympic Gold Medallist Stein Ericksen as Ski School director. Apart from the lake, what is unusual about Heavenly (as it has been known since 1990) is that the slopes are – like the lake – in two states, and the resort has base areas in both. If you find yourself in Nevada at the end of the day rather than California, there's a bus link back to South Lake Tahoe.

From the top of Monument Peak (3,068m/10,067ft), as you traverse into Nevada, the view becomes even more extraordinary: Lake Tahoe on one side, and the desert scrub of the Carson Valley on the other. The most recently built California base area, where an eight-person gondola takes skiers and snowboarders from the rapidly expanding Heavenly Village almost two thirds of the way up Monument Peak, feeding a six-

passenger high-speed chair climbing to near the top of the Nevada side, is only minutes from the state line at South Lake Tahoe. Cross that line and you walk into a different world: a world of vast, Las Vegas-style gambling hotels, with glitzy shows at places like

**On a blue-sky powder day at Lake Tahoe, even the view across the lake can be neglected as skiers concentrate on helping themselves to steep, deep Heavenly powder.**

Harrah's, Harvey's and the former Caesar's, recently purchased by the Montbleu group. There are six 24-hour casinos in the South Lake Tahoe area. Together, they have a total (at the last count) of 7,051 slot machines and 411 game tables.

Apart from the intriguing contrast of magnificent scenery and bling-riddled gambling joints, the main attractions at Heavenly are the extensive slopes and – in the right conditions – some of the best tree skiing in the country. In good powder years, the extensive gladed areas dramatically increase the skiable acreage. The ubiquitous fir trees, including Douglas firs and the much more rare white-barked Western-pines, are naturally spaced out at near-perfect intervals. Even if the snow isn't right for tree-skiing, there are plenty of challenges in the legendary Mott and Killebrew canyons – steep 'gated' areas with a series of double-black diamond chutes bearing intriguing names such as Snake Eyes, Widowmaker, Hemlock and Southern Comfort. Above these areas lies the exhilarating Milkyway Bowl, a largely treeless single black-diamond bowl with impressive views of the Carson Valley from the top.

Bump skiers will be in their element on Gunbarrel, a steep, stamina-sapping mogul field billed as 'North America's toughest black-diamond bump run', with a vertical drop of 610m (2,000ft) and running all the way from the top of the Aerial Tramway down to the California Lodge. Certain skiers, who call themselves the Face Rats, do almost nothing else but ski this seemingly endless bump run, sometimes managing as many as 50 descents or more in a day. For most holiday skiers, however, once is sufficient. You can traverse into East Bowl woods if the bumps get too much – or even take the easy Round-A-Bout option.

For most visitors, Heavenly's real selling point is the plentiful high, wide and handsome trails such as Orion, Comet, Canyon, High Roller and Liz's, backed up by what is claimed to be the largest snowmaking system on the west coast. And of the dozen or more ski areas sprinkled around the lake – with a grand total of 10,926ha (27,000 acres) of ski terrain, 200 lifts and more than 1,000 trails between them – Heavenly has the longest run (9km/5½ miles) and greatest vertical drop (1,097m/3,600 feet).

Heavenly also has four terrain parks. The Low Roller park, between The Groove and Patsy's chairs on the California side, is designed for beginners. There are two medium parks: High Roller Stateline is off the Tamarack Chair on the state border, and the after-dark terrain at the High Roller Nightlife is off the World Cup run above the California Base, and opens Thursday to Saturday. Heavenly's main park, High Roller California, is located off the Canyon chair. The High Roller Superpipe is at the top of the Powderbowl chair (also on the California side).

**KEY FACTS**

| | |
|---|---|
| Pistes | 4,800 acres |
| Lifts | 30 |
| Green Runs | 20% |
| Blue Runs | 45% |
| Black Runs | 35% |
| Snowmaking | 70% |
| Resort | 1,995m |
| | 6,540ft |

Map legend:
- Main resort ● Town/village
- Peak/mtn feature --- Country border
- Station ····· Railway
- Airport / Major/minor road
- Nearby ski area / River

A firework display at Heavenly celebrated the resort's 50th anniversary in December 2005, adding even more lustre to the glitz of this Vegas-in-the-mountains corner of Nevada just across the Californian border.

# Kirkwood

BY ARNIE WILSON

In the 1960s, a US Forest Service team hiking in one of California's most dramatic mountain chains hiked up Thimble Peak (3,010m/9,876ft) and skied down to Kirkwood Meadow. They recognized that this spectacular box canyon, with an unusually high snowfall record, had the makings of an excellent ski area. The resort takes its name from Zachary Kirkwood, who arrived here along with emigrants and fortune seekers during the Californian Gold Rush Days of the mid-1800s. He stayed on and opened the Kirkwood Station, now known as the Kirkwood Inn.

By 1972 the ski area had opened, and lifts were gradually added. Crucially, the Wagon Wheel Chair – Lift 10 – opened in 1984, and began transporting skiers to the awe-inspiring and somewhat daunting top of the steep 'Wall', servicing 283ha (700 acres) of advanced and expert terrain. The Reut chair,

This typically exhilarating backcountry terrain at Kirkwood is miles from the nearest casino.

which runs parallel with much of the Wagon Wheel Chair, opened two years later, along with a sizeable section of accommodation. A new village – with the highest base area in the Lake Tahoe region – began to take shape in 1995.

Today, Kirkwood is the thinking skier's resort in the Tahoe region – and the region's most remote. Although it is only 35 minutes away (by daily shuttle bus link) from the gaudy glitz and gambling of South Lake Tahoe, through the picturesque Hope Valley, and crosses two impressive mountain passes (including Carson Pass), Kirkwood might as well be a thousand miles away from the fleshpots of Nevada. As Tim Cohee, its long-serving Resort President, puts it, 'It's a 30-second walk to some world-class skiing, but not to dinner at Spago's or a night of gambling – people come here for the stunning location, the serenity and nature.' Kirkwood is indeed remote, wildly beautiful, with exhilarating skiing and a backdrop of spectacular scenery – jagged granite peaks of volcanic origin, reminiscent of the kind of mountains you might see in many Western movies. The resort uses winch cats to groom some of the steeper slopes in its 'high angle' grooming programme.

Although there are easy runs, and most lifts have easy ways down, this is a ski area that favours the brave. There are countless hidden chutes, cliff drops, miles of cornices,

and seemingly endless pockets of powder in the trees. Many runs (such as The Wall, Headwater and Dick's Drop – all served by the Wagon Wheel chair) are steep, and most have a healthy pitch. By traversing skier's left from the top of The Wall, strong skiers and riders can access a sprinkling of challenging double-black diamond gladed chutes. These include All The Way, Notch Chute, Sister Chute, Shaffer's Chute, Saddle Chute and Cliff Chute, clustered below The Sisters (2,865m/9,400ft). Continuing beyond Wagon Wheel Bowl and Sentinel Bowl – way out beneath Glove Rock – is another group of easier chutes, including Sentinel, Rabbit Runs and Fireball. The most difficult here is the double-black diamond Chamoix chute.

More comfortable skiing can be found on the 'backside' of the resort, reached by the Sunrise and Iron Horse lifts. From the top of Sunrise it is also possible to access some enjoyable and quite steep chutes on the flank of Thimble Peak: in good snow. Runs like Hully Gully, Cold Shoulder and Larry's Lip are all exhilarating and quite benign single black diamond runs. The easiest slopes, at Timber Creek, are accessed by The TC Express and Bunny Lifts, just above the Mighty Mountain Children's Center, and the Snowkirk lift, close to 'Adventure Land', a park for young riders. Timber Creek also has a Learn-to-Ride Center.

There are three terrain parks, and a super-pipe, as well as 80km (50 miles) of cross-country tracks, snowshoeing, ice-skating and dog sledding. There are also regular full-moon ski and snowshoe tours. The Slide Mountain Tube Park is close to the Red Cliffs Day Lodge, and both the Mountain Dew Superpipe and the main park, DC Shoes Stomping Grounds, are accessed by the Solitude lift.

Kirkwood is keen to encourage skiers and snowboarders to explore the backcountry, and has devised an 'Expedition Kirkwood' programme (including backcountry awareness clinics) using ski patrollers and backcountry guides, to ensure it's safe. ('Beacon Basin' is billed as the only avalanche-transceiver training facility in California.) The programme includes Powder Cat tours high in the Red Cliffs area.

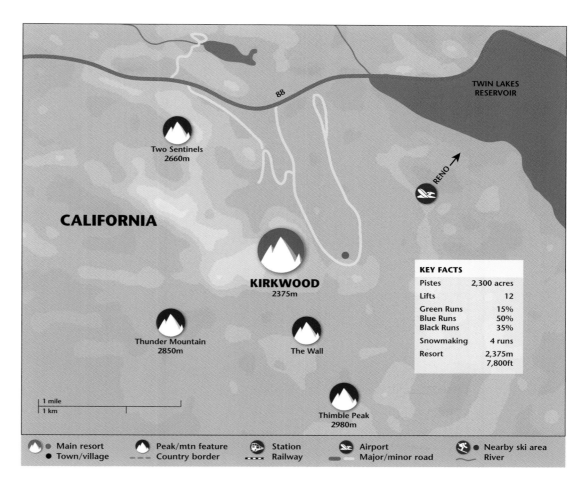

| KEY FACTS | |
|---|---|
| Pistes | 2,300 acres |
| Lifts | 12 |
| Green Runs | 15% |
| Blue Runs | 50% |
| Black Runs | 35% |
| Snowmaking | 4 runs |
| Resort | 2,375m 7,800ft |

| Main resort | Peak/mtn feature | Station | Airport | Nearby ski area |
|---|---|---|---|---|
| Town/village | Country border | Railway | Major/minor road | River |

*The village at Kirkwood, right next to the slopes, is still gradually taking shape. But the resort remains blissfully quiet and remote compared with most Tahoe ski areas.*

# Mammoth Mountain

BY ARNIE WILSON

Some ski resorts are enhanced by their surroundings and the calibre of journey required to reach them. The drive to Mammoth Mountain is awe-inspiring. This remote monolith in California's eastern Sierra Nevada is an extinct volcano perched loftily between desert and pine forest. Although Mammoth's most recent eruption was in approximately 48,000BC, the mountain continues to generate an almost primeval Jurassic-Park atmosphere, enhanced by the backdrop of the Minarets, a 'mini'-range whose jagged teeth tower above the forested valleys nearby.

The nearby town of Mammoth Lakes used to be the focal point for accommodation, although there were always options close to the slopes. As a result of Mammoth's partnership with Intrawest, the giant Vancouver-based ski-resort development company, a major new pedestrian village has been built at Juniper Ridge. However, although it was generally assumed that Intrawest would take over the resort following the eventual retirement of Dave McCoy, Mammoth's legendary founder, the resort was unexpectedly sold in October 2005 to the Starwood Capital Group Global. The selling price was based on a $365-million enterprise value.

There's an airport a few miles away at the town of Mammoth Lakes, but it's small, and in spite of grandiose plans to enlarge it and run regular services with big jets from big cities, it's never really happened on a permanent basis. So most people drive to the resort, and most people who ski here are from Los Angeles (a journey of six or seven hours, although the blurb says five) or San Francisco (more like five hours). Mammoth is about three hours' driving from Reno, Nevada. Partly because of the dramatic and remote scenery, however, even such journeys don't deter keen Californian skiers, who make Mammoth busy at weekends, and whose departure make it quieter during the week.

*Some lodging at the mountain base is so close to the lower slopes you can be skiing within minutes.*

The key to getting here is Highway 395, a road that traces the eastern slope of the Sierra Nevada from just north of San Bernardino almost all the way to Carson City, Nevada. Once you have cut across from LA to join it, 395 takes you on a spectacular journey through the beautiful Mojave Desert, passing Edwards Air Force Base and skirting Yosemite National Park. For long stretches, as you admire the scenery, it may feel as though you are alone, but beware of putting your foot down: the road is renowned for drivers picking up speeding tickets.

## All in the name

The resort's name provides a great marketing tool, but no one can be certain of how the mountain got its name. There are no fossilized prehistoric tusks lurking beneath the slopes, and although the resort is undeniably big – with more than 150 trails spread across four different areas, and a 10-km (6-mile) 'footprint' – it's not that either. The most likely explanation is that Mammoth was named after an old mining company during the 1870s gold rush that brought thousands of prospectors to the region. They set up home in what became known as Mammoth City. The rush eventually became a trickle, and it was not until a few die-hard skiers brought portable

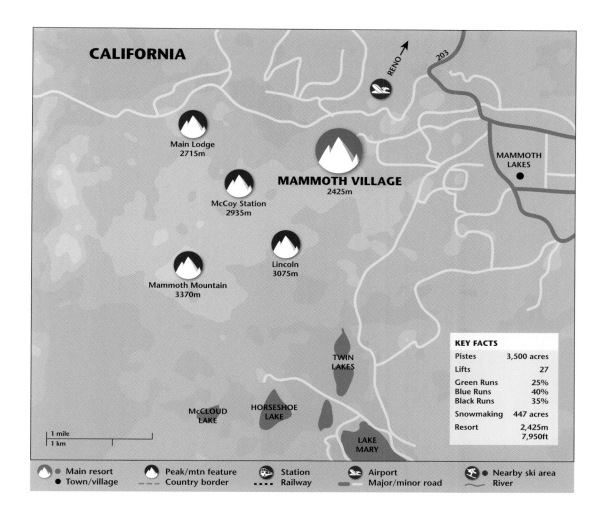

CALIFORNIA

Main Lodge
2715m

MAMMOTH VILLAGE
2425m

McCoy Station
2935m

MAMMOTH LAKES

Lincoln
3075m

Mammoth Mountain
3370m

TWIN LAKES

McCLOUD LAKE

HORSESHOE LAKE

LAKE MARY

| KEY FACTS | |
| --- | --- |
| Pistes | 3,500 acres |
| Lifts | 27 |
| Green Runs | 25% |
| Blue Runs | 40% |
| Black Runs | 35% |
| Snowmaking | 447 acres |
| Resort | 2,425m |
| | 7,950ft |

1 mile
1 km

● Main resort
● Town/village

Peak/mtn feature
- - - Country border

Station
..... Railway

Airport
Major/minor road

● Nearby ski area
River

rope-tows into the mountains – powered by Ford Model-A trucks – that a new economy and a different kind of rush began.

From this point, the history of Mammoth became inextricably linked with Dave McCoy, a one-time Californian state ski champion. In 1945, McCoy, then a snow surveyor with the Los Angeles Department of Water and Power, and a member of the Eastern Sierra Ski Club, obtained the rights from the US Forest Service to build a permanent rope tow on Mammoth Mountain. Ten years later, he personally installed the first chairlift. Although some critics had warned him that the mountain was too high, too remote and too stormy, he proved them wrong. There were storms, of course, but they were welcome, occasionally depositing as much as 2m (5ft) of snow in a single night. Mammoth's enviable snow record allows the resort to remain open, almost every year, until into June, and sometimes even later.

With four contrasting areas, there is skiing for all levels – otherwise people wouldn't spend seven hours getting here. However it

has to be said that perhaps Mammoth favours the bold. Fortunately there is a sister mountain, June, which by and large has mellower slopes. At Mammoth, the lifts will drop you off at some of the most challenging terrain there is – if you want them to!

There are double-blacks galore from Panorama Lookout, at almost 3,370m (11,056ft), where the Panorama Gondola accesses the top of the mountain. Many are not even marked on the trail map. Challenges that are marked include runs with such exotic names as Huevos Grande, Climax, Hangman's Hollow, Wipe Out Chutes and Paranoid Flats. Other lifts, like Goldrush and Broadway Express, access more double-black diamond runs like Avalanche Chutes and Gravy Chute. The locals will tell you that even more extreme skiing is possible on the backside of Mammoth Mountain, but you'll need to hike, preferably with a guide, to find it. The backside is also the gateway to the Mammoth Crest, a cluster of chutes and lips that will challenge anyone.

All this gives the mountain, mistakenly, the appearance of being essentially for experts only, but of course only a fearless few will want to go looking for this kind of terrain. Mammoth has miles of groomed runs for the average holiday skier. There is plenty for the intermediate skier and boarder, with 'easy-does-it' cruising runs like St Anton, Broadway and Forest Trail. And that's without taking into consideration Mammoth's somewhat more benign sister mountain June, which features predominantly lower-intermediate terrain, and was purchased by McCoy in 1986.

Mammoth is very much the haunt of snowboarders, particularly early in the season when they sometimes outnumber skiers reluctant to risk their skis in early snow conditions. There are three parks and three pipes. The Unbound Terrain Parks comprise more than 28ha (70 acres) dedicated to 40 rails and boxes. There's a Wall Ride, 50 jumps and a world-class system of pipes. There are two Family Fun Zones at Discovery and Canyon, along with South Park's Jibs Galore. All in all, Mammoth certainly lives up to its name.

**When it snows in Mammoth – it snows. Storm clouds coming over the High Sierras have been known to deposit 1.5m (5ft) of powder in a single night.**

# Taos Ski Valley

BY CLAIRE WALTER

Taos Ski Valley is one of America's iconic resorts, and is known as a skiers' mountain, literally and figuratively. Its legendary terrain is heavy on the challenging end of the spectrum, and it still doesn't – and perhaps never will – permit snowboarding. As such, it is one of only four ski areas in the US to prohibit snowboarding, and its exceptional glades and formidable hike-to steeps draw genuine expert skiers.

Located in the Sangre de Cristo range of the Rocky Mountains, this family-owned, family-run resort has lured skiers for nearly half a century. Attractions are bewitching terrain, cloud-light snow stripped of moisture by the nearby desert and abundant, brilliant sunshine between snowstorms. Visitors treasure the mystique of the nearby town of Taos, and its unique Anglo-Hispanic-Indian culture shows up in food, art and music. People don't come here for nightlife, because the Ski Valley is quiet as such things go, and the town isn't very lively in comparison with other ski destinations either.

The first lift, a high-speed drag lift (a Poma 'platter-pull'), whisked skiers up the nose of the ridge above the vest-pocket resort. It was built directly on Al's Run, still the resort's in-your-face signature mogul trail. The new visitor's intimidating first sight of the area is this steep, arrow-straight trail given to sprouting enormous bumps. It is ironic that the first lift was so speedy – reportedly twice as fast as a fixed-grip lift today – because Taos is the only significant North American ski area without a single high-speed, detachable chair-lift. No complaints – conventional lift speed is appropriate for this ski area, and something that people tend to savour.

Because Taos is a complicated mountain with two major bowls bracketing the frontside ridge, traverses between them and long run-outs at the base, skiers tend to pick a couple of close-together lifts and ski those trails before moving onto another section of the mountain. Everyone except beginners start directly from the base area boarding one of a pair of parallel chairs (No. 1 Lift or No. 5 Lift). To reach the highest lift-served point, it is necessary to drop down to the right into West Basin via High Five or White Feather

**Cloud-light powder, southern sunshine and skiable trees for those who can tame them are the beguiling mix at Taos Ski Valley.**

and catch one of another pair of parallel chairs (No. 2 Lift or No. 6 Lift) that continue upward. Continue beyond those lifts to the farthest-west chair (No. 8 Lift) and its handful of green-circle and blue-square runs. The high point unloading area for No. 2 and No. 6 area offers three options: ski to the right and follow the High Traverse to eight chutes of heart-stopping steepness, check out with the Ski Patrol and climb to the West Basin Ridge or Highline Ridge too for greater verticals and several additional chutes. Skiing to the left down a blue-square trail called Bambi directly accesses some of Taos's best glade skiing, notably in the Lorelei Trees and Sir Arnold Lunn.

Heading to the right on Honeysuckle leads to Taos' eastern section. First comes another chairlift (No. 7 Lift) offering up more glades and a few relatively easy trails. One of these is Maxie's, and though Taos does not allow snowboarding, it does have a terrain park here. Winkelried, an easy traverse from the bottom of No. 7 Lift, leads to Kachina Bowl, Taos's easternmost sector. The quad chairlift (No. 4 Kachina Lift) reaches toward Kachina Peak, at 3,804m (12,481ft), one of the New Mexico's highest summits. It offers hiking terrain for those with the legs and lungs for the ascent and provides a beautiful backdrop for everyone else. The lift serves varied ground: one long easy trail, some hidden steeps and the resort's best open-slope terrain. Shalako, just below the lift's top station, is a blue-square winner in anyone's book.

One on-mountain self-service cafeteria (Whistlestop Café) nestles at the base of No. 6 Lift and there are two at the bottom of the No. 4 Kachina Lift (Phoenix Grill operated by the resort and The Bavarian, which is independent). But many people return to the base area for lunch, and everyone does so at day's end. Except for experts who still have the legs for the steep, narrow lower-mountain runs below West Basin, everyone skis Porcupine to White Feather to the base. From the Kachina side, the egress trail is Rubezahl.

The base village, a cluster of welcoming lodges brimming with tradition, is slowly

| KEY FACTS | |
|---|---|
| Pistes | 1,295 acres |
| Lifts | 12 |
| Green Runs | 24% |
| Blue Runs | 25% |
| Black Runs | 51% |
| Snowmaking | 49% |
| Resort | 2,805m |
| | 9,207ft |

Main resort
Town/village
Peak/mtn feature
Country border
Station
Railway
Airport
Major/minor road
Nearby ski area
River

evolving into a more outwardly upscale resort, with new condominiums around the village core and condo conversions. Children from six weeks of age are well cared-for in a spacious, cheery nursery called the Kinderkäfig Children's Center. Ski lessons begin at age three, utilizing isolated little lifts right outside the door. Adult beginners start off on a nearby short chair-lift and soon graduate the big mountain.

Après-ski is enthusiastically, though often briefly, practiced at the day-lodge bar and at some of the inns at the base. Guests of Taos Ski Valley lodging often make it brief to rest up before dinner, while skiers commuting from town generally stay just long enough for the traffic down Taos Canyon to let up. A visit to the nearby Taos Pueblo, a timeless Native American community, makes a ski trip to Taos truly unique.

## ERNIE BLAKE

*The late Ernie Blake – who became a true North American ski pioneer – spotted the valley from a small plane in the early 1950s. He moved there and installed his family in a 3m (11ft) camper. Though they had three young children, he and his wife Rhoda scouted the mountain on foot and on skis and intuitively laid out the early trails. The area opened in 1956 with one run. Nearly half a century later, Ernie's imprint remains solidly stamped on the Taos firmament. Many of the runs bear names of people with a Blake connection. The Ernie Blake Ski School, one of North America's last bastions of the traditional ski week, is one of the few regularly attracting high-level skiers who want to ski even better. The school is known for its exceptionally high level of instruction.*

# COLORADO

# Aspen and Snowmass

BY CLAIRE WALTER

Aspen isn't a single place, but rather two resort towns and four ski mountains that together form one of the most engaging, compelling destinations in North America. The former mining town of Aspen is a place to see and be seen, especially during the celebrity-laden holidays. Snowmass, 19km (12 miles) away, is a purpose-built ski resort undergoing a massive, early-21st-century upgrade that is grandly called 'The Renaissance of Snowmass'.

Together, Aspen Mountain, Aspen Highlands, Buttermilk and Snowmass offer every level of terrain, from super-gentle beginner runs to almost death-defying steeps. Although these four ski areas are not linked, they are skiable on fully interchangeable lift passes and are connected by a fleet of free ski buses that run frequently. In addition, the Aspen-Snowmass area offers miles of free cross-country ski trails.

The Aspen Skiing Company's current promotional slogan is 'The Power of Four', created to convey the sense that four very different ski areas offer skiers and riders a variety of experiences, all on the same lift ticket. It's the rare slogan that is borne out by

Aspen's Silver Queen gondola was refurbished in 2006, with 147 spacious new cabins.

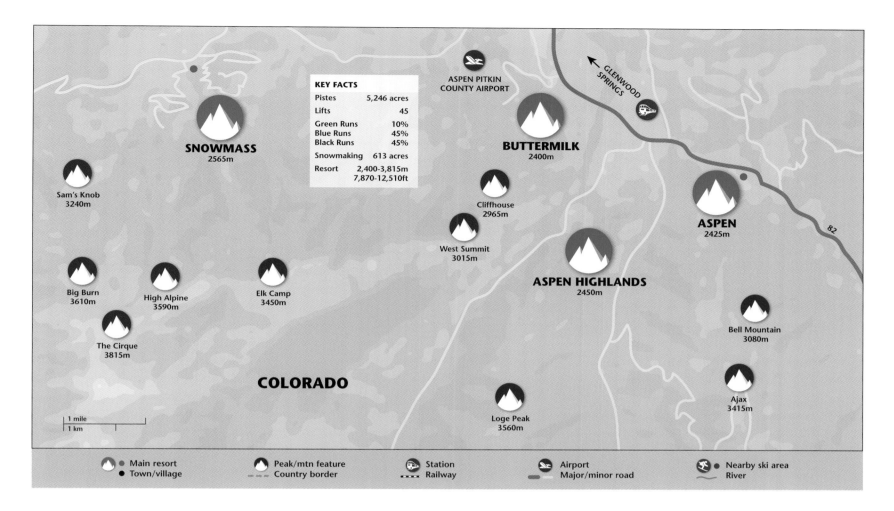

**KEY FACTS**

| | |
|---|---|
| Pistes | 5,246 acres |
| Lifts | 45 |
| Green Runs | 10% |
| Blue Runs | 45% |
| Black Runs | 45% |
| Snowmaking | 613 acres |
| Resort | 2,400-3,815m |
| | 7,870-12,510ft |

SNOWMASS 2565m

Sam's Knob 3240m

Big Burn 3610m

High Alpine 3590m

Elk Camp 3450m

The Cirque 3815m

COLORADO

1 mile
1 km

ASPEN PITKIN COUNTY AIRPORT

BUTTERMILK 2400m

Cliffhouse 2965m

West Summit 3015m

ASPEN HIGHLANDS 2450m

Loge Peak 3560m

GLENWOOD SPRINGS

ASPEN 2425m

82

Bell Mountain 3080m

Ajax 3415m

| | | | | |
|---|---|---|---|---|
| ● Main resort | ▲ Peak/mtn feature | Station | Airport | Nearby ski area |
| ● Town/village | --- Country border | ···· Railway | Major/minor road | River |

reality. Aspen Mountain's lifts take off on the south edge of town, where the sidewalks end. Aspen Highlands and Buttermilk, just a few miles west of town, offer very different ski experiences and are spawning their own modest slopeside lodging. Snowmass intertwines with its own purpose-built village and abundant ski-in/ski-out lodging.

The town of Aspen offers a matchless array of expensive retail stores emblazoned with international designer names, fine art galleries, an epicure's fantasy world of gourmet dining options, vibrant nightlife and an unsurpassed year-round cultural scene. Accommodation in the Aspen-Snowmass area ranges from a few remaining simple, old-fashioned ski lodges to super-luxurious hotels and, of course, an abundance of condominium apartments offering guests a combination of spaciousness and privacy.

## Aspen Mountain

Looming over downtown Aspen and rising nearly 1,006m (3,300ft) to an often cobalt-

blue sky, Aspen Mountain is the picturesque grande dame of Colorado ski mountains. It has long been known as a skier's mountain (and now a snowboarder's mountain, too), for it has no novice terrain at all – partly because there is no easy way down. It demands strong intermediate skills at the very least. The mountain is tall and lean, with three steep ridges and deep valleys between them.

On the trail map, the ski area shows as a Y-shaped layout. The main lift, the newly upgraded six-passenger Silver Queen gondola, is the stem of the Y, reaching the summit in 13 minutes. The upper-mountain chairlifts are embraced in the arms of the Y. Ruthie's, Bell and Gentleman's are the names of the ridges. Skiers and riders explore the cut trails and skiable glades along the ridgetops, more slopes, trails and glades down the steep sides, and huge natural halfpipes in the gullies between them. In addition to the gondola, the Shadow Mountain and Ruthie's chair-lifts rise to Aspen Mountain's western shoulder. Ruthie's chair is an unusual high-speed double, installed

because the mountain company felt that the intimacy of a two-seater lift ought to be maintained even in this high-speed age.

Aspen Mountain is a grown-up's ski area, for there is no children's ski school and, in fact, relatively few children. Most people ski and ride the upper mountain, which consists primarily of short, demanding trails and connectors linking them. Bell Mountain, the middle ridge, is effectively the ski area's centre. Its runs wear single- and double-black diamonds. Gentleman's Ridge to the west mixes blue squares and black diamonds, and it also snares the morning sun. Some people love its languorous chair-lift, which permits a rest during the ride. Others avoid it for the same reason. They prefer the Ajax Express, whose speed permits fast laps on Bell's legendary steeps, bumps and glades. The F.I.S. Chair is a short lift just across the top of Spar Gulch, reaching Ruthie's and directly serving tight trees and bumps collectively called the Mine Dumps. These runs are legacies from old mining days on Ajax

ABOVE: **The distinctive banded cliffs of the Maroon Bells are iconic peaks. None are lift-served, but visitors take snowmobile tours or a long ski tour to get a good look.**

LEFT: **Snowmass is known for wide trails, generous glades and abundant open slopes, so it's often possible to find an untracked line well after the powder flies.**

mountain, with names like Bear Paw, Zaugg Dump, Perry's Prowl, Last Dollar and Short Snort. They are fairly short, sharp and challenging descents built on the steep slopes where miners once tunnelled their way into the mountain leaving piles of shale and other debris behind. The long gully between Bell and Ruthie's is a heavily trafficked run back to town, especially at the end of the day. Trails on the Ruthie's side tend to be milder, wider and often less used.

## Aspen Highlands

At no place at a major Rockies resort do fewer lifts access more skiing than at Aspen Highlands, treasured by locals and too often overlooked by holidaymakers. Its vertical drop exceeds that of Aspen Mountain. The lower section mountain's narrow frontside runs are a medley of cruising runs, connector roads and glades. The ski area's main ridge is the side of a huge cirque, narrowing to razor sharpness at the top of the Loge Peak chairlift.

A few years ago, the ski area began allowing skiers to hike up the ridge to ski the improbable steeps of Highland Bowl. After a lung-busting hike of up to nearly 213m (700 feet), skiers and riders dropped into this awe-inspiring – and awesomely steep – bowl. (A more congenial option is to take the free snowcat along the lower section.) After plunging down open snowfields, chutes or glades with pitches as steep as 48 degrees, there was an anticlimactic 3.3km (2 miles) traverse back via the lift. The Deep Temerity triple chair, added in 2005-06, shortcuts the return to the top of Loge Peak and eliminates the traverse.

## Buttermilk Mountain

Buttermilk is the gentle child of Aspen skiing. Located just across the Maroon Creek Valley from Highlands, the two ski areas are polar opposites. Where Aspen Highlands is tall, narrow and tends toward challenge, Buttermilk is broad, with a vertical of just over 610m (2,000ft) and modest acreage, the smallest of the four Aspen areas. But for the small children and adult beginners who dominate at Buttermilk, the mountain is a grandiose universe.

The terrain wraps around three sides of Buttermilk Mountain. The lower runs are wide, beautifully groomed and designed for new skiers to get their ski legs under them and progress quickly. The children's ski school is one of the best anywhere. The upper and side-mountain runs are congenial intermediate cruisers. The Summit Express leads to the top, from which it is possible to make laps on the Savio chairlift and a broad bowl-like parcel near the summit. The adjacent Tiehack Mountain offers slightly more challenging trails and also fine tree skiing, especially treasured on a powder day.

## Snowmass

In many ways, Snowmass is the sum of the other three Aspen area mountains – and more. The census of 90 named trails diminishes the grandeur of the terrain, whose skiable acreage approaches twice that of the other three mountains combined. On the map, the frontside appears fan-shaped, with Assay Hill at the point (site of a new purpose-built village), the original slopeside Snowmass Village slightly up and to the right, Sam's Knob and the Big Burn high up to right, and Elk Camp high up on the left. Two series of chair-lifts serve the core of the area: Fanny Hill to Burlingame or Coney Glade to Big Burn is one, and Wood Run, Alpine Springs and High Alpine is the other. Spectacular, beautifully groomed intermediate terrain predominates in the generous core of the ski area. With abundant, high-speed chairlifts simply eating up the lift queues, Snowmass is a resort where you can cover so much territory that boredom is rarely an issue.

The Big Burn is a legendary slope, as much as a 0.5km (¼ mile) wide and 2.5km (1½ miles) long. Cleared by a long-ago fire, it earned a reputation as a wide-open slope, but now the trees have grown to a point where much of it now offers fabulous glade skiing. The Campground trails hang below the Sam's Knob trails like streamers off the right-hand side of the fan. Narrower than most of the Snowmass runs, but not narrow by other standards, they aren't groomed all the time and are therefore favoured by mogul skiers. Way across the ski area, beyond Elk Camp, is the Two Creeks high-speed chair-lift, which rises from a second base. Ski its handful of runs for glimpses of some of the resort's high-priced homes.

Snowmass boasts two legitimate extreme areas. A control gate above the Big Burn or Sheer Bliss chairlifts, plus a vertical 122-m (400-ft) ride on a draglift, accesses The Cirque, a large bowl featuring a series of double-black lines down the headwall and funneling through stands of trees. A traverse from the High Alpine chair leads to the additional double blacks of Hanging Valley. These superlative steeps in the wild alpine zone seem light-years away from Snowmass' gentle, condo-flanked lower slopes.

# COLORADO

# Vail and Beaver Creek

BY FELIX MILNS

Vail vies with Aspen for the title of Ski King of Colorado. Both are world-famous, expensive and extensive resorts by North American standards, but Vail can claim the accolade of America's largest single ski mountain, and it has excellent and varied terrain, with a large proportion perfect for flattering intermediates. Since 2001, expert terrain has been greatly enhanced by the addition of Blue Sky Basin. Both ski school and infrastructure are excellent, but the mock-Tyrolean architecture of the centre and sprawling condo-land suburbs alongside the Interstate 70 freeway (clearly visible from the slopes) lack the essential ambience of nearby frontier towns.

In many ways, Vail epitomizes the American dream. After the gold rush, the powder rush began and visionary pioneers like the World War II veteran Pete Seibert set out to create the perfect ski area. What began as idealism has turned into rampant capitalism, however, as the supreme marketing force of Vail Resorts, Inc. spreads the gospel of a ski area that seems primarily designed to increase the value of real estate at the foot of the hill. On the plus side, the rather unsightly Lionshead area is being completely redeveloped for 2007/08, the centre has been pedestrianized – the Austrian influence, though perhaps out of place, works beautifully in the centre of the resort. The free local bus service is also excellent. And, like any good business, there is also continual investment and improvement in both the slopes and infrastructure.

## CUTTING EDGE MOUNTAINS

*The signage at Vail is extremely clear and technologically advanced, with computerized boards detailing which lifts have queues and when different pistes were last prepared. The grooming system is excellent and European resorts could learn a lot from Vail. A good proportion of runs are always left to develop moguls but are periodically rotated so they can be enjoyed in various states throughout the season. The lift system is one of the best in North America – just as well, as queues here can be worse than almost anywhere on the continent. They are never as bad, however, as some of the more famous European bottlenecks. Innovations that some foreign visitors find overzealous are the yellow-jacketed speed police who patrol the lower nursery slopes.*

Vail's streets are paved with powder not gold. The clapboard fronts and period streetlamps add to the charm.

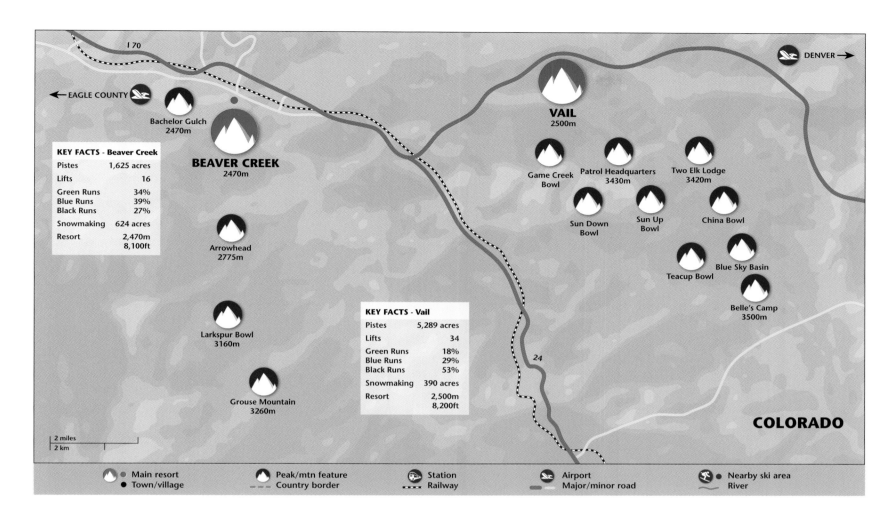

Map legend:

| KEY FACTS - Beaver Creek | |
| --- | --- |
| Pistes | 1,625 acres |
| Lifts | 16 |
| Green Runs | 34% |
| Blue Runs | 39% |
| Black Runs | 27% |
| Snowmaking | 624 acres |
| Resort | 2,470m 8,100ft |

| KEY FACTS - Vail | |
| --- | --- |
| Pistes | 5,289 acres |
| Lifts | 34 |
| Green Runs | 18% |
| Blue Runs | 29% |
| Black Runs | 53% |
| Snowmaking | 390 acres |
| Resort | 2,500m 8,200ft |

2 miles
2 km

Main resort
Town/village
Peak/mtn feature
Country border
Station
Railway
Airport
Major/minor road
Nearby ski area
River

## Up to the bowls

There are three main ways up Vail's North Face (rising to 3,430m/11,253ft), a broad flank of gladed runs cut into the lodgepole pines and aspens above the town. They rise from Vail Village, Golden Peak and Lionshead, respectively. The majority of the many runs on this side are excellent for intermediates, particularly the quieter blues like Simba above Lionshead, which runs from top to bottom. They cut picturesque paths through the trees which act as natural dividers between separate pistes. There are three high-altitude bowls, of which Game Creek has some particularly characterful terrain.

Cutting through the trees between pistes are some short but fun double diamond-blacks; Cheetah Gulley and Hairbag Alley are both tight, intriguing tracks. Advanced terrain on the front face usually means lots of bumps, and when the snow is good the

*Hold on to your hats: twin-tippers and freestyle boarders like to take an aerial view of Vail's slopes.*

backcountry route of Minturn Mile (accessed through a gate in the Game Creek Bowl) takes you out of the ski area to a wonderful powder bowl and bottoms out along a riverside path, at the end of which is a lively and atmospheric Saloon.

Before the addition of Blue Sky Basin, Vail was famous for its seven back bowls which, unusually for North America, are almost entirely above the tree line. In fresh snow they are an absolute delight but, with no shade from the trees and a south-facing aspect, they can tire pretty quickly. Most of the trails here are marked as black diamonds but, in reality, they are relatively gentle and get quickly pisted by skiers. Confident intermediates should have no fear here. Both these bowls and Blue Sky Basin generally open later in the season and the back bowls are liable to closure throughout the season on the rare occasions when there is a scarcity of fresh snow. The Sundown bowl is best for experts.

Behind the back bowls, Blue Sky Basin totally revitalized Vail for the advanced skier. Largely north-facing and thickly wooded, the emphasis is completely on free-skiing. Aside from a handful of characterful blues, the terrain is unprepared, with just a few signposts indicating named trails. There are no piste poles and you are positively encouraged to follow your own line. Cliffs, gullies and cornices make it an extreme playground, with drop-offs like Lover's Leap guaranteed to set the pulse racing. Free tours of the area, available to both intermediate and advanced skiers and riders, are offered daily. Alternatively, explore it for yourself. In fresh snow, the light powder here and in the back bowls is perfect snow for those looking to develop their off-piste skills.

## Rich and famous

Along with snow, Vail gets regular sprinklings of celebrity stardust. Many Hollywood figures are regular visitors both here and at Vail's sister resort of Beaver Creek. Consequently, standards of accommodation are high (the Lodge, Chateau Vail and Sonnenalp are the best hotels), and the diversity and quality of food in town makes up for the paucity of the mountain-side offerings while carrying a similarly hefty price tag. There is plenty to do off the slopes and a fairly lively après-ski scene. The Red Lion – where the owner sings lyrics like 'we're just two lost souls skiing Vail's back bowls' to Pink Floyd's Wish You Were Here – is worth a visit.

Vail is centrally situated in a group of resorts which are included on the lift pass and it is definitely worth at least a day trip to some of these. Beaver Creek, Breckenridge and Keystone are all owned by Vail Resorts. Arapahoe Basin is the only independent resort included on the pass, with exhilarating slopes for strong skiers.

## Beaver Creek

Real exclusivity and blissfully quiet trails are found a 20-minute drive away at Beaver Creek. Former US President Gerald Ford is one of many illustrious residents and the wood-built resort was sympathetically developed in the 1980s and makes no apologies for aiming strictly at the top end of the market. The pavements are heated and the whole place oozes both luxury and wealth. If you need to ask how much it costs this is not the place to stay, but that should not stop you spending at least one or two days skiing the well-groomed and absorbing slopes.

The skiing is divided into four main areas and rises from the resort base of 2,469m (8,100ft) to the summit of Beaver Creek Mountain 3,497m (11,473ft) where, unusually, most of the beginner terrain is found alongside some excellent intermediate terrain. The other side of a steep, forested gulley is Grouse Mountain, a steep and challenging mountain which is designated experts-only – as are the celebrated Birds of Prey runs across the valley. Working your way skier's left along the flank are two further ski areas, Strawberry Park and Arrowhead Mountain, resplendent with intriguing intermediate terrain plus the occasional steep mogul field and powder stash.

**Beaver Creek's party centre includes heated pavements, ice rinks and trees lit up for life, not just for Christmas.**

ABOVE: **Take your time on the perfectly prepared corduroy pistes, a highlight of both Vail and Beaver Creek.**

RIGHT: **Alternatively, follow the example of this USA racer and aim warp speeed – just not in the speed restriction area.**

As you would expect from a recent high-end purpose-built resort, the lift system is excellent with almost all lifts high-speed. Couple this with beautifully prepared trails, few crowds and scenic tree-lined skiing and it is easy to see the attraction. Typically, the downside is lunch. Unusually for America there are several very good mountain restaurants, but unfortunately these are members-only so the giant self-service refectory beckons once more.

# Keystone

BY CLAIRE WALTER

Keystone has long been a Colorado Rockies pioneer. It was one of the state's first purpose-built resorts, the first with a really major snowmaking system, the first (and still only) major Colorado resort with night skiing, the first to incorporate fine on-mountain dining at lunch and in the evening, and a leader in developing the full resort experience, with abundant off-slope activities and carefully designed nightlife.

This cluster of base villages and three mountains, one strung behind the other, ranks as one of Colorado's consistently most visited resorts. Being less than two hours from Denver means that it attracts hordes of 'Front Range' (the closest mountains to the state capital) skiers and snowboarders, and makes it more convenient for those flying in from a distance. Keystone, along with Breckenridge and Copper Mountain, ranks as one of Summit County's 'big three' – sizeable mountains with abundant lifts, trails and acreage.

Additionally, it is the first major ski mountain to open for the season, generally in October, and any Keystone lift pass is also good at nearby Arapahoe Basin, one of America's highest ski areas, where the ski season stretches into May, June and sometimes even July. Owned by Vail Resorts, Keystone shares a fully interchangeable lift ticket programme with Breckenridge, and multi-day passes also include Vail and Beaver Creek. Visitors who can't get enough skiing can do so practically around the clock: Keystone is Colorado's only big-time resort with night skiing; the lights shine on 15 trails, and the A51 Terrain Park is the state's largest day and night-lit park.

## Three peaks

Keystone's layout is unique to the state, with three mountains lying one behind the other. Dercum Mountain (formerly Keystone Mountain) is the main portal to North Peak and The Outback. Of the three, Dercum offers the greatest proportion of the ski area's easiest terrain; North Peak has the best cruisers and moguls; and The Outback has more cruisers and the best tree skiing, plus above-the-tree-line terrain.

The six-passenger River Run Gondola and a parallel high-speed quad near the eponymous River Run Village are the lifts by which most skiers and riders access the slopes. The trail map reads like a history book of Summit County's raucous mining heritage. Montezuma, Argentine, Peru and Hunkidori and others were mines and mining camps. Paymaster, Single Jack, Double Jack and Jackwhacker are mining terms. The front side offers mostly long, meandering classic trails cut through the thick forest. Snowmaking and meticulous grooming turn them into feel-good cruisers, mostly designated green circle or blue square. Abundant snowmaking means

An extreme skiier is too engrossed to notice the spectacular Rockies scenery.

these are the first runs to open each season, as well as where Keystone's night skiing takes place. The Montezuma Express serves just the upper runs, so it's easy to avoid the 'firmer' snow down at the base.

People disperse quickly from the summit. Some board a second gondola that dips into a valley and rises again to North Peak, the second summit. A gondola would not be necessary for daytime skiers, but it is vital to bring diners (and the food on which they dine) to the two restaurants in The Outpost, an elegant mountain-top lodge. The Alpenglow Stube, at 11,444ft (3,488m) is both the highest restaurant in Colorado and the highest haute cuisine restaurant in the country. Most skiers make a day of it: by the time five or six courses have been consumed, there is little time left for skiing, at least in daylight!

At Dercum Mountain, many skiers drop off the back – and most of those continue down the heavily trafficked run called Mozart, where another chairlift rises to North Peak. This middle mountain boasts intermediate and advanced terrain, including Keystone's best and most consistent mogul runs. Runs off the back of North Peak feed toward The Outback, Keystone's third mountain. Its dozen high-intermediate trails, beautiful glade skiing, and access to high-mountain bowls give The Outback a remote and wild feeling that is absent elsewhere at the resort. A short

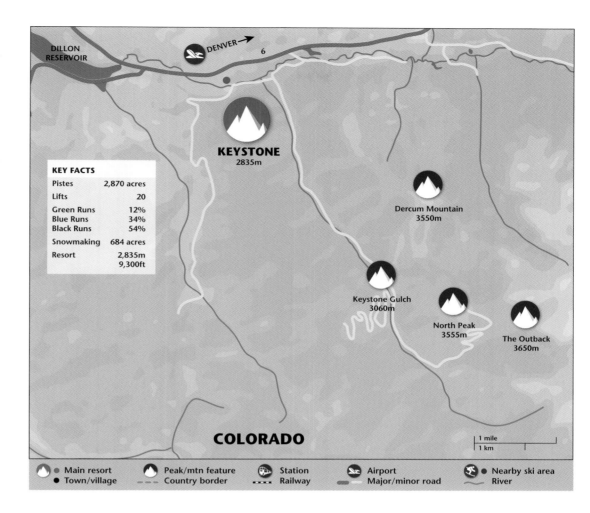

**KEY FACTS**

| | |
|---|---|
| Pistes | 2,870 acres |
| Lifts | 20 |
| Green Runs | 12% |
| Blue Runs | 34% |
| Black Runs | 54% |
| Snowmaking | 684 acres |
| Resort | 2,835m 9,300ft |

| | | | |
|---|---|---|---|
| ⛷ ● | Main resort | 🔺 ● | Peak/mtn feature |
| | ● Town/village | | - - - Country border |
| 🚉 | Station | ✈ | Airport |
| | ··· Railway | | Major/minor road |
| ✈ ● | Nearby ski area | | |
| | ● River | | |

but breath-sapping hike to the very top offers a view across the Blue River Valley towards Breckenridge, as well as access to the Outback Bowls.

Back at Dercum Mountain, three more lifts ascend from a second entry point that was Keystone's original base area. Like The Three Little Bears' lifts, one serves only a beginner slope, one angles across to mid-mountain, and one reaches a high shoulder on the north side of the mountain where A51, a large day-and-night park lit for night sliding and riding, is located. The newer A51 Incubator is a beginner park adjacent to its larger sibling. Though relatively late in welcoming snowboarders, it is now a leader.

**SNOWCAT SKIING**

*The Dercum summit is also the meeting place for snowcat skiing and riding. Instead of hiking for 30 or 40 minutes, advanced and expert skiers and riders can now reach untouched powder in a heated snowcat (see photo right) that accesses 348ha (860 acres) of bowls in less than a quarter of an hour. Guided cat skiing not only gives a tantalizing glimpse of Keystone's future expansion area, but also provides sensational bowl skiing right now.*

# Breckenridge

BY CLAIRE WALTER

Summit County – 160km (100 miles) or less from Denver – is the 800-pound gorilla of Colorado skiing. Its three largest ski areas each welcome more than one million snowriders every season – and among them, Breckenridge is the giant with Colorado's second-greatest number of lifts, third-highest summit elevation and the fourth-greatest vertical. Breckenridge's legion of fans love its variety and its verve, on the hill and off.

Breckenridge's skiing spreads across four linked mountains – the southernmost peaks in the Ten Mile Range – and boasts a massive lift capacity, tremendous vertical and lively town composed of modern hotel and condominium complexes, many of them ski-in/ski-out. The resort accommodations surround a historic downtown core with 350 registered Victorian buildings. With an abundant choice of non-ski and après-ski options, Breckenridge is positioned as an ideal ski vacation destination. As a member of the Vail Resorts family, any Breckenridge lift pass is fully interchangeable with nearby Keystone and Arapahoe Basin; there is also limited interchangeability with Vail and Beaver Creek, to the west on the other side of Vail Pass.

Breckenridge has been on the cutting edge in many arenas. It installed the first detachable, four-place chair-lift in the US – now replaced by a newer, faster version. It was one of the first to welcome snowboarders and host snowboarding competitions. 'Breck' (as the locals call it) was also among the first US resorts to actively court skiers from the UK, and it consistently ranks as one of the favourites with international skiers. Located roughly a two-hour drive from Denver International Airport, it combines convenience, congeniality and light Rocky Mountain snow.

## The peaks

The Breckenridge ski area consists of Peaks 7, 8, 9 and 10 of the Ten Mile Range. These mountains collectively stir snowriders' imaginations and make their heartbeats quicken. Any one of these by itself would make a worthy ski area, but together they form a ski arena of impressive size. Taken in consort with the resorts with which Breckenridge shares a lift pass, it makes for a skiing experience unsurpassed for variety, scope and accessibility. High-capacity cross-area lifts link Peaks 8 and 9, making these two particularly easy to combine during a ski day. Peak 7 is an easy hop from Peak 8, and likewise Peak 10 connects well from Peak 9 – though accomplished Peak 10 skiers tend to consider Peak 9 merely an access area, not worth skiing.

Peak 7, the most recent to be lift-accessed, is the northernmost. Its six-passenger, high-speed chair-lift also appeals to advanced and expert skiers who are often content to yo-yo for hours, mixing fine trail skiing with flirtations in and out of the trees. The Breck Connect, a six-passenger gondola, debuted in 2006–07 to link the town with peaks 7 and 8.

*The meticulously manicured halfpipes and terrain parks are a magnet for snowboarders and twin-tip skiers.*

**PARKS AND PIPES**

*Breckenridge caters for snowboarders and their 'New School' skiing brethren with five parks and pipes, including some of the West's best. Peak 8's Freeway boasts tabletops, boxes, rails and a halfpipe within it. Peak 7's Trygve's Park has similar features, but smaller. El Dorado on Peak 9 – similar, but smaller still – is great for the youngest tricksters and for ski and ride classes. Gold King features rails, kickers and jumps for experienced riders, while Country Boy is a mid-size pipe.*

The Breckenridge ski area started on Peak 8. Its base is high above town, and visitors are anticipating lift service eventually to eliminate the need to drive or take a shuttle bus to the long-established Peak 8 base. This mountain still has the greatest variety of terrain – from mild beginner slopes near the base to a handful of off-centre trails which have long enticed advanced and expert skiers (and now snowboarders). There's also fine mid-mountain cruising, the resort's best on-mountain restaurant and a 162-ha (400-acre) crown of challenging above-the-treeline bowls, snowfields and chutes. The winter of 2005-06 witnessed the long-anticipated debut of the Imperial Express SuperChair, North America's highest-reaching chair-lift, unloading at 3,913m (12,840ft) and a gateway to this concentration of demanding terrain.

The deep drainage between Peaks 8 and 9 provides long, steady and steep fall-line runs that sprout enormous moguls. But Peak 9 itself is the resort's 'Mellow Mountain'. With a lower base elevation than its older sibling, Peak 9 offers the lion's share of Breckenridge's easy skiing. Legions of novices slide down languorous green-circle runs on the lower mountain. Another high-speed chair-lift whisks riders to the upper reaches of Peak 9 and more pleasing intermediate runs. Additionally, the upper reaches also proffer several double-diamond parcels collectively known as the North Face. Finally, on Peak 10, the southernmost mountain, a high-speed chair-lift runs up the ridge crest with high-end blue-square and black-diamond runs dropping off on each side. Most of the precipitous north flank is called The Burn.

The town of Breckenridge is also Summit County's liveliest – by far. Holidaymakers and locals from elsewhere flock there for lively après-ski, the most interesting array of restaurants and nonstop nightlife.

---

**Sometimes Breckenridge's powder is so deep that skiers practically need ploughs to blast through it and snorkels to keep breathing.**

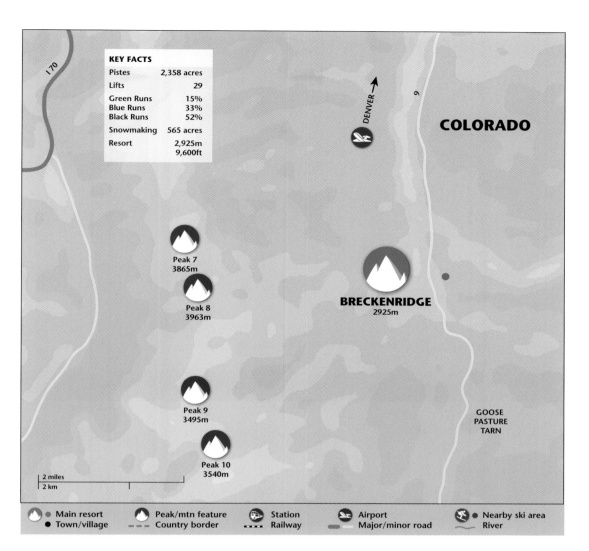

| KEY FACTS | |
|---|---|
| Pistes | 2,358 acres |
| Lifts | 29 |
| Green Runs | 15% |
| Blue Runs | 33% |
| Black Runs | 52% |
| Snowmaking | 565 acres |
| Resort | 2,925m |
| | 9,600ft |

I-70

DENVER →

9

COLORADO

Peak 7
3865m

Peak 8
3963m

BRECKENRIDGE
2925m

Peak 9
3495m

GOOSE
PASTURE
TARN

Peak 10
3540m

2 miles
2 km

| | | | | | |
|---|---|---|---|---|---|
| ● Main resort<br>● Town/village | ▲ Peak/mtn feature<br>--- Country border | Station<br>.... Railway | Airport<br>Major/minor road | ● Nearby ski area<br>~ River |

# COLORADO

# Crested Butte
BY CLAIRE WALTER

Crested Butte is just 27km (17 miles) south of Aspen, but there are no roads through the wilderness between them and only one nearby unpaved, unploughed road. The two resorts share a mining heritage but otherwise are quite dissimilar. Instead of glitz and exclusivity, Crested Butte doesn't judge visitors by their wardrobes or their wallets. There is much scenic beauty, good snow, just enough off-slope activities for variety, and the winning combination of a charming old purpose-built resort. Crested Butte long languished as the Cinderella of Colorado ski resorts.

**Extreme terrain at the summit mellows out to gentler runs below.**

Wonderful, varied, complicated terrain once rose above a cobbled-together base village – purpose-built, but not really well designed. Snowmaking needed improvement, grooming wasn't state of the art, and the lift system begged to be upgraded. That all began to change in 2004–05, the first full season under the ownership of Tim and Diane Mueller, who previously transformed Vermont's Okemo from a minor-league ski area to a top New England resort. The Muellers poured millions into lift upgrades, new grooming equipment, improvements in snowmaking, base village makeover and more. It means Crested Butte is coming of age as a ski resort in the manner that Rocky Mountain visitors expect.

In addition to the usual beginner slopes, easy novice trails, intermediate cruisers, mogul runs and terrain parks, Crested Butte offers some of the most extensive, most challenging off-piste terrain anywhere in North America. It pioneered in-bound, lift-served extreme terrain and extreme skiing competitions. Nevertheless, Crested Butte is as congenial for families and for occasional skiers and snowboarders as for those who eat black diamonds for lunch.

When you look up at the ski terrain from Crested Butte's evolving, improving base village, most of it is up to the left and out of sight. Two high-speed quad chairlifts get you there. The Red Lady Express on the left serves mostly beginner and low intermediate terrain. The Silver Queen on the right is the gateway to just about everything else, directly accessing the best mogul runs and most of the Extreme Limits' double-diamond terrain, and indirectly, the rest of the trail system.

Parallel to Silver Queen's upper section is the Twister chairlift. Good skiers often do laps there, alternating between cruising the groomers attacking trails with bumps. *Really good* skiers and riders hop on the High Lift (a drag) to Upper Peel, the formidable Headwall, the steep, tree-studded Teocalli Bowl (brought inbounds in early 2005), and the hike-to summit of Crested Butte Mountain itself, some 213m (700ft) above the High Lift unload.

### Paradise and beyond

An easy traverse from the top of Silver Queen opens into Paradise Bowl, not visually imposing as far as Rockies' bowls go, but in many ways the ski area's hub. It is wide enough to contain some packed cruising terrain, bump sections, the Canaan Terrain Park and an impressive 152-m (500-ft) Superpipe for boarders and 'New Schoolers'. The high-speed Paradise Lift and the Paradise Warming House at the bottom make it an area-within-an-area. With generously cut, groomed cruising runs, the terrain park and the big pipe,

and a place to warm up and fuel up at lunch, Paradise alone satisfies many skiers and riders.

Popular as it is, however, Paradise represents a fraction of Crested Butte's variety. Just to skier's right of Upper Paradise Bowl is a surface lift that hauls skiers and riders to the North Face, 162ha (400 acres) of steep, gladed, cliff-banded terrain so challenging that, in parts, double-diamond designation does not seem to suffice. More extreme than the Extreme Limits, the North Face likewise is avalanche-controlled but never groomed.

Halfway down, several trails split off, some returning to the base area and others angling off other lifts and trails. One of these is the East River lift, the farthest from the base area, with half-a-dozen of Crested Butte's most consistent trails for intermediate and advanced skiers. On any given day, some will have been groomed, some not; some years back, the resort opted for a clever technique called split grooming, so that skiers could choose the smooth or bumpy side for an entire run, or pop in and out of the moguls at whim. It allows people with different tastes and abilities to ski together.

Crested Butte's traditional beginner area is to the right (looking up) of the Silver Queen lift. Its short chair-lift and T-bar are both slated for replacement with a more modern lift. In addition to its gentle open slopes, the Prospect/Gold Link area on the other side of the complex has two chairlifts and easy open slopes that provide doorstep ski access for homeowners in a growing slopeside development on what, until now, has been considered the backside of the mountain.

There was a real town called Crested Butte long before there was a Crested Butte development. The resort is convenient for skiing, and the charming town provides ample scope for dining, partying and shopping. Only 3km (2 miles) separate the town and the mountain resort.

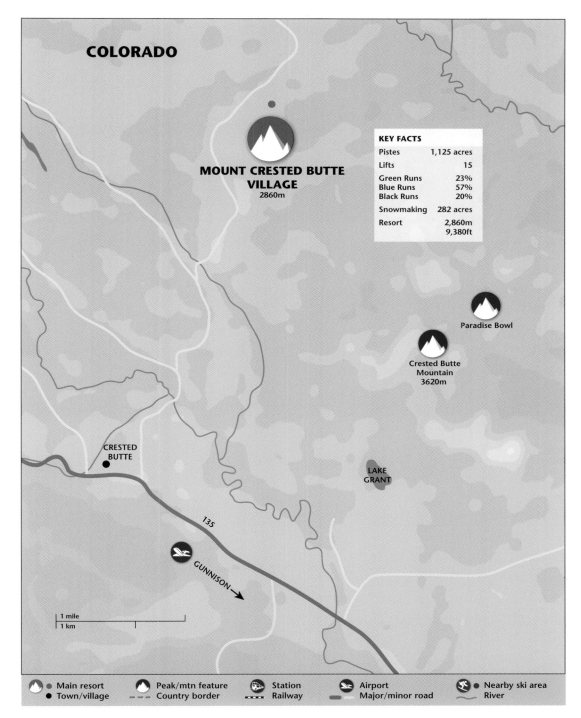

**COLORADO**

**MOUNT CRESTED BUTTE VILLAGE**
2860m

Paradise Bowl

Crested Butte Mountain
3620m

CRESTED BUTTE

LAKE GRANT

135

GUNNISON →

| KEY FACTS | |
| --- | --- |
| Pistes | 1,125 acres |
| Lifts | 15 |
| Green Runs | 23% |
| Blue Runs | 57% |
| Black Runs | 20% |
| Snowmaking | 282 acres |
| Resort | 2,860m |
| | 9,380ft |

1 mile
1 km

| | Main resort | | Peak/mtn feature | | Station | | Airport | | Nearby ski area |
| --- | --- | --- | --- | --- | --- | --- | --- | --- | --- |
| | Town/village | - - - | Country border | ▪▪▪ | Railway | | Major/minor road | | River |

COLORADO

# Copper Mountain
BY CLAIRE WALTER

Copper Mountain is a large purpose-built resort located on Interstate 70 in central Colorado. Copper Peak and Union Peak are adjacent summits, stitched together by lifts and runs into one harmonious and well-balanced ski area. The resort offers a good mix of everything from beginner terrain to snowcat-accessed backside steeps. Each lift serves pods of runs of similar levels of difficulty. This is good for groups of the same ability skiing or riding together, but not quite so good for those of varying abilities who like to meet for the lift ride.

The lower portions of both mountains are textured with ridges, valleys, and fine fall-line slopes. In addition to cut trails, several gladed parcels drop down the sides of the ridges. Copper is also topped with scooped bowls and white-coned peaks poking above the treeline.

Skiers and riders can almost read Copper Mountain like a book. When facing the slopes from the base village, the easiest terrain is to the far right; most of the intermediate runs are in the middle; and the toughest trails are to the left. A special feature is Union Creek, a gentle beginner area that is off to the side, protecting new skiers and riders and small children from the speeding skiers descending from higher slopes. Crowning the web of long frontside cruising runs are several mountain-top bowls, ranging from small scoops out of the summit to imposing high-alpine cirques. The biggest and best is Copper Bowl, on Copper's backside, with access via two summit lifts.

During ownership by Intrawest (also owners of Whistler Blackcomb and others), Copper boasts a redeveloped base village at the original base area and a second, subsidiary portal with an attractive day lodge and the resort's first six-passenger chairlift. The long purpose-built development stretches along the base, with the slopes on one side and Interstate 70 on the other. New buildings are interspersed among older ones, and cross-country trails are nearby. The original core, now called the Village at Copper, contains the loading stations for two high-speed quad chairlifts, American Eagle and American Flyer, the main feeder lifts. The resort's biggest terrain park and awesome Superpipe are close to this base where riders put on a good show.

The Flyer angles to the right, ascending lower Union Peak to a small plateau just before the mountain steepens seriously. It serves

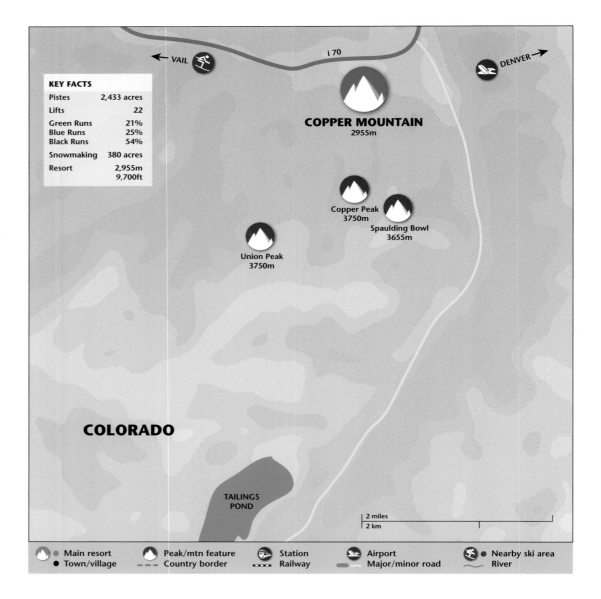

**KEY FACTS**

| Pistes | 2,433 acres |
| --- | --- |
| Lifts | 22 |
| Green Runs | 21% |
| Blue Runs | 25% |
| Black Runs | 54% |
| Snowmaking | 380 acres |
| Resort | 2,955m 9,700ft |

COPPER MOUNTAIN
2955m

Copper Peak
3750m

Spaulding Bowl
3655m

Union Peak
3750m

COLORADO

TAILINGS
POND

2 miles
2 km

| | Main resort | | Peak/mtn feature | | Station | | Airport | | Nearby ski area |
| --- | --- | --- | --- | --- | --- | --- | --- | --- | --- |
| | Town/village | | Country border | | Railway | | Major/minor road | | River |

some of the resort's easier trails – wide, ego-boosting cruisers that make novices feel like intermediates. Ski down to the right to the Timberline Express and its septet of intermediate trails which many skiers happily yo-yo for hours, stopping for breaks at the T-Rex Grill near the loading area. Down to the left from the Flyer unload area is Union Bowl. The Sierra triple chair continues to the top of Union Peak, moving up a headwall featuring a series of double-black diamond lines. Nestled into one of Copper's farthest corners below the main Union Peak runs is Union Creek, a good spot for beginners. Its user-friendly day lodge, Schoolhouse, houses a ski school desk, food service and kids' centre.

The American Eagle climbs from the base to another web of long intermediate runs. A short glide from its top station is Solitude Station, a busy mid-mountain cafeteria, and also the loading area for the Excelerator and its half-dozen high intermediate and advanced runs. The Excelerator unloads on a windy ridge near the top of the Super Bee, Copper's longest chairlift. This six-passenger lift takes just eight minutes to rise 700m (2,300ft) from East Village, a second base area with another day lodge, more housing lodging and Copper's busy tubing park.

## Up to the bowls

Copper Mountain is crowned with bowls, and all of the upper lifts reach one or more of them. Grooming is sparse and powder abounds on these high-alpine runs. In addition to directly accessing Union Bowl on the frontside, the Sierra triple chair ferries skiers to the top of Union Meadows, a double-black parcel that resembles a flattened-out powder bowl, tree-free at the top and gladed lower down. This area is never crowded, and the run-out feeds back to the Timberline Express or continues down to Union Creek.

A traverse from the top of the Excelerator leads to the Storm King drag lift. Spaulding Bowl is on one side and Enchanted Forest on the other. The same general area where the Excelerator and Super Bee unload are the four

gnarly, mogully runs of Resolution Bowl. Copper Bowl, 364ha (900 acres) on the backside and accessed through control gates at the top both Union and Storm Peaks. This is a huge north-facing cirque with two double chairlifts and a dozen roughly defined and ungroomed routes. Free snowcat access takes skiers and riders to Tucker Mountain for still more thrilling steeps.

Located directly adjacent to Interstate 70, Copper Mountain is one of the West's easiest

TOP: **The monumental Copper Station day lodge is the centrepiece of the East Village development.**

ABOVE: **Tucker Mountain dominates Copper Bowl, the backside, backcountry-style, steep-and-deep terrain at Copper Mountain, that flirts with the treeline.**

drive-to resorts. The lift capacity is generous enough to accommodate Denver locals as well as vacationers. A Copper lift pass is also valid at Winter Park, two mountain passes distant, but a feasible day trip.

# Steamboat

BY CLAIRE WALTER

No resort has a firmer reputation for bottomless powder and open-hearted Western hospitality than Steamboat, Colorado's northernmost resort. Steamboat coined – in fact, trademarked – the term 'Champagne Powder' to describe the abundant, cloud-light snow that falls consistently and abundantly on beefy, rounded mountains bracketing broad valleys. Steamboat's five-peaked *massif* looms commandingly over the Yampa Valley. Its mostly open topography, rounded summits and wooded slopes give it the appearance of a gentle giant. There are steep runs, challenging terrain and commendable glades, but the overall impression is one of unintimidating friendliness.

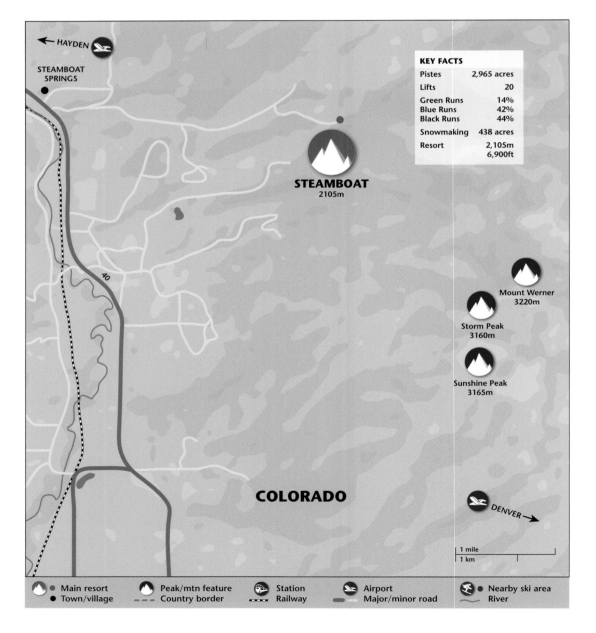

| KEY FACTS | |
|---|---|
| Pistes | 2,965 acres |
| Lifts | 20 |
| Green Runs | 14% |
| Blue Runs | 42% |
| Black Runs | 44% |
| Snowmaking | 438 acres |
| Resort | 2,105m 6,900ft |

**Main resort** / **Town/village** — **Peak/mtn feature** / **Country border** — **Station** / **Railway** — **Airport** / **Major/minor road** — **Nearby ski area** / **River**

## Two squares

The purpose-built resort at the base orbits around tandem hubs: Gondola Square, at the bottom of North America's first eight-passenger gondola, and Ski Time Square, offset slightly from the gondola plumb line. The chair-lifts from the base include short ones for beginners and a longer quad all the way to 2,768m (9,080ft) Thunderhead, a rounded mid-mountain plateau that is also the gondola's top station. It is crowned by a day lodge and restaurant and is the place to meet the Olympic silver medalist Billy Kidd for his daily run with guests down the mountain. When not following Billy, skiers can head a short way down then up much further to reach Mount Werner, Storm Peak or Sunshine Peak.

The runs to the left from Thunderhead lead into the Burgess Creek drainage. Lifts climb out of it to Storm Peak, back up to Thunderhead, or on to Mount. Werner. The Storm Peak and Bar UE lifts climb to the Storm Peak summit, from which experts tackle a ridge rilled with steep chutes, while intermediates angle over to dance down Mt Werner's Big Meadow. The Pony Express, Steamboat's westernmost lift, accesses intermediate and advanced terrain that sees less traffic and less grooming than elsewhere.

On powder days, nothing surpasses Morningside Park on the backside of Storm Peak. Between Storm and Werner is Buddy's Run, a Steamboat classic named after Buddy Werner, a local hero ski racer who perished in an avalanche in the Alps. The Four Points chair-lift enables skiers and riders to yo-yo a quartet of challenging runs on lower Storm Peak. The mountain's eastern flank is composed of broad trails alternating with open glades that provide an exciting introduction to the joy of powder skiing in the trees.

The trails dropping off to the right from Thunderhead lead to Priest Creek. From there, the Sundown Express climbs to the top of a subsidiary mountain called Sunshine Peak. Elkhead is the name of the lift that returns to Thunderhead. It is possible to ski between Sunshine and Storm, two almost equally high summits. While not the highest point of the Steamboat ski area, these are the twin giants of Steamboat skiing, forming the loftiest protrusions on a long ridge sloping off Mount Werner, and their mix of intermediate cruisers and powdery glades epitomizes the Steamboat experience. Closet and Shadows are routes through a forest of firs and aspens that are so perfectly spaced that they seem to have been planted by the god of glades. No place in Colorado can claim better tree skiing. Sunshine's trail skiing isn't too shabby either. Three O'Clock and Twilight lure skiers of the steep, while Two O'Clock and One O'Clock are more congenial for those who like their trails a little tamer.

Snowboarders love Steamboat's textured natural terrain for free-riding, and also its 5-ha (12-acre) terrain park, with its own chair-lift, sound system and snowmaking. The monarch of the park is Mavericks, a 198-m (650-ft) long, 15m (48ft)-wide monster superpipe with 4.5m (15ft) walls, 5m (17ft) transitions, and a quarter-pipe kicker at the end. Mini-Mav, a miniature version of the superpipe with 3-m (10-ft) walls, suits novice riders.

Steamboat and the nearby ranching town of Steamboat Springs in the Yampa Valley between them offer outstanding on-slope

facilities and excellent off-slope diversions as well. Steamboat's pioneering Kids Ski Free programme has made ski vacationing affordable for families since 1982 with free lift tickets, free lodging and even free rental equipment for children aged 6 to 12 when accompanying their parents. The tradition of Steamboat Springs' annual Winter Carnival dates back to 1912. Visitors share locals' enthusiasm for ski racing, ski jumping at the historic Howelsen Hill and a downtown parade featuring America's only high-school band that 'marches' on skis. Not to be missed is the annual Cowboy Downhill, in which a

**Powder and trees are two of Steamboat's signature experiences for those who like their snowriding on the wild side. Groomers, cruisers and bumps draw traditionalists.**

horde of real rodeo competitors navigate a racecourse with more courage than skiing skill. But real skill on snow is not a rare commodity in Steamboat Springs, whose nickname is Ski Town USA, because it has sent nearly 60 of its sons and daughters to the Olympic Games – more than any other community in the country, remarkable for such a small town.

# COLORADO

# Telluride

BY LESLIE WOIT

Telluride has style, it has atmosphere, and from day one, it will have your heart. Once a gold-and-silver mining town, more than a century on the town retains its colour – and not only in the deep-green pine trees and stunning iron-red mountains that surround it. It was in this south-western Colorado mining town that Butch Cassidy staged his first bank heist. Just 12 blocks from end to end, the town's Victorian clapboard houses have been tastefully converted into charming shops and galleries, funky bars and restaurants.

Eclectic and full of charm, these days Armani mixes with 10-gallon hats, and in the Old Sheridan poolroom you could easily find yourself two-stepping with a wealthy Texan oilman one moment and a snow-plough driver the next.

Connected by a gondola (free to foot passengers and running until midnight) the Mountain Village is a virtual second resort located mid-mountain at a snow-sure 2,895m (9,500ft) above sea level. In addition to dozens of massive trophy chalets and condos, the deluxe Wyndham Peaks Resort & Golden Door Spa makes this alpine ski-in/ski-out enclave a modern high-end complement to the western chic of Telluride proper. If privacy and ski-in/ski-out is your priority, you can even hire a whole chalet located mid-mountain,

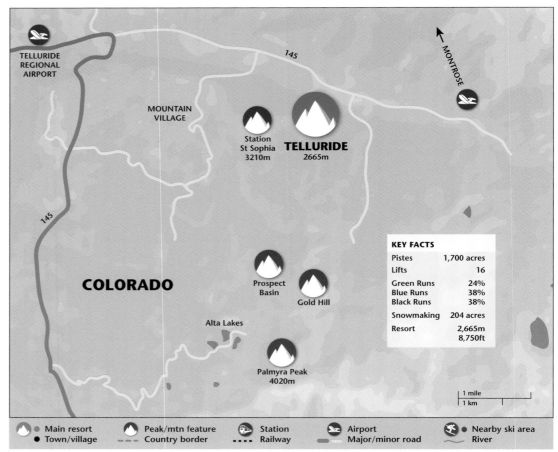

**From narrow chutes to well-spaced glades, Telluride has slopes for all abilities.**

| KEY FACTS | |
|---|---|
| Pistes | 1,700 acres |
| Lifts | 16 |
| Green Runs | 24% |
| Blue Runs | 38% |
| Black Runs | 38% |
| Snowmaking | 204 acres |
| Resort | 2,665m 8,750ft |

Tempter House, and be delivered by snow-mobile to the door.

The thing about Telluride is you have to want to be there. A seven-hour drive from Denver, 1.25 hours drive from Montrose Airport, or just a few minutes from the private charter airstrip favoured by the likes of Tom Cruise and Oprah Winfrey, it's sufficiently removed from the grind of ordinary life to dissuade day skiers, and lift capacity rules out queues. Looking up from town at the east-side runs, which represent a fraction of the total terrain, you get a good snapshot of the steeps and bumps they're known for here. Taking the Plunge is not just an expression, but a classic black-diamond mogul run that plummets vertically more than 914m (3,000ft) straight into Telluride.

Just over a third of the terrain is dedicated to intermediates. You can see and ski forever on See Forever – or at least over to Utah – and more than 5km (3 miles) down. Sheltered in the woods are a variety of groomed runs, glades and short chutes. For novices, long mellow greens and blues off Lift 10 below the Mountain Village, and Ute Park in Prospect Bowl are good ego-building areas. Galloping Goose, named after a bizarre and long-obsolete train-van hybrid, runs for almost 8km (5 miles) from the top of the Prospect Lift to the bottom of the mountain.

For powder seekers, Prospect Bowl's Mount Quail, a guided hike-to area, was opened in 2005. A half-hour hike from Lift 12, it's a remarkable 335-m (1,100-ft) chute, to which shovel and beacon-wearing skiers are delivered by ski instructors or patrollers. For those wishing to venture further afield, Helitrax offers the only heliskiing in the state. Telluride maintains 30km (19 miles) of scenic cross-country trails.

Off-slope, there is a lot of action to cover. From dog-sledding and snowmobiling, to horse riding and ice climbing, Telluride does

**The restored mining town oozes Wild West character.**

something for everyone and does it all with style. After burning all those high-altitude calories in the fresh mountain air, you won't starve either. Restaurants with groovy bars serve sophisticated menus with regional variations. Ascend on the gondola into the starlit night for a superb dinner at Allreds, 3,200m (10,500ft) above sea level and a fork away from heaven. The New Sheridan has billiards and beer, and the Last Dollar Saloon will satisfy your cowboy fantasies.

Exclusive, somewhat remote, with a perfect blend of Wild West rustic and modern decadence, Telluride belongs on everyone's must-ski list. From Hollywood A-listers to married-with-kids, this relaxed stylish resort ticks all the boxes and, as they've been known to say out there, it also kicks ass. Quite right too.

# Snowbird and Alta

BY ARNIE WILSON

It was a marriage that almost all Utah skiers – but few snowboarders – wanted: that between the ski areas of Snowbird (a modern resort in the high-altitude French purpose-built genre) and Alta, one of the oldest, with a studied determination to stay old-fashioned and funky. Only a mile of Little Cottonwood Canyon road, but a completely different culture, separated them. That, and snowboarding – which is, bizarrely in such a funky resort, banned in Alta. What united them, in essence, before the final get-together was the truly remarkable skiing.

For the simple reason that these exhilarating Utah resorts are next-door neighbours in the Wasatch Range, just east of Salt Lake City, the creation of a link between them was always likely, and perhaps even inevitable. That day finally came in 2001. Now, particularly for skiers, for whom steep and deep and plenty of it is their only mantra, the combined terrain has created one of the most exciting prospects in the Rockies – north or south of the border.

The link was achieved thanks to new lifts in Mineral Basin, a large bowl at the back of Snowbird's Hidden Peak and Alta's Sugarloaf mountains. The new area was dubbed 'Altabird' by some.

## Alta

Even today, most people discover Alta in the process of skiing Snowbird, yet it's an absolute must for any even halfway serious skier. Why would you travel so far and yet not go the extra mile or two (literally) to what some would rank as the greatest powder resort of them all? Alta, once a busy mining

**Powder unlimited: ungroomed slopes like these and plenty of Utah's 'greatest snow on earth' attract skiers the world over.**

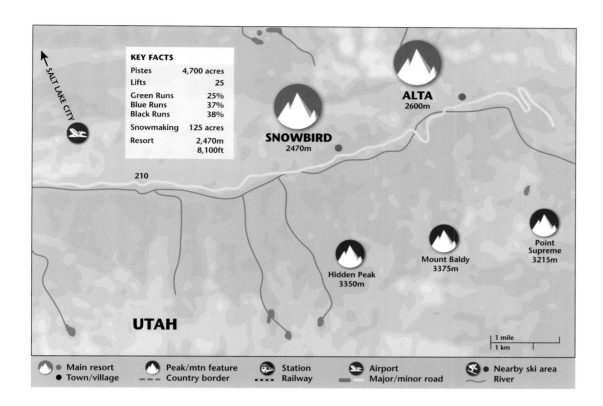

**KEY FACTS**

| | |
|---|---|
| Pistes | 4,700 acres |
| Lifts | 25 |
| Green Runs | 25% |
| Blue Runs | 37% |
| Black Runs | 38% |
| Snowmaking | 125 acres |
| Resort | 2,470m<br>8,100ft |

SALT LAKE CITY

ALTA
2600m

SNOWBIRD
2470m

210

Hidden Peak
3350m

Mount Baldy
3375m

Point
Supreme
3215m

**UTAH**

1 mile
1 km

| | | | | |
|---|---|---|---|---|
| ● Main resort<br>● Town/village | ● Peak/mtn feature<br>- - - Country border | Station<br>Railway | Airport<br>Major/minor road | ● Nearby ski area<br>River |

*With its soaring alpine peaks and challenging terrain, Snowbird sometimes has to use a howitzer and shells left over from the Korean War to blast the more avalanche-prone slopes. The resort seemed a certainty as a key location for the 2002 Salt Lake City Winter Olympics, but much to Dick Bass's chagrin, it was ruled out because it was felt that Little Cottonwood Canyon was too narrow – and possibly too avalanche-prone – to accommodate the inevitable heavy traffic and supply of extra provisions. Snowbird could have run a downhill following Chip's Run down Peruvian Gulch, but lost the prize to Snowbasin (see pages 222–223).*

community, opened its first lift as long ago as January 1939, offering a single ride on the chair for 25 cents, or a full day pass for $1.50. Many of its chair-lifts are still comparatively ancient, and none – even the modern replacements – have safety bars, emphasizing Alta's 'old school' ethos.

Like many ski areas in the Rockies, Alta's history goes back to the silver mining days of the late 19th century. The town of Alta was established in 1871, and soon distinguished itself by acquiring one of the worst murder rates in the West. Life was cheap, and riotous behaviour was always on tap. The resort had its genesis when miners started to access the slopes on primitive skis riding the lifts formerly used to bring ore down from the mountains.

Today, although there is an intriguing restaurant called the Shallow Shaft (slang for a miner who slacked during his shift) and a lodge called The Goldminer's Daughter, there is little trace of the mining town, which was periodically battered by fire, avalanche or both. With the decline of mining, Alta eventually became a ghost town. In the 1920s, a huge landslide came churning down the mountainside and wiped out almost the entire village. Yet still it didn't quite die. And skiing would give it the kiss of life. In 1971 – exactly

a century after Alta was founded – the space-age resort of Snowbird opened beneath the spectacular landmark of Utah's very own Twin Peaks.

## Sublime snow

Apart from more-than-adequate beginner slopes, what the two so-different resorts of Alta and Snowbird had (and have) in common is sublime skiing, particularly for those in search of that elusive combination of light and plentiful powder and exhilaratingly steep cirques and chutes. This is the kind of terrain that, when it snows heavily, any skier with a little guts and technique can leap into without fear (as long as the chosen slope is not prone to avalanche). The dryness and quantity of Utah's snow is so celebrated that the state proclaims it 'The Greatest Snow on Earth' on car licence plates, and it is claimed that 1,270cm (500in) falls each winter. This is a result of the two resorts' location just east of the Great Salt Lake, where the so-called 'lake effect' triggers storms that deposit copious falls, especially in Little Cottonwood Canyon,

**Light, dry and copious: once skied, the snow at 'The Bird' and neighbouring Alta is never forgotten – and always sought after by off-piste enthusiasts.**

just 48km (30 miles) from Salt Lake City international airport. (No other American airport is so close to so much skiing: there are seven Utah resorts within an hour's drive of the state capital).

Alta, known to some aficionados as the 'Cadillac' of skiing, has pretty much thrown off its funky, cheap and old-fashioned image and has begun to acquire an international reputation. Some 60 per cent of its visitors are now destination skiers. The 'secret' is out: Alta is now known across the world for its deep powder skiing and remarkable steeps. Although there are some delightful and easy runs for beginners, many in the trees, there is no doubt that Alta's best terrain favours the bold. The Baldy Chutes (accessible from the Sugarloaf lift, and then a hike) and Catherine's area (accessible from the Supreme lift) are renowned for their excellent pitches, difficulty and superb snow. The Greeley Chutes and the Rustler pitches are also well known, and were among the favourite slopes of Alf Engen, the Norwegian who pioneered skiing here and lent his name to the local ski school. Devil's Castle, a peak with open steeps and excellent powder skiing, also accessible from Sugarloaf, and the Wildcat Steeps, accessed from Wildcat lift, also have excellent deep-powder glade skiing.

Alta's two base areas – Wildcat and Albion – are linked along a long, flat stretch by a transfer tow. Most of the easy skiing, with green trails like Crooked Mile, Sweet'n Easy and Sunnyside, is reached from the Albion side. Another green, Sugar Way, also takes stronger skiers to the Sugarloaf Lift. From the top of this chair skiers survey most of the ski area and can choose whether to remain above Albion, and perhaps move onto some tougher skiing from Point Supreme, or move over into the big valley area that divides the ski area – dotted with all kinds of gullies, chutes and cruising runs – and on down towards Wildcat. Some runs are not on the trail map: Glory Hole is an unassuming little trail that starts steep – and gets steeper. Angina Chute is one of a cluster of little chutes named after heart ailments (presumably because they get your heart pounding).

Although Snowbird and Alta do get some of the best powder in the world, they also (like any resorts) occasionally have an off-day (or week), but given a deep blanket of light powder, some challenging runs become 'do-able' by skiers who might not otherwise be tempted. In deep snow, and even falling snow, as long as there is no avalanche danger, almost anything is possible.

Snowbird's 'tram' (cable-car) – one coloured blue, the other red – takes 125 skiers and boarders quickly to the top of Hidden Peak, at 3,352m (11,000ft). There is one fairly easy way down: Chip's Run (named after a young soldier killed in Vietnam), which returns all the way to the base, is a fairly accommodating blue. Otherwise, try the popular Mark Malu Fork, a steep cruiser, continuing down Bassackwards (a play on the name of Snowbird's garrulous owner, Dick Bass, a Texan oil millionaire) and onto Big Emma. This is one of the finest – and widest – upper beginner/intermediate trails in the Rockies. But the brakes do need to be applied: a sign warns: 'Ski Fast – Lose Pass'.

A new high-speed quad, the Peruvian Express, carries skiers and riders to the top of Peruvian Gulch, emerging next to the bottom of the steep Chip's switchbacks. After offloading, skiers and boarders are now able to make their way down the Peruvian side of the mountain or hop on a conveyor belt travelling to Mineral Basin through a new 183m

(600ft) tunnel. Some 3.6m (12ft) wide and 5m (16ft) high, the tunnel is claimed to be the first of its kind in a US ski area.

Snowbird's Cirque Traverse, accessed by either the tram or by traversing from the Little Cloud lift, is a must for any hard-core skier or boarder. From the Cirque you can pretty much ski wherever you like, particularly when the snow is good, dropping off almost at will on either side in chutes like Regulator Johnson, Gad Chutes, Barry Barry Steep and Mach Schnell. Those seeking off-piste in slightly less dramatic circumstances might enjoy Alice Avenue off the Baby Thunder quad. For intermediates wanting to stay on piste, there are blue cruisers all over the mountain.

Snowbird, the brash, jet-set destination, and Alta, the grande dame (although much more funky than grand), are strange bedfellows. Even though they are now linked, they remain very different animals, but the skiing is equally exciting. You can also ski Snowbird and Alta by joining the Utah Interconnect Tour, an all-day backcountry tour that also

takes skiers through Deer Valley, Park City, Brighton and Solitude. It's an exciting day out, mostly off-piste, and the only tour in the US that truly mimics the European concept of skiing all day from resort to resort.

ABOVE: **Itching to get to the top for another run: high-speed lifts ensure that skiers clock up as much vertical as possible in their day on the slopes.**

BELOW: **Devil's Castle, Alta: once you have negotiated the resort's highest trails or chutes, there are acres of powderfields to enjoy en route to the base areas.**

# Park City, Deer Valley and The Canyons

BY ARNIE WILSON

The skiing at Park City could almost be a tale of *two* cities, in the sense that – rather like the contrast between the other two Utah resorts of Snowbird and Alta (see pages 212–215) – there is such a difference in ambience between Park City Mountain Resort and its next-door neighbour, Deer Valley Resort, that the two ski areas could be in different countries instead of being joined at the hip. Fundamentally Deer Valley tends to be the playground of the not-so-idle rich, while its neighbour attracts the younger, brasher set. One cannot help thinking that if the miners from the great bonanza days were still around, and had learned to ski (as some did), Park City Mountain Resort – rather than Deer Valley – is where they'd do it!

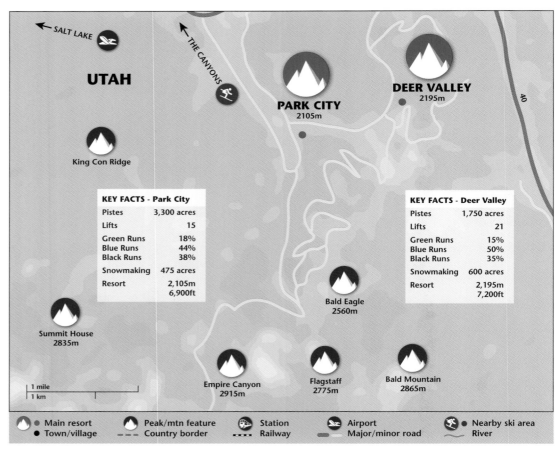

| KEY FACTS - Park City | |
|---|---|
| Pistes | 3,300 acres |
| Lifts | 15 |
| Green Runs | 18% |
| Blue Runs | 44% |
| Black Runs | 38% |
| Snowmaking | 475 acres |
| Resort | 2,105m |
| | 6,900ft |

| KEY FACTS - Deer Valley | |
|---|---|
| Pistes | 1,750 acres |
| Lifts | 21 |
| Green Runs | 15% |
| Blue Runs | 50% |
| Black Runs | 35% |
| Snowmaking | 600 acres |
| Resort | 2,195m |
| | 7,200ft |

LEFT: **Park City staged the majority of the 2002 Salt Lake City Winter Olympic events.**

Once the poor relation among Park City's ski areas, The Canyons, formerly Park West and then Wolf Mountain, has expanded to become Utah's largest single ski resort.

Deer Valley started life in 1946 as Snow Park. Park City Mountain Resort opened as 'Treasure Mountain' in1963. It's easy to generalize, but nonetheless true to say that these resorts are slightly uneasy neighbours. Although in some sections skiers on either side of the perimeter fence can see each other, and could easily ski from one resort to the other if the fence weren't there, the odds against them joining forces one day are unlikely. Yet that's what happened with Snowbird-Alta, so you can never really tell. The comparisons with Snowbird-Alta don't quite end there. One of the two central Park City resorts (the third, the Canyons, is some way out of town) does not allow snowboarders. In the Snowbird-Alta set up it's the funkier of the two that imposes the ban; at Park City it's the up-market Deer Valley which keeps boarders off the slopes.

In Utah they rave about 'The Greatest Snow On Earth', and indeed the state is uniquely placed: winter trade winds push clouds full of moisture east from the Pacific Ocean. As the clouds are swept across the desert, the heat bakes out the moisture. When the clouds meet Utah's Rocky Mountains, the remaining moisture rapidly cools to produce dry, powdery snow. This is coupled with the so-called 'lake effect' – precipitation sweeping in from the Great Salt Lake.

For those skiers or boarders who have never visited Park City, known during the Salt Lake City Winter Olympics as the 'Alpine Heart of 2002', a little geography might be helpful. The town, packed with more than 100 bars and restaurants, is the most significant skiing gateway in Utah outside Salt Lake City itself. In years gone by, the ski area now known as Park City Mountain Resort was known simply as Park City, but there was always a little confusion about whether that meant the town or the resort.

So today Park City strictly refers to the town, which provides most of the accommodation and nightlife for the ski areas of Park City Mountain Resort, its immediate, up-market and more expensive neighbour, Deer Valley, and The Canyons, formerly known (very briefly) as Wolf Mountain, which in turn started life as Park West.

It would be physically possible to lift-link all three resorts, but there are no official plans to do so at present. Such a link would create the largest single ski area in North America. There has even been speculation that it would be possible to go further, and link the three Park City resorts with Brighton and Solitude in Big Cottonwood Canyon, but there seems to be little enthusiasm for such a scheme at present. Brighton and Solitude were in fact the first two Utah ski areas to offer a joint lift ticket – the 'Big Cottonwood Ticket' – but it was scrapped in 1996 due to lack of interest. In any case, all these resorts can be skied in the same day by embarking on the Ski Utah Interconnect Adventure, an exciting all-day backcountry tour in the spirit of European-style 'joined-up resorts' skiing – a rarity in the USA, where they envy this Alpine concept.

Park City Mountain Resort was conceived in the wake of the town's hugely important mining history. Long before it gave its name to one of the three local ski resorts, the old silver-mining community was memorably described as 'a wonderful mixture of precariously-perched homes, false-fronted shops,

smoky saloons, theatres, churches and a China Town'. Its main street, almost a living museum (albeit a very lively and sometimes raucous one), reflects the days when it was the site of the largest silver-mining camp in the country. Legend had it that no one ever managed to call in at every bar in the street, have a drink, and remain standing when they reached the other end. Perhaps that remains true to this day – perhaps not!

**STRIKING A BLOW**

*On one celebrated occasion during the mining era, a British mechanic was sent for to deal with a huge pump, which had frozen overnight, causing a costly hold-up in production. What happened next was later documented in the town's tourist magazine,* Lodestar: *'the Cornishman eyed the stubborn engine, climbed its towering flywheel, and struck it a single, ringing blow with a sledge-hammer. The huge machine shuddered into action. To the chagrin of his superiors, he billed them $100 for this simple act. When an itemized bill was demanded, the mechanic wrote: 'For hitting the flywheel with the hammer, 50 cents. For knowing where to hit it, $99:50.'*

Jupiter Peak, where today skiers and boarders swirl through the powder in chutes and gullies in Puma Bowl, McConkey's Bowl and East Face, was once at the centre of the huge mining operation: ore worth more than $400 million was extracted from mines on the mountain and 23 men became millionaires as a result. They included George Hearst, founder of the Hearst mining and newspaper dynasty, whose son William Randolph Hearst was famously depicted by Orson Welles in the film *Citizen Kane*. To this day, there are still something like 1,609km (1,000 miles) of old silver-mine workings and tunnels beneath the slopes at Park City Mountain Resort.

## Deer Valley

Deer Valley, which hosted the Olympic slalom and freestyle events in 2002, is one of America's most up-market ski resorts. From the moment you arrive, as the brochures testify, the resort attempts to mollycoddle you, both with superb trail grooming and fine dining. An attendant helps unload your skis, both on the way in and the way out, and, untypically in America these days, they do not even accept tips.

One of America's most up-market resorts, Deer Valley, hosted the slalom and freestyle events in the 2002 Salt Lake City Winter Olympics.

Even out on the slopes, everything is made as easy as possible. The resort 'caps' its daily intake at 6,500 skiers, and prides itself on some of the most meticulous grooming in the country. All this pampering comes at a price, though. Deer Valley is not the cheapest resort in the Rockies. For many years it had a rather genteel reputation, and although it always undeniably had some exhilarating and steep cruising trails (like Stein's Way, named after its famously imported son, Stein Eriksen, the Norwegian Olympic champion, and Jordanelle, now one of Stein's own favourites) it had comparatively little in the way of easily reachable off-piste. But more and more ungroomed terrain has gradually been opened up, giving it more credibility among serious skiers.

Along with Deer Valley Resort's traditional wish to make its skiing experience as smooth and serene as possible for those who like to be pampered comes a desire to give experts something to get their teeth into. Both groups find what they want in Empire Canyon: the challenging Daly Chutes and bowl skiing in Daly and Lady Morgan Bowls, along with a family area too. Those in search of powder usually find it in abundance in the Triangle Trees area, where the trees have been thinned out to perfection and the angle of descent is just the right pitch to let your skis roam free. There's now no longer any reason to be dismissive about Deer Valley's once-bland terrain or to under-estimate its off-piste.

While opening challenging new terrain makes Deer Valley's choice of skiing more eclectic than of old, the resort never forgets the needs of beginners and early intermediate guests (they are never referred to as 'customers' or 'clients'). Today the current breakdown of slopes in terms of difficulty is: easier, just 15 per cent; more difficult (intermediate) 50 per cent; and most difficult, 35 per cent.

## Park City Mountain Resort

Park City Mountain Resort, right on the boundary with Deer Valley, is a funkier, more down-to-earth resort more in keeping with Park City's colourful past. Many of the trails in the resort, which hosted the giant slalom and snowboarding events at the Winter Olympics, have names which echo some of the ambience of the old mining days: Silver Cliff, The Hoist, Prospector, Bonanza and Shaft are just a few. Old mining buildings and relics can still be seen from some parts of the mountain, and there are more across the perimeter fence with Deer Valley – one of the few aspects that are common to both areas. These relics seem slightly out of place in such a sophisticated area as Deer Valley, and easier on the eye in Park City Mountain resort where they truly belong, and complement the funkier nature of the old mining area.

The major lifts from both of the main base areas take skiers and boarders over mainly intermediate terrain: the most difficult skiing is off the ridge between the two, with black runs like Silver King, Erika's Gold and Crescent tumbling down from Claim Jumper towards the resort centre. Claim Jumper also accesses a clutch of blacks on the other side of the ridge, The Hoist and Glory Hole among them. Lower down, King Con Access is the gateway to a whole face of blue cruising runs, including Eureka, Climax and, intriguingly, a trail called Courchevel.

For hard-core skiers and boarders, the chair to the top of Jupiter Bowl, at around 3,050m (10,000ft) is the key to the really interesting terrain, accessing steep tree-skiing in Fortune Teller, Silver Cliff, 6 Bells and Indicator, as well as Scott's Bowl and Puma Bowl. Snowbird/Alta doesn't have a powder monopoly!

**Once one of America's most successful mining communities, Park City is now home to three of Utah's most successful ski resorts.**

## The Canyons

The Canyons, 3km (2 miles) from Park City, and 53km (33 miles) from Salt Lake City International Airport, is a fascinating place. Although dramatically enlarged since the 2002 Winter Olympics were first announced, with a high-speed network and brand new village centre, The Canyons did not host any of the Olympic events. However, like Snowbird and Alta, it did attract a lot of skiers who wanted to stay away from neighbouring Olympic venues. As Park West, The Canyons was once very much the poor relation of the other Park City areas. It had a brief renaissance as Wolf Mountain, and in the mid-1990s was purchased by the American Skiing Company, who re-named it The Canyons and reinvented the rest of it, too. It was the subject of a massive expansion programme, and now has more trails than its two neighbours, making it Utah's largest single ski and snowboard resort. Most of the runs, named after threatened species during the brief incarnation as Wolf Creek, were renamed, but the names of two lifts, Golden Eagle and Condor (now Super Condor) survive. Others, like Falcon and Pelican lifts, and, eventually Raptor, themselves become extinct and were removed.

The American Ski Company had bought the resort for the skiing that *wasn't* on the trail map – hundreds of acres of terrain just waiting to be developed, much of it excellent intermediate/advanced skiing in bowls, gullies and chutes. The new name of the resort was inspired by the nearby White Pine Canyon and Red Pine Canyon.

When the initial facelift was complete, skiers and snowboarders who were regular visitors could hardly recognize the place. The initial $18.2 million improvement programme included six new lifts. Senior management figures enthused: 'It's basically a new ski resort.' Utah's first gondola, Flight of the Canyons, took skiers from the north side of the base lodge up and across Doc's Knob into the mid-mountain region of Red Pine Canyon. A new beginner area, High Mountain Meadow, was opened, and a number of old trails that had become overgrown were cleared and re-opened. All this brought The Canyons' total skiable terrain to 74 trails and more than 890ha (2,200 acres). Under its new ownership, the area has just about doubled in size. It now claims eight 'peaks' served by 16 lifts; however, some critics say there's too much south-facing terrain, and that the runs, in spite of the size of the resort, are on the short side.

The Canyons is not part of the Utah Interconnect Tour, which gives advanced skiers the opportunity to experience the magnificent beauty and superb backcountry terrain of the mighty Wasatch Range. Tours operate seven days a week, weather and conditions permitting, and are open to advanced skiers in good physical condition. Guests ski on backcountry routes between and through as many as six resorts in one day. Snowboarding is not permitted. The tour

Part of the backcountry area accessible from the Canyons – an insignificant ski area until a huge development programme made it Utah's largest single area.

ABOVE: **There she blows! A young female skier at the Canyons proves that gung-ho tricks are not the monopoly of testosterone-fuelled men!**

RIGHT: **The judges at a Canyons big-air competition approve of the height – but not the distance!**

includes guide service, lunch, lift access, transportation back to point of origin and a 'finisher's pin'. The organizers stress that the tour is not designed for the timid. 'It requires some walking, traversing and the ability to ski in diverse snow conditions', they stress. The Utah Interconnect Tour is run from mid-December through mid-April, conditions and weather permitting. For those who like organized backcountry skiing, it's an exhilarating way to put the whole region into perspective.

# Snowbasin

ARNIE WILSON

The name 'Snowbasin' was selected by Mrs Genevieve Woods in 1940 from 1,100 competition entries. At that time, there was a dog-sled taxi service to the slopes, located in the Wasatch-Cache National Forest of northern Utah. Snowbasin officially opened after a road was constructed from Ogden, 20 minutes away, and two rope tows were installed to pull skiers up Becker Hill. On opening day, Alf and Sverre Engen, two of the three celebrated Engen brothers (Norwegian ski pioneers in Utah), dropped flowers as they celebrated with a big ski jump on Bjorngaard Hill. The other brother, Corey, ran the ski school.

Not far from the site of the legendary Golden Spike, where the nation's railway network finally linked east with west in 1869, Snowbasin is one of the most naturally exciting ski areas in the US, with terrain that lends itself to spectacular fall-line descents and excellent powder skiing. There are long, cruising intermediate runs, high alpine bowls, steep chutes, deep powder glades and expert downhill courses, along with two terrain parks (a small one near the Powder-Puff nursery slope, the other high on Porcupine), a super-pipe with its own lift, and 26km (16 miles) of cross-country tracks.

With almost breathtaking chutzpah, the little-known – but locally venerated – ski area turned itself from the so-called 'best-kept Utah secret' into a globally famous Olympic downhill location during the 2002 Winter Games held in Salt Lake City. Yet the transition was by no means so dramatic as that of the embryonic Californian ski area of Squaw Valley, which took a huge gamble by offering itself as the host of the 1960 Winter Olympics when it only had a couple of lifts.

Until it was named as the host for both the men's and women's downhills, Snowbasin was a name whispered in awe by the cognoscenti as one to watch for the future. The future came to meet Snowbasin in 1995, when Utah landed the 2002 Olympics. Whether it would have emerged as such a force in the land without the games is hard to tell. One reason that Snowbasin was awarded the Olympic downhills and the Super Gs was that its much more famous rival Snowbird was unable to host any of the Olympic events; it was thought that the problems of supplying the extra armies of spectators, officials, media and athletes would stretch the resources along the narrow and avalanche-prone Little Cottonwood Canyon too far.

## Racing terrain

Snowbasin was duly transformed with a clutch of gleaming new lifts. The John Paul Express Quad (named not after the last pope, but John Paul Jones, a dedicated local skier killed during World War II) took the Women's Downhill racers to the top of the Wildflower course, while the Olympic Tram (cable-car) took the men to the fiercely steep start of the Grizzly course, high on Mount Allen at an elevation of 2,830m (9,288ft). There the

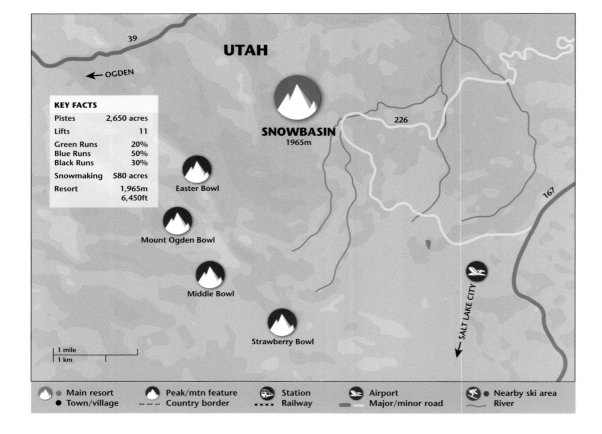

**KEY FACTS**

| Pistes | 2,650 acres |
|---|---|
| Lifts | 11 |
| Green Runs | 20% |
| Blue Runs | 50% |
| Black Runs | 30% |
| Snowmaking | 580 acres |
| Resort | 1,965m 6,450ft |

Olympic athletes would likely have been too preoccupied to have noticed the breathtaking views – the Ogden Valley to the east, and Taylor Canyon, downtown Ogden and the Great Salt Lake to the west.

Snowbasin always had exciting terrain – it was moulded that way by nature's generosity. The British skier Graham Bell, a veteran of the previous five Olympic downhills described the Grizzly downhill as being 'built down a large ridge, and which looped and jumped its way down the mountain'. To put it less prosaically, the men flashed down a vertical drop of almost 884m (2,900ft), first plunging down the extremely steep Ephrain's Face, where they quickly picked up speeds of 113–121km/hr (70–75 mph). After the John Paul Traverse, they took off at Flintlock Jump, where they billowed into the air for a considerable distance, continuing through Bear Trap, Hibernation Hole, another jump at Arrowhead, on through Three Toes, Trappers, Muzzleloader Jump, Off Track Canyon, Sling Shot, and hit violent G-forces at Buffalo Jump before gliding down Rendezvous Face to the finish line.

## Image makeover

Snowbasin's makeover from cult status to full-on Olympic downhill location was equally spectacular. Witnessing all the new lodges, gondolas, tram and new trails, Peter Shelton, a prominent ski writer and Snowbasin aficionado, famously described the resort's make-over as 'a little like coming home to find my mother had had breast implants, a nose job, laser eye surgery and hair extensions'.

The transformation was orchestrated by a man who knew a thing or two about running a major destination resort: the oil magnate Earl Holding, who had owned the far more prestigious Sun Valley, Idaho, since the mid-1970s. Holding purchased Snowbasin in 1984 (18 years before the Salt Lake City Winter Olympics), and wanted to change its name to Sun Valley, Utah – if not Sun Valley, then anything with Sun in it (Sun Light was another

Until the 2002 Winter Olympics, Snowbasin was the least well known of Utah's principal ski areas. But by staging the blue-riband events, the men's and women's downhills, the resort achieved overnight fame. This photo shows the downhill courses from top to bottom.

option). He was overruled on Sun Valley, Utah, and the resort has kept its original name, although is it now known as Snowbasin – A Sun Valley Resort. Snowbasin's three new lodges, the Day Lodge, the John Paul Lodge and the Needles Lodge (all of which can be reached easily on skis) were inspired by Sun Valley's splendid River Run Plaza lodge.

### THE FLYING KANGAROOS

*Among the more intriguing facts about Snowbasin is that the resort is the North American home of the Australian Women's Aerial Ski Team, aka 'The Flying Kangaroos'. Equally intriguing is the fact that the water table in the Ogden region of Utah has a tendency to absorb mineral deposits of a reddish hue, such as iron oxide (hematite). So when the resort makes artificial snow, it often comes out pink.*

# WYOMING

# Jackson Hole and Grand Targhee

BY ARNIE WILSON AND ALF ALDERSON

For many, the exhilarating Wyoming resort of Jackson Hole is the finest ski area in the US. The resort is in the heart of the most photographed mountain range in the Rockies – the inspirational Teton chain. These jagged peaks, which resemble giant sharks' teeth (though not properly visible from the ski area itself, a little to the south), dominate the valley, or 'hole' in the mountains where trappers like Davey Jackson, after whom the area is named, used to trade with the Shoshone, Crow, Blackfoot and Gros Ventre Indians.

Other trappers were French, hence the preponderance of French names. The word Tetons itself is an old French name for breasts, an analogy which is more understandable when you view the mountains from the other side of the range at Grand Targhee, (see pages 226–227) a much smaller cult resort celebrated for its phenomenal powder.

Unless thick cloud intervenes (or you arrive at night) the main Teton Peaks – the so-called 'cathedral group', comprising the Grand, Upper and Middle Tetons, plus Mounts Owen, Teewinot and Nez Perce Peak – will tower above you as you arrive at the small Jackson Hole airport. The mountains create such an impression of wonder and awe as they rear skywards like a 'frozen tidal wave of granite' that your entire ski holiday will be enriched by this unforgettable encounter. The experience is also enlivened by the town of Jackson, some 16km (10 miles) from the ski area at Teton Village. This is a genuine Old West community, with wooden sidewalks and rowdy cowboy bars. During the summer months, Jackson is also a very busy gateway to nearby Yellowstone National Park.

The problem – and it's a happy one – is deciding whether to base yourself in town and make a daily bus (or car) journey to the slopes, or to stay in Teton Village, and trundle into Jackson by night for the best of the valley's après-ski. One possible solution is to stay midway between the two, either at the Spring Creek Ranch condominiums, or, if you can afford it, the luxurious Amangani Hotel.

The slopes are centred on two mountains: Rendezvous (Jackson's signature peak) and Après Vous (the more mellow mountain, but certainly not without its challenges). As well as these, Jackson is celebrated for its superb backcountry. The Bridger-Teton National Forest offers 2,023ha (5,000 acres) of legendary terrain outside the main slopes, which is available to good holiday skiers throughout the winter. Jackson Hole was one of the first resorts in the litigious USA to reverse the trend of discouraging skiers and snowboarders from venturing outside the ski area boundaries, and possibly the first to introduce a European-style guiding service.

So don't go alone. A sign at the top of Rendezvous tells you all you need to know

about the dangerous elements you might encounter if you wander off under a rope or without local knowledge: 'Our mountain is like nothing you have skied before', it says. 'It is huge, with variable terrain, from groomed slopes to dangerous cliff areas and dangerously variable weather and snow conditions. You must always exercise extreme caution. You could make a mistake and suffer personal injury or death. Give this special mountain the respect it demands.'

There is no cause for such anxieties on neighbouring Après Vous, where beginners and intermediates who find some of the Rendezvous slopes unnerving can enjoy some long, exhilarating cruising on trails like Werner and Moran, which, although steep in places, are always beautifully groomed and wide enough for most visitors to set their own agenda, with plenty of room for gentle traversing.

The Bridger Gondola, between the two mountains, is a sort of halfway house, providing links with both peaks. Until recently, Jackson Hole's biggest icon apart from Rendezvous Mountain was its red cable-car, or 'tram'. The ski area was conceived more than 40 years ago by Paul McCollister, who loved the Alps and designed a simple Swiss-style village. The tram, a classic Alpine cable-car, was the final touch. But the aging lift was retired in 2006, leaving local skiers feeling deprived of what they had come to feel was the soul of their ski area. A temporary chair now takes skiers to the top of Rendezvous until a new tram is unveiled.

Rendezvous Peak is the gateway to all things exhilarating in Jackson Hole, both in-

bounds and backcountry. It is not for beginners, or even nervous intermediates: there is no really easy way down. Even by traversing the East Ridge, sooner or later skiers and boarders are forced down Rendezvous Bowl, which in difficult conditions will unnerve the inexperienced.

The straightforward route from the top after negotiating Rendezvous Bowl is Rendezvous Trail, but even this exhilarating rollercoaster is not without its difficulties – mainly because of its steeper sections. The

run also offers confident skiers and snow-boarders a variety of off-piste variants on the way down – short, sharp, steep pitches like Central Chute or Bivouac. Even better, it's the route you will need to take to reach the Hobacks – Jackson's most famous in-bounds backcountry ski area.

The resort's most infamous challenge is Corbet's Couloir, a rather terrifying gash in the rocks near the top of Rendezvous, which lures the brave and the bold into its jaws, and the not-so-sure to the brink from which some

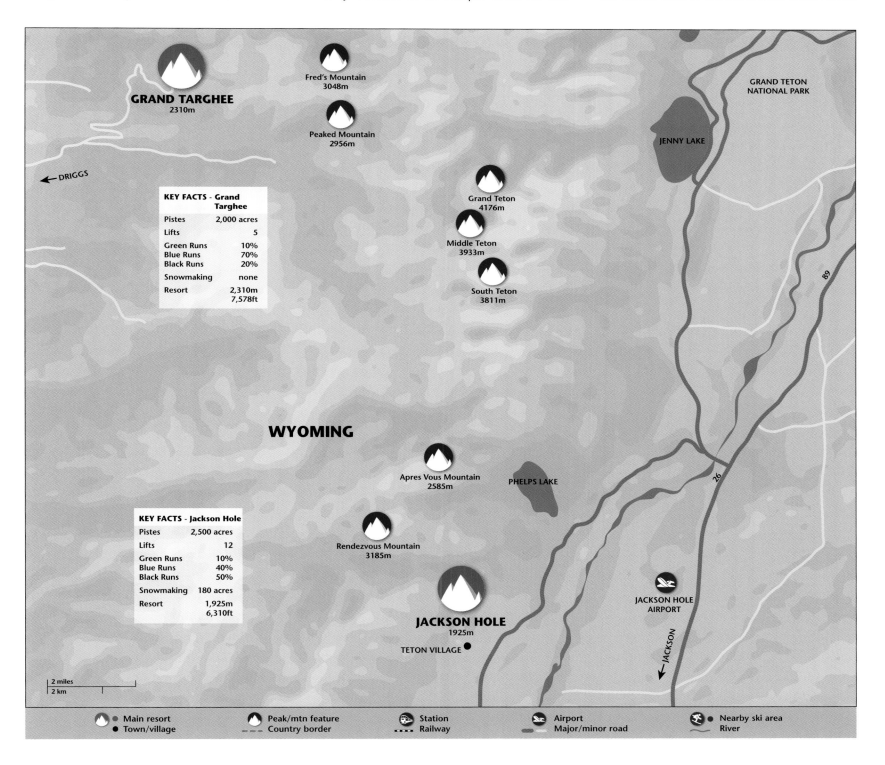

GRAND TARGHEE
2310m

Fred's Mountain
3048m

Peaked Mountain
2956m

← DRIGGS

GRAND TETON
NATIONAL PARK

JENNY LAKE

Grand Teton
4176m

Middle Teton
3933m

South Teton
3811m

89

| KEY FACTS - Grand Targhee | |
|---|---|
| Pistes | 2,000 acres |
| Lifts | 5 |
| Green Runs | 10% |
| Blue Runs | 70% |
| Black Runs | 20% |
| Snowmaking | none |
| Resort | 2,310m 7,578ft |

**WYOMING**

Apres Vous Mountain
2585m

PHELPS LAKE

26

| KEY FACTS - Jackson Hole | |
|---|---|
| Pistes | 2,500 acres |
| Lifts | 12 |
| Green Runs | 10% |
| Blue Runs | 40% |
| Black Runs | 50% |
| Snowmaking | 180 acres |
| Resort | 1,925m 6,310ft |

Rendezvous Mountain
3185m

JACKSON HOLE AIRPORT

JACKSON

**JACKSON HOLE**
1925m

TETON VILLAGE ●

2 miles
2 km

| | Main resort | | Peak/mtn feature | | Station | | Airport | | Nearby ski area |
|---|---|---|---|---|---|---|---|---|---|
| ● | Town/village | ---- | Country border | ···· | Railway | | Major/minor road | ~ | River |

turn back and others leap in, in an act of faith. Except for rare conditions when they can half-slither and half fall in, skiers must jump at least 3m (10ft) before they land. If they can keep their skis on at this point, all should be well – the actual couloir is steep, but not terrifyingly so. It's that initial jump that is difficult to make.

Apart from Corbet's, there are many rather less fearsome 'chutes', gullies and cirques to be found all over the mountain. Alta, Expert and Tower Three Chutes are steep, sometimes double-fall-line (when the angle of the slope conflicts with the way your skis want to run) gladed runs that are hugely enjoyable when the snow is good but unnerving when it's not. Other testing chutes include Paint Brush, Toilet Bowl and the Headwall.

For the committed (and usually 'local') hard-core skier, Cody Peak (not in the ski area and not served by ski-lifts) has descents that should not be attempted by holiday skiers – and certainly not without a guide. Cody has some of the most serious challenges in the Rockies, and a guide is essential to differentiate between the merely challenging and the near-suicidal. Falling in some spots is not an option. Four Shadows and No Shadows are not hugely demanding. Once Is Enough and Twice Is Nice are potential deathtraps for inexperienced skiers.

For the adventurous who nevertheless do not relish such daunting terrain, there are numerous alternatives: Rock Springs and Green River Canyons – with steep pitches like Space Walk and Zero G – are much easier valleys below Cody Peak, which run parallel with the Hobacks. You will need a knowledgeable companion to attempt the likes of Endless Couloir, Air Force Couloirs, Mile Long Couloir and Cardiac Ridge on the opposite side of the ski area in Grand Teton National Park, where the guide service does not operate.

---

**The glorious Tetons: Grand, Upper, and Middle, plus Mounts Owen, Teewinot and Nez Perce Peak. These are America's most-photographed mountains.**

## Grand Targhee

Few North American ski resorts are situated in such a spectacular location as Grand Targhee, and even fewer rejoice in the kind of talc-dry powder for which Targhee is famed, with annual snowfalls burying the resort under an average 1,270cm (500in) of snow.

Tucked beneath the awe-inspiring pinnacle of the 4,197-m (13,770-ft) Grand Teton, Grand Targhee is a friendly and welcoming little resort that revels in being something of an alter ego to its bigger neighbour, Jackson Hole. Locals are proud of their location 'on the other side' of the Tetons, and the glitz and glamour that accompany certain aspects of the Jackson Hole ski experience are refreshingly absent here; telemark skis and duct-taped gear are as likely to be seen in the lift queues as this season's new skis and outfits.

By a curious quirk of geography, you can only reach Grand Targhee from Idaho; the only road to the resort, from the small, unassuming town of Driggs, takes you on a

spectacular drive from the 'Potato State' into Wyoming and Targhee, but the barrier of the Teton Mountains prevents any access from the resort's home state of Wyoming.

Once at Targhee you'll find two peaks: 3,048-m (10,000-ft) Fred's Mountain and the slightly lower and relatively less 'busy' 2,957-m (9,700-ft) Peaked Mountain. There's also a fine 405-ha (1,000-acres) cat-skiing area off to the side of Peaked (pronounced 'peak-ed') Mountain. The small base area can be checked out in minutes, and has limited (but good) accommodation plus bars, eateries and shops.

Beginners will find a small area above the base set aside for them to learn on, after which the easier blues should be well within reach. There's a long, winding green all the way from the summit of Fred's Mountain, which has to-die-for views of the surrounding mountains and the wide, flat Teton Valley.

Given its reputation as a major attraction for powder-hounds, Grand Targhee nevertheless has 70 per cent of its terrain designated as intermediate. This varies from the well-groomed cruisers of Dreamweaver on Peaked and Wild Willie on Fred's Mountain to the steeper and more challenging Blackfoot Bowl or blue/black Floyd's Fantasy, both on Fred's Mountain.

Advanced skiers will find Targhee offers more exciting skiing after a heavy fall of snow, as the vertical drop is modest and the inbound slopes are not generally that steep (the Patrol and Instructor chutes on Fred's notwithstanding), although there are some good bumps to be found on Arrowhead. However, if you're up for some backcountry action your options expand enormously. Hike up to Mary's Nipple from the top of the Dreamcatcher Chair to access some demanding terrain, or head for the seriously challenging Das Boot from the Sacajawea Chair; check out the trees of Shadow Woman on the lower slopes of Peaked; or check in with the resort's snowcat skiing, or a guide who can show you the famed backcountry terrain of nearby Teton Pass.

**The powder at Jackson Hole's neighbouring resort of Grand Targhee, on the other side of the Tetons is legendary.**

# IDAHO

# Sun Valley
BY ALF ALDERSON

Sun Valley is a phenomenon; set miles from anywhere in the Idaho Rockies, it has nevertheless been attracting skiers, movie stars and media moguls since the first chair-lift in the US was installed here in the 1930s.

The resort's early history is in keeping with the high-roller image that is now part and parcel of the place: a former sheep ranching area made up of the Wood River Valley towns of Ketchum, Warm Springs and Hailey, it was served by the Union Pacific Railroad, which was obliged to provide a passenger service as well as one for freight out west. Company owner Averell Harriman hit upon the idea of developing a ski resort, thus giving people a reason to use the otherwise virtually redundant passenger service. He hired the services of an Austrian ski champion, Count Felix Schaffgotsch, to search out an appropriate location, who eventually hit upon the slopes above Ketchum as the ideal spot. (According to one celebrated ski pioneer, the late Friedl Pfeiffer, it was actually the count's brother Freidrich who was supposed to decide on the location. 'But instead of the very qualified Count Friedrich, Harriman acquired the very sociable Count Felix' said Pfeiffer, one of Sun Valley's earliest ski school directors. 'Who would know the difference?')

## A high profile

Marketing men came up with the name Sun Valley, the opulent Sun Valley Lodge was constructed a couple of miles from Ketchum, the first chair-lift was erected (based on a banana boat hoist) and Harriman invited Hollywood stars to the opening to garner media attention. It worked. Check out the photos around Sun Valley Lodge and in Mount Baldy's Lookout Restaurant of stars like Gary Cooper, Marilyn Monroe and latterly Clint Eastwood and Jamie Lee Curtis on Sun Valley's slopes – for Hollywood this became *the* place to be seen in winter.

More glamour was added by Ernest Hemingway, who wrote some of his novels while staying at Sun Valley Lodge (although he never skied here) and eventually moved to Ketchum, committing suicide in the town in 1961 (he was buried in Ketchum Cemetery and a memorial can be seen on Trail Creek Road).

Sun Valley has remained high-profile (and high-cost) ever since. Chic boutiques and galleries line the streets of Ketchum, real estate here is the most expensive in Idaho, and lift ticket prices can put a severe strain on your wallet. In short, Sun Valley is not the

**The Run River Lodge between Big Wood River and the base of Bald Mountain is ideal for skiers and non-skiers to meet for lunch.**

place for budget skiers. However, in return for your dollars you do get some excellent skiing, some of the most impressive ski lodges in North America, a fast and efficient lift system and – should snow ever be in short supply – one of the world's biggest computerized snowmaking systems.

## Bald Mountain

The main ski area, Bald Mountain (Baldy), stands broad-shouldered and steep-sided above Ketchum and Warm Springs, with 1,036m (3,400ft) of consistently steep slopes plunging down from its 2,789-m (9,150-ft) summit. A much smaller beginner area, Dollar Mountain (2,023m/6,638ft), sits a couple of miles away and close to the original ski area and Sun Valley Lodge.

This separation of ski hills and ski lodge isn't the logistical problem it might sound because of the excellent free bus system between Sun Valley Lodge, Dollar Mountain, Ketchum, Warm Springs and Baldy. These days, the majority of the resort's accommodation is in Ketchum and Warm Springs, from which Baldy can be accessed quickly and easily.

Dollar offers the perfect introduction to skiing – its gentle slopes, slow lifts and friendly instructors are the ideal combination for getting anyone up and running on skis. However, it's advisable to be completely confident on the blue runs as well as the greens here before heading over to Baldy, because there's a massive jump in the nature of the terrain when you reach the slopes of Dollar's big brother.

Baldy is, in essence, a steep mountain; there are green runs here that would undoubtedly be graded blue on most other mountains and are capable of providing a serious test to novice skiers. Ease yourself in on the relatively gentle inclines off the top of the Exhibition and Sunnyside chairs and on Lower River Run and Lower Warm Springs

**KEY FACTS**

| Pistes | 2,054 acres |
| --- | --- |
| Lifts | 14 |
| Green Runs | 36% |
| Blue Runs | 42% |
| Black Runs | 22% |
| Snowmaking | 73% |
| Resort | 1,750m 5,750ft |

before heading higher up the mountain to the more testing greens beneath Seattle Ridge and Lookout Restaurant.

You should at all costs try to get up to these points, for two reasons: firstly, for the spectacular wild views north into the mighty Sawtooth Mountains and south to the flat, dusty Snake River Plain, and secondly, for the

Mountain high: a lone skier drifts effortlessly down towards the valley floor.

luxurious surroundings when dining in Seattle Ridge Lodge. This log, rock and glass edifice is more reminiscent of a high-quality hotel than somewhere to clomp around in ski boots. River Run Lodge and Warm Springs Lodge at the base of the mountain are equally opulent.

For intermediate skiers, Baldy is the perfect mountain; it has a selection of long blue cruisers that are just made for honing your technique, as well as more challenging terrain on which you can push yourself – and also

LEFT: **Bald Mountain – the slopes are steeper and more challenging than they first appear from the valley.**

BELOW: **Sun Valley resort offers style and elegance in the heart of Idaho's magnificent wild mountains.**

escape from, if necessary. Start off with Warm Springs Face, or Christmas Bowl and Canyon beneath Christmas and Cold Springs chairs. They're real leg burners, but if you have any energy left after bombing down these a few times you can move onto more testing terrain easily; try the blacks of Upper Greyhawk, Upper Hemingway and Upper Cozy on the Warm Springs Face. But stick it out if you find them hard work, as they revert to blues lower down the mountain. Or try the blues of Mayday, Lefty, Farout and Sigi's bowls off the top of Mayday Chair.

For advanced and expert skiers, Baldy is a pure delight. Just looking at the consistently steep pitch of the mountain as you ascent on a lift is enough to get the adrenalin flowing, and by the time you unload from the lift you'll be positively fired up. Lookout and Easter Bowls have exciting black terrain where you can choose your own line; long, challenging bump runs can be found on Limelight on Warm Springs Face, and more secluded skiing can be found off the delightful Firetrail below

Seattle Ridge. On a powder day, half the fun of skiing Baldy is searching out new lines between trails, and the short lift queues of skiers and boarders that develop after a good snowfall are rapidly dispersed all over the mountain once everyone hops off the lifts.

On the subject of powder, however, it's worth noting that Sun Valley lives up to its name, so there's a reason for the resort's investment in state-of-the-art snowmaking systems. Top-notch snow conditions are by no means guaranteed, although there are few resorts that know better how to make the most of things if conditions aren't at their best, and even when there hasn't been any fresh snow for longer than you'd like you'll still find some fabulous skiing.

## When the sun goes down

Sun Valley's après-ski scene is rather more low-key than you might expect from such a 'glamorous' resort, tending to revolve more around dining than dancing, clubbing and gigging. However, since you'll need

*Deep powder is not that commonplace at Sun Valley, but if you do come across it you can expect some of the best skiing and boarding in North America.*

refuelling after a day of skiing Baldy you'll be pleased to know there's an excellent range of options, from bustling beer-and-burger joints to the atmospheric old Pioneer Saloon or attractive pine-panelled Sawtooth Club, both in the middle of town. And even if you're not staying there you should visit Sun Valley Lodge, an elegant echo of 1950s America with uniformed staff, huge chairs and sofas and crackling log fires; you can also dine here at the Duchin Bar & Lounge where an orchestra will serenade you as you sip cocktails.

Sun Valley is really more than just skiing. It's also the chance to leave everyday life behind for a while and indulge in a little of the high life that is so often associated with skiing but for most of us remains little more than a dream. At Sun Valley you can actually live that dream, even if only for a few days.

# MONTANA

# Big Sky

BY ALF ALDERSON

Big Sky, big mountain, big landscape – everything about this resort revels in its location in the heart of Montana's wild west. For committed skiers Big Sky is a resort that has to be ticked off at some point in your ski career – with quiet slopes, reliable snow and some of the most extreme in-bound skiing in North America, it holds a magnetic attraction despite its relatively isolated location.

And in recent years the 'addition' of Moonlight Basin Resort (formerly part of Big Sky) and the option to purchase joint lift tickets allowing unlimited access to both resorts has offered adventurous skiers one of the biggest ski areas in the US, with over 220 runs, 24 lifts and 2,146ha (5,300 acres) of terrain – indeed, this is that rare thing in North America: skiing on a European scale.

## Lone Mountain

At 3,404m (11,166ft), Big Sky's Lone Mountain stands proud above the surrounding peaks, and helps give the resort one of the biggest vertical descents in the US. And since every run off the top is a double-black diamond only accessible via a 15 person 'tram' (cable-car), you can be pretty sure that it's never going to suffer from overcrowding.

Even if the scarily steep runs down from the summit are beyond you, you should take the thrilling return ride up in the tram just for the tremendous view over three states – Montana, Idaho and Wyoming.

When skiing here, you can ease yourself in with the 'gentler' double-blacks of Marx or Lenin before dropping into a range of challenging runs through the trees beneath Shedhorn, whilst if you really want to test your skills, sign in with the ski patrol and hike off to the expert-only terrain of Big Couloir or A–Z Chutes – full avalanche gear is required for these runs and your progress will be monitored every inch of the way by the lift queue below.

Lone Mountain's South Face is not quite so daunting, but you can still find slopes of up to 50 degrees, and the lower-altitude terrain beneath the Challenger chair also provides in-bound skiing as challenging as any in North America. Less demanding but still exciting terrain can be found below Turkey Traverse from the Lone Peak Triple Chair – this gives access to the wide open bowl of South Wall, a relatively forgiving black run with a long run out at the bottom.

Big Sky has terrain to challenge the very best skiers – and plenty of easier options for the rest of us.

## The glades

Although not noted for its tree skiing, there are still some fine glades to be found at Big Sky – check out Andesite Mountain's Blue Room (north facing, so the snow stays in good condition), Congo, Bear Lair, Ambush and Wounded Knee. Andesite also has some excellent wide, undulating blue intermediate runs which vary in quality and difficulty – on some you may find bumps due to relatively heavy usage. East of Andesite is Flat Iron Mountain, the lowest of Big Sky's three peaks and another spot with wide, open runs cutting through heavy tree cover.

On Lone Mountain's lower slopes, runs such as the blue Crazy Horse and Calamity Jane provide a good warm up, although they can be relatively busy – if so head for the quieter open glades of Blue Moon or the more challenging runs beneath the Shedhorn Chair, which can be quite steep and are not always groomed.

Beginners will also find sunny, easy angled runs on the lower slopes of Lone Mountain and on Andesite's south side that are perfectly suited to them, although these trails tend to get busy at the end of the day as everyone heads off the mountain. There's also a small area set aside for first timers at the base of Lone Mountain.

Just to round off this excellent resort, freeriders will also enjoy the terrain park and halfpipe on Andesite and a natural halfpipe on Lower Morningstar on Lone Mountain.

And just in case all this still isn't enough, the really well heeled can hop across to the exclusive private Yellowstone Club resort, which can be seen from Big Sky's slopes, although the only way to get to ski here is to be invited by a member, or if you're considering building a property there.

## Winding down

The nightlife at Big Sky may seem low key after the adrenalin rushes available during the day. Opulent accommodation options such as Huntley Lodge at the base of Lone Mountain and the delightful Moonlight Basin Lodge at

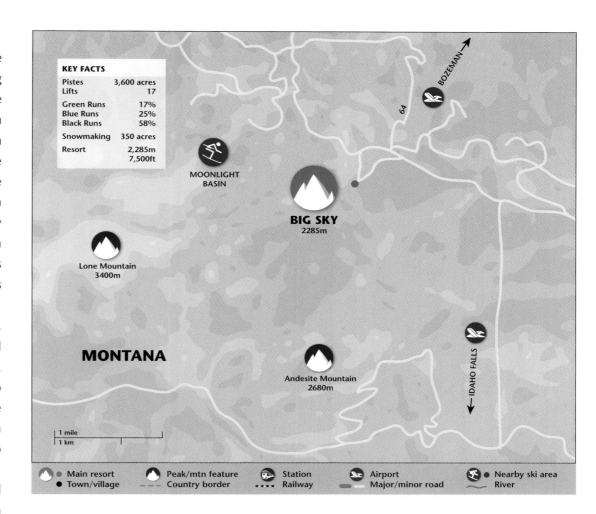

**KEY FACTS**

| | |
|---|---|
| Pistes | 3,600 acres |
| Lifts | 17 |
| Green Runs | 17% |
| Blue Runs | 25% |
| Black Runs | 58% |
| Snowmaking | 350 acres |
| Resort | 2,285m 7,500ft |

the base of Powder River Run also offer fine dining. There's not the vibe of lively European resorts, but on the other hand, European resorts are rarely so quiet and are certainly not a mere 45-minute drive from Yellowstone National Park, an unmissable option if the weather closes in or you need a rest day.

**Big Sky's base area is set in the heart of Montana's wild mountains.**

# The Big Mountain
BY ALF ALDERSON

The Big Mountain sits on the edge of the truly magnificent Glacier National Park in far northern Montana, just above Whitefish, one of the state's most characterful little towns. Although The Big Mountain has been skied since the 1930s, when locals hacked trails out of the wild forests above the town, it's only in recent years that the area has come to prominence as northern Montana's best (and biggest) ski resort.

There's a backcountry feel to the mountain (telemark skis are a common sight in the virtually non-existent lift queues) with people coming here to ski, pure and simple. Being seen in this season's styles is an irrelevance at The Big Mountain; it's what you can do on the hill that counts. And some of the locals can do plenty – the former Olympic downhill champion Tommy Moe is a local boy.

The storms that track in from the Pacific Northwest dump snow that's very often light and deep, and it doesn't get tracked out too quickly. On the other hand, cold foggy weather is a bugbear of The Big Mountain's climate, although it does help to create the beautiful 'snow ghosts' that occur higher on the mountain – fir trees coated with a thick layer of ice, rime and snow.

**You'll discover some of the finest Rocky Mountain views in the US from the summit of The Big Mountain.**

## Intermediates upwards

The Big Mountain is particularly suited to experienced skiers as opposed to beginners, who will find little more than a bunch of green runs around the base of the mountain (although the lifts here are free) and two more challenging runs (Caribou and the harder Russ's Street) running off the 2,134-m (7,000-ft) summit. Whatever your ability, you should take the Glacier Chaser lift up here at some point during your stay for the magnificent views north towards the Canadian Rockies, east into Glacier National Park and south to the Flathead Valley; the views can be enjoyed at your leisure from the warmth of the Summit House cafeteria, the highest eatery in Montana.

For intermediates, The Big Mountain is a lot of fun. Despite a relatively modest vertical drop of only 762m (2,500ft), there are plenty of long open blues and more than enough blacks if you want to push yourself. In particular the open slopes and continuous pitch of trails such as Big Ravine and Toni Matt are perfect for exciting fast runs on which you can practise your carving. And if you can't get enough during the day, the slopes off chairs 2, 3 and 6 and the beginner's platter are open until 9pm for night skiing.

For advanced and expert skiers, there's enough exciting and challenging terrain here to ensure you're never likely to get bored, with tree-skiing enthusiasts in particular being well catered for. Whether you're after a mix of steep, more open glades and tighter groves (East Rim Face), the tight and challenging (Good Medicine) or just want to explore (try Hellroaring Basin's Tepee and Connie's Couloir), you'll find plenty to go at. And it doesn't just end with trees, for there are some serious steeps such as Schmidt's Chute and Bighorn, along with a good terrain park for freestylers, including a 107-m (350-ft) half-pipe, plus Knox Landing, a freestyle jump hill. With a little judicious exploration, adventurous skiers can expect to come across fresh stashes of powder for several days after a snowfall.

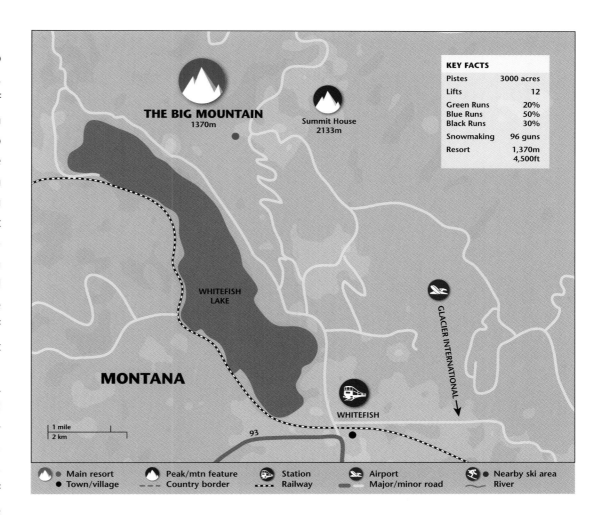

| KEY FACTS | |
|---|---|
| Pistes | 3000 acres |
| Lifts | 12 |
| Green Runs | 20% |
| Blue Runs | 50% |
| Black Runs | 30% |
| Snowmaking | 96 guns |
| Resort | 1,370m 4,500ft |

| | | |
|---|---|---|
| Main resort | Peak/mtn feature | Station |
| Town/village | Country border | Railway |
| | Airport | Nearby ski area |
| | Major/minor road | River |

Good slopeside accommodation is available at The Big Mountain, but if you choose to stay on the mountain don't neglect the chance to visit nearby Whitefish, which regularly crops up on lists of 'best small towns'. It's not just the picturesque lakeside location of this former logging town (once known as 'Stumptown' because of the tree stumps that spiked the early settlement's streets) which gets the vote, but the attractive town itself and the excellent selection of shops, bars and restaurants to be discovered in its compact downtown area. And there's a good bus service up to the resort too, so you don't have to worry about driving the 13km (8 miles) – much of it twisting and turning – after a downtown visit.

If you're skiing at The Big Mountain, it's also well worth considering taking a day off to visit Glacier National Park; it's only 25 minutes away and you'll be hard pushed to find more scenic snowshoe and cross-country ski trails anywhere in America and gear can be rented locally.

Racing is a big part of the scene at The Big Mountain – Olympian Tommy Moe started his ski career here.

# Bridger Bowl

BY ALF ALDERSON

Bridger Bowl is a very rare species – a non-profit operation that also happens to have some of the most challenging skiing in the Rockies. The non-profit tag is good news since it means lift tickets are great value, and, despite its reputation for providing skiing to challenge the very best, Bridger also has a perfectly adequate selection of trails for intermediates and beginners; indeed, over 50 per cent of the mountain is dedicated to them.

Named after both the local mountains and the legendary mountain man Jim Bridger, who once wandered this corner of southern Montana, Bridger Bowl is located some 20 minutes north of the buzzing, outdoor-oriented university town of Bozeman, which attracts many students as much for the quality of the local skiing as for the quality of its courses. In fact, a good tip is to try to ski here mid-week when the students are – or should be – in class (fresh falls of powder snow may blow this theory out of the water, however).

Bridger's ski area is flanked by the North Bowl and South Bowl, which feature a good variety of terrain, including long, open cruiser slopes, steep chutes and gullies, some fine glades and a terrain park. The testing ground at Bridger is The Ridge, which stands proud of the pistes below and can only be accessed by skiers with full avalanche gear who have signed in with the ski patrol, then hiked 122

**Small and relatively unknown, Bridger Bowl has some of the most challenging and exciting skiing in the Rockies.**

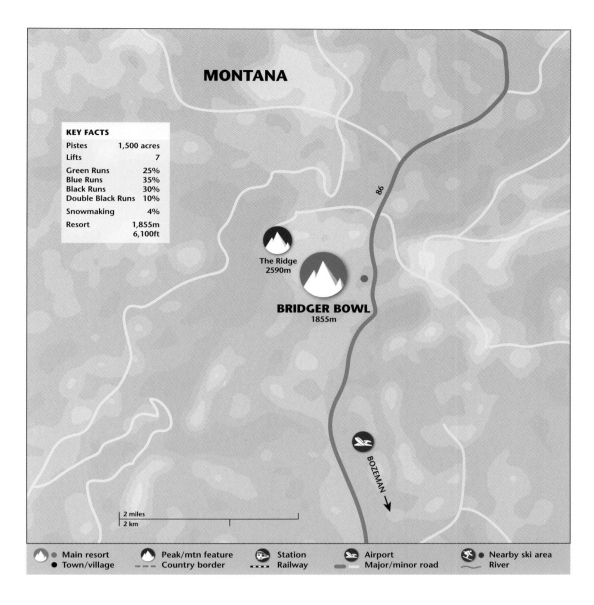

## MONTANA

**KEY FACTS**

| | |
|---|---|
| Pistes | 1,500 acres |
| Lifts | 7 |
| Green Runs | 25% |
| Blue Runs | 35% |
| Black Runs | 30% |
| Double Black Runs | 10% |
| Snowmaking | 4% |
| Resort | 1,855m |
| | 6,100ft |

The Ridge
2590m

**BRIDGER BOWL**
1855m

86

BOZEMAN →

2 miles
2 km

- Main resort
- Town/village
- Peak/mtn feature
- Country border
- Station
- Railway
- Airport
- Major/minor road
- Nearby ski area
- River

vertical metres (400ft) up vertiginous slopes from the top of the Bridger Lift. Once up on The Ridge you'll find powder-choked chutes, cliffs and steep snowfields that are the stuff of dreams – or nightmares, if you overestimate your ability.

Fear not, however, for there are plenty of easier options beneath The Ridge, including the double black runs beneath the Nose which run into South Bowl, and the thrilling blacks of North Bowl, while for intermediate skiers there's huge fun to be had cruising wide, rolling runs such as Emil's Mile and other similarly open trails which cut between the blacks and lovely sunny glades. The lower half of the mountain consists primarily of green runs and is a great playground for novice skiers. At some point in the day it's worth stopping for refreshments at either the attractive post-and-beam mid-mountain Deer Park Chalet, or the new and equally welcoming Base Lodge, both of which are easily accessible to all levels of skier.

Snow quality at Bridger is generally good since the resort is located on the eastern side of the Continental Divide and thus picks up frequent heavy falls; one storm in December 2004 deposited 180cm (71in) of powder in 24 hours!

There's no slopeside accommodation at Bridger (although a couple of good B&Bs are located nearby), but Bozeman has a great range of accommodation for all budgets, along with some of the best bars, restaurants and clubs in Montana. And if you should tire of skiing Bridger, there are two excellent options for a day's excursion: Big Sky, Montana's premier ski resort, which is around an hour south of Bozeman, and Yellowstone National Park, a further 45 minutes south of Big Sky.

ABOVE: **Regular dumps of deep powder are what draw expert skiers to Bridger Bowl.**

BELOW: **Bridger's base area is a taste of old school Rocky Mountain skiing – small, local, low-key and friendly.**

# ALASKA

# Alyeska

BY CLAIRE WALTER

Alyeska, which means 'the great land' in Aleut (the language of the Aleutians, Alaska's Inuit people) was an early name for Alaska. It lives on at Alyeska Resort, by far the largest ski area in America's largest state. Lifts and trails inhabit a glacier-carved bowl practically at sea level. Because it is located so far north, Alyeska's tree line is low. The upper mountain is a wide-open bowl, and below are conventional trails cut through thick coastal trees near the base. No other resort combines true high-mountain ski terrain, an oxygen-rich low elevation and splendid views of the nearby Pacific Ocean. The frontier spirit of Alaska lives on too.

**Skier blasts through new snow, seemingly headed straight for Turnagain Arm, shown here at low tide.**

Alyeska is both accessible and spectacular. Its expansive summit proffers a sense of see-for-ever, ski-forever terrain, with countless peaks stretching to the horizon. This statistically mid-size mountain combines remoteness, scenic splendour and a vast percentage of above-the-tree line terrain, so that it looks big and skis big. With a modest summit elevation, altitude sickness is not a problem.

The ski area has two access points. The Main Face, with a day lodge, chair-lifts and skier parking, lies at the wooded bottom of an impressive glacier-carved basin. The more recently developed North Face features a European-style 60-passenger aerial tram (cable-car) departing just steps from the Alyeska Prince Hotel and rising quickly up the 'outside' of the bowl. It is used both by skiers and sightseers.

The mountain is blessed with abundant snow – more than 1,600cm (630in) at the top in an average year, nearly twice that in a record year. Snow is dependable from December through April, but the good skiing really begins in February, when days are longer. Crowds are rarely an issue here; queues are short on weekends and most holidays, and non-existent during mid-week. Midwinter days are short. Early in the season, the night skiing lights go on in mid-afternoon, but as the calendar turns toward the equinox, steadily increasing hours of daylight make for longer and longer days.

For heliskiing enthusiasts, the wild and wonderful Chugach Range provides some amazing possibilities. Chugach Powder Guides, headquartered at Alyeska, offer a great day of heliskiing.

The tram's top station, high on a shoulder of the mountain, provides the only access to the North Face – with a vertical drop of 689m (2,260ft) – an area of open slopes and cliff-bands with a handful of double-black-diamond routes to the hotel area. On the other side is the Main Face, the original ski area built long before the tram or the hotel. The lower section is primarily novice and intermediate terrain. Chair 3 – the farthest on the left, looking up – serves the gentle beginner area. The short Tanaka lift on the far right accesses limited intermediate terrain.

The two chairlifts in the middle – numbers 1 and 4 – ascend partway up the mountain, directly serving the web of trails cut through the trees, some lit for night skiing. Chair 1 unloads at the same area as the tram, which comes up from the other side, and Chairs 1 and 4 both also feed into the upper chair-lift, Chair 6, a high-speed quad that reaches the ski areas to the lower part of Glacier Bowl. A few marked blue-square (intermediate) routes feed back to the mid-mountain, but most of the terrain up there is pure black-diamond steeps. When skiing the open bowls, skiers and riders can adjust each run to their skill and comfort level by traversing until they find a line that they like and conditions they prefer. On powder days, the skiing feels limitless.

Aggressive skiers and riders hike from Chair 6 to the super-steep upper Glacier Bowl or the Headwall (when they are open), climb to Mount Alyeska's 1,200-m (3,939-ft) summit or continue to the High Traverse and onto the double diamonds of Max's Mountain. Another option from the top of Chair 6 is to drop back into the North Face via the New Year's or Christmas Chutes, narrow passages that empty into the face like inverted funnels.

## DISCOVER THE 49TH STATE

*Alyeska Resort is not just about skiing. It is also a way to begin discovering America's eternally fascinating 49th state. From the resort, it's an easy 64km (40 miles) to Anchorage, Alaska's largest city. In mid-February, people from all over Alaska come for the annual Fur Rendezvous, a three-week, mid-winter carnival nicknamed the Fur Rondy. March brings the start of the Iditarod, a legendary dogsled race from Anchorage to Nome. The skiers' commute along Turnagain Arm is very scenic – and very Alaskan. You are likely to see Dall sheep on the cliffs just above the road, and moose sightings are not unheard-of. This, after all, is a land where the mountains meet the sea, and where the wilderness is just out of sight.*

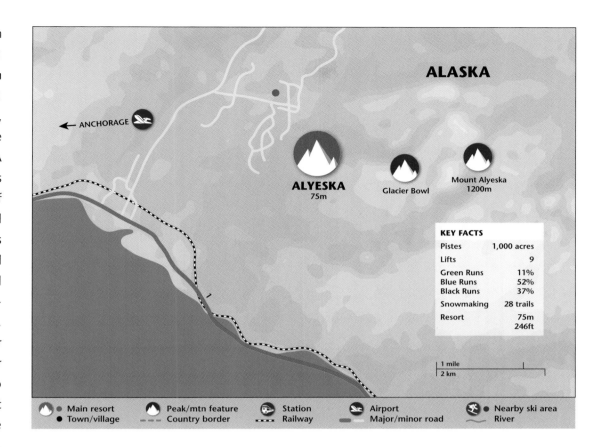

**ALASKA**

ANCHORAGE

**ALYESKA**
75m

Glacier Bowl

**Mount Alyeska**
1200m

| KEY FACTS | |
|---|---|
| Pistes | 1,000 acres |
| Lifts | 9 |
| Green Runs | 11% |
| Blue Runs | 52% |
| Black Runs | 37% |
| Snowmaking | 28 trails |
| Resort | 75m |
| | 246ft |

1 mile
2 km

| | | | | |
|---|---|---|---|---|
| ● Main resort | ▲ Peak/mtn feature | Station | ✈ Airport | Nearby ski area |
| ● Town/village | - - - Country border | ···· Railway | Major/minor road | River |

Alaskans are tough – at least some of them are. Alyeska's Spring Carnival and Slush Cup, begun in 1977, remains a late-April crowd pleaser.

BEAUFORT

SEA

*Devon Island*

*Banks Island*

BROOKS RANGE

*Yukon*

*Porcupine*

*Victoria Island*

*Mackenzie*

● Dawson

● Norman Wells

*Great Bear Lake*

YUKON

● Fort Norman

NORTHWEST

N U N A V U T

TERRITORY

TERRITORIES

▲ *Mt. Logan*

● Baker Lake

● Whitehorse

*HORN MOUNTAINS*

● Yellowknife

*Dubawnt Lake*

*Liard*

**C**

Skagway ●

*Great Slave Lake*

Juneau ●

● Fort Resolution

Fort Smith ●

**A**

*CARIBOU MOUNTAINS*

BRITISH COLUMBIA

*Lake Athabasca*

**N**

Churchill ●

*Peace*

*Reindeer Lake*

*Churchill*

Hazelton ●

● Peace River

**A**

*Nelson*

*Queen Charlotte Islands*

● Prince Rupert

Prince George ●

ALBERTA

SASKATCHEWAN

MANITOBA

*N. Saskatchewan*

● Edmonton

● Prince Albert

*Lake Winnipegosis*

*Mt. Waddington* ▲

▲ *Mt. Columbia*

● Saskatoon

*Lake Winnipeg*

*Vancouver Island*

*Fraser*

● Calgary

*S. Saskatchewan*

*Lake Manitoba*

Vancouver ●

● Regina

Victoria ●

Medicine Hat ●

Winnipeg ●

Seattle ●

**ALBERTA/BRITISH COLUMBIA: p.252**

*Columbia*

*Missouri*

Duluth

UNITED STATES

*Snake*

OF AMERICA

Minneapolis ●

0          200          400          600          800 miles

500                    1000 kilometres

BAFFIN BAY

GREENLAND

•Angmagssalik

Baffin Island

Davis Strait

Godthåb•

FOXE
BASIN

QUEBEC: p.244

uthampton
Island

Hudson Strait

LABRADOR

SEA

Coats
sland

Mansel
Island

Feuilles

Nairn•

NEWFOUNDLAND

DSON

BAY

Belcher
Island

Smallwood
Reservoir

Goose Bay•

D

A

La Grande Rivière

OTISH
MOUNTAINS

Gander•
St John's•

vern

JAMES'S BAY

•Fort George

Newfoundland

Akimiski
Island

QUEBEC

Péribonca

Ile d'Anticosti

Gulf of St. Lawrence

Albany

•Fort Albany

PRINCE
EDWARD
ISLAND

ONTARIO

Charlottetown•

NOVA SCOTIA

Lake Nipigon

Quebec•

NEW
BRUNSWICK

St John
•

•Halifax

Thunder Bay•

Fredericton•

Lake Superior

Montreal•

ATLANTIC OCEAN

Georgian Bay

Lake Michigan

Lake Huron

Ottawa

Toronto•

Lake Ontario

Boston•

•Buffalo

Lake Erie

Milwaukee•

Detroit•

New York•

ssissippi

•Cleveland

Chicago•

Philadelphia•

# CANADA

BY LESLIE WOIT

ABOVE: **All across ski areas of North America you can learn to mush your own team of Huskies.**

BELOW: **As dusk descends over Mt Tremblant, the Gallic delights of the town's many French-Quebecois restaurants come into their own.**

Oh, Canada. Land of the Mountie, the maple leaf…and snow, wonderful snow. If it's unspoiled wilderness you're after, Canada has it covered from coast to coast. From the craggy drama of the Rockies in the west, to the frosty rounded Laurentians in the east, the diversity of ski areas in the world's second largest country is as varied as her peoples.

There's been a steady stream of visitors sharing these great outdoors ever since John Cabot first made landfall at the end of the 15th century. From skiing's origins as useful transport for goods and people, over the years winters here have become something to enjoy – not merely survive – and thanks to a few hundred ski areas across the country (and the replacement of sealskin with Gore-tex®), anything is possible.

Most famously, the western provinces of British Columbia (BC) and Alberta are ridged for pleasure by the edgy peaks of the Rocky Mountains, as well as by smaller ranges like the Purcells, the Monashees and the Cariboos – the centre of heliskiing, the most sought-

after and expensive form of skiing in the world (see page 18). Indeed, heliskiing was invented in the Bugaboos in 1965 when Hans Gmoser, the founder of Canadian Mountain Holidays (CMH), discovered that having your own set of blades is the ideal way to reach the area's famously dry champagne powder.

Alas, most of us are destined to ride the resort chair-lifts. Which is fine, too, with so many modern, customer-friendly lift systems and convenient town developments from which to choose. No resort is more sophisticated than Whistler Blackcomb, the ultimate in peak-to-pavement planning from the real-estate giant Intrawest. A repeat winner of favourite ski-destination polls, its reputation for great skiing over two mountains and one mile of vertical is matched only by its nightlife and range of activities on offer. For natural beauty, Banff-Lake Louise is tough to beat. Situated in the midst of Canada's first national park, a sea of green rises up to the sky and elk wander casually through town. In the southern interior of BC, the rise of a network of smaller resorts that includes Kicking Horse, Red and Fernie have made road-trip ski holidays a popular way to try several mountains in one week. Those who go in search of fresh powder and adventurous backcountry tours are rewarded with steep terrain and snow to match; so too are beginners who are well-served by excellent ski schools and dedicated novice areas. Intermediates will find state-of-the-art grooming on wide trails. On-mountain hotels and condominiums are spacious and affordable compared with their European counterparts. In and around towns, which have their origins in mining and logging, crowds are a rarity, apart from weekends and holidays.

Four hours flying time to the east and a world away, the province of Quebec is,

surprisingly to some, still in the same country. Proud of their French language and culture, the Quebecois people are also mad about all things winter. Skiing started here in the 1950s and 60s on rope tows and T-bars in the Laurentians, an area that includes some of the oldest mountains on earth. Skiers who frequent them have been known to endure ferocious temperatures of -30°C (-22°F) and lower, though this is certainly not the norm. The highest is Mont Tremblant, just over 914m (3,000ft) in height, where runs are shorter than out west and powder is replaced by smooth groomers and challenging bumps. Tremblant, like Whistler, is an Intrawest purpose-built village, but its traffic-free Old Quebec design gives it a festive, welcoming feel. To the northeast, Le Massif might only stretch to 806m (2,645ft) on its toes but it descends almost to sea level, with stunning views of the icy St Lawrence River and the highest vertical drop east of the Rockies. One of the greatest attractions of Mont-Ste-Anne is its 30-minute proximity to the delights of Quebec City, the only walled fortress city in North America and a bistro-bejewelled outpost of Gallic charm. While nearly everyone working in the province's service industry will speak English, the Quebecois dialect is fiercely protected and the sense that one is in a much more exotic land, though still scarcely a hamburger's hurl from the American border, cannot be avoided.

In the wilderness, of course, going wild is relative. Compared to Europe, Canadian après-ski is a tame affair, likely to involve a beer and a band or possibly a soak in your outdoor whirlpool, but the low cost of eating, drinking and accommodation is a sure attraction. So too is the universal friendliness of the locals. Canadians are renowned for being polite and their cities rank among the top in the world for cleanliness and quality of life (Vancouver is currently number one, but being Canadian they're unlikely to boast about it). So bundle up and head to the great white north. Going native has never been so civilized.

ABOVE: **The snow keeps on coming in Panorama. Big spaces and few people mean fresh tracks are often in sight.**

BELOW: **The spectacular Rocky Mountains are the reason people come back every year to enjoy the natural beauty of Canada's first national park – Banff.**

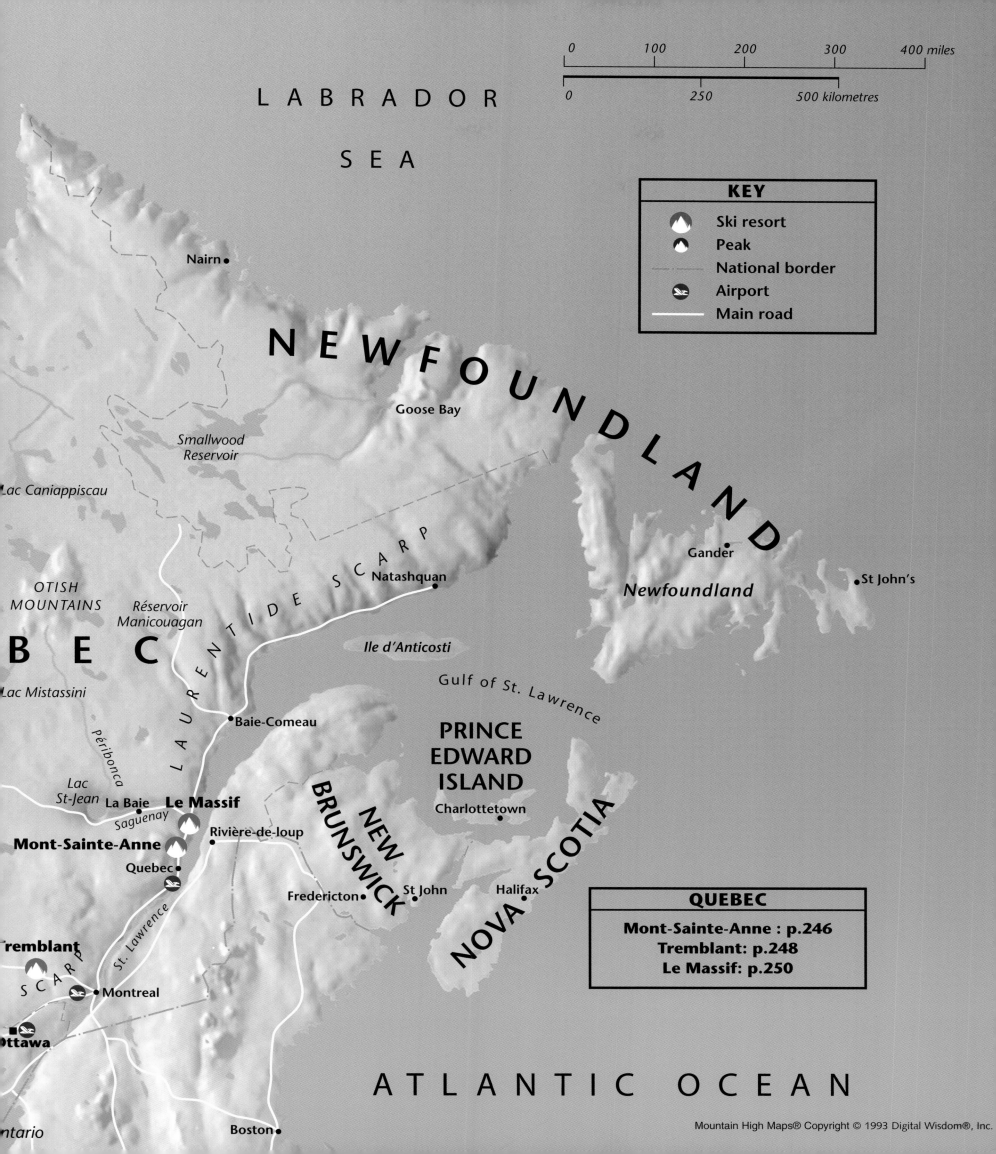

LABRADOR

SEA

NEWFOUNDLAND

Nairn

Goose Bay

*Smallwood Reservoir*

*Lac Caniappiscau*

*OTISH MOUNTAINS*

*Réservoir Manicouagan*

LAURENTIDE SCARP

Natashquan

Gander

*Newfoundland*

St John's

BEC

*Lac Mistassini*

*Ile d'Anticosti*

Gulf of St. Lawrence

*péribonca*

Baie-Comeau

*Lac St-Jean*    La Baie    **Le Massif**

**Mont-Sainte-Anne**

*Saguenay*    Rivière-de-loup

PRINCE
EDWARD
ISLAND

Charlottetown

NEW
BRUNSWICK

NOVA SCOTIA

Quebec

**Tremblant**

Fredericton    St John

Halifax

SCARP

*St. Lawrence*

Montreal

Boston

**Ottawa**

*ntario*

ATLANTIC OCEAN

Mountain High Maps® Copyright © 1993 Digital Wisdom®, Inc.

**KEY**

| | |
|---|---|
| 🔺 | Ski resort |
| 🔺 | Peak |
| ----- | National border |
| ✈ | Airport |
| ——— | Main road |

0    100    200    300    400 miles

0    250    500 kilometres

**QUEBEC**

**Mont-Sainte-Anne : p.246**
**Tremblant: p.248**
**Le Massif: p.250**

# QUEBEC

# Mont-Sainte-Anne

BY MINTY CLINCH

Mont-Sainte-Anne is the largest resort in the Quebec City area, a purpose-built complex off the main highway running east from the provincial capital. The hotels and condos in the base area have accommodation for 2,000, much of it moments away from the Summit Lodge gondola station, but the smart choice is to stay in Old Quebec – French-speaking, with food to match – within half an hour's drive of the slopes.

In Eastern Canada, the terrain is undulating and densely forested, hilly rather than mountainous, but at Mont-Sainte-Anne, sweeping views over the moving ice pack in the St Lawrence River turn the routine into the exceptional. The downside is the intense cold, but the gondola and a covered chair make skiing possible even when the mercury plummets.

The runs are on the front and back of the mountain, with impeccably groomed trails fanning out in three directions from the domed summit. The most extensive network, served by nine of the 13 lifts, is on the south side, directly above the base area. When the sun shines, this is the warmer option, though the snow is often heavier or icier than on the north and west faces over the back. By way of underlining its status as Quebec's biggest town hill, Mont-Sainte-Anne has night skiing on nearly half the south side, a total of 15 pistes starting from the shoulder below the summit.

The lift system makes the most of an area with a modest 625-m (2,050-ft) vertical drop. Complete beginners benefit from three free draglifts on the nursery slopes at the base of the mountain, and can then progress to the long loopy cruiser, Le Chemin du Roy, from

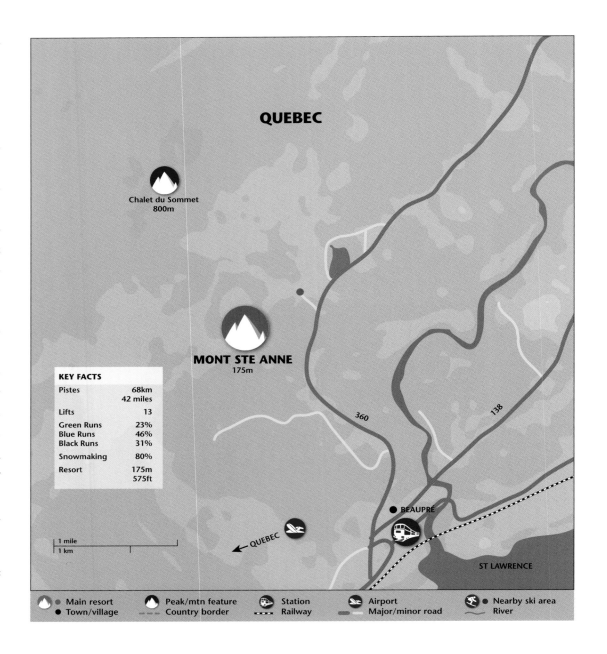

**QUEBEC**

Chalet du Sommet
800m

**MONT STE ANNE**
175m

| KEY FACTS | |
|-----------|--------|
| Pistes | 68km |
| | 42 miles |
| Lifts | 13 |
| Green Runs | 23% |
| Blue Runs | 46% |
| Black Runs | 31% |
| Snowmaking | 80% |
| Resort | 175m |
| | 575ft |

360

138

← QUEBEC

● BEAUPRÉ

ST LAWRENCE

1 mile
1 km

| | | | | |
|---|---|---|---|---|
| ● Main resort | Peak/mtn feature | Station | Airport | Nearby ski area |
| ● Town/village | - - - Country border | ···· Railway | Major/minor road | River |

## UNMISSABLE ALTERNATIVES

*Wherever you stay, it's worth buying the Carte Blanche multi-pass and spending at least one day in the other main resorts in the area. Stoneham, under the same ownership as Mont-Sainte-Anne and even closer to Quebec City, is a huge car park with a large day lodge, a single hotel and a selection of restaurants and bars. The ski area is set in a horseshoe-shaped amphitheatre on the valley floor, a naturally protected location that makes it the obvious choice when the wind blows. Stoneham has more of a buzz than Mount-Sainte-Anne, thanks to an enthusiastic youth element and nightskiing that pulls people into the pubs.*

*For Quebec's cognoscenti, Le Massif (see p 000), an hour's drive to the east of the city, is the undisputed regional star. This is a genuine original, a resort where you park at the day lodge near the top of the slopes, step into your skis and blast off towards the St. Lawrence 770 vertical metres (2,526ft) below. If you only have time for one add-on, make sure Le Massif gets the nod.*

the top of the gondola. There are several high-octane intermediate pistes, notably Gros Vallon and Le Beaupré. La Pichard is a 'must ski', not least for its Sugar Shack pitstop, Mont-Sainte-Anne's number one, all-Canadian experience. Your host pours liquid maple-syrup strips into long troughs filled with snow, then twists them into lollipops as the sugar cools – it's sin on a stick, but self-indulgently delicious.

At a more advanced level, there are choices for all sliders. The steepest bumps are on La 'S' or, more publicly, La Gondoleuse: as its name suggests, it runs right under the gondola so ritual humiliation can't be ruled out. There are some challenging glades with tight trees, especially in La Forêt Noire, and the west-facing slopes have powder potential, though only when snow conditions are right, by no means a certainty in such a cold climate.

Boarding is big time, with two impressive

terrain parks, a boarder-cross course and two halfpipes, all floodlit at night. The Mont-Sainte-Anne Cross Country Centre, the largest in Canada, has 224km (139 miles) of marked trails winding through the dense Laurentian forest. Alternatively, there are wildlife spotters' snowshoe trails, plus facilities for paragliding, skating, dog sledding and sleigh rides on the golf course.

The most convenient sleepovers are the Château Mont-Sainte-Anne, a full service hotel, or the Chalets Mont-Sainte-Anne next door. Otherwise the choice is between the

*When it's good, it's very, very good. If he needed to catch his breath, this expert tree skier would have a fine overview of the Mont-Sainte-Anne base complex.*

Swiss-style Chalets Montmorency, 750m (2,460ft) from the lifts with a free shuttle, and the Quebecois-style Chalets Village, each with fireplace and whirlpool or sauna. If you opt for Old Quebec, the French-speaking Auberge St. Pierre boutique hotel is highly recommended. There is also a regional ice hotel on the shores of Lake Saint-Joseph 30km (19 miles) northwest of the city.

# QUEBEC

# Tremblant

BY MINTY CLINCH

Tremblant is eastern Canada's leading residential resort, a complex of cheerful building blocks devised by Intrawest, the country's premier ski-resort developers. The firm pioneered its integrated designs in Whistler Village in British Columbia and exported them extensively to the United States and Europe, but none of its other projects quite matches Tremblant's colourful spectrum of cobbled pedestrian streets and squares. The architecture is allegedly inspired by old Quebec, but more as painted by an imaginative child than as it is in real life.

The core of this long-established resort (the first chair-lift was built in 1939) is simple and convenient – a large semi-circle built around Place St Bernard, with the imposing Fairmont Tremblant hotel at one extremity and the Kid's Club at the other. The Place is the starting point for the heated express gondola, a comfortable nine-minute ride to the top of skiing on Le Grand Manitou, and the high-speed covered chair to mid-mountain.

The layout means that as long as you stay in the central zone, you will be within five minutes' walk of both lifts, a key factor in a region where temperatures routinely fall to -35°C (-31°F) in mid-winter. The user-friendly nursery slope is right on-site as well – a 0.8ha (2 acre) enclosure served by two magic carpets and a warming hut.

The majestic landscape of the Laurentian Mountains is heavily wooded, more rolling hills than peaks and troughs, with snowfall guaranteed more by the prevailing climate than by altitude or latitude. Light powder is not unknown, but it is certainly rare in the kind of cold that would generate sheet ice were it not for the huge investment in grooming and snow cannons, which cover 75 per cent of the pistes. French is the official language, but it is much less all-embracing than in Quebec City, where English may not always be understood.

## Chasing the sun

With skiing on four slopes facing in different directions, it is possible – and perhaps sensible – to work out a game plan to make the most of the sunshine. The gondola goes up the South Side, but provides rapid access to the less crowded North Side, (in reality north-easterly and therefore exposed to the morning rays). The Duncan and Expo Express chairs open up some long mogul fields and a rich haul of pistes cut through the woods, most of them rated black, though many would be red or even blue in a major European resort. Boarders get to strut their stuff in the 7.3 ha (18 acre) Gravité terrain

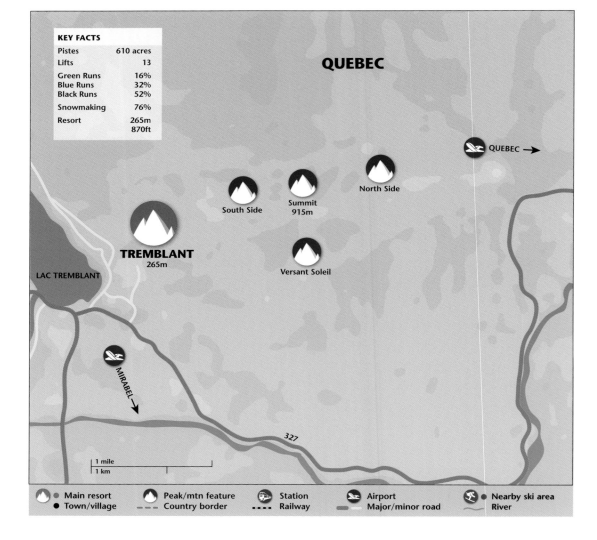

**KEY FACTS**

| Pistes | 610 acres |
| --- | --- |
| Lifts | 13 |
| Green Runs | 16% |
| Blue Runs | 32% |
| Black Runs | 52% |
| Snowmaking | 76% |
| Resort | 265m 870ft |

QUEBEC

QUEBEC →

North Side

South Side

Summit
915m

TREMBLANT
265m

LAC TREMBLANT

Versant Soleil

MIRABEL →

327

1 mile
1 km

| | Main resort | | Peak/mtn feature | | Station | | Airport | | Nearby ski area |
| --- | --- | --- | --- | --- | --- | --- | --- | --- | --- |
| | Town/village | | Country border | | Railway | | Major/minor road | | River |

park and the Super Demi-Lune halfpipe on the upper slope.

Beginners will appreciate the lone green run, Le P'tit Bonheur, from the top of the mountain. Halfway down, it funnels into a network of equally encouraging pistes below the Lowell Thomas triple chair. The North Side base station is little more than a large car park, with a lodge for refreshments and rentals. The Edge area, another face linked to the North Side at mid-mountain level, provides tree runs, several of them genuinely double black diamond, but getting any pleasure out of them requires the kind of snow cover that is by no means guaranteed.

In the middle of the day, experts should head for the encouragingly named Soleil face, a tight network of challenging chutes and tree shots with a single blue descent from top to bottom. Later on, the South Side, which actually faces southwest, is the warmest option. Again, there is an encouraging green run, the 6km (4 mile) Nansen – Tremblant's longest – from the summit back to the village, plus a range of intermediate and advanced

runs. As these are easily skied from the heated gondola, they encourage enthusiasts to stay out until the lifts close. Accommodation is either in hotels or self-catering apartments, but be aware that the nearest supermarket is not within easy walking distance – and shuttle buses are fairly rare. Intrawest's second pedestrian village at Versant Soleil features six hotels totalling 1,500 condo-hotel units, including one 500-room hotel and a 200-room luxury spa hotel, a multifunctional convention centre, boutiques and restaurants, a park, lake and new chair-lifts. The capacity of the ski slopes is also being expanded there.

Eastern Canada has two major advantages over its Rocky Mountain rivals: a six-hour flight time from Europe (four hours less than Calgary or Vancouver), and French – or fairly French – food. At Tremblant, it is easy to eat in a relaxed Gallic ambiance at very affordable prices. Look for the most authentic French cooking at La Savoie (for *raclette, pierrades* and fondue); Aux Truffes for *foie gras* and game; and La Grappe à Vin for regional specialities backed by an extensive wine list.

At lunchtime, many prefer to sit out on a terrace in the village over steak-frites or pasta

and a glass of wine rather than tackle the cafeteria-style Grand Manitou, the only on-mountain restaurant. The downtown atmosphere is all the more cheerful for the bands that play in the main square, both at lunchtime and after skiing. The best après-ski bars are the Forge and the Shack, which brews its own beer, with October Rock coming on stream later in the evening.

As is customary in action-packed Canada, the hyper visitor can work off any post-skiing excess energy – or indeed excess calories – with snowshoeing, ice climbing, tubing, dog sledding, snowmobiling, skating and even equestrianism. In a more pampering mode, the Aquaclub La Source – its interior designed as a lake set in a forest – offers indoor and outdoor swimming, whirlpools and fitness programmes for the whole family. Fed up with the kids? Try the Scandinavian Baths for a range of Nordic experiences – sauna, steam bath, thermal waterfalls, swimming in the river – plus treatments and massage, all reserved for over-18s. And leave time to visit Montreal: it's more than worth the detour.

# Le Massif

BY ARNIE WILSON

There are river views – and river views. By and large, when you go skiing the classic scenery is usually one variant or another of snowy mountain peaks and idyllic villages down in the valley. Le Massif – or, to give it its full name, Le Massif de Petite-Rivière-Saint-François – is different. The scenery here is no less jaw-dropping, but it is all about the frozen St Lawrence. It's billed as a 'mountain by the sea' experience, with the picturesque Isle-aux-Coudres in the starring role – the river as backdrop and passing shipping the main actors (when the winter ice allows). The area marks the point where the mighty St Lawrence becomes salty – the so-called 'portal to the oceans'.

Le Massif, part of the Charlevoix World Biosphere Reserve, is without doubt the most scenic of Quebec City's ski areas (which include the better-known Mont Sainte-Anne, see pages 246–47, and Stoneham, with which Le Massif has a joint lift pass arrangement). The ski area has the biggest vertical drop (769m/2,526ft, almost 5km/3 miles,

**Massive views: with the exception of Lake Tahoe, it's hard to think of anywhere with more stunning waterfront scenery than this exhilarating Quebec resort.**

top to bottom) in Eastern Canada, spreads around more than 121ha (300 acres) of skiable terrain and boasts some of its most challenging slopes. The runs are genuinely spectacular, partly because of the gradient, but mainly because many swoop down almost to the attractive waterfront village of Petite-Rivière-Saint-François on the edge of the St Lawrence, where huge ice floes make their way towards the Gulf of St. Lawrence – or back again on the tide. And as you hurtle down runs like La Martine, La

Lavoie or La Petite Rivière, you sometimes just have to pause and look out across the magnificent river.

The St Lawrence is so wide here that it does indeed resemble a sea, and when the light is right, the innumerable chunks of ice drifting gently up or downstream glitter like a sea of fool's gold in the afternoon sun. One of the best vantage points is from the blue La Gagnon run. From here, you could almost imagine for a second that you are gazing out across a frozen version of a south-Pacific

scene. The easiest runs – which allow you to take your mind off any serious challenges and just enjoy the view – include Anse, Jean-Noël, Gagné, Combe and Ancienne.

Another unusual aspect of Le Massif is that most of the skiing is below the resort centre (the *chalet du sommet*, or summit lodge) area. Between the mountain opening in 1980, and 1992 when the first lifts opened, skiers used yellow school buses to get to the terrain. They were led by a team of guides who also provided entertainment during transit. The first skiers were towed around the mountain to the five ungroomed 'trails' by snowmobile. At the bottom they would catch a bus back to the top. Until 2001, when a direct road was constructed to access the summit of the ski area, the slopes were reached from the base area, at just 40m (131ft) above sea level. You can now get to the slopes from either location. These days, there are as many as 43 named trails and glades at Le Massif.

The resort's most famous run, La Charlevoix, a double-black diamond trail 2,200m (7,217ft) in length, is used for official races. Conceived by Bernhard Russi, the celebrated designer of Olympic downhill courses, and FIS-classified for downhill and Super G events, La Charlevoix is known for its technical attributes, including a wall with a 64 per cent pitch. The trail is used by Le Massif's National Alpine Skiing Training Center, and is featured in national and international races. Until this run opened in 2001, the parallel La 42 was Le Massif's signature slope: a steep, moguls-all-the way trail from top to bottom – more than 610 vertical metres (2,000 vertical feet) of thigh-burning terrain. (Before they were given names, the runs only had numbers, and this trail has kept the original numerical designation).

In 2005–06, Le Massif celebrated its first 25 years by introducing an improved terrain park, The Zone (305m/1,000ft in length) for intermediate and advanced riders, and a Mini Park almost 122m (400ft) long at the Summit Bunny Slope aimed at 're-thinking the beginner experience' for beginners and children.

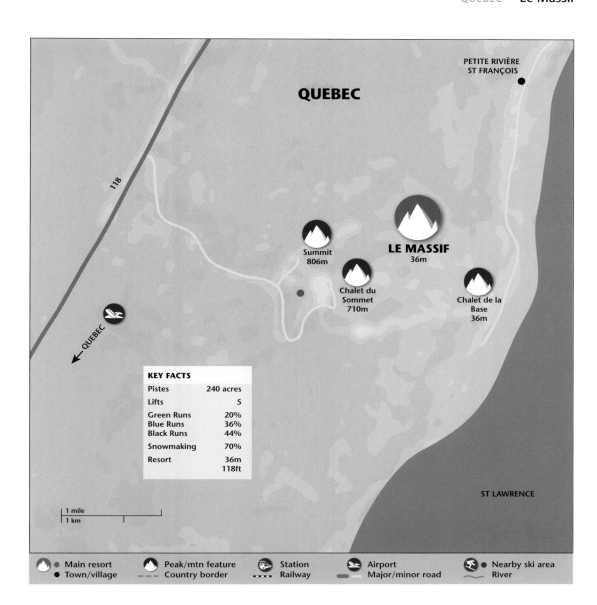

**KEY FACTS**

| | |
|---|---|
| Pistes | 240 acres |
| Lifts | 5 |
| Green Runs | 20% |
| Blue Runs | 36% |
| Black Runs | 44% |
| Snowmaking | 70% |
| Resort | 36m |
| | 118ft |

| | | |
|---|---|---|
| ● Main resort | ▲ Peak/mtn feature | Station |
| ● Town/village | Country border | Railway |
| | | Airport |
| | | Major/minor road |
| | | ● Nearby ski area |
| | | River |

Both are at the summit of the mountain, and both are groomed daily. Free guided tours are available daily at any time, led by a "passionate team of guides who share the mountain's best-kept secrets."

The 70 instructors at the Snowsports School are "slide sports enthusiasts who teach the finer points of skiing, snowboarding, telemarking and sit-skiing" (a way for paraplegics to ski on a low-slung 'toboggan' with small outrigger skis), "while childcare workers enchant children from two months to 10 years old with educational activities and ski programmes."

Other things to do apart from downhill skiing include cross-country, snowshoeing, dog-sledding, snowmobiling and ice climbing (all at the Sentier des Caps de Charlevoix, just five minutes from the summit lodge). Or just admiring the astonishing view.

**THE FUTURE**

*By 2012, Le Massif's owners are expected to have invested a total of approximately $230 million since 2002. This will include new hotels, inns, chalets and other lodging, and will create more than 600 jobs. The charming village of Petite-Rivière-Saint-François has plenty of accommodation, but many skiers base themselves downstream at Baie-Saint-Paul, just 18km (11 miles) or so away, or in Quebec City itself, 72km (45 miles) away. For some 50 days each winter, there's a shuttle service between Quebec City (from Sainte-Foy and Quebec City train stations) and the slopes. There are also plans to introduce a passenger service on the freight railway between Quebec City and La Malbaie, east of Baie-Saint-Paul.*

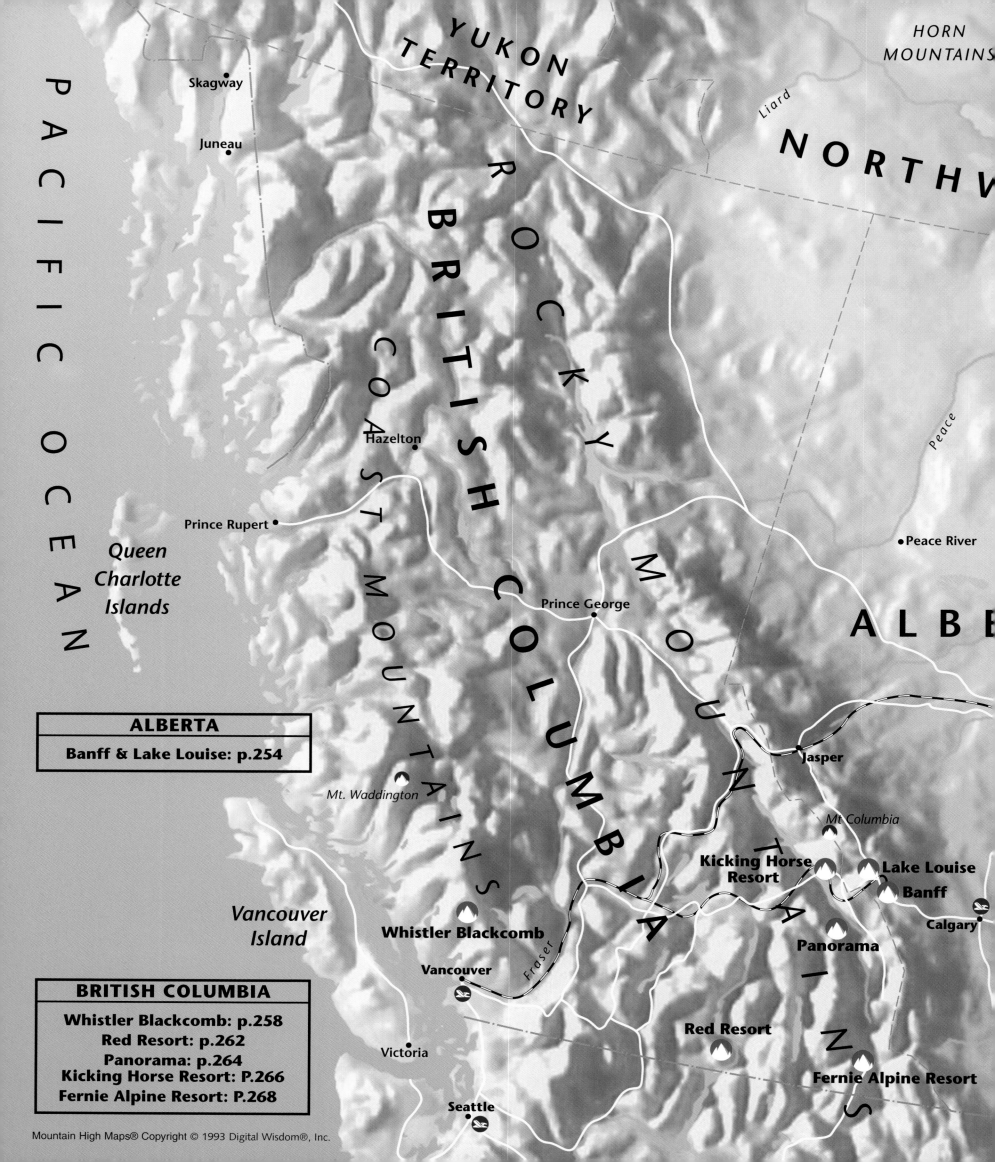

PACIFIC OCEAN

Skagway

Juneau

YUKON TERRITORY

HORN MOUNTAINS

NORTHW

Liard

R
O
C
K
Y

Hazelton

C
O
A
S
T

M
O
U
N
T
A
I
N
S

Prince Rupert

*Queen Charlotte Islands*

BRITISH COLUMBIA

Peace

Prince George

Peace River

M
O
U
N
T
A
I
N
S

ALBE

**ALBERTA**

**Banff & Lake Louise: p.254**

Jasper

Mt. Waddington

*Mt Columbia*

**Kicking Horse Resort**

**Lake Louise**

**Banff**

*Vancouver Island*

**Whistler Blackcomb**

**Panorama**

Calgary

Vancouver

Fraser

Victoria

**Red Resort**

**Fernie Alpine Resort**

Seattle

Mountain High Maps® Copyright © 1993 Digital Wisdom®, Inc.

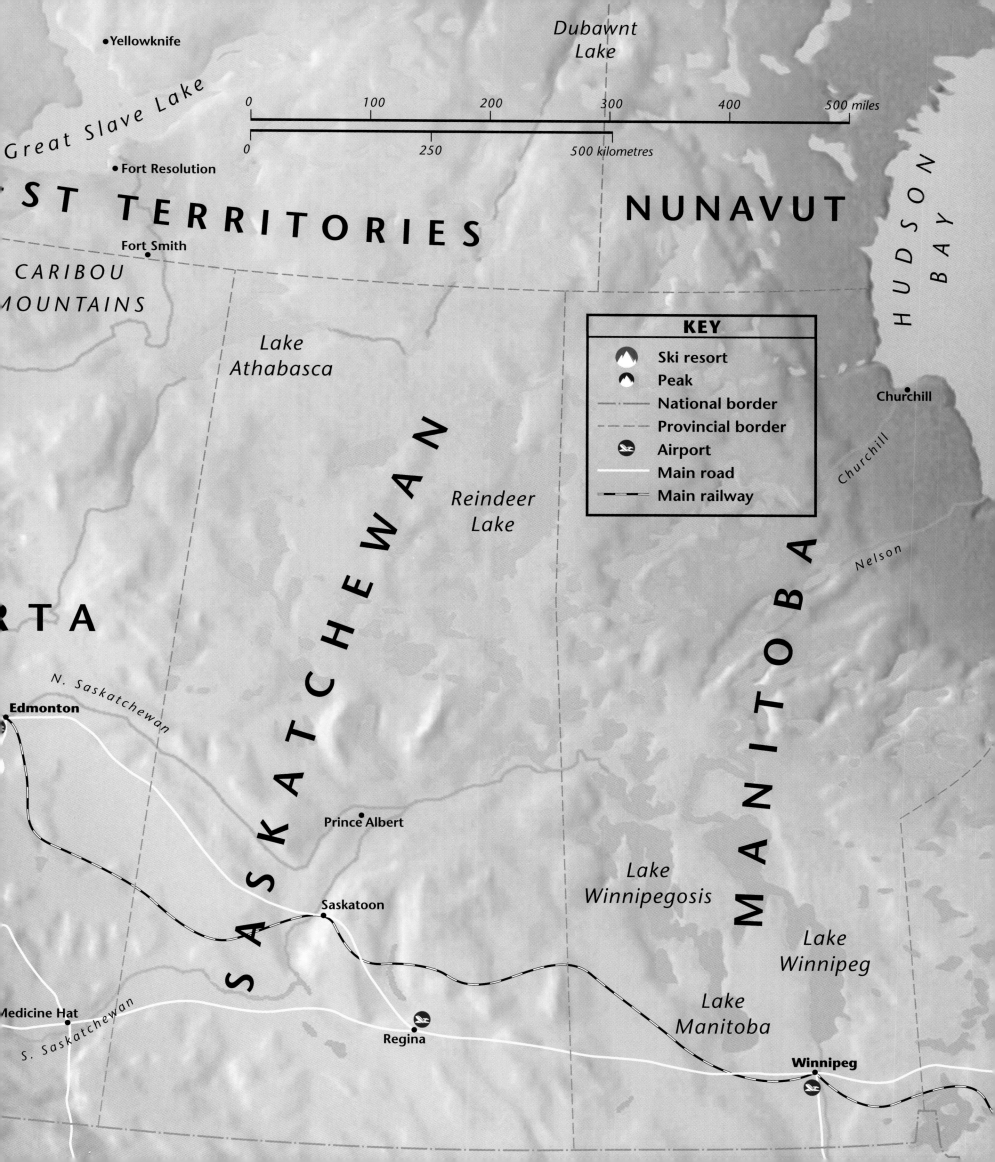

•Yellowknife

Dubawnt
Lake

Great Slave Lake

•Fort Resolution

**ST TERRITORIES**

**NUNAVUT**

HUDSON

BAY

Fort Smith•

CARIBOU
MOUNTAINS

Lake
Athabasca

Churchill

Churchill

| KEY | |
|---|---|
| Ski resort | |
| Peak | |
| National border | |
| Provincial border | |
| Airport | |
| Main road | |
| Main railway | |

Reindeer
Lake

Nelson

**S A S K A T C H E W A N**

**M A N I T O B A**

RTA

N. Saskatchewan

Edmonton•

Prince Albert•

Lake
Winnipegosis

Lake
Winnipeg

**S A S K A T C H E W A N**

Saskatoon•

Lake
Manitoba

Medicine Hat•

S. Saskatchewan

Regina•

Winnipeg•

# Banff and Lake Louise

BY FELIX MILNS

If it weren't for the crisp, cold air and occasional ski shop you would not know you were in a ski town. Winter here is low season and, bar the tourist shops selling maple syrup, Canadian Mountie outfits and replica bears, most of the shops on the wide, low-slung high street are what you would find in any North American town. What you may not find everywhere else, however, are elk and deer wandering along the sidewalk and a backdrop of some of the most emblematic peaks in the Rockies.

Then again, Banff is far from your typical ski resort. For a start, there are no ski lifts in town. The locals' favourite, Mount Norquay, has a small collection of well-groomed tree-lined runs up the hill from town. It is small but characterful and worth a morning's visit for strong skiers, and a day for others. But the nearest major skiing is at Sunshine Village, a 20-minute car journey. The other main ski area served by the town is Lake Louise, a 45-minute drive away. What's more, you have to take a long gondola at Sunshine just to access the base of the ski area, meaning in real terms it is not much closer than Lake Louise. However, don't be put off; together these ski areas offer some of the best skiing in

Sunshine Village has an average snowfall of 10m (400in) per winter, so powder days are the norm not the exception.

the world; a sedate drive through the awe-inspiring national park is a pleasure, not a chore, and the frontier town itself has a lively, laid-back and friendly feel.

Universally acknowledged as North America's most scenic ski area, the Banff resorts sit in the Banff National Park, the first area to achieve such status in Canada and also recognized as a UNESCO World Heritage site. The expansive skies and wide open valleys

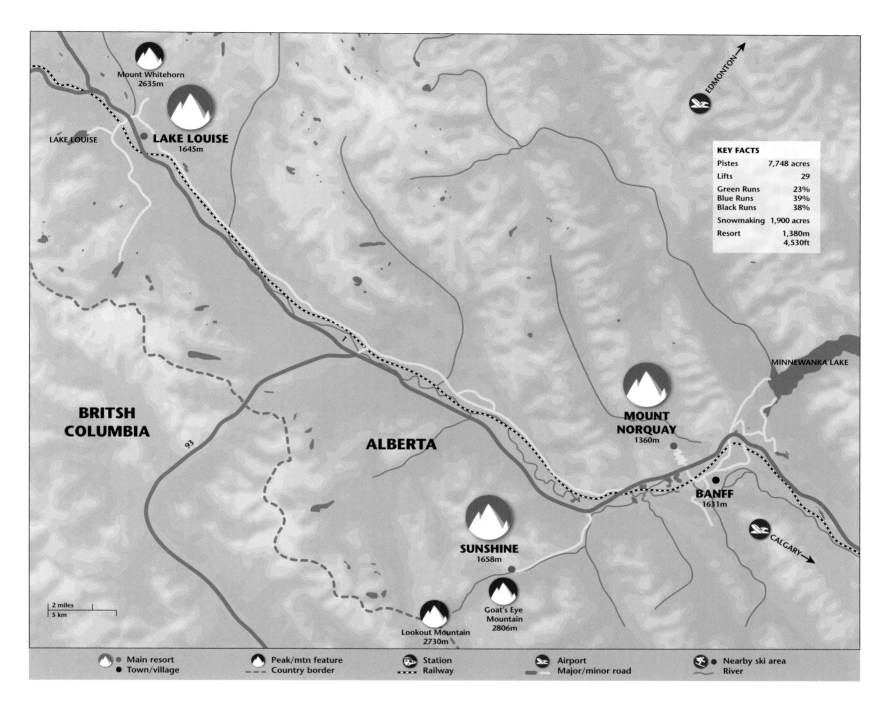

give an immediate feeling of space and serenity, while the snow-laden forests of pine, spruce and larch only add to the mysticism. This is a place for the soul as much as the ski.

Skiing began at Norquay in the 1920s, with the other ski areas opening up in the following decade. There is a tri-area skipass, and 29 lifts service the 3,135ha (7,748 acres) of skiable terrain. This may not sound like a lot of lifts, but this is a significant part of the area's charm. The national park does not allow the endless construction of lifts; Sunshine has 12, but an equivalent area in the Alps would have double this figure. What this means is far more terrain and fewer lifts – excellent

news for powder lovers happy to trade in a short traverse or trek for deserted slopes.

## Sunshine Village

Sunshine sits right on the Continental Divide, which produces an excellent snow record. Annual falls of up to 1,016cm (400in) are not uncommon, and the resorts make a virtue out of not having any artificial snowmaking facilities. Their slogan, 'three times the snow' refers to their snow record in comparison with neighbouring Lake Louise. In contrast, 90 per cent of Norquay and 40 per cent of Lake Louise have snowmaking, so lack of snow is extremely rare.

Sunshine's ski area comprises three mountains, and has the largest vertical drop (1,072m/3,517ft) in the Canadian Rockies. Lookout Mountain (2,730m/8,956ft) is the exposed peak at the head of the resort with some steep blacks at the summit. Lookout is right on the divide, and off the back of the main slopes is the famous freeride area, 'Delirium Dive', where a 40-degree pitch is considered gentle. This should not be attempted by the faint-hearted or inexperienced. This area is strictly patrolled, and you are only allowed in with an avalanche transceiver and a partner. Be warned: it is also liable to closure if conditions are not perfect.

Canadian standards, the annual snowfall of 355cm (140in) is comparatively low, but 40 per cent of slopes have snowmaking and the north-facing back bowls and Larch area hold their snow well. Almost all the major lifts have easy ways down.

There are a few ways up the south-facing front side of Whitehorn mountain, and three high-altitude lifts from where you can drop over into the back bowls and Larch area. There is plenty of good skiing on the south side, predominantly below the tree line, though treeless treats include the out-of-bounds West Bowl (guide essential) and runs down from the summit drag. There is also plenty for intermediates, but the best way to explore the area is to work round the circuit. The terrain park just above the main lodge is one of the most comprehensive anywhere.

The back bowls are the jewels in Lake Louise's crown. Accessed from the summit drag is a kilometre-wide steep ridge, cut with myriad chutes and couloirs known as the Whitehorn 2 Gullies, opening out onto steep bumpy terrain. Winding round the flanks are gentler, open slopes far from any sign of lifts. Off the back of Eagle Ridge are yet more

Less extreme thrill-seekers have over 50 intermediate runs to choose from. Check out the World Cup downhill from the top of the Continental Divide Express. Opposite Lookout is Mount Standish, a pleasant tree-lined mountain with a good mix of terrain spread over generally shorter runs. The central ski area sees a network of greens through the trees; those serviced by the Wolverine chair are particularly characterful.

The newest addition to the resort is Goat's Eye Mountain, serviced from the first stage of the main gondola with epic views across to Delirium Dive. There is only one lift but a handful of decent blues and blacks plus a seriously impressive colonnade of steep chutes and double-black-diamond trails.

## Lake Louise

Lake Louise has the allure of the most spectacular high-mountain scenery in North America and the largest single collection of slopes in the Canadian Rockies, spread over high, open flanks and tree-lined trails below and the justifiably renowned back bowls. By

ABOVE: **This view of the jagged peaks above Banff town is as good a reason as any to visit Norquay.**

BELOW: **The base lodge at Lake Louise is one of the prettiest in North America.**

gullies of equal pitch as well as a great mix of terrain in the Paradise Bowl. Along and round the ridge, there is some excellent gladed skiing under the Ptarmingan Chair. Both this and the Paradise Chair link back to the south face and have gentle runs running back into the bowls and round to the Larch area. Again serviced by one lift, there are lots of shorter routes down this pretty, tree-lined mountain for all levels.

There is also accommodation in Lake Louise, in the shape of a small peaceful village and the large neo-Gothic Fairmount Chateau Lake Louise, idyllically situated across the valley floor from the ski area with a view over the frozen lake and Victoria Glacier that is positively breathtaking. That apart, however, there is not much life in the village and most people tend to stay in Banff, which has its own neo-Gothic Fairmount, several other excellent hotels plus lots of accommodation and entertainment in town. Check out the live music at Wild Bills, which can be anything from punk to line dancing. There is plenty to do for non-skiers, with beautiful walks, hot springs and snowmobiling just a taster.

Queues, particularly mid-week, are never that severe, and there is a good ski school programme, including video analysis, allowing you to ski in all the different areas. Mountain restaurants are the usual depressingly average North American fare, but at least they are reasonably cheap. There are fairly efficient buses that run between the ski areas but your own 4x4 vehicle is definitely recommended, particularly as it is also worthwhile moving onto some of the other ski areas nearby, such as Panorama, Kicking Horse or Fernie. For a true taste of Canadian powder, treat yourself to a couple of days of heliskiing nearby. Bear in mind it can be very cold, particularly in the early season.

**Vast, tree-lined plains roll out across the wide valley at the foot of Lake Louise's slopes.**

257

# BRITISH COLUMBIA

# Whistler Blackcomb

BY LESLIE WOIT

Over the years, Canada's most famous resort has been awarded truckloads of prizes for its extensive skiing and boarding, its luxury hotels, its happening nightlife. Thanks to innovative recycling programmes, even Whistler's garbage has won accolades. What's so special about a resort that 30 years ago, scarcely even existed?

Look up, way up. These two mountains – from a village standpoint Whistler is on the right, Blackcomb on the left – boast more area and vertical than any other area in North America; one long lovely white mile, in fact. More than 200 marked runs are served by 37 lifts, covering some of the longest runs on the continent, many cut through scenic fir and pine forests that stretch almost to the top of their respective 2,285-m (7,497-ft) and 2,180-m (7,152ft) mountains. Part of the westernmost Coast Mountain range, these peaks are the first to get the snow-laden weather systems that rage in from the Pacific Ocean. It's a mixed blessing; these systems are known to occasionally bring rain as well as snow. The resort has been known to hand out plastic slickers (raincoats) to diehards who don't mind a bit of wet with their edge set.

Located just two hours north of Vancouver on the dazzling Sea to Sky Highway, past the rainforests and waterfalls, Whistler Blackcomb (WB) will play host to alpine races and to sliding events (bobsleigh and the like) when Vancouver hosts the Winter Olympic Games in 2010. It may come as a surprise to find that snowboarding events will be held in neighbouring resorts, but that just means more slope-time for those who are not (yet) of

LEFT: **Powder, powder everywhere: freeriding is a way of life out here.**

BELOW: **The Blackcomb and Whistler mountains are set deep in the wilderness of the Coast range.**

world calibre. Even in non-Olympic years, in addition to skiers and boarders of all levels, the place attracts more than its share of international names. From Hollywood A-listers and royals to heads of small countries and big companies, WB is a landing strip for all sorts of shooting stars – as well as clever non-skiers and avid ski bums alike.

What's the draw? The engineers stayed up late building this place – and will be rewarded in heaven for their good work on earth. As the flagship resort of mega-developers Intrawest, who have interests in 10 North American resorts as well as in the Alps, you'd be hard pressed to find a more advanced high-speed lift system anywhere. Criss-crossing wide open bowls, super-long cruisey pistes, broad gentle beginner areas and chutes and glades steep enough to curl your hair, WB's network of 37 high-speed quads, six-packs and gondolas will get you to the top – though at busy periods you will not be short of company in the neatly organized lift lines.

## All things to all skiers

No matter what your level, you can be sure that your heart's desires have been lovingly factored into The Grand Plan. Fully 20 per cent of the terrain on Whistler Mountain is suitable for beginners, and numerous slow skiing zones on both mountains create a stress-free environment for learners. A special Family Zone with gentle terrain is located at Ego Bowl and a kids-only area on Whistler Mountain comes complete with tunnels, tree forts and slides. In addition to all the standard ski and snowboard school programmes, teens can join the Ride Tribe programme, a cool and challenging way to push the boundaries. And of course it's no secret that WB is at the cutting edge of boarding culture, with nine beginner, intermediate and expert terrain parks and pipe zones,

| KEY FACTS | |
|---|---|
| Pistes | 8,171 acres |
| Lifts | 37 |
| Green Runs | 18% |
| Blue Runs | 55% |
| Black Runs | 27% |
| Snowmaking | 565 acres |
| Resort | 675m |
| | 2,210ft |

GREEN LAKE

ALTA LAKE
99

WHISTLER BLACKCOMB
675m

Creekside
650m

Blackcomb Mountain
2284m

VANCOUVER

Whistler Mountain
2182m

BRITISH COLUMBIA

1 mile
2 km

CHEAKAMUS LAKE

● Main resort
● Town/village
Peak/mtn feature
Country border
Station
Railway
Airport
Major/minor road
Nearby ski area
River

including a new 5m (16ft) walled superpipe built for the 2005 Snowboard World Championships at Blackcomb's Base II.

But don't be scared of the groovy scene that throbs through the resort. Run-of-the-mill intermediates are also treated like kings and queens. They have it long: both mountains boast a snaking 11km (7 mile) long run each, starting at Burnt Stew on Whistler and Green Line on Blackcomb. They have it challenging: gentle bowls like Harmony and Ego let even timid types get a feel for Whistler's

---

**Another powder day: backcountry boarders and skiers form a major community around Whistler.**

famous powder on easy pitches. A total of 45 per cent of groomed terrain is graded intermediate, and daily reports let you know what's smooth and what's not.

Of course, for boarders and skiers alike, the real selling point here is the in-bounds backcountry. Easily accessed by hikes from just two to 20 minutes, hundreds of acres of avalanche-controlled terrain is spread over 12 bowls. If you can see it you can ski it – and it's white as far as the eye can see.

Except when it's grey. There is a cloud for every silver lining and Whistler's is rain. It happens at least once a year; in 2004–05 it fairly wiped out a week's worth of high-

season skiing. On balance, however, a spot of potential drizzle is not a good enough reason to miss all the terrific things on offer.

Renowned for its après-ski offerings, skiers and non-skiers have no problem keeping busy with outdoor activities like slip-sliding in the tubing park, snowshoeing, or bungee jumping above a rushing river. Sign up for a day-trip of Vancouver shopping and sightseeing or take in an NHL hockey game with the Vancouver Canucks. There are massages and spa treatments guaranteed to turn you into a noodle. There's all that and more, provided you can make it past bottom-of-the-piste pubs and outdoor terraces like

the GLC, Merlin's and Longhorn at the end of the day.

Come evening, there is a huge choice of bars and restaurants, from no-reservations at Sushi Village, to fine Italian fare at Umberto's and star-spotting at Barefoot Bistro. Dancing and drinking at Tommy Africa's and the Savage Beatle will keep you up late, though when bedtime calls you will once again be well tended. Top hotels with all the bells and whistles such as ski valets and driver service include the slope-side Fairmont Chateau Whistler, the Four Seasons and the all-suite Westin Hotel. There is a large selection of smaller hotels and self-catering condos. As all conceivable shops and services have been engineered into the pedestrian village master plan, there's a good chance your bed will be within easy walking distance of both ski and après-ski destinations.

In 2006, the birthday cakes came out for the 25th anniversary of Blackcomb Mountain and the 40th of Whistler Mountain. Over just a handful of decades, the Terrific Two have taken their place in skiing's hall of fame. With two mountains, three glaciers and 9m (30ft) of snow every year, they have what it takes to join the jet set of international wintersports destinations. For anyone who thinks the Terrific Two's popularity may kill their appeal, there is help at hand. Just over the hill, there is also great heliskiing to be had. Didn't I say this place has it all?

### THE BIGGER THE BETTER?

*Can WB get any bigger? Some people wonder. As if to bait the anti-development lobby, in 2004-05 a further 445ha (1,100 acres) was added to its existing 2,861ha (7,071 acres) of skiable terrain. The opening of the Peak to Creek zone, on the west side of Whistler Mountain, has created four new runs and more opportunities for skiing new bowls, glades and old-growth forest. At the foot of it all, Whistler's original base, Creekside, has also been redeveloped. In addition to the base areas at Whistler and Blackcomb villages, Creekside provides a pedestrian-only family-friendly zone.*

ABOVE: **Whistler and Blackcomb have more area than any other resort in North America.**

BELOW: **Gearing up for the 2010 Winter Olympics – professional and amateur events occur all season long.**

# Red Resort

BY ALF ALDERSON

Skiing at Red has become something of a rite of passage for many. The standard of skier the place turns out is attested to by the fact that Rossland, a town of just a few thousand snow-mad souls, has produced more Olympic and World Cup skiers than any other town in North America. The quality of the trails at Red is commensurate with the quality of the local skiers. Scarcely a winter goes by that this unpretentious resort perched above this former gold-mining town doesn't rack up yet another award for the quality of its slopes, and its tree skiing in particular.

**Red revels in its justified reputation for offering some of the most exciting skiing in North America.**

Red Resort consists of two mountains: 1,587m (5,208ft) Red Mountain and 1,764m (5800ft) Granite Mountain – which is actually the main attraction rather than the eponymous Red. Its location in the interior of the province, just a few miles north of the Canada–US border is rather off the beaten track, which means the slopes are rarely too busy and lift queues are generally non-existent. The slopes stand some 5km (3 miles) above Rossland, a soulful little settlement where people live for the outdoors and where, unlike many resorts south of the border, utility and not fashion is the be-all and end-all of the local ski scene.

The down-home atmosphere of Rossland is reflected on the slopes, where form and function take priority over glitz and glamour. Although new developments are moving forward, the base lodge remains resolutely old school (and much the better for it), some of the chair-lifts are from the same mould and the locals are happy to let the mountain speak for itself in terms of the quality of the skiing to be had.

And what Red tells you is that the tree-skiing is comparable to the best in the world. A popular, if apocryphal, tale is that of the hardened local with decades of experience of the mountain who will find a great line

through the trees and then never be able to locate it again. Granite Mountain is draped in double black-diamond tree runs, which can contain hidden powder stashes for days after the last snowfall. Short Squaw is a good introduction to the mountain's more challenging terrain, and if you find this easy have a go at Cambodia, where tight trees and 5m (16ft) drop-offs will test the best. Also on Granite are the devilish 1st, 2nd and 3rd Slide, while over on Red, Hole in the Wall drops into Upper War Eagle, two more double blacks that are more open than those on Granite. Also on Red is Towers of Red, a tricky bump run beneath Red Chair. You'll get plenty of free advice from above as you descend.

With its harum-scarum reputation, Red can easily scare off anyone other than advanced or expert skiers, but it would be wrong of intermediates to assume they won't enjoy themselves here as almost half the terrain is set aside for them. The Paradise Area on Granite Mountain has a fine selection of fun, open blue and black runs, such as Southern Comfort, Ruby Monday and Ruby Tuesday, along with the gregarious Paradise Lodge, a real throwback to the 1970s, where the food is cheap and cheerful and the clientele warm and friendly. There's also the chance to test yourself here on black tree-runs such as Alder Gully and Jumbo, which drop into Southside Road cat track, ensuring an easy escape route if you bite off more than

you can chew, while on Red Mountain the Face of Red is an excellent trail on which to practise your carving skills. 'Red' is a place where intermediates can challenge themselves to push their skiing to the next level.

For beginners, it has to be said that the options at Red are limited, although the gentle, open green runs above the base lodge are ideal learning territory, and there is a green run off the top of every lift for more confident novices, which also provide the chance to enjoy the surrounding views of mountains, forest and the Columbia River valley.

It will come as no surprise to find that Red is also popular with backcountry skiers, who will find plenty of terrain that's easily accessible from the ski area, in particular Mount Roberts, Record Mountain, Gray Mountain and Kirkup Mountain.

Red Resort has big plans to expand into a further 1,699ha (4,200 acres) of terrain as and when skier visits increase, which would make it one of the largest ski areas in North America. Quite how much this will affect the soulful atmosphere that pervades the place remains to be seen. However, those involved in these developments seem to be well aware that atmosphere and character are almost as

big a draw here as the fine skiing, so hopefully both Red and Rossland will retain their unique charm.

**Steeps, trees and deep powder are Red Resort's stock in trade.**

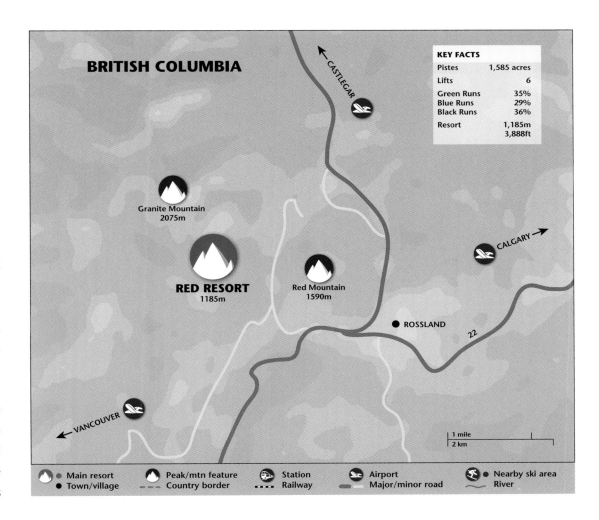

# Panorama

BY CLAIRE WALTER

Panorama Mountain Village, a purpose-built resort west of Banff and Kootenay National Parks in a sparsely populated part of eastern British Columbia, feels a world away from the busy Vancouver–Whistler stretch along the coast. The resort is a family-friendly, civilized and welcoming island surrounded by an untamed landscape known for wildlife, rugged beauty and unspoiled nature. For skiers and riders, Panorama's interior location makes for colder temperatures but drier snow than at the coast.

With Canada's second-greatest vertical (after Whistler Blackcomb), the mountain is a large and looming giant. Terrain ranges from wide-open slopes and cruising trails to super-steep chutes (and a couple of bowls for good measure), appealing to a wide range of skiers and riders. It is a place where novices and small children feel comfortable on gentle, manicured and uncrowded terrain, but where gonzo off-piste skiers can find terrain that is steep, ungroomed and also uncrowded.

Panorama Mountain Village's rambling wooden buildings might not win any architectural prizes, but they can't be beaten for convenience. Many lodgings are ski-in/ski-out, while those down the hill are easily accessible via a transit gondola. Après-ski and evening activities are right there too.

Like Whistler, Tremblant, Copper Mountain, Stratton and others, the resort was shaped by Intrawest, a company in transition at the time of writing, but it was not developed or heavily redeveloped by Intrawest, so the corporation's signature regional architecture, a village layout with open plazas and underground parking, are absent. Still, comfortable and convenient lodging – mostly condo apartments, several in complexes with inviting steaming hot tubs and swimming pools – occupy tiers at the base of the mountain. The resort is mellow and civilized at the bottom, but rugged, wild and uncrowded at the top.

## The mountain

When you look up from the base, it is easy to lose sight of the fact that Panorama has a vertical drop of 1,310m (4,300ft). This classic ski area is configured with the easiest terrain at the bottom and the most challenging on top. Wrapped around this single-peak layout are splendid fall-line trails, fabulous glades and even a mid-mountain snowfield. Additional black diamonds are etched onto the backside and on lower slopes partway

**The village at Panorama is compact and family-friendly, but the drop-in chutes, walls, cornices and steep glades of Taynton Bowl represent the resort's wild side.**

around the mountain that is broad at the base and both tapers and steepens at the top. Reaching the summit is accomplished by a series of three quad chairlifts. You can yo-yo on any one of them or link the rides and runs together to ski the entire imposing vertical.

From the base area, the green-circle (easy) and blue-square (intermediate) freeways off the Mile 1 Quad Express are perfect for racking up vertical footage with minimal chair-lift time. Nearby are the resort's easiest beginner slopes and also the halfpipe. This lift unloads on a small plateau, from which you can continue skyward on the mid-mountain Champagne Express, which offers upper-level skiers and riders a variety of blue-square cruisers and steep short runs that merit their black diamonds (difficult). Those in the know plug a stop or two at the mid-mountain Cappuccino Hut into their day. Another option is to follow Triple Traverse to the Sunbird triple chairlift, a separate but connected mountain sector. With a different exposure, different snow conditions and even a different look to the terrain, it appeals to intermediate and advanced skiers and riders.

To access Panorama's crowning runs, angle down to the Summit Quad. Roy's Run, Top of the World and a glade called Tight Spots wear single black diamonds. Nearly everything else up there is double-black (most difficult) territory, including tight chutes etched into cliff bands. Farther down, near and below the lower section of the lift, are additional glades and snowfields that never get crowded, because it takes a while to work your way back to the summit.

If that isn't enough expert territory, the backside splendour of Taynton Bowl beckons from the Summit Quad unload. View of 1000 Peaks is the evocative name of the easiest, most straightforward route. It divides into Stumbock's, Elmo, 1st Chance, Fat Chance or Last Chance and eventually returns to the main trail system. Hardcore experts continue from the summit along the Outback Ridge and drop into any of the dozen or so named double-black chutes, mini-bowls or glades of

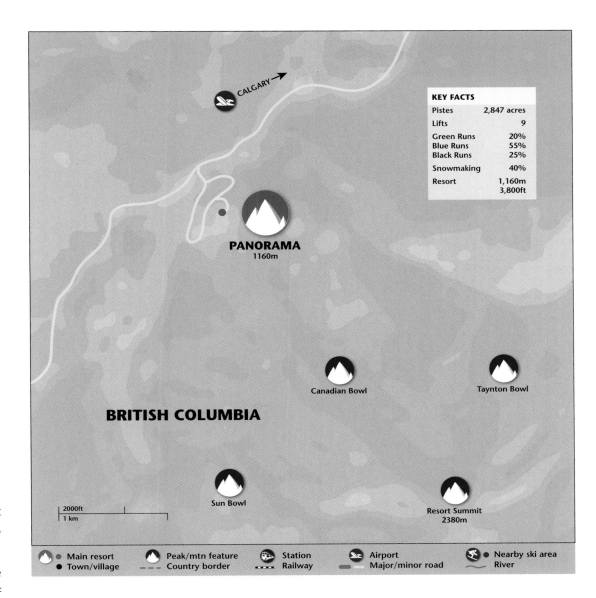

**KEY FACTS**

| | |
|---|---|
| Pistes | 2,847 acres |
| Lifts | 9 |
| Green Runs | 20% |
| Blue Runs | 55% |
| Black Runs | 25% |
| Snowmaking | 40% |
| Resort | 1,160m 3,800ft |

Main resort — Town/village · Peak/mtn feature — Country border · Station ···· Railway · Airport — Major/minor road · Nearby ski area — River

choice. These super-steeps funnel into Landing Strip and then Taynton Trail back to frontside reality.

For strong skiers and riders, especially those travelling with less-skilled companions, Panorama boasts the unsurpassed convenience of a heliskiing operation based right out of the village. At no other North American resort can you walk out of your condo and board a chopper for so memorable a backcountry adventure. RK Heliski has been in business since 1970, ferrying skiers and now snowboarders into the heart of the Purcell Range. And when the heliskiing day is done, it's just a short walk back to the condo and a soak in one of those inviting hot tubs.

**Visitors treasure abundant ski-in/ski-out lodging. The condominium apartments comfortably accommodate families and groups of friends.**

## BRITISH COLUMBIA

# Kicking Horse Resort

BY ALF ALDERSON

Canada's 'newest' ski resort has to be something pretty special to compete with the country's many world-class resorts, and so it is. British skiers who discover it are apt to remark that 'Kicking Arse' might be a better name. Scurrilous as that may be, it's also a pretty accurate description of the kind of skiing to be had here.

The resort, which was actually developed on the back of the small exisiting ski area of Whitetooth, is a veritable adventure playground for advanced to expert skiers, who will find no end of challenges in its inspiring selection of bowls, ridges, chutes and trees, while the lower half of the mountain is crisscrossed by a good network of green and blue runs suited to less experienced skiers. Although good intermediates may become frustrated at the sparseness of top-to-bottom blues, novice skiers will relish the easy 'It's A

Ten', 10km (6 miles) from the 2,346m (7,700ft) top station of the Golden Eagle Express gondola. Indeed, you could easily ski all day at Kicking Horse using only the gondola – actually only one of the resort's four main base-to-summit lifts – particularly if you're searching for black and double-black diamond runs or some exciting off-piste action. To reach the resort's highest point, the 2,448m (8033ft) Blue Heaven, you need to hop on the mid-mountain Stairway to Heaven quad, which, apart from one blue

ABOVE: **Kicking Horse is based in what was once heliskiing terrain – spectacular, steep and deep.**

RIGHT: **The resort's Eagle's Eye Restaurant has one of the best menus and some of the finest views in Canada.**

266

run, provides access to a fantastic selection of black and double-black diamond trails.

It's the upper mountain that experienced skiers will fall in love with. However good you are, you'll find something to challenge you in Bowl Over off CPR Ridge, or the prosaically monikered runs 98 to 106 that spill into Feuz Bowl; all are steep double-black chutes, some narrower than others – just choose your angle of descent and go for it. The fun continues as you emerge from the bowls onto the option of a variety of open blacks, or some fun tree-skiing where there's a good chance of finding hidden powder stashes. If it's moguls you're after, there's no shortage, especially under the Pioneer Chair.

Some of the slopes that make up Kicking Horse Resort were once heliskiing territory, (and the bowls to either side of the resort are still used for that purpose) so if you've never actually been heliskiing this is a chance to ski the kind of terrain that's used for the sport. Or you could actually try a day at Purcell Helicopter Skiing while you're there!

The lower mountain is busier than the upper, since this is where the majority of intermediate and novice skiers will find terrain to suit them, with a whole sequence of green and blue runs beneath Catamount and Pioneer chairs, while complete beginners have an area beneath the Catamount chair.

Irrespective of your ability, make at least one trip up in the Golden Eagle Express gondola for the truly magnificent panoramas to

## WHAT'S IN A NAME?

*The resort's colourful name was inspired by an incident during an expedition to the Canadian Rockies in 1858 by Sir James Hector and a team sent to find a rail route across the Great Divide. When one of the expedition's packhorses got loose and escaped into the river, the plucky geologist swam after it and managed to drag it out of the water. But his own horse attacked it, and during the ruckus, Sir James was kicked unconscious. Convinced he was mortally wounded, his native guides were about to bury him when he regained consciousness.*

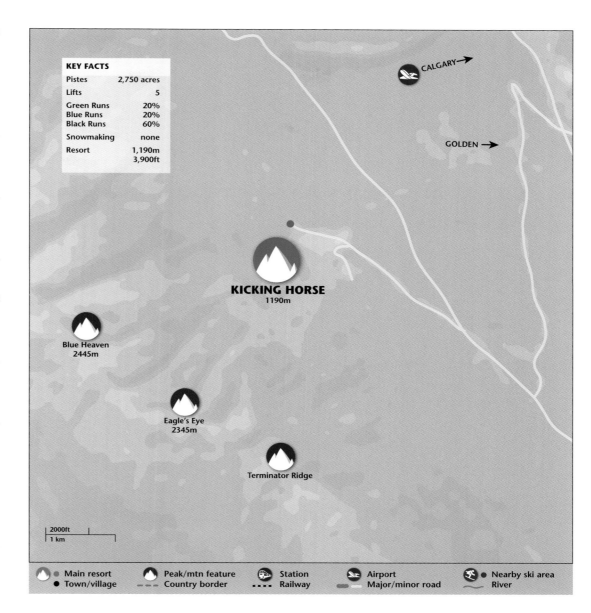

| KEY FACTS | |
|---|---|
| Pistes | 2,750 acres |
| Lifts | 5 |
| Green Runs | 20% |
| Blue Runs | 20% |
| Black Runs | 60% |
| Snowmaking | none |
| Resort | 1,190m |
| | 3,900ft |

KICKING HORSE
1190m

Blue Heaven
2445m

Eagle's Eye
2345m

Terminator Ridge

2000ft
1 km

| | | |
|---|---|---|
| ● Main resort | ● Peak/mtn feature | ▣ Station |
| ● Town/village | --- Country border | ···· Railway |
| ✈ Airport | ⚡ Nearby ski area | |
| ▬ Major/minor road | ~ River | |

be viewed from the summit. If you want to get technical, what you can see are the Rocky Mountains to the north and east, divided from the Purcell Mountains and Kootenay Ranges to the south by the Rocky Mountain Trench, through which flows the Columbia River. To the west are the Selkirk Mountains. For the non-technical, it's simply a whole lot of mountains, forest and river, and some truly glorious wild Canadian landscapes.

Another unmissable attraction adjacent to the gondola's top station is the Eagle's Eye Restaurant, which combines elegant dining with tremendous views and a superb menu based on Canadian Rocky Mountain produce. This is the best dining to be had at the resort or in the nearby town of Golden, because the options at Kicking Horse's base and in the town are, as yet, fairly limited.

The same is true of accommodation options. You can stay in truly luxurious (and correspondingly expensive) suites above the Eagle's Eye, or there are very comfortable but limited ski-in/ski-out options at the base. Otherwise you're restricted to a modest range of motels and B&Bs in the blue-collar lumbering and railroad town of Golden. However, the ongoing expansion plans of the resort will see this situation change in the future.

These plans extend to the slopes, which can only mean that a resort that already has world-class skiing is going to get even better. And because of Kicking Horse's relative isolation (some three hours from Calgary and no resort-access on public transport) the already quiet pistes are likely to remain that way, which is great news for skiers who don't mind a bit of a trek.

# Fernie Alpine Resort

BY ARNIE WILSON

Just under a decade since a makeover costing millions of dollars transformed Fernie from a little-known cult ski area to a celebrated destination resort, with luxurious mountain homes and twice as much terrain, it is no longer a diamond in the rough – but one which seems set to grow and sparkle more as the decade continues. The transformation is far from over. But a further upgrade of some of the lifts may now become something of a priority.

In a good snow year (and it enjoys many) this resort in the heart of the Lizard Range – in the south-eastern tip of British Columbia – offers skiing that is the epitome of steep and deep.

An old coal-mining town, Fernie – 5km (3 miles) from the resort and linked with the ski area by bus – is still refreshingly glitz-free with a funky, gung-ho image, and plentiful cafes, bars, restaurants and shops. It was founded a little over a century ago by William Fernie, an British adventurer who discovered coal here (or rather realized that the local Native Americans had discovered it without realizing what it was).

The somewhat run-down old community produced abundant coal and, eventually, some avid skiers. They enjoyed exceptional slopes, and little interference from the outside world. But word of this 'best kept secret' eventually got out, and in 1996 Fernie was purchased by Resorts of the Canadian Rockies, determined to expand a portfolio that already included the high-profile Lake Louise Mountain Resort.

Almost immediately, the new owners doubled the size of Fernie's remarkable terrain by building new lifts in the magnificent bowl areas which until then had been almost entirely the reserve of snowcat skiers. Now, thanks to the Timber Bowl chair, which takes skiers and snowboarders into the heart of Siberia Bowl and Timber Bowl, and the White Pass quad, which opened up some excellent terrain in Currie Bowl – they can ski old favourites like Deep Sea and Heartland to their hearts' content. Altogether there are now five lift-served bowls and 107 marked runs beneath the evocatively named mountains of Elephant Head, Polar Peak and Grizzly Peak.

Fernie has always been famous for its steep 'front-face' trails high above the base area: it is almost as if the powers-that-be built

**More and more of Fernie's magnificent natural bowl areas are now accessible to skiers and snowboarders, thanks to new lifts.**

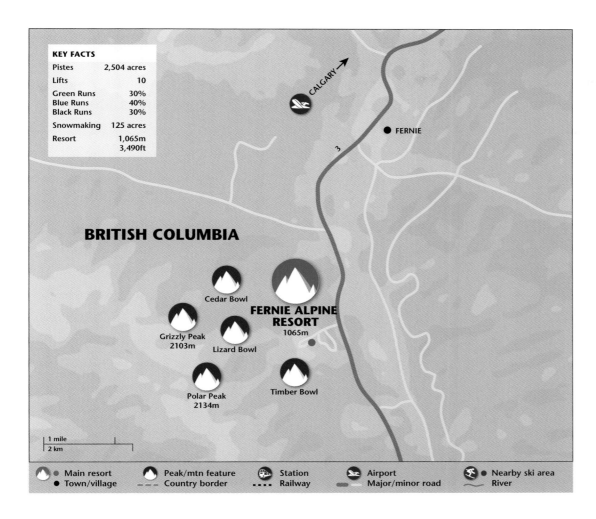

**KEY FACTS**

| Pistes | 2,504 acres |
| --- | --- |
| Lifts | 10 |
| Green Runs | 30% |
| Blue Runs | 40% |
| Black Runs | 30% |
| Snowmaking | 125 acres |
| Resort | 1,065m |
| | 3,490ft |

CALGARY →

FERNIE

3

**BRITISH COLUMBIA**

Cedar Bowl

**FERNIE ALPINE RESORT**
1065m

Grizzly Peak
2103m

Lizard Bowl

Polar Peak
2134m

Timber Bowl

1 mile
2 km

| | Main resort | | Peak/mtn feature | | Station | | Airport | | Nearby ski area |
| --- | --- | --- | --- | --- | --- | --- | --- | --- | --- |
| | Town/village | - - - | Country border | · · · · | Railway | | Major/minor road | | River |

an ordinary ski area and then went around with a huge invisible crane and jacked most runs up an extra ten degrees. Deep Space and Sunnyside 44 (so called because of its 44-degree slope) are good examples. The twin peaks you gaze up at from the Timberline Village base area gaze back at you like disapproving gods. The appropriately named Sky Dive trail towers above you like a huge frozen waterfall. Stag Leap and Boomerang Ridge look daunting too. But fortunately for startled newcomers to the resort, if they manage to stifle their anxiety and inspect these runs from the top, they will find, to their relief, they're not quite as steep as they look.

The Great Bear Express Quad chair is another gateway to some steep but exhilarating skiing. It gets you to the somewhat tricky and uncomfortable Face Lift rope-tow (sometimes affectionately known as the Lift From Hell or the Meat-Hook), which brings you to Lizard Bowl. From here you can take a blue run called Cruiser, until you reach the top of the Boomerang Chair and beyond, where there's

a wonderful variety of steep, exhilarating pitches through the trees like Boomerang and Linda's Run. If you ski to the right at the top of the Face Lift, you can access a steep ridge with some of Fernie's classic glade runs, including Gorbie Bowl, Steep & Deep, Red Tree and Wally's Follies.

But not everyone who rides the Face Lift has to ski such daunting terrain. The tow also accesses an assortment of blue runs, including Cascade, Bow, Weasel, Bear and Cruiser. And in spite of Fernie's steep-and-deep reputation, there is certainly no shortage of runs for beginners. The Elk Quad services a whole network of green runs, and novices can enjoy the wonderfully long Falling Star all the way from the top of the White Pass Chair to the base area – a vertical drop of almost 915m (3,000ft).

Although there is enough here to keep skiers and boarders happy for much more than a week, there are also opportunities for some excellent cat skiing, with a number of operations in the vicinity.

**Powder almost up to your knees: that's what attracts riders from around the world to this snow-sure resort in a remote part of British Columbia.**

**Gobi Desert**

*Huang He*

Sea of Okhotsk

*Hokkaido*  • Sapporo
**Niseko**

**Gassan**

**JAPAN**

**Happo One**  **Shiga Kogen**
Nagano• •**Tokyo**
*Honshu*

*Yangtze Kiang*

*Mekong*

*South China Sea*

*Philippine Sea*

Tropic of Cancer

*Hawaiian Islands*

**P A C I**

*Indonesia*

**O C E**

*Melanesia*

**INDIAN**

**OCEAN**

•Darwin

**NORTHERN**

**TERRITORY**

*Macdonnell Ranges*

*Mt Bruce*

**WESTERN**

**AUSTRALIA**

**AUSTRALIA**

**SOUTH**

**AUSTRALIA**

•Perth

*Coral Sea*

*Great Barrier Reef*

**QUEENSLAND**

•Brisbane

**NEW**
**SOUTH**
**WALES**

•Sydney

**Canberra**

Adelaide•

*Murray*

**VICTORIA**

**Perisher Blue**
**& Thredbo**

*Mt Kosciuszko*

Melbourne•

**Mount Buller**

**Falls Creek &**
**Mount Hotham**

TASMANIA

*Tasman Sea*

**NEW**
**ZEALAND**

*North Island*

Auckland• •Hamilton

*Mt Ruapehu*

**Whakapapa & Turoa**

**Wellington**

*Mt Cook*

*South Island*

•Christchurch

**Mount Hutt**

**Coronet Peak,**
**The Remarkables,**
**Treble Cone,**
**Cardrona**

**S O U T H E R N**

1000   2000   3000
2500   5000 kilometres

4000 miles

Rocky Mountains

Great
Plains

Appalachian Mountains

Mississippi

Sierra Madre

Gulf of
Mexico

West Indies

Caribbean
Sea

NORTH

ATLANTIC

OCEAN

F I C

A N

Equator

Cordillera

Guiana Highlands

Chimborazo

Amazon

Basin

Amazon

Huascaran

Andes

Mato
Grosso

Brazilian Highlands

Tropic of Capricorn

CHILE

Andes

ARGENTINA

Aconcagua

Valle Nevado,
La Parva &
El Colorado

Portillo

Santiago

Mendoza

Las Leñas

Malargue

Buenos Aires

Pampas

Termas de
Chillán

Llaima

Villarica

Pucon

SOUTH

Osorno

San Carlos de Bariloche

Antillanca

Gran
Catedral

ATLANTIC

OCEAN

Andes

Patagonia

OCEAN

Mountain High Maps® Copyright © 1993 Digital Wisdom®, Inc.

# THE REST OF THE WORLD

BY ARNIE WILSON

Which skier or snowboarder with the merest hint of adrenalin coursing through his or her veins could fail to be excited by the thought of skiing in some distant mountain range? Just the names of some of the Himalayan, Andean and New Zealand peaks – visible, if not always skiable from the slopes – are electrifying. Indrasan, Deo Tibba and Shiukar Beh tower above Manali, in Himachal Pradesh. Aconcagua, El Plomo, and Tronador pierce the Andean sky. Mounts Aspiring and Cook, aka Aoraki ('the cloud piercer') dominate the New Zealand skyline.

Those of us in the Northern hemisphere are so used to the idea of skiing in the Alps and perhaps in North America that the thought of skiing in such exotic places as Japan, Chile, Argentina, New Zealand and especially Australia seems wildly exotic – even if we have rather more conventional skiing on our doorstep. And yet, of course, for skiers and snowboarders actually living in these countries it is simply their 'local' skiing.

Just as Northern hemisphere skiers forget that Christmas in Australasia is usually celebrated on the beach in a heatwave (some Australians actually celebrate it in June when things are a little cooler) they also tend to think of skiing in the Andes as "summer" skiing when of course to the Chileans and Argentineans it is very much winter, and there is usually plenty of snow to prove it. So visitors from north of the equator should not think of it as skiing in sketchy, slushy conditions – but in a full-on winter. The question is, is it really worth travelling such vast distances during the Northern hemisphere summer to try skiing south of the Equator?

ABOVE: **Victoria Jealouse, from Whistler, BC – one of the best backcountry snowboarders in the world – romps through the powder at Valle Navado, Chile.**

BELOW: **The easy-does-it slopes of the Shiga Plateau, Shiga Kogen, Japan. This particular run is more suitable for a gentle cruise than a steep downhill!**

Japan, with its fascinating customs and cuisine, is probably worth a skiing visit in its own right, and Santiago, with almost immediate access to the Chilean and even Argentinean slopes, certainly is. By contrast, the Argentinean capital, Buenos Aires – beautiful city though it is – is a very long way indeed from the mountains!

Tokyo is also a long way – both from Europe and from Japan's own Alps. Being in the northern hemisphere its winters occur at fundamentally the same time as those in the Alps and the Rockies. This also applies to the Himalayas, where although there is limited 'resort' and lift-accessed skiing, there are superb opportunities to heliski in the Himalayas. Cultural differences alone make the journey to these places well worthwhile. How many temples do you get to visit in the Alps or the Rockies? And what an opportunity to see the sights of such intriguing cities as New Delhi and Tokyo en route.

The same goes for Santiago, with dramatic views of the mighty Andes which almost encircle this European-style city (providing the pollution allows you a few glimpses). And there is no doubt that the Andes skiing experience is richly rewarding and universally acclaimed, whichever side of the great cordillera you chose to explore. If current trends are anything to go by, skiing and snowboarding in Chile and Argentina seem to be the next big thing, and although it is a long journey (and even feels as though you are almost falling off the very edge of the world) it is obviously not as far as New Zealand and Australia, which are just about as far as you can travel round the globe before the curvature of the earth sends you winging your way north again.

For skiers in Europe and even North America, the notion of visiting such exotic resort destinations is probably best considered as adjuncts to business trips or general travel trips. Skiers who happen to find themselves in Tokyo during the winter months, for example, or Auckland, Christchurch, Sydney or Melbourne, during the northern hemisphere summer, would unquestionably enjoy taking time out to go skiing. Although New Zealand's slopes are worth journeying to the other side of the world for, the same cannot always be said for Australia, if only because its snow record is far less dependable than its neighbour's. But given good conditions, the resorts of New South Wales and Victoria are certainly rewarding. And if you can throw in a visit to Sydney, one of the most beautiful cities in the world, who really cares if the skiing in the Snowies is not quite up to Val d'Isère or Verbier standards?

# The Andes

BY ARNIE WILSON

It is almost unheard of for any skier or snowboarder to venture into the wonderfully impressive Andes, which divide South America's only real skiing nations of Chile and Argentina, without being captivated by both countries' resorts. Sir Arnold Lunn, the British ski pioneer, once famously said: 'An Englishman is at home in the Alps, but an intruder in the Andes'. An intruder not necessarily in a malevolent sense, but as a visitor from another world.

The Andes, in other words – a magnificently remote mountain range – are almost other-worldly compared with the Alps: a place where the human race, or at least westerners, seem to be relative parvenus and outsiders. From a casual glance at a map, it seems almost as though one can visit both Argentinean and Chilean resorts in a systematic way as one journeys south along the stunning cordillera that provides such a spectacular backbone to both countries. But unfortunately you can't just drift, as it were, from Chilean slopes to those in Argentina at will. It has to be carefully planned.

There are only two mountain passes linking the two countries in winter – the Puyehue pass, where lush, sub-tropical vegetation bowed down with snow lines the route, giving it a wintry, surreal feel, and the fiercely bleak and desolate Uspallata pass, which culminates at Chile's oldest resort of Portillo just before dropping across the Argentine border. Trucks, engines screaming, use this route to ply between the central valley of Chile and the Argentinean city of Mendoza. The Puyehue pass links both countries' Lake Districts from Argentina's San Carlos de Bariloche to Chile's Osorno district. So for those who wish to work their way down the Andes, taking in as many resorts as possible, the practical modus operandi is to start on one side of the mountains and ski there until the opportunity arises to cross one of the two passes, and then linger on the other side until the next opportunity arises to change countries. In fact the best solution might well be to

LEFT: **The swimming pool at the Hotel Portillo, right on Chile's border with Argentina, with its splendid view of the Laguna del Inca.**

BELOW: **This is the purpose-built resort of Valle Nevado, inspired by French architecture, which offers some of the closest skiing to the Chilean capital of Santiago.**

do all your Chile skiing before crossing into Argentina – or vice versa. Mix and match doesn't really work.

## Around Santiago

For the most immediate introduction to skiing in the Andes, the best plan is to make for Santiago, the Chilean capital: there are four resorts within immediate striking distance. The three closest, a mere 48km (30 miles) or so from the capital, are linked: Valle Nevado, the French-designed purpose-built ski centre which is the only genuine destination resort of the three; La Parva, an up-market resort where wealthy Chileans have second or even third homes; and El Colorado, a more prosaic ski area, whose custom is drawn mainly at weekends from day trippers from Santiago. These three areas are often referred to, a touch optimistically, as Chile's version of France's vast Trois Vallées system. A little further afield (some 160km/100 miles from Santiago) is Portillo, a resort in a spectacular location on the shores of the Laguna del Inca. In the days when the only way to reach Mendoza from Santiago was the Trans Andean Railway, Portillo, at almost the highest point the railway reached, was linked with it via a short spur line. To this day, with sufficient blown-in snow, you can ski through an old tunnel along the now long-abandoned track by making a short detour from the Bajada Del Tren run.

## Further south

Because Chile is such an extraordinarily long and thin country, getting to the other resorts involves travelling considerable distances to the south. As you move down the seemingly endless cordillera, the terrain becomes more and more interesting, with volcanoes rearing up (mainly on the Chilean side) and gradually the ski areas you reach become more and more exotic – but less alpine. Termas de Chillán is on the cusp of this transition, and it is fortunate to have the best of both worlds – a truly extensive, reasonably modern ski resort combining a fascinating volcanic flavour

The linked resorts of Valle Nevado, La Parva and El Colorado are called the 'Three Valleys'. This seemingly endless chute provides expert snowboarders and skiers with one of the backcountry highlights of the region.

– and smell! (Even the mild stench of sulphur has a curious attraction once you realize it's not the drains of the mountain restaurant.)

The nearby city of Chillan was the birthplace of Chile's first president, Bernardo O'Higgins (b.1778), the illegitimate son of an Irish born governor of Chile and Viceroy of Peru and Isabel, a young Chilean aristocrat almost 40 years his junior. To this day his name lives on: every major city in Chile has something named after him, be it a street, a hotel and even a football team (Club Deportivo O'Higgins of Rancagua). If you don't fancy the longish haul down the Pan American Highway there's now a train service from Santiago to Chillan, which takes four hours and is rarely late: good going for a South American train.

From Chillan, you can move on to investigate other Chilean volcano resorts like Villarrica Pucon, Llaima and Antillanca before crossing the border to Bariloche, or Gran Catedral (the resort's official name), the most European of the Argentine resorts, way down near the shores of Lake Nahuel Huapi in the heart of the Argentine Lake District. If you decide to cross into Argentina via Portillo, you can (eventually) get to Bariloche that way too (it's a fearsomely long drive!). But first you can head for the distant Argentinean resort of Las Leñas, revered as the Chamonix of the southern hemisphere, with its phenomenal off-piste opportunities. If you want conventional skiing with plenty of cruising and delightful scenery, with outstanding lake views, Bariloche will not disappoint. It has the additional advantage of being close to the cosmopolitan city of San Carlos de Bariloche. Las Leñas, on the other hand – not far from the spot where a plane-load of Uruguayan rugby players crashed in 1972, inspiring the book *Alive!* and a subsequent film – is not really near anywhere, although there is a small airport at Malargue.

# Australasia

BY ARNIE WILSON

They're a long way away. At least they are if you happen to live in the northern hemisphere. But don't underestimate the skiing in New Zealand – or even Australia. New Zealand claims to have more mountains in the Southern Alps on South Island than there are in the entire European Alps. That is questionable. Nonetheless, it does have a vast mountainous area.

## New Zealand

The big difference between the Southern Alps and those in the northern hemisphere is that ski resorts in the New Zealand 'version' are few and far between. The vast majority of New Zealand's ski areas are in South Island: North Island, without a major alpine range of its own, has two commercial fields, on either side of a huge, sprawling and active volcano – Mount Ruapehu. The main centres for skiing in the Southern Alps are the bustling lakeside town of Queenstown (close to one of the country's oldest ski areas, Coronet Peak, and its newest, The Remarkables), Wanaka, close to Treble Cone, by consensus South Island's best commercial field, and Cardrona (mainly beginner–intermediate slopes with some contrastingly wild, serious experts-only all-mountain terrain thrown in) and Methven, not too far from Christchurch, and the base for the country's legendary Mount Hutt. Apart from these principle centres of the skiing world, there's a scattering of smaller areas like Porter Heights, Mount Lyford and Rainbow, many of which started out as 'club fields' – an intriguing New Zealand concept which precipitated up to a score of small, fairly basic ski areas with little or no grooming and primitive 'nutcracker' lifts as often as not powered by car or tractor engines. Most of these areas remain club fields to this day – only a handful have become semi or fully 'commercial'. Club members pay cheap rates for the limited lifts and subsidise the clubs by sharing daily duties such as cooking, washing up, cleaning and keeping the heating systems going.

New Zealand's commercial fields have virtually no on-mountain accommodation (you simply drive to the slopes – often along rather precarious winding roads, particularly the infamously unnerving route to Mount Hutt – and drive back down again after the lifts have shut). Club fields are the exception. Almost all of them have lodging – some a little ramshackle – and club members also share in their upkeep. This may sound a little unglamorous for skiers used to five-star hotels and luxury chalets in places like Courchevel, Lech and Zermatt, but club fields provide hardcore skiers with cheap but often excellent skiing, most famously in Craigieburn.

Apart from commercial and club fields, there is also some first-class helicopter skiing in the Harris Mountains, some exceptional heliskiing terrain around Mount Cook (at 3,000m/9,842ft the country's highest peak) and in the Arrowsmith mountains around Methven. In good visibility, the resorts on North Island's Mount Ruapehu (Whakapapa and Turoa) provide some of the best skiing in Australasia. But the volcano, which erupts on average every 50 years or so (most recently in 1995 and 1996), is a magnet for unsettled weather. Turoa has the biggest vertical drop in the country (722m/2,369ft). Whakapapa's is 675m (2,215ft). On South Island, Treble Cone just edges Whakapapa with a vertical drop of 697m (2,287ft).

**Down-under delight: off the beaten track at Coronet Peak, New Zealand, this skier can hardly believe that the conditions are so exhilarating.**

## Australia

Although New Zealand's commercial resorts and club fields are not that extensive, their reliable snow lures many Australian skiers across the Tasman Sea – particularly to Coronet Peak and The Remarkables – even though Australia itself has some excellent skiing. Australia's resorts are confined to just two states – New South Wales and Victoria, along with some skiing in Tasmania. Altogether Australia has about a dozen ski areas, the principal ones are Thredbo and Perisher Blue in New South Wales, where Australia's highest peak, Mount Kosciuszko (7,310ft/2,228m) dominates the scenery, and Falls Creek, Mount Hotham and Mount Buller in Victoria. Perisher Blue has the largest ski area in the country. It is in fact an amalgam of four ski areas. Perisher Valley-Smiggin Holes were once big rivals of neighbouring Blue Cow (Australia's newest ski resort), which itself was linked with the country's oldest ski area of Guthega. Perisher – said (probably apocryphally) to be so named after an Australian cattleman's remarks when he and a friend were caught in a blizzard he described as 'a perisher') – ended up purchasing its rivals.

No matter which ski resort you visit, you will find yourself skiing through the country's ubiquitous eucalyptus trees, known locally as 'snow gums'. In a good snow year, the skiing in Australia is certainly not to be sniffed at. Intriguingly, thanks to Scandinavian miners who journeyed here during the gold rush, Australia has what is claimed to be the oldest ski club in the world – The Kiandra Snowshoe Club. But the sport really took off when Europeans came here to work on the Snowy Mountain hydro-electric scheme in the 1950s. Some were from Austria and the then Czechoslovakia, and they soon popularized skiing. Some runs and lifts at Thredbo – the most alpine of Austria's resorts – are named after these European exponents of the sport.

RIGHT: **High plains drifter: a lone Australian skier surveys an extensive view of the Victoria Alps above the resort of Falls Creek.**

ABOVE: **Way above the eucalyptus treeline, a snowboarder executes a grab high above Thredbo, New South Wales – Australia's most alpine ski area.**

BELOW: **Almost a cricket team – skiers and snowboarders congregate happily on an eight-person chair at Perisher Blue, Australia's biggest ski resort.**

# Japan

BY ARNIE WILSON

Few skiers or snowboarders think of the Japan Alps when they are planning their winter schedule – yet this surprisingly large island complex (Japan is only slightly smaller than California) has a surprising number of ski resorts – more than 600 – and an equally surprising amount of snowfall each year. In fact one resort – Gassan – has so much snow that it can only operate during the summer months. In winter the handful of lifts are simply buried in the snow. So May becomes a good month to visit – with the best of both worlds.

Japan's ski areas are scattered across northern Honshu, the biggest of some 3,000 islands which make up this island nation, and Hokkaido, the second largest – which, in a more northerly location, has colder winters and even more reliable snow which blows in direct from Siberia.

Japan has a long history of skiing dating back almost a century, and has twice hosted the Winter Olympics – first at Sapporo (Hokkaido), in 1972, and much more recently at Nagano (Honshu) in 1998, when the resorts of Happo One in the splendidly scenic Hakuba Valley, and Shiga Kogen – a complex of 21 small, more-or-less linked resorts – became briefly famous.

Although the Japanese are fanatical skiers, traditionally changing their ski suits and equipment on an almost annual basis (as their culture seems to demand in all sports) the country's ski industry has been suffering something of a decline, with fewer visitors, and some resorts struggling for survival. But this has more to do with the country's long economic recession than any diminished fascination with the sport – although there was an inevitable peak of interest during the 1998 Olympics.

Skiing in Japan has become popular with Europeans and Americans based in Tokyo, and is starting to attract tourists too. Shiga Highlands is part of the huge Shiga Kogen network of 21 linked resorts which hosted most of the events at the 1998 Nagano Winter Olympics.

## A different view

One intriguing difference between skiing in Japan and the 'mainstream' ski areas of the northern hemisphere is the Japanese attitude to skiing off-piste. Until fairly recently, although Japanese skiers were happy to go heliskiing in British Columbia, the whole notion of off-piste in their own land was anathema. So much so that some resorts erected signs on the towers of their ski-lifts warning skiers of avalanche danger off-piste. These signs are a permanent deterrent to skiers venturing off-piste, with no account taken of genuine avalanche risk on a day-to-day basis. In other words, off-piste has been strongly and rather arbitrarily discouraged, regardless of any genuine consideration of danger. Things finally came to a head before the Nagano games in one resort when New Zealand guest workers – used to making the most of the extensive off-piste (including cliff-jumps!) in their own Southern Alps – were involved in a fight with Japanese ski patrollers when they tried to do the same in some tempting Japanese powder. What has changed things in recent years is that local snowboarders have forced Japanese resorts to change their philosophy. Riders – particularly in the high, wide-open glades of the upper slopes of Shiga Kogen – have put into practice what many of them learned from visits to New Zealand, laying down huge, sweeping arcs away from the main pistes. Skiers, watching their one-board 'cousins' enjoying this exhilarating phenomenon, have started to follow suit, and the process continues. At one Hokkaido area in particular, Niseko, Australian visitors have 'infiltrated' the resort in such numbers that a 'ski the powder' culture has evolved, and the resort now boasts of being the 'powder capital' of Japan – something almost unheard of a decade or so ago.

## Reaching the slopes

Unlike in Europe, few if any Japanese skiers access their ski areas by plane. By far the most popular methods of reaching the slopes are by 'Shinkansen' (bullet-trains) or bus. In Japan, where 'salarymen' will regularly remind you that in Japan more than anywhere 'time is money', the general idea is to pack as much skiing into a weekend as possible – allowing them (also if possible) to be back at their desks by Monday morning. This can be achieved with great success at such bustling ski areas as Naeba, one of Japan's busiest weekend resorts, where some slopes are floodlit from 4.30am, allowing skiers to complete 'double shifts' on both Saturdays and Sundays before climbing back into their coaches and trains late on Sunday, and heading back to the big city. Sometimes they don't even bother to book a hotel room. Instead, they may well simply get their heads down for a brief few hours in a locker room. Naeba, which once experienced 41,000 skiers on an unusually busy Sunday, also has 40 or so restaurants, at least one of which usually opens at around 3.30–4am to provide a hot breakfast for those skiers and snowboarders braving pre-dawn temperatures.

A word or two of warning about travelling by train from Tokyo to any of the ski areas: Japanese taxis rarely, if ever, carry ski racks. You will have to put your skis inside the taxi, which will probably have white linen sheeting draping the seats. Be prepared for dark looks and mutters from the not-always-friendly cab drivers. The other problem you'll encounter is that Japanese railway stations seem to have neither porters or trolleys – but they *do* have long walks to get to the platforms. So if you are carrying skis, poles, boots and assorted luggage, be prepared for a struggle.

Yamagata prefecture, home of Zao, one of Japan's best ski resorts. Zao is famous for its acres of 'snow monsters' – fir trees on which wet snow has frozen solid.

# Resort Profiles

It is sometimes almost impossible to unravel the differences in the classification and groupings of lifts and runs that various resorts and resort 'clusters' use in different parts of the world. Linked resorts such as Val d'Isère and Tignes in France give joint figures, and even resorts that are not linked but nearby may prefer to give 'grand totals' for entire 'regions'. In the Italian Dolomites and Austria's Salzburgerland, there are regional lift tickets that enable skiers and snowboarders to access scores of resorts and hundreds of lifts in the vast Dolomiti Superski region, the Skirama Dolomiti Adamello-Brenta region and Austria's Ski amadé region. Ski amadé includes resorts like Schladming, which has a relationship with both local resorts (some linked, and some not) and resorts further afield. Such problems make standardizing these resort profiles almost impossible. Of necessity, some categories within this directory have had to remain inconsistent.

There are also inconsistencies caused by differing skiing nomenclature in various parts of the world – particularly between Europe and North America. The Americans, for example, refer to trails or groomed runs rather than pistes, to ungroomed or backcountry rather than off-piste, and to trams rather than cable-cars. Austrian resorts often refer to ropeways and cableways. For ease of reference the names have generally been standardized, and the variations within different lift categories have been reduced: for example, there is no distinction between single, double, triple, quadruple or 'six-pack' chairlifts, or gondolas of various shapes and sizes.

| SPAIN | ANDORRA | ANDORRA |
|---|---|---|
| **Baqueira-Beret** | **Soldeu-El Tarter** | **Pas de la Casa** |

## Baqueira-Beret (SPAIN)

**Location** Baqueira-Beret is 2 hours from Toulouse Airport (146km/91 miles) in France, and 340km (211 miles) from Barcelona in Spain. The nearby town of Vielha is just under 14km (9 miles) from the resort; Lerida is 180km (112 miles) away.

**Resort details**
www.baqueira.es
+349 973 63 90 10

**Elevation** 1,500–2,509m (4,920–8,230ft)

**Vertical drop**
1,009m (3,310ft)

**Number of lifts**
Drags 11
Chairs 19
Gondola 1
Total 31

**Marked runs** 1,923ha (4,750 acres); 77 trails (104km/64 miles)

**Off-piste** ****

**Ski areas** The resort's 1,923ha (4,750 acres) of skiable terrain are divided into the separate sections of Baqueira, Beret and the recently developed Bonaigua section.

**Snowmaking** 36km

**Night skiing** No

**Length of season**
Mid-December–late April

## Soldeu-El Tarter (ANDORRA)

**Location** The villages of Soldeu and El Tarter lie on Andorra's arterial CG2 road, less than half an hour from the capital, Andorra la Vella (17km/11 miles). The nearest international airports are at Toulouse in France (192km/119 miles) and Barcelona in Spain (186km/116 miles). There are several coach services daily from and to Andorra la Vella, with Barcelona having the most frequent links. Andorra has no trains. A car is recommended.

**Resort details**
www.grandvalira.com
+376 808 900

**Elevation** 1,710–2,640m (5,609–8,659ft)

**Vertical drop**
930m (3,050ft)

**Number of lifts**
Drags 26
Chairs 28
Gondolas 3
Cable-car 1
Moving carpets 5
Total 63

**Marked runs** 193km (119 miles), 108 trails

**Off-piste** ***

**Ski areas** There are three sectors to the Soldeu-El Tarter ski area: the core Soldeu sector, the open El Tarter snowbowl and the compact El Forn area in the Valls de Canillo – all lift-linked. Soldeu-El Tarter is also lift-linked with Grau Roig at Pas de la Casa-Grau Roig, included on the Grandvalira area skipass.

**Snowmaking** 68km

**Night skiing** No

**Length of season**
Mid-December–early April

NB: figures for elevation, vertical drop, number of lifts and pisted runs are for the whole of the Grandvalira domain, including Pas de la Casa-Grau Roig.

## Pas de la Casa (ANDORRA)

**Location** The town of Pas de la Casa is in northeastern Andorra, on the border with France, around three-quarters of an hour from the capital. Andorra la Vella (31km/19 miles). The nearest international airports are at Toulouse in France (160km/99 miles) and Barcelona in Spain (174km/108 miles). There are several coach services daily both from and to Andorra la Vella, Barcelona having the most frequent links. Andorra has no trains, and a car is recommended.

**Resort details**
www.grandvalira.com
+376 808 900

**Elevation** 1,710–2,640m (5,609–8,659ft)

**Vertical drop**
930m (3,050ft)

**Number of lifts**
Drags 26
Chairs 28
Gondolas 3
Cable-car 1
Magic carpets 5
Total 63

**Marked runs** 193km (119 miles), 108 trails

**Off-piste** ***

**Ski areas** There are two main ski areas: the core Pas de la Casa area and the lift-linked and more varied area at Grau Roig to the south. Grau Roig is also lift-linked with Soldeu-El Tarter, included on the Grandvalira area skipass.

**Snowmaking** 68km

**Night skiing** Occasionally

**Length of season**
Mid-December–early April

NB: figures for elevation, vertical drop, number of lifts and pisted runs are for the entire Grandvalira domain, including Soldeu-El Tarter.

| ANDORRA | FRANCE | FRANCE | FRANCE | FRANCE | FRANCE | FRANCE |
|---|---|---|---|---|---|---|
| **Arcalis** | **Val d'Isère (Espace Killy)** | **Tignes (Espace Killy)** | **Les Trois Vallées** | **Les Trois Vallées** *continued* | **Chamonix/ Argentière** | **La Plagne/Les Arcs (Paradiski)** |

## Arcalis

**Location** Arcalis is tucked away in the remote north-western corner of Andorra, around half an hour from the capital Andorra la Vella (22km/14 miles). The nearest international airports are at Toulouse in France (247km/153 miles) and Barcelona in Spain (242km/150 miles). There are several coach services daily both from and to Andorra la Vella, with Barcelona having the most frequent links. Andorra has no trains. A car is strongly recommended.

**Resort details**
www.vallnord.com
+376 739 600

**Elevation** 1,940–2,640m (6,363–8,659ft)

**Vertical drop**
700m (2,296ft)

**Number of lifts**
Drags 8
Chairs 5
Total 14

**Marked runs** 24km (15 miles), 25 trails

**Off-piste** ****

**Ski areas** There are two sectors to the main ski area: the core Cirque d'Arcalis and the higher La Coma Valley snowbowl. The Vallnord area skipass also includes access to Pal-Arinsal-La Massana, which is not lift-linked with Arcalis – 16km (10 miles) from Arcalis to the nearest lift at La Massana.

**Snowmaking** 74 guns

**Night skiing** No

**Length of season**
Mid-December–early April

## Val d'Isère (Espace Killy)

**Location** At the end of the Tarentaise Valley in France's Savoie *département*, around half an hour from Bourg-St-Maurice (31km/19 miles). TGV and Eurostar services run direct to Bourg-St-Maurice, from where there are daily coach services to Val d'Isère. Regular airport coach services also connect with Lyon and Geneva; the nearest airport is Chambéry (146km/91 miles). A car is useful but not essential.

**Resort details**
www.valdisere.com
+33 479 06 06 60

**Elevation** 1,550–3,456m (5,084–11,336ft)

**Vertical drop**
1,906m (6,252ft)

**Number of lifts**
Drags 36
Chairs 44
Gondolas 4
Cable-cars 4
Funiculars 2
Total 90

**Marked runs** 300km (186 miles), 131 trails

**Off-piste** *****

**Ski areas** Three linked sectors: the Pissaillas Glacier above the village of Le Fornet; the core Solaise sector; and the extensive Bellevarde/La Daille sector linked with Tignes – all covered on the Espace Killy skipass. The off-piste possibilities from all sectors are some of Europe's best.

**Snowmaking** 22km

**Night skiing** No

**Length of season**
Early December–early May

NB: figures for elevation, vertical drop, number of lifts and pisted runs are for the entire Espace Killy domain, including Tignes.

## Tignes (Espace Killy)

**Location** High in the Tarentaise Valley in France's Savoie *département*, around half an hour from Bourg-St-Maurice (30km/19 miles). TGV and Eurostar services run direct to Bourg-St-Maurice, from where there are daily coach services to Tignes. Regular airport coach services also connect with Lyon and Geneva; the nearest airport is Chambéry (145km/91 miles). A car is useful but not essential.

**Resort details**
www.ski-tignes.net
+33 479 40 04 40

**Elevation** 1,550–3,456m (5,084–11,336ft)

**Vertical drop**
1,906m (6,252ft)

**Number of lifts**
Drags 36
Chairs 44
Gondolas 4
Cable-cars 4
Funiculars 2
Total 90

**Marked runs** 300km (186 miles), 131 trails

**Off-piste** *****

**Ski areas** Four linked sectors: the picturesque Aiguille Percée sector down to the villages of Les Boisses and Les Brévières; the wild Palet sector; the glacial Grande Motte sector; and the Tovière sector linked with La Daille/Val d'Isère – all covered on the Espace Killy skipass.

**Snowmaking** 22km

**Night skiing** Occasionally on national and school holidays.

**Length of season**
Mid-November–early May (plus July and August for summer skiing on the Grande Motte glacier)

NB: figures for elevation, vertical drop, number of lifts and pisted runs are for the entire Espace Killy domain, including Val d'Isère.

## Les Trois Vallées

**Location** Les Trois Vallées is the collective name for the interconnecting resorts of the Courchevel, Méribel and Val Thorens Valleys. Centrally located in the Haute Savoie, all the resorts are lift-linked and conveniently situated for many nearby large French ski resorts. The nearest valley town is Moutiers, from where there are regular bus services to all of the resorts. Méribel is the nearest resort to the valley. The nearest airports are Chambéry (1.5 hours, 95km/59 miles), Geneva (2.5 hours, 135km/84 miles) and Lyon (2.5 hours, 185km/115 miles). Times and distances measured from Méribel; add an extra half an hour for other resorts. All are clearly signposted from Moutiers.

**Resort details**
www.courchevel.com
+33 479 08 00 29

www.latania.com
+33 479 08 40 40

www.meribel.net
+33 479 08 60 01

www.valthorens.com
+33 479 00 08 08

www.lesmenuires.com
+33 479 00 73 00

www.st-martin-belleville.com
+33 479 00 20 00

**Elevation**
Courchevel Valley: 1,260–2,738m (4,134–8,983ft); Méribel Valley: 1,400–2,950m (4,593–9,678ft); Val Thorens Valley: 1,400–3,230m (4,593–10,597ft)

**Vertical drop**
1,970m (6,463ft)

**Number of lifts**
Drags 81
Chairs 68
Gondolas 34
Cable-cars 3
Funiculars 3
Total 189

**Marked runs** 600km (373 miles), 328 trails

**Off-piste** *****

*continued*

## Les Trois Vallées *continued*

**Ski areas** Les Trois Vallées is incredibly diverse and is the largest lift-linked ski area in the world. All three valleys have good beginner areas. Courchevel is the most varied, Val Thorens the most snow-sure and Méribel the best positioned.

**Snowmaking** 90km

**Night skiing** Yes: Courchevel: 1650 Wednesdays; Les Menuires: Thursdays Saint Martin: one night weekly

**Length of season**
Early December–late April

## Chamonix/ Argentière

**Location** Chamonix is a major town just over an hour away from Geneva (85km/53 miles). TGV services link to Annecy, from where there is a direct SNCF service. A car is recommended.

**Resort details**
www.chamonix.com
+33 450 53 00 24

**Elevation** 1,035–3,840m (3,400–12,605ft)

**Vertical drop**
2,807m (9,209ft)

**Number of lifts**
Drags 18
Chairs 16
Gondolas 5
Cable-cars 8
Total 47

**Marked runs** 152km (94 miles), 80 trails

**Off-piste** *****

**Ski areas** There are five main ski areas: le Tour, les Grands Montets, the linked areas of le Brévent and la Flégère and the famous off-piste of the Vallée Blanche. Nearby but not on the cham'ski pass is Les Houches.

**Snowmaking** 96 guns

**Night skiing** Yes: Thursday nights, Les Houches

**Length of season**
November–May

## La Plagne/Les Arcs (Paradiski)

**Location** Paradiski is the collective name for the neighbouring Upper Tarentaise resorts of La Plagne and Les Arcs. Les Arcs' nearest town is Bourg-St-Maurice (linked by funicular to Arc 1600) and La Plagne lies between here and the town of Aime. Geneva airport is around 150km (93 miles) away, Lyon 200km (124 miles).

**Resort details**
www.paradiski.com

www.lesarcs.com,
+33 479 07 12 57

www.la-plagne.com,
+33 479 09 79 79

**Elevation**
Les Arcs: 1,200–3,226m (3,937–10,584ft); La Plagne: 1,250–3,250m (4,101–10,663ft)

**Vertical drop**
2,226m (7,303ft)

**Number of lifts**
Drags 58
Chairs 66
Gondolas 12
Cable-cars 3
Funiculars 2
Total 141

**Marked runs** 425km (264 miles), 239 trails

**Off-piste** *****

**Ski areas** Les Arcs comprises the main western flank and the Arc 2000 Valley behind. La Plagne similarly spreads along the mountainside with the Champagny Valley behind.

**Snowmaking** La Plagne 98 Hectares / Les Arcs 12km

**Night skiing** Yes: Les Arcs: Tuesday/Thursday La Plagne: Tuesday/Thursday/Sunday

**Length of season**
Early December–late April

| FRANCE | FRANCE | ITALY | ITALY | ITALY | ITALY | ITALY |
|---|---|---|---|---|---|---|
| ## La Grave | ## Les Deux Alps | ## Cortina d'Ampezzo | ## Madonna di Campiglio | ## Selva Gardena | ## Cervinia (Val d'Aosta) | ## Courmayeur (Val d'Aosta) |

**La Grave**

**Location** La Grave straddles the N91 road between le Bourg-d'Oisans and Briançon, in France's Haute-Alpes *département*, around an hour from Grenoble (78km/48 miles) and just under 2 hours from Turin (137km/85 miles). The nearest international airport and TGV services are located at Grenoble, from where there are infrequent coach services. A car is strongly recommended.

**Resort details**
www.lagrave-lameije.com
+33 476 79 90 05

**Elevation** 1,400–3,550m
(4,592–11,644ft)

**Vertical drop**
2,150m (7,052ft)

**Number of lifts**
Drags 2
Chair 1*
Cable-cars 2
Total 5

*Only operates when lower slopes are impassable

**Marked runs** Other than four Blue-graded link pistes on the Glacier de la Girose, all routes are off-piste.

**Off-piste** ****

**Ski areas** There are three distinct ski areas: the uppermost limited pisted area on the Glacier de la Girose, which links into Les Deux Alpes; the classic Vallons de la Meije route and the parallel Vallons de Chancel route, both descending towards La Grave.

**Snowmaking** No

**Night skiing** No

**Length of season**
Mid-December–early May

---

**Les Deux Alps**

**Location** Les Deux Alpes occupies a high col between the Romanche and Vénéon valleys in France's Isère *département*, around an hour from Grenoble (75km/ 46 miles). The nearest international airport and TGV services are at Grenoble, from where there are several daily coach services. A car is recommended.

**Resort details**
www.les2alpes.com
+33 476 79 22 00

**Elevation** 1,300–3,600m
(4,265–11,812ft)

**Vertical drop**
2,300m (7,546ft)

**Number of lifts**
Drags 20
Chairs 23
Gondolas 3
Cable-cars 3
Funicular 1
Total 50

**Marked runs** 220km
(137 miles), 102 trails

**Off-piste** ****

**Ski areas** There are two main ski areas: the compact Pied Moutet sector on the western side of the resort and the core ski area extending above the eastern side of town towards the Mont-de-Lans glaciers and high-altitude link with La Grave/Vallons de La Meije.

**Snowmaking** 191 guns

**Night skiing** Yes: Tuesdays and Thursdays, central town slopes

**Length of season** Late November–late April (plus late June–late August for summer skiing on the glaciers)

---

**Cortina d'Ampezzo**

**Location** Cortina is a stand-alone resort in the Dolomites, purely Italian unlike its Sud Tirolean neighbours, where German is widely spoken. Fly into Venice (160km/99 miles) or Treviso (132km/82 miles). Trains go to Dobbiaco (32km/20 miles) or Calalzo (35km/22 miles), with frequent buses to Cortina. A car is recommended, though parking is difficult.

**Resort details**
www.cortina.dolomiti.org
+39 0436 866252

**Elevation** 1,225–2,930m
(4,020–9,610ft)

**Vertical drop**
1,705m (5,590ft)

**Number of lifts**
Drags 13
Chairs 29
Cable-cars 5
Total 47

**Marked runs** 140km
(87 miles), 97 trails

**Off-piste** **

**Cross country** 85km
(53 miles)

**Ski areas** Cortina has three main ski areas and four outlying ones, none of them near the town centre and none of them linked. The resort is also covered by the Super Dolomiti lift pass, valid on 450 lifts accessing 1,220km (750 miles) of piste, including the Sella Ronda resorts of Selva (Val Gardena), Canazei, San Cassiano, Corvara and Arabba.

**Snowmaking** Yes: 130km (81 miles)

**Night skiing** No

**Length of season**
Early December–mid-April

---

**Madonna di Campiglio**

**Location** Brenta Dolomites, northern Italy. The nearest airports are Bergamo (4 hours) Verona (3 hours), Milan Malpensa and Milan Linate (5 hours). The nearest train station is Trento (70km/ 44 miles). By road take the SS239 south from the SS42 Bolzano-Bergamo road.

**Resort details**
www.campiglio.to
+ 39 0465 447501

**Elevation**
1,520–2,505m (4,990–8,220ft)

**Vertical drop**
980m (3,215ft)

**Number of lifts**
Drags 7
Chairs 13
Gondolas 4
Cable-car 1
Total 25

**Marked runs** Madonna, including Marilleva and Folgarida: 90km (56 miles)

**Off-piste** **

**Ski areas** Campo Carlo Magno, Cima Fioccio di Neve, Dosson di Vagliana, Folgarida/Marilleva, Grostè, Pradalago, Spinale, 5 Laghi

**Snowmaking** 276km

**Night skiing** Yes

**Length of season**
December–April

---

**Selva Gardena**

**Location** Val Gardena is located in the Dolomites, in northern Italy. The nearest airports are Innsbruck (1.5 hours), Verona (2.5 hours), Milan (3.5 hours), Munich (3.5 hours). The nearest train stations are at Chiusa (27km/17 miles), Bressanone (35km/22 miles) and Bolzano (40km/25 miles), with a bus service from each. If coming by road, from A22 Innsbruck-Bolzano autostrada take SS49, then SS244.

**Resort details**
www.val-gardena.com
+ 39 0471 792277

**Elevation** 1,235–2,520m
(4,050–8,270ft)

**Vertical drop**
955m (3,133ft)

**Number of lifts**
Drags 32
Chairs 43
Gondolas 6
Cable-cars 2
Total 83

**Marked runs** Val Gardena: 175km (109 miles); Dolomiti Superski area: 1,220km

**Off-piste** **

**Ski areas** Arabba, Armentarola, Campitello, Canazei, Colfosco, Corvara, Ortisei, Pedraces, San Cassiano, Santa Cristina, La Villa (Cortina d'Ampezzo)

**Snowmaking** Yes

**Night skiing** Yes

**Length of season**
Late November/early December–April

---

**Cervinia (Val d'Aosta)**

**Location** Italy's highest resort at 2,050m (6,726ft), Cervinia is a 2.5-hour drive from both Turin (118km/73 miles) and Geneva (220km/138 miles).

**Resort details**
www.montecervino.it
www.cervinia.it
+39 0166 949136

**Elevation** 1,525–3,480m
(3,885m including Zermatt)

**Vertical drop**
1,955m/2,350m
(6,412ft/7,708ft)

**Number of lifts**
Drags 3
Chairs 14
Gondolas 2
Cable-cars 3
Moving carpets 2
Total 24

**Marked runs** 130km
(81 miles)

**Off-piste** *

**Ski areas** There are two principal ski areas in Cervinia: the large west-facing central bowl and the shoulder that drops down to neighbouring Valtournenche. Off the back is Zermatt.

**Snowmaking** Yes

**Night skiing** Yes

**Length of season**
October–May

---

**Courmayeur (Val d'Aosta)**

**Location** At the mouth of the Italian side of the Mont Blanc tunnel, the pretty town of Courmayeur is 105km (65 miles/2 hours) from Geneva and 150km (93 miles/ 2 hours) from Turin.

**Resort details**
www.courmayeur.net
+39 0165 842060

**Elevation** 1,224–2,755m
(4,015–9,038ft)

**Vertical drop**
1,531m (5,022ft)

**Number of lifts**
Drags 3
Chairs 8
Gondolas 2
Cable-cars 4
Total 17

**Marked runs** 200km
(124 miles), 24 trails

**Off-piste** ***

**Ski areas** There are two main pisted ski areas in Courmayeur, the east-facing central plain and the shoulder that drops down to Val Veny. Across from here is the unpisted expanse of Mont Blanc.

**Snowmaking** Yes

**Night skiing** Yes

**Length of season**
December–April

| ITALY | ITALY | ITALY | ITALY | SLOVENIA | AUSTRIA | AUSTRIA |
|---|---|---|---|---|---|---|
| **Monterosa Ski** | **Sestriere** | **Sauze d'Oulx** | **Sansicario** | **Kranjska Gora** | **St Anton** | **Ischgl** |

## Monterosa Ski

**Location** The Monterosa ski area, on the Italian side of the border with Switzerland, stretches from Champoluc in the west to Alagna in the east, with Gressoney in between. The nearest airports are Milan (165km/102.5 miles) and Turin (100km/62 miles). There are trains to Verres (26km/16 miles) for Champoluc, Pont St Martin (32km/20 miles) for Gressoney and Varallo Sesia (40km/25 miles) for Alagna, with onward bus connections to each resort. A car is not necessary as there are no direct road links between the resorts.

**Resort details**
www.monterosa-ski.com
+39 0125 303111

**Elevation** 1,200–3,260m (3,940–10,700ft)

**Vertical drop**
2,060m (6,860ft)

**Number of lifts**
Drags 15
Chairs 14
Gondolas 8
Cable-cars 4
Bucket lift 1
Total 42

**Marked runs** 180km (112 miles), 82 trails

**Off-piste** *****

**Cross country** 30km (18.5 miles)

**Ski areas** The Monterosa skipass covers three linked resorts: Champoluc and Gressoney in the Aosta Valley, and Alagna in the Valsesia, plus three small outlying areas, Antagnard, Brusson and Gressoney-St-Jean. The Aosta Valley pass is also valid in Courmayeur, La Thuile, Pila and Cervinia.

**Snowmaking** Yes

**Night skiing** No

**Length of season**
Early December–early April

## Sestriere

**Location** Sestriere straddles a high col at the top end of the Chisone Valley in Italy's Piemonte region. The town of Oulx, just 25km (15 miles) away in the neighbouring Susa Valley, has the nearest major motorway exit and railway station, with numerous high-speed train links with Turin, Rome, Lyon and Paris; frequent daily bus services from Oulx to Sestriere. A car is recommended.

**Resort details**
www.vialattea.it
+39 0122 755444

**Elevation** 1,350–2840m (4,428–9,315ft)

**Vertical drop**
1,490m (4,887ft)

**Number of lifts**
Drags 46
Chairs 38
Gondolas 4
Total 88

**Marked runs** 400km (258 miles), 214 trails

**Off-piste** **

**Ski areas** There are two core sectors at Sestriere: the slopes on Monte Sises immediately above the resort and the more extensive ski area on Monte Motta above the linked hamlet of Borgata. A gondola links Borgata with the neighbouring Sauze d'Oulx and Sansicario ski areas – covered on the full Milky Way skipass.

**Snowmaking** 90km

**Night skiing** Yes: Wednesday nights

**Length of season**
Late December–early April

NB: figures for elevation, vertical drop, number of lifts, snowmaking and pisted runs are for the entire Milky Way domain, including Sauze d'Oulx, Sansicario, Cesana, Claviere and Montgenèvre (France).

## Sauze d'Oulx

**Location** Perched above the Susa Valley in Italy's Piemonte region. Nearby Oulx (5km/3 miles) has the nearest major motorway exit and railway station, with numerous high-speed train links with Turin, Rome, Lyon and Paris. The nearest international airport at Turin is around an hour's drive away (65km/40 miles). A car is not necessary.

**Resort details**
www.vialattea.it
+39 0122 858009

**Elevation** 1,350–2,840m (4,428–9,315ft)

**Vertical drop**
1,490m (4,887ft)

**Number of lifts**
Drags 46
Chairs 38
Gondolas 4
Total 88

**Marked runs** 400km (248 miles), 214 trails

**Off-piste** **

**Ski areas** Sauze d'Oulx's ski area fans out over four distinct zones: the separate Monte Genevris area; the core Clotes slopes flowing down to the resort; the high Sportinia plateau; and the uppermost Col Basset area. A single draglift links with the neighbouring Sansicario ski area and a gondola links to Borgata at Sestriere – all accessible on the full Milky Way skipass.

**Snowmaking** 90km

**Night skiing** No

**Length of season**
Late December–early April

NB: figures for elevation, vertical drop, number of lifts, snowmaking and pisted runs are for the entire Milky Way domain, including Sestriere, Sansicario, Cesana, Claviere and Montgenèvre (France).

## Sansicario

**Location** Just above the town of Cesana Torinese in Italy's Piemonte region, close to the French border. The nearest major motorway exit and railway station are at Oulx (14km/9 miles), which has numerous high-speed train links with Turin, Rome, Lyon and Paris. The nearest international airport at Turin is just over an hour's drive away (74km/46 miles). A car is recommended.

**Resort details**
www.vialattea.it
+39 0122 811343

**Elevation** 1,350–2,840m (4,428–9,315ft)

**Vertical drop**
1,490m (4,887ft)

**Number of lifts**
Drags 46
Chairs 38
Gondolas 4
Total 88

**Marked runs** 400km (248 miles), 214 trails

**Off-piste** **

**Ski areas** A single ski area fanning out over attractive forested slopes. The uppermost pistes link into the neighbouring Sauze d'Oulx ski area; a seldom accessible red piste links directly to Sestriere; and a two-stage gondola links via the valley floor at Cesana Torinese with a chairlift towards Sagnalonga in the Claviere ski area – all accessible on the full Milky Way skipass.

**Snowmaking** 90km

**Night skiing** No

**Length of season**
Late December–early April

NB: figures for elevation, vertical drop, number of lifts, snowmaking and pisted runs are for the entire Milky Way domain, including Sauze d'Oulx, Sestriere, Cesana, Claviere and Montgenévre (France).

## Kranjska Gora

**Location** Kranjska Gora, Slovenia's leading resort, lies in the Julian Alps, within a few miles of the Austrian and Italian borders. The nearest airport is Ljubljana (60km/37 miles), with bus transfers to the resort.

**Resort details**
www.kranjskagora.com
+386 (0) 4588 1768

**Elevation** 810–1,295m (2,660–4,268ft)

**Vertical drop**
485m (1,627ft)

**Number of lifts**
Drags 12
Chairs 5
Total 17

**Marked runs** 30km (18 miles), 20 trails

**Off-piste** **

**Cross country** 40km (25 miles)

**Ski areas** Kranjska Gora's simple lift system links three faces on the same mountain. Add variety with a day trip to Mount Vogel near the lakeside town of Bled.

**Snowmaking** 75%

**Night skiing** Yes

**Length of season**
End November–beginning of May

## St Anton

**Location** St Anton is a traditional resort at the bottom of the Arlberg Pass on the main railway line from Zürich to Vienna. The nearest airport is Innsbruck (100km/62miles). It is not essential to have a car.

**Resort details**
www.stantonamarlberg.com
+43 5446 22690

**Elevation** 1,304–2,650m (4,280ft–8,690ft).

**Vertical drop**
1,346m (4,410ft)

**Number of lifts** (Arlberg Ski Area)
Drags 35
Chairs 38
Cable-cars 10
Total 83

**Marked runs** 260km (162 miles), 53 trails

**Off-piste** *****

**Cross country** 38km (24 miles)

**Ski areas** St Anton is the major player in the high-profile Arlberg ski area, with links to St Christoph and Stuben. Lech and Zurs also share the Arlberg lift pass.

**Snowmaking** 72km

**Night skiing** No

**Length of season**
Late November–early May

## Ischgl

**Location** Ischgl is a large, compact village in the Pazaun Valley 100km (62 miles) from Innsbruck, which has the nearest airport. There are trains to Landeck (30km/19 miles), with bus connections to the resort.

**Resort details**
www.ischgl.com
+43 5444 5266

**Elevation** 1,400–2,870m (4,590–9,420ft)

**Vertical drop**
1,470m (4,830ft)

**Number of lifts**
Drags 15
Chairs 22
Gondolas 3
Cable-cars 2
Total 42

**Marked runs** 210km (130 miles), 82 trails

**Off-piste** ***

**Cross country** 48km (30 miles)

**Ski areas** Ischgl shares a mountain and a lift pass with Samnaun, an isolated duty-free resort in Switzerland. The 6-day flexi pass allows two days in the neighbouring Paznaun Valley resorts of Galtur, Kappl and See.

**Snowmaking** 168km

**Night skiing** No

**Length of season**
End November–early May

| AUSTRIA | AUSTRIA | AUSTRIA | AUSTRIA | AUSTRIA | SWITZERLAND | SWITZERLAND |
|---|---|---|---|---|---|---|
| ## Saalbach-Hinterglemm | ## Schladming | ## Bad Gastein | ## Lech and Zürs | ## Kitzbühel | ## Zermatt | ## St Moritz (Engadin) |

### Saalbach-Hinterglemm

**Location** Saalbach-Hinterglemm is in south-western Austria. By train: buses leave every hour from Zell am See station. The journey takes 40 minutes – by car just 20 minutes or so. By air: Salzburg's W.A. Mozart Airport is 1.5 hours away. Munich is 3 hours away.

**Resort details**
www.saalbach.com
+43 6541 680068

**Elevation** 1,003–2,096m (3,290–6,876ft)

**Vertical drop**
1,166m (3,825ft)

**Number of lifts**
Drags 25
Chairs 16
Gondolas 14
Total 55

**Marked runs** 200km (125 miles)

**Off-piste** **

**Ski areas** Major ski circus with separate resort of Leogang as add-on; 90km (56 miles)

**Snowmaking** 100%

**Night skiing** At the fun park Unterschwazach, Hinterglemm

**Length of season**
Early December–mid-April

### Schladming

**Location** Schladming is 90km (56 miles) from Salzburg. From Salzburg, go south on the A-10 autobahn, exiting at junction 63 on route E-651/B-99. From Munich Airport (260km/162 miles), take autobahns A-9, A-99 (bypass), A-8 and A-10 from Salzburg, and then exit on to the B-99. By train: from Salzburg (1.5 hours). There's a regular shuttle and bus transfer to Salzburg train station from Salzburg Airport. A direct rail connection goes from Munich's FJ Strauss Airport to the city. From there, trains take around 3–4 hours to the resort.

**Resort details**
www.schladming.at
+43 3687 22777

**Elevation** 745–2,015m (2,444–6,611ft)

**Vertical drop**
1,270m (4,167ft)

**Number of lifts**
Drags 22 (145 in region)
Chairs 18 (88 in region)
Cable-cars 6 (37 in region)
Total 46 (270 in region)

**Marked runs** 114km (71 miles) in Schladming (4-mountain-resort) 860km (535 miles) over Ski amadé region

**Off-piste** **

**Ski areas** Extensive 4-mountain-resort area, part of the even bigger Ski amadé region.

**Snowmaking** 100%

**Night skiing** Yes: Schladming has a floodlit World Cup slalom course lit by 230 lights

**Length of season**
November–April

### Bad Gastein

**Location** Salzburg Airport is about an hour by road: take the Tauern motorway (A10) to Bischofshofen, then via B 311 and the B 167 into the Gastein Valley. Innsbruck and Munich are both about 2 hours away. From Innsbruck take the motorway via Wörgl, B 312 via St Johann/Tirol to Lofer, B 311 via Zell am See, and at Lend via the B 167 into the Gastein Valley. Inter-city and Eurotrains stop at Bad Gastein, Bad Hofgastein and Dorfgastein.

**Resort details**
www.skigastein.com
+43 6432 3393-560

**Elevation** 830–2,650m (2,723–8,694ft)

**Vertical drop**
1,820m (5,971ft)

**Number of lifts**
Drags 18
Chairs 19
Gondolas 9
Cable-car 1
Funicular 1
Total 48

**Marked runs** 201km (125 miles)

**Off-piste** ***

**Ski areas** Badgastein (1,000m/3,280ft) is one of three villages lying in the valley – Bad Hofgastein (850m/2,788ft) and Dorfgastein (830m/2,723ft) are the others. Sportgastein (1,600m/5,249ft) is a high-altitude alternative in poor snow years. The main areas are: Stubnerkogel-Angertal-Schlossalm, Sportgastein, Graukogel and Dorfgastein-Grossarl. These ski areas are part of the vast Ski amadé region, which has a total of 270 lifts and 860km (534 miles) of pistes.

**Snowmaking** 93km

**Night skiing** Yes, at Bad Gastein

**Length of season**
Early December–late April

### Lech and Zürs

**Location** Lech and Zürs are 10 minutes' drive apart. There are three airports nearby: Zurich is 200km away (124 miles/2.5 hours), Innsbruck 120km away (74 miles/1.5 hours), and Friedrichshafen 130km (81 miles) and a 1.5-hour drive away.

**Resort details**
www.lech-zuers.at
+43 5583 2161

**Elevation** 1,450–2,450m (4,756–8.036ft)

**Vertical drop**
1,000m (3,280ft)

**Number of lifts** (for entire Arlberg ski area)
Drags 37
Chairs 39
Gondolas/cable-cars 10
Total 86

**Marked runs** 117km/276km (73/171 miles)

**Off-piste** ****

**Ski areas** There are three main mountains, the large Oberlech sector with good off-piste and plenty of intermediate cruising, the west-facing slopes above Zürs and another broad flank across the valley. It is not possible to buy a separate ski pass just for the Lech/Zürs area, so the total number of lifts detailed above covers the whole Arlberg.

**Snowmaking** 72km

**Night skiing** No

**Length of season**
December–April

### Kitzbühel

**Location** Kitzbühel is situated 1.5 hours from Salzburg, 2 hours from Innsbruck and 2.5 hours from Munich. There is a train station in the resort.

**Resort details**
www.kitzbuhel.com
+43 5356 777

**Elevation** 800–2,000m (2,624–6,562ft)

**Vertical drop**
1,200m (3,937ft)

**Number of lifts**
Drags 17
Chairs 28
Gondolas 7
Others 2
Total 54

**Marked runs** 145km (90 miles), 49 trails

**Off-piste** ***

**Ski areas** There are four main ski areas: the Hahnenkamm is the largest and is now linked to Jochberg-Pass Thurn; The Kitzbüheler Horn is on the other side of town; and the nearby Bichlalm is now devoted to off-piste runs and serviced only by snowcat.

**Snowmaking** 65km

**Night skiing** Kirchberg – Thursday, Friday

**Length of season**
December–April

### Zermatt

**Location** Zermatt is at the foot of the Matterhorn in the Valais Alps in southern Switzerland. The resort lies at the end of the Vispa Valley, and is reached by train via the town of Visp. Zermatt's ski area is linked with the Italian ski resort of Breuil-Cervinia. Zermatt is car-free, and all visitors access the resort by train or taxi – 4 hours from Geneva Airport, 3 hours from Zürich Airport. Cars can be parked at Täsch, 5km (3 miles) away, where there are shuttle trains up to the resort every 20 minutes.

**Resort details**
www.zermatt.ch
+41 27 966 81 00

**Elevation** 1,620–3,883m (5,314–12,739ft)

**Vertical drop**
2,263m (7,424ft)

**Number of lifts**
Drags 9
Chairs 8
Gondolas 5
Cable-cars 9
Funiculars 2
Total 33 (74 including Cervinia)

**Marked runs** 313km (194 miles)

**Off-piste** *****

**Ski areas** There are three main ski areas: Matterhorn/Schwarzsee, Gornergrat and Rothorn. Ski into Cervinia and the Val d'Aosta from the Klein Matterhorn.

**Snowmaking** 48km

**Night skiing** Yes: Rothorn – arranged trips only

**Length of season** Year round

### St Moritz (Engadin)

**Location** St Moritz is the biggest wintersports area in Switzerland. Locations like St Moritz, Pontresina and Sils make the valley popular and famous.

**Resort details**
www.bergbahnenengadin.ch
+41 818 300 000

**Elevation** 1,750–3,303m (5,741–10,836ft)

**Vertical drop**
1,553m (5,095ft)

**Number of lifts**
Drags 27
Chairs 18
Gondolas 8
Cable-cars 3
Total 56

**Marked runs** 350km (217 miles)

**Off-piste** ***

**Ski areas** There are three principal ski areas: Corvatsch/Furtschellas, Corviglia and Diavolezza/Lagalb, all available on the Snowsafari skipass. This gives you access to three 3,000m (9,842ft) peaks and 99km (61 miles) of slopes.

**Snowmaking** 70km

**Night skiing** Yes: every Friday at Corvatsch from 7pm to 2am

**Length of season**
Mid-November–early May

| SWITZERLAND | SWITZERLAND | SWITZERLAND | SWITZERLAND | SWITZERLAND | GERMANY | GERMANY |
|---|---|---|---|---|---|---|

## Gstaad

**Location** Gstaad is in south-western Switzerland, easily accessed by train or car from Lake Thun, Lake Geneva or the Gruyère region. The nearest airports are at Zürich, Basle and Geneva. By train it is 2.5 hours from Geneva, and 3.5 hours from Zürich. By road the journey from Berne (A6 motorway – Spiez: exit Wimmis: main road (Simmen Valley) to Boltigen – Zweisimmen – Saanen – Gstaad) is 1.25 hours. Geneva is 2 hours away, Zürich 2.5 hours away. The nearest major town is Montreux, with a direct link by MOB (panorama train).

**Resort details**
www.gstaad.ch
+41 33 748 81 81

**Elevation** 950–3,000m (3,117–9,842ft)

**Vertical drop**
2,000m (6,561ft)

**Number of lifts** (in Gstaad region)
Drags 30
Chairs 17
Gondolas/cable-cars 19
Total 66

**Marked runs** 250km (155 miles), 84 trails

**Off-piste** ***

**Ski areas** There are six main ski areas in the region:

1. Rinderberg-Zweisimmen, Lengebrand-St Stephan, Saanersloch-Saanenmöser, Horneggli-Schönried, Rellerli-Schönried;

2. Wispile-Gstaad, Eggli-Gstaad, Videmanette-Rougemont, Wasserngrat-Gstaad;

3. La Braye-Château d'Oex;

4. Glacier 3000 (Diablerets Glacier)

5. Heiti-Gsteig;

6. Lauenen.

**Snowmaking** limited

**Night skiing** Yes: at Rinderberg

**Length of season**
Early December–late April

## Verbier

**Location** Verbier is in the heart of the Swiss Alps, 170km (106 miles) from Geneva and less than 30km (19 miles) from the Valais motorway. The nearest airports are Geneva or Zürich. By train: take the Simplon line, get off at Martigny, change to the Martigny-Le Châble line, then go from Le Châble to Verbier by bus or gondola. If arriving by car: from Martigny, take the Grand-St-Bernard main road up to Sembrancher, then take the road to the Bagnes Valley. At Le Châble, take the road to Verbier.

**Resort details**
www.verbier.ch
+41 27 775 38 88

**Elevation** 1,500–3,330m (4,920–10,925ft)

**Vertical drop**
1,800m (5,905ft)

**Number of lifts** (in Verbier's 4-valley region)
Drags 46
Chairs 27
Gondolas 11
Cable-cars 5
Moving carpets 3
Total 92

**Marked runs** 412km (256 miles), 30 trails

**Off-piste** *****

**Ski areas** Verbier is the main gateway to the Four Valleys area (La Tzoumaz, Nendaz, Veysonnaz, Thyon, Bruson, Evolène), comprising over 410km (255 miles) of ski runs and 92 lifts, all covered by a single skipass.

**Snowmaking** 50km

**Night skiing** Yes: some evenings on the slope of Les Esserts (organized by the Maison du Sport, +41 27 775 33 63)

**Length of season**
Early November–late April

## Davos and Klosters

**Location** Davos and Klosters are in the Grisons region of eastern Switzerland. The nearest airport is Zurich (2.5 hours). By rail to Davos Dorf and Davos Platz; Klosters Dorf and Klosters Platz. Klosters is on Hwy 28 to the north of St Moritz, while Davos is just to the southwest off the 28 on a minor road.

**Resort details**
Davos: www.davos.ch
+41 81 415 21 21

Klosters: www.klosters.ch
+41 81 410 20 20

**Elevation** Davos: 1,560m (5,118ft); Klosters: 1,192m (3,910ft)

**Vertical drop**
2,031m (6,663ft)

**Number of lifts**
Drags 27
Chairs 9
Gondolas 3
Cable-cars 9
Funicuclars 2
Total 50

**Marked runs** 370km (230 miles)

**Off-piste** ****

**Snowmaking** 19km

**Night skiing** Yes

**Length of season**
December–April

## Jungfrau Region

**Location** The Jungfrau region is in the Bernese Oberland, Switzerland. The nearest airports are Geneva (3 hours) and Zürich (3 hours). Each resort is served by rail connections. To get here by road, take the A6 motorway from Bern to Interlaken, then a steep drive to resorts. Mürren and Wengen are traffic free.

**Resort details**
Grindelwald:
www.grindelwald.ch
+41 33 854 1212

Wengen: www.wengen-muerren.ch
+41 33 855 1414

Mürren:
www.wengen-muerren.ch
+41 33 856 8686

**Elevation** Grindelwald: 1,034m (3,392ft); Wengen: 1,274m (4,179ft); Mürren: 1,650m (5,413ft)

**Vertical drop**
2,174m (7,132ft)

**Number of lifts**
Drags 13
Chairs 13
Gondolas 2
Cabel-cars 3
Funiculars 3
Total 34

**Marked runs** 215km (134 miles)

**Ski areas** Grindelwald, Wengen (Lauterbrunnen), Mürren,

**Snowmaking** Yes

**Night skiing** No

**Length of season**
November/December–April/May, with some summer skiing on Jungfraujoch

## Andermatt

**Location** Andermatt is 67km (41 miles) southeast of Lucerne and 140km (87 miles) from Zürich near the junction of four alpine passes: the St Gotthard, Furka, Susten and Oberalp. Andermatt is in the Canton of Uri, on a plateau above the main Chiasso railway line between Zürich and Italy. Take the express from Zürich to Göschenen (near the entrance to the Gotthard tunnel), where you switch trains for the quick climb to Andermatt. Some trains continue beyond Andermatt to Brig.

**Resort details**
www.andermatt.ch
+41 41 887 14 54

**Elevation** 1,445–2,965m (4,740–9,730ft)

**Vertical drop**
1,521m (4,990ft)

**Number of lifts**
Drags 7
Chairs 4
Gondolas 2
Cable-car 1
Total 14

**Marked runs** 80km (46 miles)

**Off-piste** *****

**Ski areas** Skiing is geared towards intermediate and expert skiers, with 80km (46 miles) of alpine runs and 40km (24 miles) of groomed cross-country trails running along the valley floor towards Realp.

**Snowmaking** Yes: 11km (7 miles)

**Night skiing** Certain days in February and early March

**Length of season**
Early December–early May

## Garmisch-Partenkirchen

**Location** Garmisch-Partenkirchen is at the base of Germany's highest mountain, the Zugspitze (2,962m/9,721ft). It is 96km (60 miles) south of Munich, close to the Austrian border. Innsbruck and Munich Airports are each 1 hour away by car. A free ski bus takes skiers to the lifts.

**Resort details**
www.garmisch-partenkirchen.de
+49 8821 180 700

**Elevation** 702–2,830m (2,303–9,825ft)

**Vertical drop**
1,350m (4,429ft)

**Number of lifts**
Drags 25
Chairs 4
Cable-cars 11
Funicular 1
Total 41 (131 in region)

**Marked runs** 118km (73 miles), 43 trails

**Off-piste** ***

**Ski areas** Three lift-served areas: Zugspitze (highest), Kreuzeck (some difficult terrain) and Garmisch main ski area, including the Hausberg, Kreuzwankel and Osterfelder mountains. Ski areas of Lermoos and Seefeld in Austria can be accessed with the full area lift pass.

**Snowmaking** Yes

**Night skiing** No

**Length of season**
Early December–early May

## Oberstdorf

**Location** Oberstdorf is 186km (115 miles) from Munich via Kempten or Kreuzlingen. Innsbruck (156km/97 miles) is nearer, but Munich has better motorway connections. Drivers from Innsbruck should head east towards Imst and cross the Fernpass to Reutte. Here, in good weather, they can take the small mountain road via Nesselwängle to Sonthofen – or cross into Germany via Pfronten. Oberstdorf is 1.5 hour's drive from Friedrichshafen – a useful option for skiers using budget airlines. They can reach Oberstdorf via the northern shore of Lake Constance and Immenstadt. Oberstdorf has a mainline railway station.

**Resort details**
www.oberstdorf.de
+49 8322 700 120

**Elevation** 813–2,224m (2,667–7,297ft)

**Vertical drop** 1,390m (4,560ft)

**Number of lifts**
Drags 12
Chairs 8
Gondolas 2
Cable-cars 5
Total 27

**Marked runs** 44km (27 miles), 38 trails; 120km (74 miles), 103 trails including Kleinwalsertal

**Off-piste** ***

**Ski areas** Three ski areas linked by a shuttle bus service. The biggest – (Fellhorn/Kanzelwand) which crosses the Austrian border – is 3km (5 miles) from town on the Fellhorn. Oberstdorf's most convenient ski area is on the Nebelhorn reached by cable-car from the town centre The third area is on the family ski area of Schönblick, with gladed, sunny slopes.

**Snowmaking** Yes

**Night skiing** Yes: At Kanzelwand, Ifen and the Walmendinger Horn

**Length of season**
Early December–early May

| SWEDEN | SWEDEN | NORWAY | NORWAY | NORWAY | NORWAY | NORWAY |
|---|---|---|---|---|---|---|
| # Åre | # Sälen | # Hemsedal | # Oppdal | # Lillehammer | # Voss | # Trysil |

## Åre

**Location** Åre is in western Sweden. It takes about 1.25 hours to drive here from Östersund (100km/ 62 miles). A more romantic route is to go by train. The high-speed ski train link from Stockholm (640 km/ 398 miles) takes 6.5 hours.

**Resort details**
www.skistar.com
+46 647 177 20

**Elevation** 380–1,274m (1,247–4,180ft)

**Vertical drop**
894m (2,944ft)

**Number of lifts**
Drags 31
Chairs 6
Gondola 1
Cable-car 1
Funicular 1
Total 40

**Marked runs** 96km (60 miles), 102 trails

**Off-piste** ***

**Ski areas** Four areas: Duved, Tegefjäll, Åre and Åre Björnen (the Bear)

**Snowmaking** Yes: 21 runs

**Night skiing** Good floodlit slopes at Gästrappet and Lundsrappet. Seven runs in total

**Length of season**
Mid-November–May 1

## Sälen

**Location** Sälen is in west-central Sweden. Most visitors arrive by car. Stockholm is 410km (255 miles) away, Gothenburg 450km (280 miles) and Malmö 720km (447 miles). You can also go by express bus (Fjällexpressen or Säfflebussen) from these cities. Fly to Mora, or go by train to Mora or Malung. The transfer time from Mora is 1.5 hours. The easiest way to complete the journey is to rent a car. From Malung a local bus takes about an hour.

**Resort details**
www.skistar.com/salen
+46 280 187 00

**Elevation** 557–860m (1,827–2,822ft)

**Vertical drop**
303m (994ft)

**Number of lifts**
Drags 75
Chairs 7
Moving carpets 10
Total 92

**Marked runs** 112 trails

**Off-piste** **

**Ski areas** There are four main resorts divided into two linked pairs, and a sprinkling of other resorts. If you wish to ski them all, having a car is pretty essential.

**Snowmaking** Yes: 60 runs

**Nightskiing** Yes:

**Length of season**
Mid-November–late April

## Hemsedal

**Location** Hemsedal is 220km (137 miles) from Oslo – around 3 hours' journey by express coach, car or train. One of the world's longest mountain tunnels, 24km (15 miles) in length, which opened in November 2000, links Hemsedal with Bergen and western Norway, bringing many additional skiers and boarders to the resort.

**Resort details**
www.hemsedal.com
+47 32 055 030

**Elevation** 640–1,455m (2,099–4,774ft)

**Vertical drop**
815m (2,674ft)

**Number of lifts**
Drags 15
Chairs 6
Total 21

**Marked runs** 42km (26 miles)

**Off-piste** ***

**Ski areas** Skiing on three mountains, most of it on Hamaren. You can also ski at the small neighbouring resort of Solheisen

**Snowmaking** Yes: 14km (35 per cent)

**Night skiing** Yes: Four nights a week from mid-December to end of March.

**Length of season**
Mid-November–early May

## Oppdal

**Location** Oppdal is in west-central Norway. The closest airports are Trondheim (122km/76 miles), Molde (170km/106miles) and Oslo (320km/199 miles). There are regular train services from Oslo, Trondheim and Bodø (including the fast Signature service, just under 5 hours from Oslo). Drivers should take the E6 road, which links Oslo and Trondheim. There are also daily express buses from Trondheim, Oslo, Bergen (560km/348 miles) and Kristiansund (165km/ 103 miles).

**Resort details**
www.oppdal.com
+47 72 400 470

**Elevation** 550–1,325m (1,804–4,347ft)

**Vertical drop**
790m (2,592ft)

**Number of lifts**
Drags 14
Chairs 2
Moving carpet 1
Total 17

**Marked runs** 60km (34 miles)

**Off-piste** ***

**Ski areas** 4 peaks to ski, with runs mainly above the tree line.

**Snowmaking** Yes (16km/ 10 miles)

**Night skiing** Yes (6 nights a week)

**Length of season**
December–early May

## Lillehammer

**Location** Lillehammer is a small lakeside town 180km (112 miles) north of Oslo in central Norway. Oslo is the nearest international airport (145km/90 miles). There are frequent direct trains from the airport to Lillehammer, with buses to Hafjell.

**Resort details**
www.lillehammerturist.no
+47 61 28 98 00
www.hafjell.no
+47 61 27 70 00
www.kvitfjell.no
+47 61 28 36 30

**Elevation** Hafjell: 230–1,060m (750–3,470ft); Kvitfjell: 204–1,044m (665–1,044m (3,403ft)

**Vertical drop** Hafjell: 830m (2,720ft); Kvitfjell: 840m (2,736ft)

**Number of lifts**
Hafjell:
Drags 9
Chairs 3
Total 12

Kvitfjell:
Drags 5
Chairs 2
Total 7

**Marked runs**
Hafjell: 33km (21 miles), 28 trails; Kvitfjell: 18km (12 miles), 22 trails

**Off-piste**
Hafjell ***
Kvitfjell ***

**Cross-country**
Hafjell: 450km (280 miles)
Kvitfjell: 600km (372 miles)

**Ski areas** Hafjell and Kvitfjell are stand-alone resorts, with their own lift passes. A third area, the Sjusjøen Alpine Ski Centre (4 lifts, 9 slopes, 250m/820ft vertical), opened in December 2003.

**Snowmaking** Yes, Hafjell: (26km/16 miles); Kvitfjell: (16km/10 miles)

**Night skiing** Yes (7km/ 4 miles)

**Length of season**
Mid-November–end April

## Voss

**Location** Voss is in western Norway. The nearest airport is Bergen (2.5 hours). By rail: to Voss station. By road: Voss is on the E16 to the east of Bergen.

**Resort details**
www.visitvoss.no
+47 56 51 12 12

**Elevation**
91m (299ft)

**Vertical drop**
854m (2,802ft)

**Number of lifts**
Drags 5
Chairs 4
Cable-car 1
Total 10

**Marked runs** 40km (25 miles)

**Off-piste** *

**Ski areas** Horgaletten, Hanguren, Kisseldur, Middagsholo, Raugstad, Slettafjellet, Trastølen

**Snowmaking** Yes

**Night skiing** No

**Length of season**
Mid-November–mid-April

## Trysil

**Location** Trysil is 160km (99 miles) from Oslo's Gardermoen International Airport (and 210km/130 miles from Oslo itself). From Oslo it is a 2.5–3 hour drive: take the E6 highway to Rv 3 north and then Rv 25 east into the mountains. Buses leave eight times daily, bringing you right to the centre of Trysil. Elverum (11km/7 miles) is the closest railway station – linked with Trysil by the Trysilekspressen shuttle bus, which travels in both directions eight times every day. The town of Trysil is some way from the slopes (2km/1 mile), and most skiers and snowboarders stay at the ski village (Turistsenteret) or the other base areas.

**Resort details**
www.trysil.com
+47 6245 1000

**Elevation** 460–1,132m (1,509–3,714ft)

**Vertical drop**
685m (2,247ft)

**Number of lifts**
Drags 16
Chairs 5
Moving carpets 9
Total 30

**Marked runs** 64km (40 miles)

**Off-piste** **

**Ski areas** There are three areas, all linked.

**Snowmaking** 27km

**Night skiing** Yes: two nights a week on five runs

**Length of season**
End October–1 May

| BULGARIA | ROMANIA | SLOVAKIA | USA · NEW YORK | USA · NEW YORK | USA · NEW YORK | USA · VERMONT |
|---|---|---|---|---|---|---|
| ## Borovets | ## Poiana Brasov | ## Donovaly | ## Lake Placid | ## Hunter Mountain | ## Windham Mountain | ## Killington |

### Borovets (BULGARIA)

**Location** Borovets is 1 hour or so (72km/45 miles) from from the capital, Sofia.

**Resort details**
www.bulgariaski.com
+359 7226 6171

**Elevation** 1,323–2,560m (4,339–8,399ft)

**Vertical drop** 1,137m (3,729ft)

**Number of lifts**
Drags 10
Chairs 4
Gondola 1
Total 15

**Marked runs** 40km (25 miles), 24 trails

**Off-piste** **

**Ski areas** Upper (above the tree line) and lower sections of north-facing Mount Masala – soon expected to be linked.

**Snowmaking** Yes: 14 snow cannon on 9 runs

**Night skiing** Yes: At Martinovi Baraki

**Length of season** Mid-December–April

### Poiana Brasov (ROMANIA)

**Location** Poiana Brasov is located some 186km (116 miles) from the Romanian capital, Bucharest.

**Resort details**
www.poiana-brasov.com
+40 286550443

**Elevation** 1,021–1,768m (3,350–5,800ft)

**Vertical drop** 747m (2,451ft)

**Number of lifts**
Drags 7
Gondola 1
Cable-cars 2
Total 10

**Marked runs** 14km (9 miles), 12 trails

**Off-piste** *

**Ski areas** One mountain face

**Snowmaking** 95%

**Night skiing** Yes: On the Bradul slope

**Length of season** Mid-December–April

### Donovaly (SLOVAKIA)

**Location** Donovaly is in central Slovakia, 220km (136 miles) from Bratislava. It is accessible by flights into Bratislava, Budapest, in Hungary (200km/124 miles) or Krakow, Poland (185km/ 115 miles). The bus network is said to be efficient, getting you here in several hours. It is also possible to hire a car at any airport.

**Resort details**
www.parksnow.sk
+421 48 4199 900

**Elevation** 900–1,361m (2,952–4,465ft)

**Vertical drop** 461m (1,512ft)

**Number of lifts**
Drags 14
Chairs 2
Total 16

**Marked runs** 11km (7 miles), 17 trails

**Off-piste** **

**Ski areas** Záhradi_te and Nová Hol'a

**Snowmaking** Yes

**Night skiing** Yes

**Length of season** Late November–early April

### Lake Placid (USA · NEW YORK)

**Location** Lake Placid/ Whiteface is located in upstate New York, within Adirondack State Park. The nearest airports are Adirondack Airport (40 minutes), Burlington (3 hours) and Albany (2.5 hours). The nearest train station is at Westport, 64km (40 miles) away; taxi service only from here to Lake Placid. By road, take Exit 30 off Interstate 87 onto Route 9 then Route 73 to Lake Placid; from the west, take Interstate 90, then Interstate 81 to Watertown, then Route 3 to Saranac Lake and Route 86 to Lake Placid.

**Resort details**
www.orda.org or
www.whiteface.com
+1 518 946 2223

**Elevation** 366m (1,200ft)

**Vertical drop** 980m (3,216ft)

**Number of lifts**
Drag 1
Chairs 9
Gondola 1
Total 11

**Marked runs** 211 acres (16.6 miles)

**Ungroomed** **

**Ski areas** Whiteface Mountain

**Snowmaking** 98%

**Night skiing** No

**Length of season** November–April

### Hunter Mountain (USA · NEW YORK)

**Location** Hunter Mountain is 2.5 hours north of New York City in the northern Catskill Mountains of New York State. Whether you are coming from the north or the south, Hunter is a half-hour ride from New York State Thruway exits 20 or 21. The Adirondack Trailways bus service offers daily runs through Hunter from New York City. Albany is 1 hour away, Hartford 3 hours, Boston 3.5 hours, Philadelphia 4 hours, Washington, DC 5.5 hours.

**Resort details**
www.HunterMtn.com
+1 518 263 4223

**Elevation** 488–975m (1,600–3,200ft)

**Vertical drop** 488m (1,600ft)

**Number of lifts**
Drag 1
Chairs 10
Total 11

**Marked runs** 97ha (240 skiable acres); 56km (35 miles), 54 trails

**Ungroomed** **

**Ski areas** Hunter has 3 mountain faces, served by 11 lifts, with some 56km (35 miles) of trails and a vertical drop of 488m (1,600ft). Hunter One has mainly easy runs, while Hunter West and Hunter Mountain itself offer some of the steeper options – particularly Hunter West.

**Snowmaking** 100%

**Night skiing** No

**Length of season** Mid-November–mid-April

### Windham Mountain (USA · NEW YORK)

**Location** Windham Mountain is located in upstate New York, 190km (118 miles), 3 hours from Manhattan and 97km (60 miles) from Albany in the Catskill Mountain High Peaks. Take Exit 21 from New York State Thruway to Route 23 West. The resort is 40km (25 miles) further on.

**Resort details**
www.windhammountain.com
+1 518 734 4300

**Elevation** 457–945m (1,500–3,100ft)

**Vertical drop** 488m (1,600ft)

**Number of lifts**
Drag 1
Chairs 7
Total 8

**Marked runs** 103ha (245 acres), 42 trails

**Ungroomed** **

**Ski areas** The ski area at Windham Mountain covers two peaks. The main skiing is on the north face of Cave Mountain

**Snowmaking** 98%

**Night skiing** Yes (on 8 trails, Thursday through Sunday and some holiday periods)

**Length of season** Late November–early April

### Killington (USA · VERMONT)

**Location** Killington is a small town 20 minutes west of Rutland, Vermont, and just under 2 hours south of Burlington, Vermont, 132km (82 miles) away. Most major US airlines fly into the Burlington International Airport. Rutland also has a small airport with commuter service to Boston. A car is recommended.

**Resort details**
www.killington.com
+1 800 621 6867

**Elevation** 325–1,293m (1,165–4,241ft)

**Vertical drop** 957m (3,050ft)

**Number of lifts**
Drags 9
Chairs 22
Gondolas 2
Total 33

**Marked runs** 139km (90 miles), 200 trails

**Ungroomed** ***

**Ski areas** There are six linked mountains; Ramshead, Snowdon, Killington Peak, Skye Peak, Bear Mountain and Sunrise. Nearby but not linked is Pico Mountain.

**Snowmaking** 775 acres

**Night skiing** No

**Length of season** October–May

| USA · VERMONT | USA · VERMONT | USA · VERMONT | USA · VERMONT | USA · N. HAMPSHIRE | USA · N. HAMPSHIRE | USA · N. HAMPSHIRE |
|---|---|---|---|---|---|---|
| ## Jay Peak | ## Stowe | ## Smugglers' Notch | ## Mad River Glen | ## Loon Mountain | ## Waterville Valley | ## Cannon Mountain |

### Jay Peak

**Location** Jay Peak is located in northern Vermont just 10 minutes from the Canadian border. The mountain is easily accessed from airports in Burlington, a little over an hour away, and Montreal, 90 minutes from the resort.

**Resort details**
www.jaypeakresort.com
+1 800 451 4449

**Elevation** 553–1,209m (1,774–3,968ft)

**Vertical drop**
656m (2,153ft)

**Number of lifts**
Drags 2
Chairs 5
Cable-car 1
Total 8

**Marked runs** 155ha (385 acres), 76 trails

**Ungroomed** ***

**Ski areas** Jay Peak is best known for its extensive network of glades and abundant natural snowfall (902cm/355in annual average). Vermont's only aerial tramway is one of 8 lifts accessing 156ha (385 acres) of terrain, including 2 peaks, 76 trails and 4 terrain parks for skiers and riders of all abilities.

**Snowmaking** 80%

**Night skiing** No

**Length of season**
Mid-November–mid-April

### Stowe

**Location** Stowe is in north-central Vermont, 40 minutes from Burlington Airport and 225km (140 miles) from Montreal, Quebec.

**Resort details**
www.stowe.com
+1 802 253 3000

**Elevation** 390–1,109m (1,280ft–3,640ft)

**Vertical drop**
719m (2,360ft)

**Number of lifts**
Drags 2
Chairs 9
Gondola 1
Total 12

**Marked runs** 63km (39 miles), 48 trails

**Ungroomed** **

**Ski areas** There are 2 main ski areas: Mount Mansfield and Spruce Peak

**Snowmaking** 354 acres

**Night skiing**
Thursday–Saturday

**Length of season**
November–April

### Smugglers' Notch

**Location** Smugglers' Notch is located in north-central Vermont, 48km (30 miles) east of Burlington International Airport and 8km (5 miles) south of Jeffersonville on Route 108. Montreal is 150km (93 miles) away, Boston 354km (220 miles) and New York City 468km (291 miles). Smugglers' arranges shuttle services for guests arriving at Burlington.

**Resort details**
www.smuggs.com
+1 802 644 8851

**Elevation** 314–11,109m (1,030–3,640ft)

**Vertical drop**
796m (2,610ft)

**Number of lifts**
Drags 2
Chairs 6
Moving carpets 2
Total 10

**Marked runs** 125ha (310 acres), 78 trails

**Ungroomed** **283ha (700 acres)

**Ski areas** Smugglers' Notch has three linked areas: Madonna, Sterling and Morse

**Snowmaking** 62%

**Night skiing** No

**Length of season** End November–early April

### Mad River Glen

**Location** Mad River Glen is located in central Vermont's Mad River Valley, 5km (3 miles) from the Sugarbush ski area, and 45 minutes from Burlington, Vermont, via Interstate 89. The nearest airport is at Burlington. The resort is 3 hours from Boston, 2 hours from Montreal and 5.5 hours from New York City.

**Resort details**
www.madriverglen.com
+1 802 496-3551

**Elevation** 488–1,109m (1,600–3,637ft)

**Vertical drop**
621m (2,037ft)

**Number of lifts**
Drag 1
Chairs 4
Total 5

**Marked runs** 45 marked trails, plus 324ha (800 acres) of boundary-to-boundary ungroomed access.

**Ungroomed** *** 283ha (700 acres)

**Ski areas** Stark Mountain

**Snowmaking** Minimal (15%)

**Night skiing** No

**Length of season**
Mid-December–mid-April

### Loon Mountain

**Location** Loon Mountain is in Lincoln, New Hampshire, 2 hours from Boston along the Kancamagus Highway, 3 hours from Montreal and 5.5 hours from New York.

**Resort details**
www.loonmtn.com
www.loonsnowboarding.com
+1 603 745 8111

**Elevation** 290–930m (950–3,050ft)

**Vertical drop**
640m (2,100ft)

**Number of lifts**
Drags 2
Chairs 6
Gondola 1
Moving carpet 1
Total 10

**Marked runs** 111ha (275 acres), 45 trails (just under 32km (20 miles), plus 5 tree-skiing areas

**Ungroomed** **

**Ski areas** Loon's skiing is on one mountain face. Loon has one of the longest halfpipes in New Hampshire, at 122m (400ft). There are 5 tree skiing areas; 64 per cent of the ski area is suited to intermediates.

**Snowmaking** 96%

**Night skiing** Yes

**Length of season**
End November–early April

### Waterville Valley

**Location** Waterville Valley is located in central New Hampshire, at the base of Mount Tecumseh in White Mountain National Forest. It is 2 hours (209km/130 miles) north of Boston, 3.5 hours from Montreal (362km/225 miles) and 6 hours (523km/325 miles) from New York City.

**Resort details**
www.waterville.com
+1 603 236 8311

**Elevation** 605–1,220m (1,984–4,004ft)

**Vertical drop**
616m (2,020ft)

**Number of lifts**
Drags 5
Chairs 7
Total 12

**Marked runs** 214ha (259 acres), 52 trails (longest 5km/3 miles)

**Ungroomed** **

**Ski areas** There are 5 gladed areas. The 'Threedom' lift pass offers skiing at Waterville Valley, Loon and Cranmore.

**Snowmaking** 100%

**Night skiing** No

**Length of season**
Mid-November–mid-April

### Cannon Mountain

**Location** Cannon Mountain is located in northern New Hampshire, on Interstate 93, 6km (4 miles) south of Franconia and 241km (150 miles) from Boston (2.5 hours), and less than 3 hours from Montreal.

**Resort details**
www.cannonmt.com
+1 603 823 8800

**Elevation** 609–1,276m (2,000–4,186ft)

**Vertical drop**
654m (2,146ft)

**Number of lifts**
Drags 1
Chairs 6
Cable-cars 1
Moving carpet 1
Total 9

**Marked runs** 36km (22 miles), 55 trails

**Ungroomed** **

**Ski areas** Many runs are narrow and steep: almost 50 per cent of the trails are intermediate (all told, 83 per cent of the trails are intermediate or expert), leaving just 17 per cent for beginners.

**Snowmaking** 96%

**Night skiing** No

**Length of season**
Mid-November–early April

| USA · MAINE | USA · MAINE | USA · CALIFORNIA | USA · CALIFORNIA | USA · CALIFORNIA | USA · CALIFORNIA | USA · NEW MEXICO |
|---|---|---|---|---|---|---|

## Sugarloaf USA

**Location** Sugarloaf is located in northwestern Maine, about 2.5 hours north of Portland, which has an airport, and about 4.5 hours northwest of Boston, which has an international airport. A car is necessary to reach the resort. From Boston or Portland, take I-95 north to Augusta, then Route 27 north to the resort.

**Resort details**
www.sugarloaf.com
+1 207 237 2000

**Elevation** 431–1,291m (1,417–4,237ft)

**Vertical drop**
860m (2.820ft)

**Number of lifts**
Drags 2
Chairs 13
Total 15

**Marked runs** 87km (54 miles), 133 trails, plus ungroomed terrain between boundaries for a total skiable area of 567ha (1,400 acres)

**Ungroomed** ***

**Ski areas** One broad mountain strewn with a huge variety of trails, Sugarloaf USA is located in the heart of Carrabassett Valley. It is Maine's second highest peak and claims the only lift-serviced above tree-line skiing in the east.

**Snowmaking** 490 acres

**Night skiing** No

**Length of season**
Mid-November–late April

---

## Sunday River

**Location** Sunday River is located in central Maine, about 1.5 hours northwest of Portland and about 3.5 hours northwest of Boston, each of which have a major airport. A car is necessary to reach the resort. From Boston, take Interstate 95 to Gray, Route 26 to Bethel and Route 2 to the resort. From Portland, take Route 26 and proceed as above.

**Resort details**
www.sundayriver.com
+1 207 824 3000

**Elevation** 244–957m (800–3,140ft)

**Vertical drop**
713m (2,340ft)

**Number of lifts**
Drags 3
Chairs 15
Total 18

**Marked runs** 77km (48 miles), on 269ha (663 skiable acres), 128 trails

**Ungroomed** ***

**Ski areas** Eight linked peaks: White Cap, Locke Mountain, Barker Mountain, Spruce Peak, North Peak, Aurora Peak, Oz and Jordan Bowl.

**Snowmaking** 607 acres

**Night skiing** No, but a lighted tubing park

**Length of season**
Mid-November–late April

---

## Squaw Valley USA

**Location** Squaw Valley USA is in northeastern California, 68km (42 miles) west of Reno, Nevada, 154km (96 miles) from Sacramento and 315km (196 miles) from San Francisco (via Interstate 80). The resort is located off Highway 89, between Truckee and Tahoe City on the north shore of Lake Tahoe, some 8km (5 miles) from the shore. The nearest airports are Reno Tahoe International (45 minutes), Sacramento International and San Francisco (2 hours). There is an Amtrak railway station at Truckee.

**Resort details**
www.squaw.com
+1 530 583 6985

**Elevation** 1,890–2,652m (6,200–8,700ft)

**Vertical drop**
869m (2,850ft)

**Number of lifts**
Drags 3
Chairs 26
Gondola 1
Cable-car 1
Moving carpet 2
Funicular 1
Total 34

**Marked runs** 170

**Ungroomed** ****

**Ski areas** Six peaks (Snow King, KT-22, Squaw Peak, Emigrant, Broken Arrow and Granite Chief), with 16 open bowls.

**Snowmaking** 400 acres

**Night skiing** Yes: On the 5km (3 mile) Mountain Run or the halfpipe in the Riviera Park from 4 to 9pm daily (mid-Dec–mid-April).

**Length of season**
Mid-November–late May

---

## Heavenly

**Location** Heavenly is on the shores of Lake Tahoe, astride the Nevada-California state line. The nearest airports are at San Francisco (274km/170 miles), Reno (88km/55 miles) and South Lake Tahoe (15 minutes).

**Resort details**
www.skiheavenly.com
+1 775 586 7000

**Elevation** 1,993–3,068m (6,540–10,067ft)

**Vertical drop**
1,075m (3,527ft)

**Number of lifts**
Chairs 28
Gondola 1
Cable-car 1
Total 30

**Marked runs** 92

**Ungroomed** ***

**Ski areas** 1,942ha (4,800 acres) spanning two states. Extensive tree-skiing.

**Snowmaking** 70%

**Night skiing** No

**Length of season**
November–April

---

## Kirkwood

**Location** Kirkwood is in northeastern California, 35 minutes by car or shuttle from South Lake Tahoe via Highway 89 South and Highway 88 West. The resort is 90 minutes from Reno/Tahoe International Airport via US 395 South and Highway 88 West, 3.5 hours from San Francisco International Airport (via Jackson, California) and a 2-hour drive from Sacramento International Airport via State Routes 16 East, 49 South and Highway 88.

**Resort details**
www.kirkwood.com
+1 209 258 6000

**Elevation** 2,377–2,987m (7,800–9,800ft)

**Vertical drop**
610m (2,000ft)

**Number of lifts**
Drags 2
Chairs 10
Total 12 (plus plans for 5 new lifts)

**Marked runs** Many unnamed bowl runs (931ha/2,300 acres), 65+ trails

**Ungroomed** ***

**Ski areas** Kirkwood sits high in a natural, steep-sided amphitheatre with jagged peaks overlooking extensive bowl-skiing.

**Snowmaking** 4 runs

**Night skiing** No

**Length of season**
November–late April/early May

---

## Mammoth Mountain

**Location** Mammoth Mountain is in central Califorrnia, in the Eastern Sierra, approximately 5 hours north of Los Angeles and 3 hours south of Reno.

**Resort details**
www.mammothmountain.com
+1 760 934 0745

**Elevation** Base elevation 7,953ft (2,424m); summit 11,053ft (3,369m)

**Vertical drop**
3,100ft (945m)

**Number of lifts**
Chairs 25
Gondolas 3
Total 28

**Marked runs** 1,417ha (3,500 acres), 150 trails

**Ungroomed** *****

**Ski areas** 1,417ha (3,500 acres) of terrain, 15 per cent expert, 20 per cent advanced, 40 per cent intermediate, 25 per cent beginner. There are also 3 terrain parks and 3 halfpipes. Mammoth's sister resort June, some 25 minutes away, features predominantly lower-intermediate terrain.

**Snowmaking** 447 acres

**Night skiing** No

**Length of season**
November–June

---

## Taos

**Location** Taos Ski Valley is in northern New Mexico, 278km (173 miles) north of Albuquerque. By road, take Interstate 25 north to NM 84 and NM 68 to town; the ski resort is 29km (18 miles) to the northeast via Taos Canyon Road (NM 150). The nearest airport is Albuquerque.

**Resort details**
www.skitaos.org
+1 505 776 2291

**Elevation** 2,805–3,602m (9,207–11,819ft)

**Vertical drop**
796m (2,612ft)

**Number of Lifts**
Chairs 12
Total 12

**Marked runs** 524ha (1,294 acres), 110 trails

**Ungroomed** ****

**Ski areas** Frontside, West Basin and Kachina Basin, all linked. Hike-to backcountry skiing from West Basin Ridge, Highline Ridge and Kachina Peak (3,804m/12,481ft)

**Snowmaking** 49%

**Night skiing** No

**Length of season**
Late November–early April

| USA · COLORADO | USA · COLORADO | USA · COLORADO | USA · COLORADO | USA · COLORADO | USA · COLORADO | USA · COLORADO |
|---|---|---|---|---|---|---|
| ## Aspen | ## Aspen Highlands | ## Buttermilk | ## Snowmass | ## Vail and Beaver Creek | ## Keystone | ## Breckenridge |

### Aspen

**Location** Aspen is in central Colorado, 354km (220 miles) west of Denver International Airport and 112km (70 miles) from Vail-Eagle County Airport, via Interstate 70 and Colorado Highway 82.

**Resort details**
www.aspensnowmass.com
+1 970 925 1220

**Elevation** 2,422–3,418m (7,945f–11,212ft)

**Vertical drop**
996m (3,267ft)

**Number of lifts**
Chairs 7
Gondola 1
Total 8

**Marked runs** 272ha (673 acres), 76 trails

**Ungroomed** ***

**Ski areas** One mountain; all lift tickets fully interchangeable with Aspen Highlands, Buttermilk and Snowmass.

**Snowmaking** 613 acres (total for all 4 resorts)

**Night skiing** No

**Length of season** Late November–mid-April

### Aspen Highlands

**Location** Easily visible from the slopes of Aspen Mountain, Aspen Highlands is 4km (3 miles) southwest of the town of Aspen and 347km (217 miles) west of Denver.

**Resort details**
www.aspensnowmass.com
+1 970 925 1220

**Elevation** 2,451–3,559m (8,040–11,675ft); hike to (top of Highland Bowl) 3,777m (12,392ft)

**Vertical drop**
1,108m (3,635ft)

**Number of lifts**
Chairs 5
Total 5

**Marked runs** 272ha (673 acres), 76 trails

**Ungroomed** ****

**Ski area** One mountain; all lift tickets fully interchangeable with Aspen Mountain, Buttermilk and Snowmass.

**Snowmaking** 613 acres (total for all 4 resorts)

**Night skiing** No

**Length of season** Mid-December–early April

### Buttermilk

**Location** Buttermilk, right next to Aspen Highlands, is 4km (3 miles) of three resorts in the Roaring Fork Valley, in the near vicinity of the town of Aspen.

**Resort details**
www.aspensnowmass.com
+1 970 925 1220

**Elevation** 2,399–3,018m (7,870– 9,900ft)

**Vertical drop**
2,030ft (619m)

**Number of lifts**
Drags 2
Chairs 5
Ski/snowboard school lifts 2
Total 9

**Marked runs** 176ha (435 acres), 44 trails

**Ungroomed** **

**Ski areas** Buttermilk Mountain (including Buttermilk West) and Tiehack Mountain; all lift tickets fully interchangeable with Aspen Highlands, Aspen Mountain and Snowmass

**Snowmaking** 613 acres (total for all 4 resorts)

**Night skiing** No

**Length of season** Early to mid-December–early April

### Snowmass

**Location** Snowmass is 19km (12 miles) northwest of Aspen and 334km (209 miles) from Denver. Although run by Aspen Ski Company, Snowmass is virtually autonomous as a separate resort.

**Resort details**
www.aspensnowmass.com
+1 970 925 1220

**Elevation** 2,473–3,813m (8,104–12,510ft)

**Vertical drop**
1,343m (4,406ft)

**Number of lifts**
Drags 2
Chairs 14
Gondola 1
Moving carpets 3
Ski/snowboard school lifts 2
Total 22

**Marked runs** 1,265ha (3,128 acres), 88 trails

**Ungroomed** ****

**Ski areas** One major massif, with three sub-peaks

**Snowmaking** 613 acres (total for all 4 resorts)

**Night skiing** No

**Length of season** Late November–mid-April

### Vail and Beaver Creek

**Location** Vail is centrally located in Colorado's Rocky Mountains 160km (100 miles) west of Denver along Interstate 70. Denver International Airport is a 2-hour drive and Vail/Eagle County Airport is only 56km (35 miles) from the resort. Beaver Creek is a further 20 minutes from Vail and both are conveniently situated for links with other Colorado resorts.

**Resort details**
www.vailresorts.com
www.vail.snow.com
+1 970 476 5601
www.beavercreek.snow.co
+1 970 845 9090

**Elevation** Vail: 2,475–3,527m (8,120–11,571ft); Beaver Creek: 2,255–3,485m (7,398–11,433ft)

**Vertical drop**
Vail: 1,052m (3,451ft); Beaver Creek: 1,230m (4,035ft)

**Number of lifts**
Vail:
Drags 5
Chairs 23
Gondolas 1
Moving carpets 5
Total 34

Beaver Creek:
Drags 1
Chairs 15
Total 16

**Marked runs** Vail: 2,140ha (5,289 acres), 193 trails; Beaver Creek: 658ha (1,625 acres), 146 trails

**Ungroomed** ****

**Ski areas** Vail can be neatly divided into the wide, intermediate-friendly front side, the unpisted Back Bowls and the advanced terrain of the Blue Sky Basin. Beaver Creek has the eponymous mountain and expert-only Grouse Mountain above the village, plus Strawberry Park and Arrowhead mountain adjacent to it.

**Snowmaking** Vail 390 acres / Beaver Creek 624 acres

**Night skiing** Yes: at Adventure Ridge, Vail.

**Length of season** Mid-November–mid-April

### Keystone

**Location** Keystone is in central Colorado, 121km (75 miles) west of Denver; from Denver, take Interstate 70, then south on US 6 to the resort. The nearest airport is Denver.

**Resort details**
www.keystone.snow.com
+1 970 496 4386

**Elevation** 2,829–3,782m (9,280–12,408ft)

**Vertical drop**
953m (3,128ft)

**Number of lifts**
Drag 1
Chairs 12
Gondolas 2
Moving carpets 4
Total 19

**Marked runs** 117 trails

**Ungroomed** ***

**Ski areas** Three linked mountains: Dercum Mountain (formerly Keystone Mountain), North Peak and The Outback, with above-the-treeline terrain and snowcat-served bowls

**Snowmaking** 684 acres

**Night skiing** Yes: 15 slopes and terrain park available every evening (high season)

**Length of season** Mid-October–mid-April

### Breckenridge

**Location** In central Colorado, 137km (85 miles) west of Denver. Take Interstate 70 from Denver and CO 9 south to the resort.

**Resort details**
www.breckenridge.com
+1 970 453 5000

**Elevation** 2,926–3,962m (9,600–12,998ft)

**Vertical drop**
1,036m (3,398ft)

**Number of lifts**
Drags 4
Chairs 16
Moving carpets 8
Total 28

**Marked runs** 146,893ha (2,208 acres), 146 trails

**Ungroomed** ***

**Ski areas** Five areas: Peak 7, Peak 8, Peak 9, Peak 10; 312ha (772 acres) of bowls above and behind cut frontside trails

**Snowmaking** 565 acres

**Night skiing** No

**Length of season** Mid-November–late April

| USA · COLORADO | USA · COLORADO | USA · COLORADO | USA · COLORADO | USA · UTAH | USA · UTAH | USA · UTAH |
|---|---|---|---|---|---|---|
| ## Crested Butte | ## Copper Mountain | ## Steamboat | ## Telluride | ## Snowbird | ## Alta | ## Park City Mountain Resort |

### Crested Butte

**Location** Crested Butte is located in central Colorado, 48km (30 miles) north of Gunnison (and its airport) via CO 135. From Denver, take US 285 south through Fairplay to Poncha Springs, then US 50 west to Gunnison, then Highway 135 north to Crested Butte. From Denver International Airport, take US 70 west, to C-470 to US 285 south, and then proceed as above

**Resort details**
www.skicb.com
+1 970 349 2211

**Elevation** 2,775–3,971m (9,100–11,875ft)

**Vertical drop**
846m (2,775ft)

**Number of lifts**
Chairs 8
Total 8

**Marked runs** 455ha (1,125 acres), 121 trails

**Ungroomed** ****

**Ski areas** Lifts and trails wrap around Crested Butte Peak; North Face, Extreme Limits and Teocalli Bowl, lift-served extreme terrain; hike to peak for additional vertical.

**Snowmaking** 282 acres

**Night skiing** No

**Length of season**
Mid-November–early April

### Copper Mountain

**Location** Copper Mountain is located in central Colorado, 121km (75 miles) west of Denver, directly off Interstate 70. The nearest airport is Denver.

**Resort details**
www.coppercolorado.com
+1 970 968 2882

**Elevation** 2,926–3,767m (9,712–12,313ft)

**Vertical drop**
793m (2,601ft)

**Number of lifts**
Drags 7
Chairs 15
Total 22

**Marked runs** 991ha (2,450 acres), 125 trails

**Ungroomed** ****

**Ski areas** Adjacent Copper Peak and Union Peak, with 4 summit bowls and 1 backside bowl (Copper Bowl); Tucker Mountain (snowcat access)

**Snowmaking** 380 acres

**Night skiing** No

**Length of season**
Early November–mid-April

### Steamboat

**Location** Steamboat is in central Colorado, 258km (160 miles) from Denver; take Interstate 70 west to exit 205, then Colorado 9 north to US 40 west to Steamboat.

**Resort details**
www.steamboat.com
+1 970 879 6111

**Elevation** 3,224m (10,568ft); top station: 2,103m (6,900ft)

**Vertical drop**
1,118m (3,668ft)

**Number of lifts**
Drags 4
Chairs 18
Gondola 1
Moving carpets 3
Total 26

**Marked runs** 1,199ha (2,965 acres), 164 trails

**Ungroomed** ****

**Ski areas** Mount Werner, Sunshine Peak, Storm Peak, Thunderhead Peak, Pioneer Ridge and Christie Peak

**Snowmaking** 438 acres

**Night skiing** No

**Length of season**
Late November–early April

### Telluride

**Location** Telluride is in central Colorado, a 7-hour drive from Denver. From Denver take Interstate 70 West to Grand Junction, and go south on Route 50 to Montrose. Continue south on Route 550 to Ridgway, then turn right onto Route 62. Follow this to Route 145 and turn left. Follow the signs into Telluride.Travel time – 7 hours. The nearest airports are at Denver and Montrose (1.25 hours).

**Resort details**
www.tellurideskiresort.com
+1 866 287 5015

**Elevation**
3,737m (12,260ft)

**Vertical drop**
1,076m (3,530ft)

**Number of lifts**
Drags 2
Chairs 11
Gondolas 2
Moving carpet 1
Total 16

**Marked runs** 84 trails

**Ungroomed** Hike to terrain on Bald Mountain and Mountain Quail.

**Ski areas** Four mountain faces. A gondola links the slopes down to the old town with the much newer mountain village, which is the base of the bulk of the skiing.

**Snowmaking** 204 acres

**Night skiing** No

**Length of season**
23 November –2 April

### Snowbird

**Location** Snowbird is in northern Utah, in Little Cottonwood Canyon, 46km (29 miles) from Salt Lake City International Airport, and 40km (25 miles) from the centre of Salt Lake City. Snowbird is a 45-minute drive from the airport. Alta is 1.6km (1 mile) further up the road.

**Resort details**
www.snowbird.com
+1 801 933 2047

**Elevation** 2,365–3,353m (7,760–11,000ft)

**Vertical drop**
987m (3,240ft)

**Number of lifts**
Drags 2
Chairs 10
Cable-car 1
Total 13

**Marked runs** 1,012ha (2,500 acres), 89 trails

**Ungroomed** *****

**Ski areas** Skiers at Snowbird can also access the resort of Alta – but snowboarders are not allowed there. Snowbird's ski areas include Mineral Basin, Gad Valley, Thunder Bowl and Peruvian Gulch. The combined resorts of Snowbird and Alta offer 1,902ha (4,700 acres) of skiable terrain.

**Snowmaking** 125 acres with Alta

**Night skiing** Yes: Wednesday, Friday, Saturday

**Length of season**
Mid-November–mid-May

### Alta

**Location** Alta is in northern Utah, 40km (25 miles) southeast of Salt Lake City at the top of Little Cottonwood Canyon, on State Highway 210. The resort is approximately 45 minutes from Salt Lake City International Airport. Snowbird is 1.6 km (1 mile away).

**Resort details**
www.alta.com
+1 801 359 1078

**Elevation** 2,600–3,216m (8,530–10,550ft)

**Vertical drop**
616m (2,020ft)

**Number of lifts**
Drags 5
Chairs 7
Total 12

**Marked runs** 890ha (2,200 acres), 116 trails

**Ungroomed** *****

**Ski areas** Alta is for skiers only (no snowboarding). Skiers can also ski at Snowbird on the Alta-Snowbird skipass and enter this ski area at the saddle between Alta's Albion Basin and Snowbird's Mineral Basin. The combined resorts of Snowbird and Alta offer 1,902ha (4,700 acres) of skiable terrain.

**Snowmaking** 125 acres with Snowbird

**Night skiing** One-off events only: e.g. New Year's Eve

**Length of season**
Mid-November–16 April

### Park City Mountain Resort

**Location** Park City Mountain Resort is in northern Utah, 45 minutes' drive from Salt Lake City International Airport, 58km (36 miles) away. The town of Park City is located at the base of the resort.

**Resort details**
www.parkcitymountain.com
www.pcride.com
+1 435 649 8111

**Elevation** 2,103–3,048m (6,900–10,000ft)

**Vertical drop**
945m (3,100ft)

**Number of lifts**
Chairs 14
Total 14

**Marked runs** 1,335ha (3,300 acres), 100 trails

**Ungroomed** ***

**Ski areas** Park City has 8 peaks and 9 bowls as well as 4 terrain parks and a large superpipe. The 4 main areas are: Pine Cone Ridge, East Side, Mid-Mountain and the Base Area. It is possible to ski back to the town of Park City.

**Snowmaking** 475 acres

**Night skiing** Yes

**Length of season**
Mid-November–mid-April

| USA · UTAH | USA · UTAH | USA · UTAH | USA · WYOMING | USA · WYOMING | USA · IDAHO | USA · MONTANA |
|---|---|---|---|---|---|---|
| ## Deer Valley | ## The Canyons | ## Snowbasin | ## Jackson Hole and Grand Targhee | ## Jackson Hole and Grand Targhee *continued* | ## Sun Valley | ## Big Sky |

**Deer Valley**

**Location** Deer Valley is 58km (36 miles) from Salt Lake City International Airport. The ski area is 1.6km (1 mile) from the centre of the mining town of Park City.

**Resort details**
www.deervalley.com
+1 435 649 1000

**Elevation** 2,003–2,917m (6,570–9,570ft)

**Vertical drop**
914m (3,000ft)

**Number of lifts**
Chairs 20
Gondola 1
Total 21

**Marked runs** 739ha (1,825 acres), 91 trails

**Ungroomed** *** 350ha (865 acres) of gladed skiing

**Ski areas** Deer Valley has skiing over five areas: Little Baldy Peak (2,423m/7,950ft), Bald Eagle Mountain (2,560m/8,400ft), Bald Mountain (2,865m/9,400ft), Flagstaff Mountain (2,774m/ 9,100ft) and up to Empire Canyon (2,917m/9,570ft). All areas are for skiers only. No snowboarding allowed.

**Snowmaking** 600 acres

**Night skiing** No

**Length of season** Beginning December–mid-April

---

**The Canyons**

**Location** There are direct flights from 70 US cities into SLC International Airport and then it is just 40 minutes on the interstate to The Canyons.

**Resort details**
www.thecanyons.com
+1 435 649 5400

**Elevation** 2,106–3,044m (6,910–9,990ft)

**Vertical drop**
972m (3,190ft)

**Number of lifts**
Chairs 15
Gondolas 2
Total 17

**M arked runs** 1,498ha (3,700 acres), 152 trails

**Ungroomed** ***

**Ski areas** The Canyons has 8 peaks, 5 bowls, 6 natural halfpipes, as well as 2 terrain parks.

**Snowmaking** Yes

**Night skiing** No

**Length of season** Mid-November–mid-April

---

**Snowbasin**

**Location** Snowbasin Resort is in northern Utah, 53km (33 miles) by road from downtown Salt Lake City and Salt Lake City International Airport. The mountain is located 27km (17 miles) from the city of Ogden.

**Resort details**
www.snowbasin.com
+1 801 620 1000

**Elevation** 1,951–2,850m (6,400–9,350ft)

**Vertical drop**
899m (2,950ft)

**Number of lifts**
Drags 4
Chairs 7
Gondolas 2
Cable-car 1
Total 14

**Marked runs** 1,076ha (2,660 acres), 53 trails

**Ungroomed** ****

**Ski areas** Although there is a cluster of 2,743m (9,000ft+) peaks, most of the skiing is in major bowls between De Moisy Peak, Needles Mount Ogden and Allen's Peak. The resort is the home of the technically intimidating Olympic men's and women's downhill and super G courses, but also has abundant beginner and intermediate terrain. There is also the Six Lane Lift assisted tubing hill, 2 terrain parks, 1 superpipe and 26km (16 miles) of cross-country skiing.

**Snowmaking** 580 acres

**Night skiing** No

**Length of season** Mid-November–mid-April

---

**Jackson Hole and Grand Targhee**

**Location** Jackson Hole Mountain Resort is 16km (10 miles) from the town of Jackson, 32km (20 miles) from Jackson Hole Airport and (0.6km)1 mile from Teton National Park. Grand Targhee is located in the Teton Mountains on the Wyoming/Idaho border, at the end of a minor road off Highway 33 through Driggs, Idaho. The nearest airports are at Jackson Hole (1 hour), Idaho Falls (2 hours) and Salt Lake City (4 hours).

**Resort details**
www.jacksonhole.com
+1 307 733 2292www.grandtarghee.com
+1 307 353 2300

**Elevation** Jackson Hole: 1,924m–3,186m (6,311ft– 10,450ft); Grand Targhee: 2,438–3,050m (8,000– 10,006ft)

**Vertical drop**
Jackson Hole: 1,262m (4,139ft); Grand Targhee: 610m (2,000ft)

**Number of lifts**
Jackson Hole:
Chairs 10
Total 10

Grand Targhee:
Chairs 4
Total 4

**Marked runs** Jackson Hole: 1,012ha (2,500 acres), 96 trails; Grand Targhee: 809ha (2,000 acres) total skiable area, plus 405ha (1,000 acres) cat-skiing and extensive backcountry, 62 trails

**Ungroomed** *****

**Ski areas** Jackson Hole: 1,012ha (2,500 acres) of bowls, steeps and rolling descents, as well as Nordic activities at the base. The temporary absence of a continuous lift from base to summit means skiers will ride the Bridger Gondola and a series of chairs to reach the top, and still be able to access the resort's notorious Corbet's Couloir and access 2,024ha+ (5,000 acres) of backcountry through marked gates.

*continued*

---

**Jackson Hole and Grand Targhee** *continued*

Grand Targhee: Fred's Mountain, Peaked Mountain, guided cat-skiing area and extensive backcountry.

**Snowmaking** Jackson Hole: 180 acres, Grand Targhee: none

**Night skiing** Jackson Hole and Grand Targhee, no; but yes at Snow King Resort in downtown Jackson.

**Length of season** Jackson Hole: December–mid-April; Grand Targhee: 1 December–8 April

---

**Sun Valley**

**Location** Sun Valley is in central Idaho. The nearest airports are at Hailey (25 minutes), Boise (3.5 hours) and Salt Lake City (5-6 hours). From Boise, take Interstate 84, US 20 and Highway 75; from Salt Lake City take Interstate 84 and US 93.

**Resort details**
www.sunvalley.com
+1 800 635 4150

**Elevation**
1,753m (5,750ft)

**Vertical drop**
1,036m (3,400ft)

**Number of lifts**
Drag 1
Chairs 17
Total 18

**Marked runs** 427ha (2,054 acres), 75 trails (65 on Bald Mountain, 10 on Dollar Mountain)

**Ungroomed** ***

**Ski areas** Mount Baldy, Dollar Mountain

**Snowmaking** 73%

**Night skiing** No

**Length of season** Thanksgiving (late November)–mid/late April

---

**Big Sky**

**Location** Big Sky is located above the Gallatin Valley, in southwestern Montana. The nearest airports are at Bozeman (1 hour) and Salt Lake City (5 hours). By road: drive 13km (8 miles) west up State Highway 64 off US 191, around 72km (45 miles) south of Bozeman.

**Resort details**
www.bigskyresort.co
+1 800 548 4486 or
+1 406 995 5000

**Elevation**
2,286m (7,500ft)

**Vertical drop**
1,326m (4,350ft)

**Number of lifts**
Drag 1
Chairs 14
Cable-car 1
Moving carpets 2
Total 18

**Marked runs** 1,457ha (3,600 acres), 150+ trails

**Ungroom ed** ***

**Ski areas** Lone Mountain, Andesite Mountain, Flat Iron Mountain. (Big Sky is linked with the separate resort of Moonlight Basin www.moonlightbasin.com: 6 chairs serving 810ha (2,000 acres)

**Snowmaking** 350 acres

**Night skiing** Yes: Christmas–mid-March

**Length of season** Late November–late April

| USA · MONTANA | USA · MONTANA | USA · ALASKA | CANADA · QUEBEC | CANADA · QUEBEC | CANADA · QUEBEC | CANADA · ALBERTA |
|---|---|---|---|---|---|---|

## The Big Mountain

**Location** The Big Mountain is located in the Whitefish Range of the Rocky Mountains in northwestern Montana. The nearest town, Whitefish, is located on US 93 16km (10 miles) north of Missoula; The Big Mountain is 13km (8 miles) north of town on Highway 487. The nearest airport is at Kalispell (30 minutes, airport shuttle available). The nearest train station is Whitefish; Amtrak's Empire Builder Seattle-Chicago service stops here.

**Resort details**
www.bigmtn.com
+1 406 862 1900

**Elevation**
1,372m (4,500ft)

**Vertical drop**
762m (2,500ft)

**Number of lifts**
Drags 3
Chairs 8
Total 11

**Marked runs** 1,214ha (3,000 acres), 93 trails

**Ungroomed** ***

**Ski areas** North Side, Hellroaring Basin

**Snowmaking** 96 runs

**Night skiing** Yes

**Length of season**
Late November–mid-April

## Bridger Bowl

**Location** Bridger Bowl is in the Bridger Mountains of southwestern Montana, 26km (16 miles) north of Bozeman on Highway 86. The nearest airport is Bozeman (20 minutes)

**Resort details**
www.bridgerbowl.com
+1 406 587 2111

**Elevation**
1,859m (6,100ft)

**Vertical drop**
797m (2,600ft), of which 610m (2,000ft) is lift-served

**Number of lifts**
Chairs 7

**Marked runs** 607ha (1,500 acres), 69 trails

**Ungroomed** ****

**Ski areas** North Bowl, South Bowl, The Ridge

**Snowmaking** Limited (4%)

**Night skiing** No

**Length of season**
December–April

## Alyeska

**Location** Alyeska is located in southern Alaska, 64km (40 miles) east of Anchorage. From Anchorage, take the New Seward Highway, then left on to the Alyeska Highway at mile 90 for 5km (3 miles). The nearest airport is at Anchorage.

**Resort details**
www.alyeskaresort.com
+1 907 754 1111

**Elevation** 76–838m (250–2,750ft)

**Vertical drop**
747m (2,450ft)

**Number of lifts**
Drags 2
Chairs 7
Total 9

**Marked runs** 567ha (1,400 acres), 68 trails

**Ungroomed** ***

**Ski areas** Main face; North face

**Snowmaking** 28 trails

**Night skiing** Yes

**Length of season**:
Mid-November–mid-April, plus weekend operations until late May, conditions permitting

## Mont-Saint-Anne

**Location** Mont-Sainte-Anne is an easy 30-minute drive to the east of Quebec City. Quebec (40km/25 miles) is the nearest international airport. There are direct flights from Europe on Air Canada and the Canadian charter, Zoom. It is recommended to rent a car to drive out from the city and explore other resorts.

**Resort details**
www.mont-sainte-anne.com
+1 418 827 4561

**Elevation** 175–800m (575–2,625ft)

**Vertical drop**
625m (2,050ft)

**Number of lifts**
Drags 6
Chairs 6
Gondola 1
Total 13

**Marked runs** 68km (42 miles), 63 trails; 224km (139 miles) of cross-country trails

**Ungroomed** **

**Ski areas** Mont-Sainte-Anne is the largest and most varied of Quebec City's town hills. It shares the Carte Blanche multipass with Le Massif, Stoneham and Le Relais.

**Snowmaking**
56km (35 miles)

**Night skiing** Yes (15 marked trails)

**Length of season**
November–April

## Tremblant

**Location** Tremblant, in western Quebec, is a 2-hour drive from Montreal International Airport (124km/ 77miles). There are direct flights from Europe to the airport on Air Canada and other major airlines. Hire car is recommended for the easiest access to the resort.

**Resort details**
www.tremblant.ca
+1 819 681 2000

**Elevation** 230– 875m (750–2,870ft)

**Vertical drop**
645m (2,120ft)

**Number of lifts**
Chairs 9
Gondola 1
Moving carpet 3
Total 13

**Marked runs** 254ha (628 acres), 94 trails; 100km (62 miles) of cross-country trails.

**Ungroomed** **

**Ski areas** Tremblant is a stand-alone resort, with skiing on four faces of Le Grand Manitou mountain

**Snowmaking** Yes (885 snow cannon)

**Night skiing** Yes

**Length of season**
Mid-November–mid-April

## Le Massif

**Location** Le Massif is located in central Quebec, 33km (20 miles) east of Mont-Sainte-Anne, and 73km (45 miles) from Quebec City. The closest airport is at Quebec City. By road from Quebec City, take Route 138 east. From La Malbaie, take Route 138 west. Le Massif is 18km (11 miles) west of Baie-Saint-Paul, and 66km (40 miles) from La Malbaie. Access is via the summit or base of the mountain.

**Resort details**
www.lemassif.com
+1 877 536 2774

**Elevation**
36–806m (118–2,645ft)

**Vertical drop**
770m (2,526ft)

**Number of lifts**
Drags 2
Chairs 3
Total 5

**Marked runs** 122ha (302 acres), 43 trails

**Ungroomed** **

**Ski areas** The carte blanche ticket allows skiers to take advantage of three mountains within 45 minutes of Quebec City: Mont-Sainte-Anne, Stoneham and Le Massif.

**Snowmaking** 70%

**Night skiing** No

**Length of season**
Early December–early April

## Banff and Lake Louise

**Location** Located in the middle of Banff National Park, Banff is a 1.5-hour drive from Calgary (122km/76 miles). The nearest airport is Calgary. The slopes of Sunshine are 20 minutes' drive away, while Lake Louise is 45 minutes away. Norquay is just above the town.

**Resort details**
www.banfflakelouise.com
www.skibig3.com
+1 403 762 4561

**Elevation** Slopes; 1,630– 2,730m (5,347–8,956ft)

**Vertical drop**
Lake Louise: 991m (3,251ft)

**Number of lifts**
Drags 2
Chairs 19
Gondolas 2
Total 23

**Marked runs** 3,135ha (7,748 acres)

**Ungroomed** ****

**Ski areas** Mount Norquay is a small but characterful tree-lined area just above the town. The more extensive Sunshine Village comprises three mountains plus the backcountry area of Delirium Dive. Lake Louise is the biggest of the three with skiing on the wide south face, tree-lined Larch and Ptarmigan and the legendary back bowls.

**Snowmaking** Not necessary at Sunshine; 40 per cent coverage at Lake Louise; 90 per cent coverage at Norquay. (Total 1950 acres)

**Night skiing** Yes; Norquay on Fridays

**Length of season**
Early November–early May

| CANADA · BC | CANADA · BC | CANADA · BC | CANADA · BC | CANADA · BC |
|---|---|---|---|---|

## Whistler Blackcomb

**Location** Whistler is nestled in the Coast Mountain Range of British Columbia, 120km (75 miles) north of Vancouver, BC, and 354km (218 miles) north of Seattle, USA. The closest airport is Vancouver.

**Resort details**
www.whistlerblackcomb.com
+1 866 218 9690

**Elevation** 650–2,285m (2,140–7,490ft)

**Vertical drop**
Whistler: 1,530m (5,020ft);
Blackcomb: 1,609m (5,280ft)

**Number of lifts**
Drags 16
Chairs 18
Gondolas 3
Total 37

**Marked runs** 486ha (1,200 acres), 200+ trails

**Ungroomed** 2,815 ha (6,971 acres)

**Ski areas** Whistler Mountain, Blackcomb Mountain

**Snowmaking** 565 acres

**Night skiing** Night Moves: Thursday, Friday, Saturday from 5 to 9pm

**Length of season** Winter through to summer; glacier skiing 24 November–end July

## Red Resort

**Location** Southern British Columbia, near the town of Rossland, located on Highway 22, some 20 minutes north of the US border. The nearest airports are Castlegar (30 minutes) and Spokane International (3 hours), in Washington State.

**Resort details**
www.redresort.com
+1 250 362 7384

**Elevation**
1,296m (4,251ft)

**Vertical drop**
970m (3,182ft)

**Number of lifts**
Drag 1
Chairs 4
Total 5

**Marked runs** 83 trails, 640ha (1,585 acres)

**Ungroomed** *****

**Total area** 648ha (1,600 acres)

**Ski areas** Red Mountain and Granite Mountain are the main ski areas, with extensive backcountry skiing on Gray Mountain, Record Mountain, Kirkup Mountain and Mount Roberts.

**Snowmaking** No

**Night skiing** No

**Length of season**
December–April

## Panorama

**Location** Eastern British Columbia, 291km (181 miles) west of Calgary, Alberta, via the Trans-Canada Highway west through Banff and Kootenay National Parks, then 10km (6 miles) south on Highway 93/95 to Invermere, then 17km (11 miles) to the resort. The nearest airport is Calgary.

**Resort details**
www.panoramaresort.com
+1 250 342 6941
RK Heliski: www.rkheliski.com
+1 250 342 3889

**Elevation**
1,160–3,800m (3,800–7,800ft )

**Vertical drop**
1,220m (4,000ft)

**Number of lifts**
Drags 2
Chairs 6
Total 8

**Marked runs** 1,152ha (2,847 acres), 120 trails, bowls, chutes

**Ungroomed** ***

**Ski areas** Frontside, Taynton Bowl on backside

**Snowmaking** 40%

**Night skiing** Yes

**Length of season**
November–late April

## Kicking Horse Resort

**Location** South of Golden, British Columbia. The nearest airport is Calgary, Alberta (3 hours). By road: from Highway 1 take Highway 95 south into Golden and follow signs to the resort (14km/8 miles). There are no train services.

**Resort details**
www.kickinghorseresort.com
+1 250 439 5400
+1 866 754 5425

**Elevation**
1,188–3,900m (3,900–8,030ft)

**Vertical drop**
1,259m (4,133ft)

**Number of lifts**
Drag 1
Chairs 3
Gondola 1
Moving carpet 1
Total 6

**Marked runs** 1,100 ha (2,750 acres), 64 trails

**Ungroomed** ****

**Total area**
1,113ha (2,750 acres)

**Ski areas** Bowl Over, Crystal Bow, Feuz Bowl, lower mountain

**Snowmaking** No

**Night skiing** No

**Length of season**
December–April

## Fernie Alpine Resort

**Location** Fernie is tucked away in the southeastern tip of British Columbia, some 320km (200 miles) from Calgary. Banff is about 4 hours away.

**Resort details**
www.skifernie.com
+1 250 423 4655

**Elevation** 1,067–1,926m (3,500–6,316ft)

**Vertical drop**
863m (2,830ft)

**Number of lifts**
Drags 4
Chairs 6
Total 10

**Marked runs** 107

**Ungroomed** Hundreds of acres of open bowl skiing

**Ski areas** A total of more than 1,012ha (2,500 acres) spread across five steep bowls with mellow nursery slopes at the base. A variety of snowcat skiing options

**Snowmaking** 125 acres

**Night skiing** No

**Length of season**
Early December–mid-April

# Contributors

## Alf Alderson

Award-winning freelance journalist and photographer Alf Alderson specializes in adventure sports and travel writing, focusing on skiing, surfing and mountain biking. His work has appeared in newspapers and magazines in the UK, USA, Canada and Australia. He was a contributor to the *Rough Guide to Skiing and Snowboarding in North America* and the *Rough Guide to the Rocky Mountains*. He is a committee member of the Outdoor Writers' Guild (www.owg.org.uk), the UK's best-established organization of professional outdoor and travel writers, and gear review editor and watersports editor at *OE* magazine (www.oe-mag.com). He lives in St David's, Pembrokeshire, Wales.

## Minty Clinch

Until 1998 Minty Clinch, as a film critic, made a living from sitting in a darkened cinema. Since then she has travelled the world in search of adventure, with the emphasis on activity sports. She has skied in five continents, leaving Africa and Antarctica as the two fields yet to be conquered. She is a freelance writer, contributing to leading newspapers and magazines.

## Nick Dalton

Nick Dalton has been writing about skiing and travel (particularly mountain destinations) for well over a decade. He has written about skiing for the *Daily* and *Sunday Telegraph*, *The Times*, and the *Daily* and *Sunday Express*. His work also appears in the *Good Ski Guide* and *Ski and Board* magazines. He has skied almost 100 resorts across North America, and many more in Europe. He revels in finding new and undiscovered resorts, using skiing as an excuse to explore beautiful high-altitude spots across the globe.

## Francis (Gary) Johnston

Francis Johnston was born in County Down, Northern Ireland and is the founder and managing director of the specialist snowsports travel guide publisher Ski*Ride Productions. Johnston was previously employed at senior management level in overseas resort operations and retail travel trade training/sales with some of the UK's leading ski, lakes and mountains tour operators. He has also worked in or visited most of the leading French, Austrian, Italian and Eastern European ski resorts, and has personally accompanied and guided well over 4,000 visitors and travel industry professionals during that time. He now divides his time between Andorra, France and Brighton in England, travelling up to five months each year in the Alps and Pyrenees.

## Felix Milns

Always keen to leap into a couloir, Felix Milns has skied everywhere from Utah to Lebanon and Morocco. A freelance travel journalist and photographer, he writes about skiing for *The Times*, the *Evening Standard* and the *Express*, as well as many ski, travel and lifestyle magazines. A writer and presenter of travel-related television productions, he has also regularly featured as a travel expert on the BBC's *Holiday 10 Best*.

## Hilary Nangle

Avid skier and former whitewater guide Hilary Nangle left college to follow her passions, working her way up to professional writer and editor. She travels widely, writing about soft adventure, arts, culture and food for magazines ranging from *Art and Antiques* to *National Geographic Adventure*. A Maine resident, she has authored two guidebooks, *Moon Acadia National Park* and *Moon Coastal Maine*, and is working on *Moon Maine*, a guide to the entire state. She can be reached through her website, www.hilarynangle.com.

## Peggy Shinn

Peggy Shinn is an award-winning freelance writer. She has skied at almost every major resort in North America, but Killington is in her backyard. A former editor of a professional environmental journal and a columnist for MSN, Peggy contributes to a number of magazines and websites in the USA, including *Ski Racing Magazine*, *Skiing* and *SKI* magazines, MSNBC.com, and several newspapers. She also combs New England for new or little-known facts to update travel guides, including Fodor's *New England Gold Guide* and *Ski Snowboard America and Canada*. She lives with her husband Andy and daughter Samantha in Rutland, Vermont in the USA.

## Claire Walter

Claire Walter is an award-winning travel and snowsports writer based in Boulder, Colorado. From there, she has explored slopes and resort communities throughout the North American West and elsewhere in the ski world. Her perspective is therefore global. Her book *The Best Ski Resorts in America* won the Lowell Thomas Award as the Best Guidebook of the Year, and her *Rocky Mountain Skiing* was honoured with the Harold Hirsch Award for the Best Snowsports Book of the Year. She also assembled *The Berlitz Ski Guide to the Alps* for North American skiers and wrote the North American section for the *Skier's Holiday Guide*, published in London for British skiers. She is a member of the American Society of Journalists and Authors, the North American SnowSports Journalists Association, the Society of American Travel Writers and the Colorado Authors' League.

## Arnie Wilson (Contributing Editor)

Arnie Wilson first put on a pair of skis during a school trip at the age of 16. He didn't ski again until he was 30 and was invited to write an article on a resort near Verbier, Switzerland. Skiing then became Wilson's passion, and in 1986 he became the *Financial Times* ski correspondent. He has since written over 500 articles for the paper and skied in 650 areas in more than 25 countries.

In 1994 Wilson skied every day for a year – a feat that took him to 240 resorts in 13 countries around the world, and into the *Guinness Book of Records*. His next mission is to ski in all 40 of America's 'skiing states' – he has 12 to go. British Ski Travel Writer of the Year in 1999, he contributes regularly to *Condé Nast Traveller*, *The Great Skiing Guide*, *Country Life*, and many other magazines. This is his firth ski book. In 2001 he also became editor of *Ski+board*. He and his Swedish wife, Vivianne, were married on the mountain at Jackson Hole, Wyoming in 2000.

## Leslie Woit

A long-time ski and travel writer, Leslie Woit has edited and contributed to an international assortment of magazines, newspapers and guidebooks. She was certified by the Canadian Ski Instructors Alliance and taught skiing for several years in Canada and Switzerland.

# Picture credits

Copyright in photographs rests with the following photographers and/or their agents:

Agence Nuts/Cathy Ribier, 58 (bottom); A.I.A.T. Monte Bianco, 68; A.I.A.T. Monte Cervino, 71; Alamy, 36, 37 (top), 38, 39 (bottom), 76, 94, 107 (top), 119 (top), 121 (bottom), 129 (bottom), 142, 196, 226, 272 (bottom), 273 (bottom left), 278, 279; Alyeska Ski Resort/© Anchorage Photography, 238, 239 (bottom); Alyeska Ski Resort/©D. Watts, 151 (bottom left), 151 (top); Alta Ski Resort, 212, 213 (bottom), 214, 215 (bottom); Andermatt Gotthard Tourismus, 119 (bottom); Andorra Tourist Board, 28, 31, 32, 33 (bottom), 35 (top and bottom); Les Arc/Erna Low/K.L. Keppens, 52; Les Arc/Erna Low/J. Favre, 55; Les Arc/Erna Low/S. Leon, 53; Les Arc/Erna Low/D. Schmitt, 54; Aspen & Snowmass/ Jeff Hanle, 192 (bottom left); Banff Lake Louise Tourism, 254, 256 (top); Banff Lake Louise Tourism/Henry George, 17 (bottom left), 243 (bottom), 256 (bottom), 257; Baqueira/Beret S.A., 26, 27 (bottom); Beaver Creek Ski Resort, 197 (bottom), 198 (bottom), 199 (top and bottom); Big Sky Resort, 232, 233 (bottom); Big Mountain Resort, 234 (bottom), 235; Bridger Bowl Ski Resort/Travis Andersen, 236 (bottom), 237 (top right); ©Bosse Lind/paragonbild.se, 126, 127 (bottom), 129 (top); Bernard Brault, 97; Bridger Bowl Ski Resort, 237 (bottom right); Breckenridge Ski Resort Colorado/Aaron Dodds, 202 (bottom left); Breckenridge Ski Resort Colorado/Dave Lehl, 203 (bottom); The Canyons Resort, 217, 220, 221 (top and bottom right); Chamonet.com, 46; Cannon Mountain/John McNamara, 174, 175 (bottom); Chilean Ski.com, 19; Copper Mountain Resort, 207 (top right), 207 (bottom right); Corbis/©Jeff Curtes, 272 (top), 275; Corbis/©Marc Muench, 194 (bottom); Corbis/©Joseph Sohm, 194 (top); 4 Corners Images, 100; Cortina Turismo, 62, 63 (top); Crested Butte Mountain Resort, 16, 150 (bottom right), 204, 205 (top); Deer Valley Resort, 218; Les Deux Alps/J.P. Noisellier, 59; Falls Creek Ski Resort, 277 (bottom); Fernie Alpine Resort/ Terry Parker, 268; Fernie Alpine Resort/©Henry George, 269 (right); ©Ken Gallard, 190 (bottom left); Gastein Tourismus, 4; Getty Images/Ilja Herb, 259 (top); Getty Images/©Mike Powell, 260; Grandvalira/Snowhunter/ Snow 24.com, 29; La Grave – La Meije Tourism, 56 (bottom left), 57 (top), 58 (top); Simon Hall – simon@soldeuonline.com, 30; Heavenly Mountain Resort/Jeff Farrell, 185 (bottom); Heavenly Mountain Resort/Corey Rich, 184; Heavenly Ski Resort/Corey Rich, 14 (bottom right); Hemsedal Ski Resort, 131; ©Hans-Peter Huber/Simephoto-4Corners Images, 103; Hunter Mountain Ski Resort, 157 (top and bottom); Grand Targhee Resort, 227; Jay Peak Resort, 13, 162, 163 (top); Jungfrau-Akeetsch-Bietschhorn, 114, 115 (bottom), 116, 117; Keystone Resort, 200, 201 (bottom); Kicking Horse Mountain Resort, 266 (left and right); Killington Resort & Pico Mountain, 161; Kirkwood Mountain Resort, 186, 187 (bottom); Kitzbuhel Tourismus, 98; Klosters

Tourismus, p. 2, 112; Lech Zurs Tourismus, 96; Lillehammer Turistkontor, 135; Loon Mountain Resort, 170 (bottom left); Loon Mountain Resort/Brian Norton, 171 (bottom); Madonna di Campiglio Pinzolo Val Rendena, 64; Mad River Glen, 168 (bottom left), 169 (top left); Mammoth Mountain Resort, 188, 189 (bottom); Le Massif Resort, 250; Les Menuires Resort, 22 (right); Mont-Sainte-Anne Ski Resort/© Christian Tremblay, 247; Mont Tremblant Quebec, 242 (top and bottom), 249 (left and right); St Moritz Tourist Board, 12, 104, 105 (bottom left and bottom right); ©Muench Photography Inc/Marc Meunch, front cover; Norge Knut, 138, 139 (top); Office de Tourisme de Val Thorens/ Mirande, 17; Oppdal Næringsforening/Oppdal kommune/Ludvig Killingberg, 132; Oppdal Næringsforening/Oppdal kommune/Nils Eric Kjellmann, 133 (top); Panorama Mountain Village, 264, 265 (bottom); Panorama Mountain Village/©Ken Bommin, 243 (top); Paradiskila Plagne Ski Resort/Tourist Board, 50; Park City Mountain Resort/©Dan Campbell, 219; Park City Mountain Resort/©Mark Maziarz, 216 (bottom left); Park Snow Donovaly, 146 (bottom), 147 (top right), 147 (bottom); Perisher Blue Resort, 277 (centre); Photolibrary, 23, 40, 43 (top and bottom), 47 (bottom), 48, 49, 102, 151 (bottom right), 210 (bottom left), 211; Photolibrary/Jon Arnold Images, 15; Red Mountain Resort, 262, 263 (top); Romanian National Tourist Office – UK & Ireland, 145; Sestriere Ski Resort, 74 (bottom), 77 (top); Ski Amade/Bad Gastein, 90, 91 (right), 92, 93 (top and bottom); Ski Portillo Chile, 274; Slovenian Tourist Board, 78 (bottom left), 79; Smuggler's Notch Resort, 150 (bottom left), 166, 167 (top right); Snow24.com, 89 (bottom), 143 (top), 176, 177 (top); Snow24.com/©Albin Niederstrasser, 85 (bottom); Snowbasin Resort, 223; Squaw Valley USA/Nathan Kendall, 182 (bottom left), 183 (top); Steamboat Ski Resort Corporation/Larry Pierce, 14 (bottom left); Steamboat Ski Town USA, 209; Stowe Mountain Resort, 164 (bottom left), 165 (bottom); Sunday River Photo., 178, 179 (bottom); Sun Valley Resort, 228 (bottom left), 229 (bottom right), 230 (top), 230 (bottom), 231 (top); Superstock, 164 (bottom right); Thedbo Ski Resort, 277 (top); La Thuille Resort, 69 (bottom), 70; Tourismusverband Paznaun, Ischgl, 84; Tourismusverband St Anton am Arlberg, back cover, 10 (bottom left), 11, 81, 82, 83, 84; Tourismuverband Saalbach Hinterglemm, 19, 87 (top and bottom); Tourismusverband Schladming-Rohrmoos, 88; Tourist Office Val Gardena, 66, 67 (bottom); Ufficio Promozione Monterosa SpA, 72 (top left), 72 (top right), 73; Val d' Isere Tourist Board/Jean-Pierre Noisiller, 39 (top); Val Thorens/Oddoux, 45; Val Thorens/A. Perier, 44; Valle Nevado Tourism, 273 (right), 274; Val Thorens/Les Trois Vallees/Oddoux, spine; Verbier/Bagnes Tourisme, 108, 109 (top), 110, 111 (top and bottom); Voss/Fjellandsby, 137 (top and bottom); Waterville Valley Resort, 172 (bottom left), 173 (bottom right); Whiteface Mountain Ski Resort, 155; Whistler Blackcomb Resort, 258, 261 (top and bottom); Arnie and Vivianne Wilson, back flap, and Turkey heliskiing, 18 ; Windham Mountain Resort, 158, 159 (bottom); World Pictures, 123.

# Index

Page numbers followed by 'p' denote resort profiles

# Index

# Index